Multilingual Literature as World Literature

Literatures as World Literature

Can the literature of a specific country, author, or genre be used to approach the elusive concept of 'world literature'? Literatures as World Literature takes a novel approach to world literature by analyzing specific constellations—according to language, nation, form, or theme—of literary texts and authors in their own world-literary dimensions. World literature is obviously so vast that any view of it cannot help but be partial; the question then becomes how to reduce the complex task of understanding and describing world literature. Most treatments of world literature so far either have been theoretical and thus abstract, or else have made broad use of exemplary texts from a variety of languages and epochs. The majority of critical work, the filling in of what has been traced, lies ahead of us. Literatures as World Literature fills in the devilish details by allowing scholars to move outward from their own areas of specialization, fostering scholarly writing that approaches more closely the polyphonic, multiperspectival nature of world literature.

Series Editor
Thomas O. Beebee

Editorial Board
Eduardo Coutinho, Federal University of Rio de Janeiro, Brazil
Hsinya Huang, National Sun-yat Sen University, Taiwan
Meg Samuelson, University of Cape Town, South Africa
Ken Seigneurie, Simon Fraser University, Canada
Mads Rosendahl Thomsen, Aarhus University, Denmark

Volumes in the Series
German Literature as World Literature, edited by Thomas O. Beebee
Roberto Bolaño as World Literature, edited by Nicholas Birns and Juan E. De Castro
Crime Fiction as World Literature, edited by David Damrosch, Theo D'haen, and Louise Nilsson

Danish Literature as World Literature, edited by Dan Ringgaard and
Mads Rosendahl Thomsen
From Paris to Tlön: Surrealism as World Literature, by Delia Ungureanu
American Literature as World Literature, edited by Jeffrey R. Di Leo
Romanian Literature as World Literature, edited by Mircea Martin,
Christian Moraru, and Andrei Terian
Brazilian Literature as World Literature, edited by Eduardo F. Coutinho
Dutch and Flemish Literature as World Literature, edited by Theo D'haen
Afropolitan Literature as World Literature, edited by James Hodapp
Francophone Literature as World Literature, edited by Christian Moraru,
Nicole Simek, and Bertrand Westphal
Bulgarian Literature as World Literature, edited by Mihaela P. Harper and
Dimitar Kambourov
Philosophy as World Literature, edited by Jeffrey R. Di Leo
Turkish Literature as World Literature, edited by Burcu Alkan and
Çimen Günay-Erkol
Elena Ferrante as World Literature, by Stiliana Milkova
Multilingual Literature as World Literature, edited by Jane Hiddleston and
Wen-chin Ouyang
Persian Literature as World Literature, edited by Mostafa Abedinifard,
Omid Azadibougar, and Amirhossein Vafa (forthcoming)
Mexican Literature as World Literature, edited by Ignacio M. Sánchez Prado
(forthcoming)
Graphic Novels and Comics as World Literature, edited by James Hodapp
(forthcoming)
Feminism as World Literature, edited by Robin Truth Goodman (forthcoming)
Modern Irish Literature as World Literature, edited by Christopher Langlois
(forthcoming)
Modern Indian Literature as World Literature: Going Beyond English,
by Bhavya Tiwari (forthcoming)

Multilingual Literature as World Literature

Edited by
Jane Hiddleston and Wen-chin Ouyang

BLOOMSBURY ACADEMIC
NEW YORK • LONDON • OXFORD • NEW DELHI • SYDNEY

BLOOMSBURY ACADEMIC
Bloomsbury Publishing Inc
1385 Broadway, New York, NY 10018, USA
50 Bedford Square, London, WC1B 3DP, UK
29 Earlsfort Terrace, Dublin 2, Ireland

BLOOMSBURY, BLOOMSBURY ACADEMIC and the Diana logo are
trademarks of Bloomsbury Publishing Plc

First published in the United States of America 2021
This paperback edition published 2023

Volume Editor's Part of the Work © Jane Hiddleston and Wen-chin Ouyang, 2021
Each chapter © Contributors

Cover design by Simon Levy / Levy Associates

For legal purposes, the Acknowledgements on p. xiv constitute an extension
of this copyright page.

All rights reserved. No part of this publication may be reproduced or
transmitted in any form or by any means, electronic or mechanical, including
photocopying, recording, or any information storage or retrieval system,
without prior permission in writing from the publishers.

Bloomsbury Publishing Inc does not have any control over, or responsibility for,
any third-party websites referred to or in this book. All internet addresses given
in this book were correct at the time of going to press. The author and publisher
regret any inconvenience caused if addresses have changed or sites have
ceased to exist, but can accept no responsibility for any such changes.

Library of Congress Cataloging-in-Publication Data
Names: Hiddleston, Jane, editor. | Ouyang, Wen-chin, editor.
Title: Multilingual literature as world literature / edited by Jane
Hiddleston and Wen-chin Ouyang.
Description: New York : Bloomsbury Academic, 2021. | Series: Literatures as
world literature | Includes bibliographical references and index.
Identifiers: LCCN 2021000983 (print) | LCCN 2021000984 (ebook) | ISBN
9781501360091 (hardback) | ISBN 9781501360107 (ebook) | ISBN 9781501360114 (pdf)
Subjects: LCSH: Multilingualism and literature.
Classification: LCC PN171.M93 M83 2021 (print) | LCC PN171.M93 (ebook) |
DDC 809–dc23
LC record available at https://lccn.loc.gov/2021000983
LC ebook record available at https://lccn.loc.gov/2021000984

ISBN:	HB:	978-1-5013-6009-1
	PB:	978-1-5013-7142-4
	ePDF:	978-1-5013-6011-4
	ePUB:	978-1-5013-6010-7

Series: Literatures as World Literature

Typeset by Integra Software Services Pvt. Ltd.

To find out more about our authors and books visit www.bloomsbury.com
and sign up for our newsletters.

Contents

List of Figures ix
Notes on Contributors x
Acknowledgements xiv

Introduction: Multilingual literature as world literature 1
Jane Hiddleston and Wen-chin Ouyang

Part I Multilingualism and modes of reading

1 Writing in the presence of the languages of the world: Language, literature and world in Édouard Glissant's late theoretical works 13
   Jane Hiddleston
2 (Sino)graphs in Franco(n)texts: The multilingual and the multimodal in Franco-Chinese literature and visual arts 27
   Shuangyi Li
3 A 'boundless creative ferocity': The *Souffles* generation, Moroccan poetry and visual art in dialogue 51
   Khalid Lyamlahy
4 The heterolingual zone: Arabic, English and the practice of worldliness 69
   Claire Gallien

Part II A multilingual ecology of world literature and modes of circulation

5 'O local sen paredes': The multilingual ecology of Manuel Rivas's *A desaparición da neve (The Disappearance of Snow)* 93
   Laura Lonsdale
6 Monolingualizing the multilingual Ottoman novel: Ahmet Midhat Efendi's *Felatun Bey ile Rakım Efendi* 111
   Keya Anjaria
7 Thinking in French and writing in Spanish: Rubén Darío's multilingualism 127
   Carlos F. Grigsby
8 Multilingual maelström: Re-reading Primo Levi's 'Canto of Ulysses' 145
   Dominique Jullien

Part III Multilingual comparative reading: Beyond translation and untranslatability

9 Ghetto, Nakba, Holocaust: New terms (of relationship) in Elias Khoury's *Awlād al-Ghītū* 167
   Nora Parr

10 Multilingual others: Transliteration as resistant translation 184
    Dima Ayoub

11 Hauntological versions in Isabel del Río's bilingual *Zero Negative/ Cero Negativo* 201
    Ellen Jones

12 *transition*, untranslatability and the 'Revolution of the Word' 215
    Juliette Taylor-Batty

Part IV Multilingual poetics of world literature

13 How each sound becomes world 233
    yasser elhariry

14 Vahni Capildeo's multilingual poetics: Translation, synaesthesia, relation 253
    Rachael Gilmour

15 'Le mystère de notre présence au monde': Monchoachi, Creole proverbs and world literature as restoration 267
    Christopher Monier

16 Configurations of multilingualism and world literature 282
    Wen-chin Ouyang

Index 304

Figures

2.1 'Montagne – Eau' (Mountain – Water), in *Et le souffle* (2001 [2010], 90–1). @FrançoisCheng-Etlesouffledevientsigne-L'Iconoclaste — 29

2.2 'Entre source et nuage' (Between Source and Cloud), in *Et le souffle* (2001 [2010], 86–7). @FrançoisCheng-Etlesouffledevientsigne-L'Iconoclaste — 33

2.3 'La Quête' (The Quest), in *Et le souffle* (2001 [2010], 44–5). @FrançoisCheng-Etlesouffledevientsigne-L'Iconoclaste — 34

2.4 'La chute' (The Fall), in *Et le souffle* (2001 [2010], 114–15). @FrançoisCheng-Etlesouffledevientsigne-L'Iconoclaste — 35

2.5 Shan Sa, 'La Falaise' (The Cliff), in *Le Miroir du calligraphe* (Paris: Albin Michel 2002, 27) — 40

2.6 Shan Sa, 'La lune auréolée' (The Glowing Moon), in *Le Miroir du calligraphe* (Paris: Albin Michel 2002, 75) — 41

2.7 Shan Sa, 'La lune' (The Moon), in *Le Miroir du calligraphe* (Paris: Albin Michel 2002, 120) — 42

2.8 The book cover of the French version of *Impératrice* ((Paris: Le Livre de Poche) 2003), the Chinese character 曌 zhao is composed by Shan herself. © Le Livre de Poche — 44

4.1 Tablet 1 in *The Iraqi Nights* (2014, 13) — 78

4.2 Tablet 10 in *The Iraqi Nights* (2014, 22) — 79

4.3 Tablet 11 in *The Iraqi Nights* (2014, 23) — 80

4.4 Tablet 20 in *The Iraqi Nights* (2014, 32) — 81

Contributors

Keya Anjaria is a senior teaching fellow at SOAS, University of London. Keya has published research on the twentieth- and twenty-first-century Turkish novel. She is currently working on a comparative project on the female *bildungsroman*, which looks to connect articulations of the imperialist self in the Ottoman and British contexts, at the turn of the twentieth century, through the female protagonist's coming of age. Keya currently teaches in the fields of comparative literature and the cinema and literary studies of the Middle East.

Dima Ayoub is an assistant professor of Arabic and C.V. Starr Junior Faculty Fellow in International Studies at Middlebury College, Vermont, USA. Her book manuscript *Paratext and Power: Modern Arabic Literature in Translation* rewrites the social and cultural history of modern Arabic literature in translation by centring the role of publishers, translators and paratexts, in addition to writers. Parallel to her book project, Dr Ayoub is developing a digital archive of modern Arabic literature in English, French, German and Spanish translation. Her most recent publications appeared in the *Journal of Translation Studies*, the *Journal of Arabic Literature* and *Middle Eastern Literatures*.

yasser elhariry is Associate Professor of French at Dartmouth College, USA. He is the author of *Pacifist Invasions: Arabic, Translation & the Postfrancophone Lyric* (2017), guest editor of *Cultures du mysticisme* (2017) and co-editor of *Critically Mediterranean: Temporalities, Aesthetics & Deployments of a Sea in Crisis* (2018). A recipient of the William Riley Parker Prize, his writing appears in *PMLA*, *New Literary History*, *Yale French Studies*, *Francosphères*, *Contemporary French Civilization*, *Parade sauvage*, *French Forum* and several edited volumes. His edited volume, *Sounds Senses*, is forthcoming in 2021.

Claire Gallien is a senior lecturer in English at the University of Montpellier 3, France. She is the author of *L'Orient anglais* (2011) and is currently working on a monograph titled *From Corpus to Canon: Eastern Literary Traditions and Orientalist Reconfigurations in Seventeenth- and Eighteenth-Century Britain* and a co-edited volume on *Islam and New Directions in World Literature*, contracted with Edinburgh University Press. She has published in the *Journal of Postcolonial Writing*, the *Journal of Commonwealth Literature* and *Translation Studies*. She also guest edited a special issue on Refugee Literature for *JPW* and on contemporary Anglo-Arab literature for *Commonwealth Essays and Studies*.

Rachael Gilmour is Professor of Contemporary Literature and Postcolonial Studies at Queen Mary University of London. Her publications include *Bad English: Literature,*

Multilingualism, and the Politics of Language in Contemporary Britain (2020); *Multilingual Currents in Literature, Language & Culture* (2017, co-edited with Tamar Steinitz); *End of Empire & the English Novel since 1945* (2011/2015, co-edited with Bill Schwarz); and *Grammars of Colonialism: Representing Languages in Colonial South Africa* (2006).

Carlos F. Grigsby is a lecturer in Spanish at the University of Oxford, UK, where he completed his DPhil thesis *Rediscovering Rubén Darío through Translation*. He has also published articles on Darío in journals including the *Bulletin of Spanish Studies* and *MLR*. Aside from his scholarly work, he is also a poet and a translator, having won the XX International Poetry Prize 'Premio Creación Joven Fundación Loewe' in 2007 for the poetry collection *Una oscuridad brillando en la claridad que la claridad no logra comprender* (2008), making him the youngest person to win that award.

Jane Hiddleston is Professor of Literatures in French at the University of Oxford, and Official Fellow in French at Exeter College, Oxford (both UK). She is the author of *Poststructuralism and Postcoloniality: The Anxiety of Theory* (2010); *Writing After Postcolonialism: Francophone North African Literature in Transition* (2017); and *Decolonising the Intellectual: Politics, Culture, and Humanism at the End of the French Empire* (2014). She is also the co-editor of several collective volumes, including, with Khalid Lyamlahy, *Abdelkébir Khatibi: Postcolonialism, Transnationalism and Culture in the Maghreb and Beyond* (2020). She has been working on a book entitled *Frantz Fanon: Literature and Invention*, to be published by Legenda.

Ellen Jones is a researcher, editor and translator from Spanish. She completed her PhD at Queen Mary University of London in 2017, and has since held postdoctoral fellowships at the School of Advanced Study and the University of East Anglia. She is Reviews Editor of *Hispanic Research Journal*, and teaches literary translation at the National Autonomous University in Mexico City. Her translations include Rodrigo Fuentes's short story collection *Trout, Belly Up* (shortlisted for the Translators Association First Translation Prize 2019) and Bruno Lloret's novel *Nancy* (2020).

Dominique Jullien is Professor of Comparative Literature and French Studies at the University of California, Santa Barbara, USA, and a fellow of the Ecole Normale Supérieure in Paris. Her most recent book is *Borges, Buddhism and World Literature: a Morphology of Renunciation Tales* (2019). She is the author of *Les Amoureux de Schéhérazade: variations modernes sur les Mille et Une Nuits* (2009), *Récits du Nouveau Monde. Les Voyageurs français en Amérique de Chateaubriand à nos jours* (1992) and *Proust et ses modèles. Les Mille et Une nuits et les Mémoires de Saint-Simon* (1989), and editor of *Foundational Texts of World Literature* (2011), among others.

Shuangyi Li is the author of *Proust, China and Intertextual Engagement: Translation and Transcultural Dialogue* (2017) (International Comparative Literature Association Anna Balakian Prize 2019). He received a PhD in French at the University of Edinburgh, and was selected as *pensionnaire étranger* at L'École Normale Supérieure, Paris (2012–13). He joined Lund University, Sweden, as a postdoctoral scholar in 2017 and is currently working as a Swedish Research Council (Vetenskapsrådet) Research Fellow, completing his second monograph titled *Travel, Translation, Transmedia Aesthetics: Franco-Chinese Literature and Visual Arts in a Global Age* (forthcoming 2021).

Laura Lonsdale is Associate Professor of Modern Spanish Literature at the University of Oxford, UK. Her research in recent years has focused on literary multilingualism and translation, and her monograph *Multilingualism and Modernity: Barbarisms in Spanish and American Literature* was published in 2018. She is also co-editor of the *Routledge Companion to Iberian Studies* (2017), which promotes a comparative approach to the multilingual cultures of the Iberian Peninsula. As a literary translator she is interested in major authors little known outside Spain, and has translated works by Ramón del Valle-Inclán and Ana María Matute.

Khalid Lyamlahy is Assistant Professor of French and Francophone Studies at the University of Chicago, USA. His research focuses on North African Francophone literature in relation to political, social and cultural debates in the region. His scholarly publications have appeared in *Research in African Literature*, *The Journal of North African Studies*, the *Irish Journal of French Studies* and *Revue Roland Barthes*. His current work explores questions of identity and alterity in post-2011 Maghrebi fiction. He has also published a novel, *Un Roman Étranger* (2017) and is a regular contributor to several literary magazines in France and the US.

Christopher Monier is currently completing his doctoral work in poetry and poetics, which has been generously funded by the Oxford-based research initiative, Creative Multilingualism. Christopher is also a new assistant professor in the Department of English, Modern Languages, and Cultural Studies at Nicholls State University in the Bayou Region of south Louisiana, USA.

Wen-chin Ouyang FBA is Professor of Arabic and Comparative Literature at SOAS, University of London. She is the author of *Politics of Nostalgia in the Arabic Novel* (2013), *Poetics of Love in the Arabic Novel* (2012) and *Literary Criticism in Medieval Arabic-Islamic Culture: The Making of a Tradition* (1997). She has published widely on *The Thousand and One Nights*. She has been working towards Arabic-Chinese comparative literary and cultural studies, including Silk Road Studies.

Nora Parr is Alexander von Humboldt fellow at the Freie Universitat Berlin, Germany, where she is working on a project called 'What is the Arabic for Trauma?' The project continues work carried out while she was Postdoctoral Research Fellow with the OWRI Creative Multilingualism Programme. Previous to this she taught at King's College, London, Bethlehem University, and was Visiting Fellow at the Kenyon Institute in East Jerusalem. She is Subject Editor for the Middle East with *The Literary Encyclopedia* and Co-Investigator with the Birmingham University-based network project Rights for Time/Time for Rights.

Juliette Taylor-Batty is Senior Lecturer in English at Leeds Trinity University, UK. Her research focuses on literary multilingualism and on the relationship between writers' work as translators and their 'original' writing, particularly in the modernist period. She is the author of *Multilingualism in Modernist Fiction* (2013) and has published articles and chapters on a range of authors including Jean Rhys, Eugene Jolas, James Joyce, Samuel Beckett, Vladimir Nabokov and Salman Rushdie. She is co-author (with Mark Taylor-Batty) of *Samuel Beckett's Waiting for Godot* (2009).

Acknowledgements

Wen-chin Ouyang and Jane Hiddleston are Co-Investigators on the AHRC-funded OWRI Creative Multilingualism Programme (2016–2020). Together they lead Strand 5, Creativity in World Literature: Languages in Dialogue.

This volume is the first of the three publications planned for the Strand.

We are grateful to AHRC for funding our OWRI project and making the research that has gone into this volume possible. We are also grateful to all the participants in our workshops and conferences for contributing to the debates explored in our strand.

Introduction: Multilingual literature as world literature

Jane Hiddleston and Wen-chin Ouyang

Debates around the thorny concept of 'world literature' have often emphasized the ways in which literary texts dramatize the dynamic relationship between the local and the global, or indeed between nation and world. 'World literature', writes David Damrosch in a much-cited phrase, is the 'elliptical refraction of national literatures', and he goes on to argue that literature is still almost always understood in relation to a national tradition that leaves its mark on the text however extensively it succeeds in circulating in the international arena.[1] Damrosch's metaphor of 'refraction' evokes a two-way dialogue between nation and world, a dialogue that is in many cases complex and difficult to disentangle, but is nevertheless based for Damrosch on this binary schema which in turn assumes some degree of security within the national framework. Equally, Pascale Casanova's ground-breaking *World Republic of Letters* theorizes world literature as the product of the hierarchical international networks through which national literatures are circulated. Yet for all her insistence on the dynamics of international literary space, Casanova's study is particularly focused on Paris as the central hub of this international network, as, from the nineteenth century, 'Paris became the capital of the literary world, the city endowed with the greatest literary prestige on earth'.[2] This suggests that although Casanova, like Damrosch, challenges the category of the nation as the defining framework of 'world' literary texts, her conception of 'world literature' nevertheless relies on a concept of national literature, conditioned, marketed, though also reinvented by international circulation. Even Franco Moretti's looser understanding of the ways in which the dual forces of the local and the global play themselves out in and around literary texts assumes that the work starts in a particular culture and then encounters and becomes enmeshed in a global system. Moretti also seeks to challenge the national literary paradigm, but laments that literary study is still mired in this struggle between the national and the international. The study of world literature must remain 'the thorn in the side, the permanent intellectual challenge to national literatures – especially the local literature'.[3]

The Bloomsbury series on 'literatures as world literature' has also tended to suggest that literatures of a particular nation, language or genre engage with or enter into 'world literature' in a structure that nevertheless assumes a degree of stability in the defining term. The existing studies of American, German, Brazilian or Romanian literature as world literature have drawn attention to the multilingualism inherent in the national or indeed linguistic category, yet are again based on the model of tension between the national and its broader imbrication in multiple cultures, traditions and forms. In his eloquent introduction to *German Literature as World Literature*, Thomas O. Beebee suggests inverting Damrosch's dictum by arguing that national literatures can be seen as the 'elliptical refraction of world literature'; what is perceived as German literature, for example, has constantly 'imbricated other cultural traditions, ventriloquized other cultures, taken them as mimetic objects, translated and transadapted their texts' and vice versa.[4] National literature is from this point of view far from monolithic and enclosed, but dialogic and porous. Nevertheless, Beebee's study evidently still focuses on the ways in which a national culture and language are engaged in a dialogue with the wider world but are still on some level determined as Germanic. Jeffrey R. Di Leo's *American Literature as World Literature* offers a slightly different model by attending to the multilingualism of American literature, since American literature is not necessarily Anglophone but is 'infused with words, images, and sounds of people from distant lands'.[5] Although the descriptor 'American' is not conceived here as the signifier of a particular culture and is indeed evoked as 'multinational', however, and although the contributors are at pains to bring to light precisely those aspects of American literature that announce its transgression of the national category, once again the volume inevitably relies on the notion of national–international exchange.

Multilingual Literature as World Literature starts from an entirely different premise. Multilingual literatures are by definition not circumscribed by a single language, nation or culture; rather, they can be construed as 'world literature' precisely because in their very fabric they resist linguistic, national or communitarian boundaries and dramatize cultural movement and blending through their manipulation and indeed redefinition of language and linguistic frameworks. These literatures take neither the nation nor a single language as their starting point but are already created out of the dynamic and constantly evolving encounter between what are often seen as established national traditions or linguistic systems. Their 'worldliness' can be conceived as their display of the resistance of the languages they deploy to specified national or cultural categories and their performance of the dynamism of linguistic usage as it travels and evolves in the world. 'Worldliness' has been described by Edward Said as the result of a text's close affiliation with place and community, 'the text's status as an event having sensuous particularity as well as historical contingency', which is in turn 'an infrangible part of its capacity for conveying and producing meaning'.[6] Both text and criticism are worldly, moreover, if in this attention to particularity and contingency they refuse to assume that one culture can be placed in a hierarchical position above others. The worldly text and the worldly critic are also aware, as Said argues in 'Travelling Theory', that 'ideas and theories travel – from person to person, from situation to situation, from one period to another', which in turn implies that cultural and historical particularity must be understood as the product of this continual movement and exchange.[7] 'Worldliness' might from this point of view also require an openness to the porosity of the language and culture of place. Said's early vision of 'worldliness' can in this way provide a backdrop for our understanding of multilingual literatures exhibiting a 'worldly', self-aware understanding of both the singularity and the transience of idiom. The present volume, moreover, takes that imbrication and heterogeneity as the starting point for its vision of a 'worldly' literature defined, rather than simply challenged, by transnational and transcultural movement.

The multilingual literatures that are the focus of this volume at the same time work to undermine the universalism that critics have increasingly denounced in some of the more celebratory theories and anthologies of 'world literature'. As Eric Hayot has shown, the 'world' assumed by theories of world literature is necessarily only ever partial, despite the promise of completion and totality that the term promises.[8] The Warwick Research Collective make of this a more pointed critique, as they build on Moretti's conception of 'world literature' as 'one and unequal' and denounce the inevitable ideological complicity between 'world-literature' and the global capitalist world-system (though their concept of world-literature seems limited to those works that directly reflect that world-system).[9] Many commentators indeed share this view of the co-implication of 'world literature' with a globalizing culture merely 'masquerading', as Graham Huggan would have it, as a 'worldly' cosmopolitanism of reading.[10] A prominent aspect of this purportedly universal global literary culture is also that it tends to be construed as dominated by writing in English, and, to a lesser extent but still significantly, by a few other hegemonic European languages (particularly French and Spanish). One of the problems of the leading studies and anthologies of 'world literature', then, is that they focus far too often on works written in English, or otherwise assume that literatures in other languages enter into the domain of 'world literature' only through translation into that language. The association between the 'world' of 'world literature' and global capitalist culture reveals its flattening cultural universalism, then, while the dominance of English means that works in other languages are marginalized or even excluded from the 'world literature' debate. In her introduction to the essays reprinted in her provocatively titled *An Aesthetic Education in the Era of Globalization*, Gayatri Spivak laments the lack of 'deep language learning', its importance as a gesture of resistance to the 'new world machine' even if it is a gesture that cannot hope to stem the globalizing tide.[11] Aamir Mufti's equally provocatively titled *Forget English!* analyses the co-implication of the resurgence of 'world literature' and the rise of English as the global vernacular, and articulates clearly the need for an enhanced commitment to writing in a wide range of languages to achieve a better understanding of the diverse literatures of the world.[12]

'World literature' must, then, do better in attending to literatures in more of the languages of the world. Even more, however, the present volume argues not only, with Spivak and Mufti, against the dominance of English, but also against a dominant concept of monolingualism that has further served to limit and skew the scope of 'world literature'. We take on board for this reason the arguments of thinkers such as Yasemin Yildiz, David Gramling and Robert Young, who reveal the pressure on literature by the publishing market to conform to the demands of either monolingualism or smooth translatability. Yildiz's study *Beyond the Mother Tongue: The Postmonolingual Condition* sets out to puncture the myth of monolingualism as an Enlightenment invention aimed at shoring up the unity of the nation state, and demonstrates at the same time how literatures in German have worked to debunk the assurances promulgated by a monolithic understanding of the 'mother tongue'.[13] David Gramling's *The Invention of Monolingualism*, published in 2016, goes further in tracing the continuity between the institutionalization of monolingualism in the eighteenth century, and the privileging of only certain, acceptable and easily translatable forms of multilingualism in the current global publishing market.[14] Insisting that monolingualism is a 'myth' in the sense that Roland Barthes attributes to it, that it is an ideological construction that presents itself as 'innocent' or 'inherent', he argues that, 'monolingualism has experienced an asymptotic spike in impact and innovation since the 1990s and has become the organizing fulcrum for a new era of human history, the linguacene'.[15] And this 'linguacene', he explains, names a society where the global market drives either monolingualism or the demand for only smooth and rapid forms of translation. In response to the 'linguacene', Gramling insists on the artificiality of the opposition between monolingualism and multilingualism, arguing that a conception of multilingualism that nevertheless rests on the assumption that languages should be kept separate perpetuates cultural segregation and isolationism. Robert Young reinforces the point, by arguing that, 'in promoting multilingualism, we are upholding and confirming monolingualism, the idea that people speak separate, classifiable and classified single languages, each of which by definition is marked by a border that ensures unity, like the boundary of a nation'.[16]

In foregrounding 'worldliness' over and above the putative particularity of national languages and cultures, 'world literature' could be conceived as a forum for a potentially more creative and dynamic encounter between linguistic systems. Yet, Gramling insists, not enough has yet been done to challenge the monolingual myth within the arena of world literature. Gramling and Young have both pointed out the conservatism of the conception of language underpinning many recent theories of 'world literature', despite their mission of inclusivity. Young argues that, while it may appear to celebrate global consciousness, world literature in fact 'look[s] for literatures written in identifiable languages and then organiz[es] each language and its literature in relation to nationality, region, or cultural origin'.[17] In his more detailed analysis of 'world literarity', Gramling notes how 'foreignizing' translation and the use of local idiom in the world literary arena actually reinforces the idea that literatures represent particular, determinate territories and introduce these in ways palatable to publishers and readers in the global market still dominated by English. According to Gramling, a form of 'soft multilingualism' 'sanctions certain kinds of translatedness at the expense of others', so that despite an apparent opening up to global linguistic diversity, languages are still conceived as set, framed sovereign entities and only certain, either exoticized or easily absorbed forms of multilingualism are welcomed or approved.[18] This 'soft multilingualism' is theorized by Yaseen Noorani as a means by which 'structural incompatibilities between languages have been or continue to be eliminated', since an acceptable multilingual literature must assume that the languages on which it plays are translatable and consumable by readers in the world's ruling nations.[19]

In response to these observations, critics have started to analyse multilingualism in literary texts produced and shaped by particular cross-cultural contexts. While interest in linguistic diversity in literature has been growing for some time, with Doris Sommer's work on *Bilingual Aesthetics* and *Bilingual Games* in 2003 and 2004 respectively making a significant intervention in its embrace of the critical significance of bilingual writing, it is relatively recently that critics have sought to bring out the deep mutual interpenetration of multiple systems rather than merely celebrating fleeting and playful insertions. Sommer's work takes a useful and productive first step towards reading literatures across linguistic frameworks, but her focus remains on texts staging an encounter always between two rather than several 'sovereign' languages, and her studies tend still to conceptualize linguistic border-crossing as transient and anomalous. Sommer's discussion of bilingualism as an occasionally challenging feature of certain literary texts is echoed in studies such as Maria Lauret's *Wanderwords: Language Migration in American Literature* published in 2014. Yet some critics have started to explore linguistic border-crossing as more integral to the 'worldliness' of a world literature capable of undermining the potential flattening and generalizing sweep of world literary criticism. In her *Shades of the Planet: American Literature as World Literature*, Wai Chee Dimock insists we separate the notion of 'world literature' from globalization and suggests we need to explore 'alternate geographies' that are constrained neither by nation-based mapping nor by a market-driven globalized culture. Her own intervention in the volume analyses the use of 'creole tongue' in African, Caribbean and American writing, to show how these uses of the vernacular 'bear witness to the planetary circuit of tongues, the mixing of syntax and phonemes across continents'.[20] Francesca Orsini's concept of the 'multilingual local' also emphasizes 'significant geographies' beyond the national and the global, and particularly in Asian literatures where the leading theoretical narratives of 'world literature' do not apply. Orsini helpfully redefines 'world literature' rather as 'situated, plural, necessarily multilingual, and always-in-the-making'.[21] Stefan Helgesson's volume *World Literatures: Exploring the Cosmopolitan-Vernacular Exchange* is also ground-breaking in its call to replace the framework of nation-world with that of the cosmopolitan-vernacular exchange.[22] The cosmopolitan is here already conceived as relational whilst the vernacular is associated with place rather than with authenticity, and both are 'dynamics' that must be understood in the context of the various power relations working upon them.

The present volume builds on such studies, but will be the first to take multilingualism in literature as its own structuring and generative principle and to combine analyses of linguistic plurality in literature across a range of contexts to provide a conceptual overview of the place and function of such plurality in literary works from different parts of the world and divergent linguistic systems within the framework of 'world literature'. The essays gathered here are, however, no longer concerned with the ways in which a national tradition and language reach out into the wider network of global connectivity, but rather construe the creative intermingling of languages in hybridized literary works as emblematic of 'worldliness' and of how languages are dynamically used and spoken in the world. Rather than assuming, moreover, that 'multilingualism' is merely the accumulation of several 'monolingualisms', a mode of thinking that continues to imply that languages should be kept separate, the volume instead conceives language itself not only as an elastic and evolving practice but also inherently multilingual whose mobility and inventiveness can be aptly dramatized in literary writing. Contributors to the volume seek to display this inventiveness both by foregrounding the interpenetration between what are ordinarily conceived as particular linguistic systems and by highlighting idiomatic and structural diversity within these 'systems'. In addition, considering language as a semiology based in word, we open out multilingualism to semiologies based in both image and sound. We take on board and also question the concepts such as those of 'plurilingualism', 'translingualism' and 'heterolingualism', and seek less to propose a new model or buzzword for multilingualism in world literature than to interrogate the very limits of language, the stability of its apparent boundaries, its ability to communicate the resonance of unintelligibility.[23] These questions, and the provocative ways in which literary works are able to extend and reimagine the very concept and borders of language, are again conceived as central to the 'worldliness' of 'world literature' in that they demonstrate the movement of language not just through the globalized network but across national and cultural classifications in various hybridized configurations. The chapters are also less interventions on the already excessively glossed theory of 'world literature', but more close and intricate literary readings of works selected for their singular linguistic challenges. They examine various particular modalities of linguistic blending, including borrowings and insertions, the use of experimental idioms and vernaculars, the cross-fertilization of genres and forms, as well as translation and untranslatability.

The juxtaposition, moreover, of studies of works combining such a wide range of languages is at the same time crucial to the innovative impetus of the volume and to its fundamental concept of multilingual literatures operating in parallel in particular geographies across different parts of the world. The choice of languages covered will, however, inevitably seem partial, as our contributors focus mostly on European languages, Arabic, Turkish, Chinese or Creole. The volume in no way sets out to offer a representative view of multilingual literatures across the world, but rather selects particular examples to offer various perspectives on the different forms, implications and challenges of linguistic border-crossing in literary texts. English translations are offered of all quotations in other languages, but the readings presented here are also committed to working not only with the transfer of meaning across linguistic borders but also with the friction always at work at the border, as multilingual literature necessarily embraces some degree of opacity. The essays gathered here are not aimed solely at the multilingual reader but also deliberately foreground unintelligibility as one of the consequences of multilingual writing. Rather than experiencing this opacity as a hindrance, however, the readings set out to foreground how linguistic border-crossing makes creative demands upon the reader, who should not be seen to be excluded by the use of foreign languages but whose role is subversively reconfigured to involve a form of co-creation based at once on partial understanding and on her own creative imagination.

The languages that contribute to these multilingual literatures are also themselves understood in a broad sense. They may in some cases be apparently national or cultural units, though the essays will endeavour to demonstrate that such units are on some level ideological constructions whose usage is in reality changeable and porous. They may also be local vernaculars, including oral languages, or hybridized local idioms, such as a creole. At the same time, however, one of the aims of the volume is to test our understanding of language through literary readings, to explore the phonetic sign in this context and its combination with other nonverbal forms of language. The signifying systems with which our works experiment are also charged and altered by nonverbal sound, bodily movement, gesture and breath, for example. Human expression as it is dramatized in the texts under consideration will at times be construed not only as the product of combinations of spoken languages but also as infused with other types of sound, with bodily movement and experience. In other examples, moreover, our contributors analyse verbal languages in dialogue with visual languages, as the form and meaning of literary works can be expanded and developed through the interspersing of word and image in ways that again serve to question assumed cultural frontiers. In addition, the languages of the world we perceive as expressive of 'world literature' necessarily include human languages as well as those of the world around us, of landscape, environment, ecology and materiality. *Multilingual Literature as World Literature* includes in this way attention to both human and nonhuman languages to offer a more expansive view of the energy and creativity released by the encounter and blending of multiple forms of expression.

Our primary concerns are conceptual and theoretical. We are keen to refine and advance further the theories and practices of world literature from as many vantage points as possible. Multilingualism allows us to move away from the 'national', 'international', 'local' and 'global' in the imaginings of how the world is constructed, and from 'translation' in the mappings of the ways in which the national or local is connected with and to the international and global. Our starting point is that the international or global is already inherent in the national or local and that world in world literature resides both inside and outside the literary work. Multilingualism in a work of literature reflects and refracts the plurilingual speaking subject and heterolingual environment in the world we live in, and also styles the poetics of worlding in the same literary work. When thought of both as lingual and semiological, it gives word both image and sound. Translanguaging knits sovereignly perceived languages and semiologies into the same fabric, and brings different locals around the globe, even 'multilingual locals', into productive literary encounters. Such a starting point occasions new strategies for reading literary texts and for tracing the avenues through which these texts circulate from the local to the global. We are now able to focus on the global within the text and see in it the cross-cultural literary encounters which give shape to its poetics outside the framework of monologically conceptualized language and nation. However, we remain committed to 'world literature' and its vision even as we question its theories and practices.

The sixteen chapters are organized around the four main inquiries in current theories and practices of world literature. Part I, in four chapters, considers different configurations of multilingualism in literary works and brings these to bear on modes of reading and on the conceptualization of world literature. Jane Hiddleston turns to Édouard Glissant's theory of 'writing in the presence of other languages' and reads his works to show how a language thrives on crossing the borders of our imagined linguistic systems, and a literary work on bringing world languages into creative intermingling. Shuangyi Li and Khalid Lyamlahy open out linguistic systems to visual semiology in their respective contemplations of French-Chinese and Arabic-French literary works and similarly see creativity in intersemiological encounters blending the verbal and the visual. Claire Gallien takes on the differences in notions of multilingual, plurilingual and heterolingual worldliness, and privileges the 'creative intermeshing between languages' of heterolingualism in her reading of what she calls Anglo-Arabic writings. These writings, she shows, mix languages without translation, to recreate the sound effect of heterolingualism and, more particularly, to bring to life the multilingual environment in which the authors live and work.

Part II naturally steers our critical sight, and site, to a multilingual 'ecology of world literature', but moves away from Alexander Beecroft's monolingually focused explorations,[24] and seeks insight into the formation of literary worlds in the creative responses to the multilingual ecology of literary works. It picks up from the political and ethical concerns raised in Part I. The four chapters look at how politics and ethics contribute to shaping the multilingual text in a particular time and place, and reflect on how to read these texts 'ecologically', with a focus on the local as a space for the interrogation of global concerns, and as a call for diversity. Laura Lonsdale connects multilingualism with biodiversity in her readings of twenty-first-century poetry in Spain, and Keya Anjaria, Carlos F. Grigsby and Dominique Jullien track creative and critical responses to the 'maelström' of multilingualism and at the same time turn the notion of 'multilingual maelström' on its head to show how multilingualism in literary works is a form of resistance to national monologism in nineteenth-century Turkey, to the monolingual French definition of modernism in Spain, and to the trauma of the Holocaust in the twentieth century.

Part III develops the current thinking about modes of circulation in world literature. Taking as a point of departure the multilingual world of a literary text, the four chapters challenge and reconsider the prevalent concepts of translation and particularly Emily Apter's 'untranslatability'.[25] Nora Parr looks at the insistent multilingualism of concepts like 'trauma' and 'ghetto' in the context of the world literature market and demonstrates the limits of translation as the primary means of the circulation of literary works around the world. Dima Ayoub similarly contests the monolingual paradigm of translation in a comparative analysis of a multilingual translation of an already multilingual text. Ellen Jones uses multilingual texts to deterritorialize translation as 'finished work' and to help us see it as a 'creative process' that is 'unfinished', 'ongoing' and 'continually in motion'. Juliette Taylor-Batty brings current notions of translation and untranslatability into conversation with multilingual texts and argues that persistent ambivalence is attendant to the exuberance of multilingual texts. The politics surrounding untranslatability in fact celebrate an interlingual creativity that eschews the writers' ability to 'know' and 'master' a language.

Part IV, also in four chapters, explores diverse instances of creativity in multilingualism. yasser elhariry explains the multilingual poetics born out of the playful combination of word and sound, and of text and performance in French and Francophone poetry. In her demonstration of the interplay between 'polyphonic fluidity and zigzagging of Trinidadian speech' and 'expatriation' in Trinidadian poetry, Rachael Gilmour shows that poetry is a game played with language as event and sound effect rather than fixed system. Christopher Monier locates cross-lingual aesthetics in the dialogue between a *première parole* inherent in proverbs and language in use, and argues that a Martinican approach to poetry holds up language as inherently multilingual and puts into practice a Caribbean 'archipelagic' conception of world literature. Wen-chin Ouyang takes advantage of the diverse configurations of multilingualism explored in the preceding chapters and brings two examples into conversation to show the ways in which multilingual experimentation produces new forms of poetics.

World literature, all the chapters in this book argue, thrives in language encounters, which are re-enacted in literary texts. They demonstrate that multilingualism in a text circulates aesthetics across languages, literary traditions and cultures, and must be taken into consideration in theorizing world literature. Translation need not be the means of circulation, and translatability, or untranslatability, should not define the terms of our engagement with world literature. The politics surrounding world literature and translation as well as their markets, including untranslatability, do have an impact on how we do 'world literature' and, more importantly, view the world. The difference between a monolingual vision of the world and a multilingual one is that the former can be exclusive of diversity and the latter is by definition inclusive. There is an ethical dimension in this difference. Human unity in diversity aside, we are also concerned with the ecology of Earth, with how monological anthropocentrism has eroded the balance and health of our habitat. Biodiversity is embedded in our multilingual worldview and practice. We see for 'world literature' an activist role. 'World literature' is languages, worldviews and cultures in dialogue, but also engagement with our environment and critical response to all forms of violence committed against our world.

Notes

1. David Damrosch, *What is World Literature?* (Princeton: Princeton University Press, 2003), 281.
2. Pascale Casanova, *The World Republic of Letters*, trans. Malcolm DeBevoise (Cambridge, MA: Harvard University Press, 2007), 24.
3. Franco Moretti, 'Conjectures on World Literature', *New Left Review* 1 (2000): 54–68, 68.
4. Thomas O. Beebee, ed., *German Literature as World Literature* (London: Bloomsbury, 2014), 4, 5.
5. Jeffrey R. Di Leo, *American Literature as World Literature* (London: Bloomsbury, 2017), 6.

6. Edward Said, *The World, the Text, the Critic* (Cambridge, MA: Harvard University Press, 1984), 39.
7. Ibid., 226.
8. Eric Hayot, *On Literary Worlds* (Oxford: Oxford University Press, 2012).
9. The Warwick Research Collective, *Combined and Uneven Development: Towards a New Theory of World-literature* (Liverpool: Liverpool University Press, 2015).
10. Graham Huggan, 'The Trouble with World Literature', in Ali Behdad and Dominic Thomas (eds.), *A Companion to Comparative Literature* (Oxford: Wiley Blackwell, 2011), 491.
11. Gayatri Spivak, *An Aesthetic Education in the Era of Globalization* (Cambridge, MA: Harvard University Press, 2012), 26.
12. Aaamir Mufti, *Forget English! Orientalisms and World Literatures* (Cambridge, MA: Harvard University Press, 2016).
13. Yasemin Yildiz, *Beyond the Mother Tongue: The Postmonolingual Condition* (New York: Fordham University Press, 2012).
14. David Gramling, *The Invention of Monolingualism* (London: Bloomsbury, 2016).
15. Ibid., 93.
16. Robert Young, 'That Which Is Casually Called a Language', *PMLA* 131.5 (2016): 1207–21, 1209.
17. Ibid., 1209.
18. Gramling, *The Invention of Monolingualism*, 25.
19. Yaseen Noorani, 'Hard and Soft Multilingualism', *Critical Multilingualism Studies* 1.2 (2013): 7–28, 9.
20. Wai Chee Dimock and Laurence Buell, ed., *Shades of the Planet: American Literature as World Literature* (Princeton: Princeton University Press, 2007), 274.
21. Francesca Orsini, 'The Multilingual Local in World Literature', *Comparative Literature* 67.4 (2015): 345–74. See also Karima Laachir, Sara Maragorza, Francesca Orsini, 'Multilingual Locals and Significant Geographies: For a Ground-up and Located Approach to World Literature', *Modern Languages Open* 1 (2018): 1–8.
22. Stefan Helgesson, Annika Mörte Alling, Yvonne Lindqvist and Helena Wulff, *World Literatures: Exploring the Cosmopolitan–Vernacular Exchange* (Stockholm: Stockholm University Press, 2018).
23. These concepts are theorized by thinkers such as Brian Lennon, *In Babel's Shadow: Multilingual Literatures, Monolingual States* (Minneapolis: University of Minnesota Press, 2010); see also Stefan Helgesson and Christina Kullberg, 'Translingual Events: World Literature and the Making of Language', *Journal of World Literature* 3.2 (2018): 136–52; Paul Bandia, *Translation as Reparation: Writing and Translation in Postcolonial Africa* (Abingdon: Routledge, 2008); Myriam Suchet, *L'Imaginaire hétérolingue: ce que nous apprennent les textes à la croisée des langues* (Paris: Classiques Garnier, 2014).
24. Alexander Beecroft, *An Ecology of World Literature: From Antiquity to the Present Day* (London: Verso, 2015).
25. Emily Apter, *Against World Literature: On the Politics of Untranslatability* (London: Verso, 2013).

Part I

Multilingualism and modes of reading

1

Writing in the presence of the languages of the world: Language, literature and world in Édouard Glissant's late theoretical works

Jane Hiddleston

Glissant's assertion that 'j'écris en présence de toutes les langues du monde' (I write in the presence of the languages of the world) is repeated multiple times in his later theoretical essays, in particular in *Traité du tout-monde* (Treatise on the Totality-World), published in 1997. The statement announces his ongoing commitment to multilingualism and his insistence that language is always defined by Relation, by which he means that our idioms are created out of the dynamic global network of languages and are not necessarily determined by a single linguistic system. Yet if Glissant so insistently celebrates this creative multilingual expression, the dominant language of his prose appears on first glance to be French. He occasionally incorporates creole terms, particularly in his poetry, and often uses the specific lexicon of the local Martinican landscape in all his writing, but his theorization of a creolized, multilingual writing nevertheless for the most part appears to take place in literary French, even if this French is lexically wide-ranging and contains evidence of his engagement with multiple cultures. The notion that the writer writes in the presence of the languages of the world, then, implies something different from a bilingual writing that stages a confrontation between languages by consistently inserting words or sentences from one language into another.

This chapter takes Glissant's statement as a starting point for a conception of multilingualism in 'world literature' that does not rest on the assumption that separate languages can be juxtaposed with one another, but that is constructed out of a more expansive and relational understanding of language usage. Glissant's assertion notes the presence in his writing of multiple languages 'dans la nostalgie poignante de leur devenir menacé' (in the poignant nostalgia of their threatened becoming), and announces a commitment to the preservation of minority languages as a principled response to global linguistic diversity and as a challenge to the repressiveness behind any insistence on linguistic hierarchy or segregation.[1] Yet the statement also announces a deep-seated ethics of writing, an approach to language whereby the writer seeks deliberately to exhibit the contingency of his usage and signals an awareness of the myriad potentially unfamiliar languages that surround and shape his writing. Glissant's conception of language itself, and of the 'world' in which it is immersed, indicates that it is possible to transcend the putative opposition between monolingualism and multilingualism and to understand language and writing in ways that are ultimately both more creative and more ethical. 'World literature', from this point of view, would be an arena for performing the creation of idiom from a dynamic world of languages and for continually testing and expanding our assumed linguistic systems.

A number of critics have in recent years attempted to come up with ways of imagining literary creativity so as to reflect the complex activity and interpenetration of languages in ways that provide a starting point for Glissant's more thoroughgoing theoretical intervention. Rebecca Walkowitz's *Born Translated* examines novels that 'have been written for translation from the start', that is, novels that stage their own indebtedness to languages other than the one in which they are written.[2] This might include works written in a second language, for example, or texts that have been translated by their authors, or that are manifestly the product of a translation process at some point. In this sense they are on some level written 'in the presence of' other languages, as Glissant would suggest, as these languages are referenced through the staging of the translation process. The difficulty with Walkowitz's model, however, is that although she insists that her readings demonstrate that 'anglophone writing operates in many languages, even when it appears to be operating only in English', her analyses do not particularly exhibit linguistic diversity and experimentalism, and her model still relies on a notion of translation from one language into another.[3] The other languages to which her chosen texts refer may be present but they are also latent, and do not necessarily generate linguistic invention.

Other critics have examined more fully the presence of other languages in literary texts by foregrounding not just 'multilingualism' in the sense of the juxtaposition of several monolingual systems, but more developed forms of linguistic interpenetration. In *In Babel's Shadow*, for example, Brian Lennon denounces the constraints on language usage applied by the publishing industry, and proposes a notion of 'strong plurilingualism', that is 'the interpolation into English of significant quantities of a language or languages other than English', usually only permitted by small independent publishing houses.[4] This 'strong plurilingualism' is theorized by Lennon as an alternative to 'multilingualism' because it describes both the mixing of linguistic systems and, importantly for my reading of Glissant, the presence of combinations of idiom within a single linguistic system. As a further alternative to 'multilingualism', moreover, Paul Bandia has examined what he calls the 'heterolingualism' of postcolonial literature, choosing this term to reflect the 'heterogeneity' of postcolonial society as well as the creative ways in which a range of postcolonial writers challenge the hegemonic language of colonization.[5] Bandia's 'heterolingualism' is reminiscent of Glissant's embrace of 'creolization', a process rather than a dialect, and one by which hegemonic languages are continually remodelled through their contact with multiple and dynamic local languages or creoles. Bandia shows how works by writers such as the Ivorian Ahmadou Kourouma offer a vision of literary heterolingualism, where 'language mixing and hybridity occur without any regard for linguistic hierarchy, in a context where languages coexist in a rhizomatic relationship'.[6] Lennon's 'plurilingualism' and

Bandia's 'heterolingualism' may, then, offer viable alternatives to 'multilingualism' in their more convincing description of non-hierarchical forms of linguistic plurality in literary works.

Édouard Glissant's highly creative poetic theory, however, is less focused on finding a new 'lingualism' and more concerned with the ways in which literary writing might challenge our notions of what a language is and of its activity in the world. Glissant proposes to think of language not in terms of monolingualism and multilingualism but in terms of a form of relational expressivity. Language can be construed, perhaps, not as a defined system but as the infinitely multiple forms of expression we create out of our varying contacts with particular systems, each conceived as more dynamic than the 'myth' of monolingualism assumes. Language is comprised of the singular idioms we put together on the basis of our dialogue with other people, cultures, languages and environments. As the critic Celia Britton has shown, the root of Glissant's linguistic theory as it evolves through his oeuvre is the distinction he makes between 'langage' and 'langue'.[7] While his thinking is clearly developed out of Saussure's distinction between 'langue' and 'parole', Glissant nevertheless undermines Saussure's privileging of identifiable linguistic systems to emphasize how individual inventions of 'langage' continually extend and reshape the 'langue' or 'langues' out of which they emerge. Rather than assuming that language is a signifier of national identity, moreover, Glissant insists instead on the dynamism of 'langage' as the trace of the speaker or writer's contact both with a specific place in the world, and with the multiple other places and cultures that infiltrate that place as well as his or her expression of it: 'un langage, c'est cela d'abord: la fréquentation insensée de l'organique, des spécifiques d'une langue et, en même temps, son ouverture sévère à la Relation' (a language is above all the senseless frequenting of the organic, of the specificity of a language, and at the same time its severe opening out to Relation).[8] A 'langue', then, should not be construed as fixed and standardized, but is constantly stretched and altered by the dynamic movement of 'langages'. Literary writing, moreover, with its creative energy is particularly well placed to drive this movement forward, as Glissant argues in a manner reminiscent of Bakhtin's 'dialogic imagination' in the novel, 'la langue ne grandit que par le langage, cette frappe du poète, et le langage a besoin de toutes les langues, qui sont l'imaginaire du monde' (language only grows through individual usages of language, the force of the poet, and individual usages of language need all languages, which are the imaginary of the world).[9] No longer a question of either monolingualism or multilingualism, literary writing is rather the inventive pursuit of ever new 'langages': idioms or forms of expression that test and push the limits of what we conceive as the existing frameworks of 'langue'.

As Celia Britton has astutely argued, Glissant's conception of 'langage' also implies an ethical stance. His insistence on the importance of inventive 'langages' stems in part from an embrace of unintelligibility: my awareness of the opacity of a language I do not understand demonstrates to me the contingency of my own language and counters dangerously reductive and exclusive notions of cultural identity. In this sense Glissant goes beyond Bakhtin in his insistence not only on the multilingual imagination but also on the ethical significance of our encounter with idioms or cultural forms we cannot necessarily assimilate, and that call upon us in turn to co-create in our reading.

Glissant's linguistic theory has, since *Le Discours antillais* (Caribbean Discourse) published in 1981, brought with it a claim for 'le droit à l'opacité' (the right to opacity), which implies both respect for unfamiliar forms of expression and a capacity to write or create in ways that might not produce meaning in predictable and established forms. The 'droit à l'opacité' challenges the demand for false clarity associated with reductive universalisms and invites a more open, risky but constructive form of complicity, as Glissant asserts: 'il ne m'est pas nécessaire de "comprendre" qui que ce soit, individu, communauté, peuple, de le "prendre avec moi" au prix de l'étouffer, de le perdre ainsi dans une totalité assommante que je gérerais, pour accepter de vivre avec lui, de bâtir avec lui, de risquer avec lui' (in order to live, build, and take a risk with an individual, a community, a people, it is not necessary for me to 'understand' them, to 'take them with me' at the cost of stifling them, of losing them in an oppressive totality that I would manage).[10] In addition, this encounter with opacity is again a driver for the creation of new and composite forms of expression, as the poet, for example, according to Glissant also recreates foreign idioms in a different form in his or her own 'langage': 'je te parle dans ta langue, et c'est dans mon langage que je t'entends' (I speak to you in your language, and it's in my language that I understand you).[11] Britton explains that this respect for opacity is also a necessary correlation of Glissant's concept of 'langage' as a singular form of expression created out of the speaker's relation with the world: '*langage*, that is, also opens up the possibility of a different mode of understanding the other's speech which does not depend either upon the reductive transparency he is opposing or upon ordinary linguistic knowledge'.[12] 'Langage' designates a form of expression that is not constrained by the rules of a standardized system, but may speak to listeners and readers in more open-ended and transformative ways. Some degree of unintelligibility is indeed in itself a trigger for discovery and invention.

Glissant's conception of the contact and blurring between 'langues' created by 'langages' is bound up, moreover, with his notion of 'mondialité' (worldliness), not in the sense of the universalizing force of globalization, but as a catalyst for creolization, hybridization and Relation. 'Tout monde' (Totality-World) precisely names not so much the world itself as the imagination of a dynamic, evolving interconnectedness across the world, the embrace of 'métissage' and the rejection of 'les absolus de l'Histoire' (the absolutes of History). 'Mondialité' in no way implies homogenization, then, but rather, as Eric Prieto puts it, a 'theory of interdependence' demonstrating the connections between particular forms of oppression across the capitalist world.[13] The apparently utopian quality of Glissant's celebration of 'mondialité', then, is offset by his repeated evocations of suffering in different parts of the world, where hierarchical and exclusivist thinking has led to violence, expressed precisely as 'le cri du monde' (the cry of the world).[14] In the face of this violence, Glissant emphatically affirms the potentially salutary effects of a world literary form of writing, the inventive 'langages' of which would contest oppressive systems of thinking. The writer's linguistic imaginary cannot be constricted by an atavistic identity but precisely requires immersion in the dynamic multiplicity of the world, and writing records the trace of this process.[15] Important for Glissant too is this contact between writing and orality, as it is oral cultures that best perform the dynamic creativity of 'langage', and that, 'conviennent tant à la diversité de toutes choses, la répétition, le ressassement, la parole circulaire, le cri en spirale, les cassures de la voix' (are so well suited to the diversity of all things, repetition, returning to, circular discourse, the cry in the form of a spiral, the breaking of voices).[16] Glissant's vision of worldly literature rejects any putative claim to encompass globality, as he suggests that the Anglophone conception of 'world literature' risks implying, but again, is the product of a more fundamentally ethical and creative approach to the inventiveness of 'langage'.[17] It is also a way of writing that does not aspire to universalism, but that deliberately displays its idiosyncrasies, its particular locality, while conceiving that locality itself as necessarily plural and interactive. Against the world literary marketplace shaped and constrained by the global publishing market, then, Glissant imagines a different worldly aesthetic energized by the relationality of its idiom and form.

It is against this background of a renewed conceptualization of both language and world that Glissant intermittently affirms, 'j'écris en présence de toutes les langues du monde' (I write in the presence of the languages of the world). The statement suggests that he composes out of an imaginary that acknowledges and embraces the vast and sprawling network of languages that jostle against one another. He may, as we have seen, not be familiar with these multiple languages, and yet, 'dans la langue qui me sert à exprimer, et quand même je ne me réclamerais que d'elle seule, je n'écris plus de manière monolingue' (in the language I use to express myself, and even though I claim only this one, I no longer write in a monolingual way).[18] To write in the presence of other languages is not necessarily to write by incorporating borrowings, but rather to foreground the work's contingent place in the global linguistic arena. Glissant's initial description of his own writing practice is also later reiterated in the plural and in italics – '*nous écrivons en présence de toutes les langues du monde*' (*we write in the presence of all the languages in the world*) – as if to describe literary production itself rather than his own particular poetics. Whatever relationship we think we might have with a language, 'nous les partageons sans les connaître, nous les convions à la langue dont nous usons. La langue n'est plus le miroir d'aucun être. Les langues sont nos paysages, que la poussée du jour change en nous' (we share them without knowing them, we invite them into the language that we use. Language is no longer the mirror of being. Languages are our landscapes, which the advancement of the day changes within us).[19] As experience alters and shifts, so too does the form of our self-expression, so that we cannot conceive ourselves as purely and securely represented in a single linguistic framework connoting a specified identity. To write in the presence of other languages means to write not in order to provide a copy of what we think we are and know, but in order to invent singular forms of expression exhibiting their situation in a world of languages in continual transit.

The creative activity of writing also gives rise to the invention of 'langages' whose form is necessarily unpredictable. The writer's interaction with existing cultures and heritages leads to unforeseen combinations of idiom, melding the old with the new: 'l'écriture, qui nous mène à des intuitions imprévisibles, nous fait découvrir les constantes cachées de la diversité du monde, et nous éprouvons bienheureusement que ces invariants nous parlent à leur tour' (writing, which leads us to unpredictable intuitions, makes us discover the hidden constants of the diversity of the world, and we happily feel that these invariants speak to us in turn).[20] The writer patches together his or her composition by drawing on the languages of his or her locality, of those speaking around him, and these languages are in turn always shaped by his or her previous and ongoing interactions. Writing necessarily builds on a linguistic heritage but combines these 'invariants' in unforeseen configurations. This patchwork creation is precisely the starting point, moreover, for the discovery of spontaneous and unanticipated idioms and forms of expression. Glissant's ethics of respect for opacity in this way also issues an assertive call for creative endeavour, again as a form of resistance to oppressive hierarchies and reductive categorizations. The unpredictable results of creolization 'nous gardent d'être persuadés d'une essence ou d'être raidis dans des exclusives' (keep us from being persuaded by an essence or from being hardened into exclusivities).[21]

Glissant's conception of the openness of writing to the unpredictable offers a compelling development of Derek Attridge's more introspective conception of creation, as he too suggests that writing resurges unplanned, not necessarily transcribing a pre-existing idea, but generating new thinking or 'otherness', as its idioms take shape.[22] Attridge's view of literary creation stresses how a creative work can emerge in ways that are mysterious to the writer, as he or she experiments with combinations of words on the page without knowing where these arrangements will take the text. Creation, for Attridge, is 'a handling of language whereby something we might call "otherness", or "alterity", or "the other" is made, or allowed, to impact upon the existing configurations of an individual's mental world – which is to say, upon a particular cultural field as it is embodied in a single subjectivity'.[23] Attridge goes on to discuss the ways in which 'idioculture' provides the backdrop for this process, and he defines this 'idioculture' as a 'changing array of interlocking, overlapping, and often contradictory cultural systems absorbed in the course of his or her previous experience, a complex matrix of habits, cognitive models, representations, beliefs, expectations, prejudices, and preferences'.[24] Attridge's model implies a sort of coherence within any particular individual's 'idioculture', and yet it is significant that his theory is based on the contribution of potentially contradictory cultures to a unique 'event' of creation that is not predetermined. Read in conjunction with Glissant, this creation can also be conceived to occur through the writer's contacts with locality and Relation in a more active, plural and worldly way than Attridge's model seems to emphasize. Writing evolves unplanned from traces of idioms captured, translated and reinvented by the writer in ways that generate their own momentum. The spontaneous inventions of the writer's 'langage' come not only from his or her solipsistic introspection but from his immersion in the languages of the world.

Although Glissant's theorization of language, literature and relationality is itself not explicitly multilingual, his own use of form offers one way to imagine what it means to 'write in the presence of the languages of the world'. In his reflection on the relationship between writing and orality quoted earlier, Glissant also associated worldly writing with the spontaneous characteristics of oral storytelling, with repetition and reworking, circularity and fragmentation. It is also through structure, then, that the writer emphasizes the contingency of his or her usage, its provisional form among other languages, and its resistance to established grammatical and syntactical structures or lexicons. Glissant's *Traité du tout-monde* is importantly itself a hybrid text, part 'theory' and part narrative, combining different sorts of prose (and some occasional verse), while also juxtaposing Glissant's analytical voice with that of the character Mathieu Béluse from his novels. This mixed and fragmented form is itself a performance of writing made up of different 'langages', and some of the theoretical sections contain poetic imagery, or convoluted syntax, or intersperse conceptual analysis with lyricism. A rich and surprising passage, for example, opens the section made up of reflections on other writers 'Ce qui nous fut, ce qui nous est', and is worth quoting in full:

> ... Les feux des lys sauvages, les clairs fourrés d'oiseaux du paradis, les maisons rousses assoupies qui veillent sur des marais semés de roses-de-porcelaine, et tout ce que la totalité-monde amasse de rires et de malheurs en une seule favela, puis les sables – Brésil – cascadant entre les murailles des fleuves-serpents, et l'évohé des chœurs d'Afrique mêlés de flûte indienne, d'où va sourdre bientôt la bossa-nova, et le jappement des usines venu lécher les mosaïques des trottoirs, toutes ces images convenues qui entrent en démesure, et les paons amazoniens qui engloutissent dans la ténèbre de leurs roues les familles de la forêt, et l'odeur rêche des cocos et des oranges amères ...²⁵

> (The fires of wild lilies, the light areas lined with birds of paradise, the sleepy red houses that watch over marshes planted with porcelain roses, and all that the totality-world amasses with laughter and misfortune in a single favela (shanty-town), then the sands – Brazil – cascading between the walls of the rivers-serpents, and the frenzy of African choirs mingled with Indian flute, from which the bossa-nova will soon dull, and the barking of factories come to lick the mosaics of sidewalks, all these images together in disproportion, and the Amazonian peacocks which engulf in the darkness of their wheels the families of the forest, and the rough smell of coconuts and bitter oranges ...)

The passage piles on top of one another a series of composite images, enumerating flora and fauna, natural and cultural phenomena, local biological and cultural terms as well as colours, textures, sounds and smells, to emphasize both proliferation and incompletion. The ellipses at the beginning and end of the passage present the description as a fragment in a greater network, and the absence of full stops too foregrounds continuity. The images at the same time are themselves richly expressive and capture hints of local 'langages' in their noisy and vibrant diversity. The colours of the lilies and the birds of paradise are juxtaposed with those of the houses, for example, and sounds of the Indian flute or the bossa-nova compete with the yelping of the factories. Each of these images represents a form of expression drawing on multiple senses, rubbing against one another in the 'totalité-monde', while the passage as a whole flouts grammatical and syntactical rules so as to situate itself outside any determined linguistic system.

Most striking in Glissant's *Traité* is the incursion of the voice of Mathieu Béluse from the novels, whose interjections both offer an additional set of 'langages' to those of Glissant and at times challenge the philosopher's arguments so as to situate them within a relational framework. Mathieu Béluse's narrative foregrounds its situation in relation to multiple histories and geographies, and sets his own experience and that of his wife Marie Celat alongside the stories of other characters. He too emphasizes incompletion and provisonality, as narratives exist alongside other narratives, just as 'langages' jostle against one another, to undermine any definitive version: 'nos récits sont des mélopées, des traités de joyeux parler, et des cartes de géographie, et de plaisantes prophéties, qui n'ont pas souci d'être vérifiés' (our narratives are chants, treatises of joyful speech, geographical maps, pleasing prophecies, which do not need to be checked).[26] Béluse's objections to the *Traité* also underline Glissant's resistance to constructing his theory as a definitive truth, and the dialogic structure again constitutes another way to perform a notion of writing in the presence of other languages: Glissant writes his *Traité* so as to display its relativity, its encounter with other points of view. The objections list conflicts and injustices across the world, the non-recognition of migrant communities and the all-consuming sweep of global capitalist culture, for example, so that it is clear that the acceptance of relationality is figured as an ongoing effort rather than a completed statement. The *Traité*'s status as a sort of supplement to the main event of the novel, *Tout-monde*, itself the result of a long and complex sequence, also underlines its provisionality and its participation in an ongoing series of narratives.

Glissant's vision of writing in the presence of the languages of the world is presented by the time of *Traité du tout-monde* as a practice not necessarily grounded in the Caribbean, though it emerges out of his earlier conception of 'Antillanité' as an intensified experience of Relation. The shifting and ambiguous status of Caribbean specificity in Glissant's thought has generated some controversy, as thinkers such as Peter Hallward and Nick Nesbitt lament the depoliticization of his work as it shifts attention away from colonialism and the history of slavery in the Caribbean to the less-grounded aesthetics of the *tout-monde*.[27] Yet Glissant repeatedly argues that it is the archipelagic form of the islands, both connected with one another and distinct, as well as the region's rapid history of migration and confluence, that creates a particularly apt example of relationality, even if this has developed more slowly and in different ways elsewhere. Glissant's dynamic 'langage' is also comparable to the conceptions of language invented by other Caribbean writers similarly capturing the dynamic movement and development of local languages as they mix influences and create rhythms, sounds and structures that resist the monolingual system. Edward Kamau Brathwaite's concept of the 'nation language' in Anglophone Caribbean poetry, for example, describes the 'language-energy' of the combination of English with traces of ancestral languages, Hindi and Chinese, and African languages. This 'nation language' may ostensibly appear to be English, 'but in its contours, its rhythm and timbre, its sound explosions, it is not English'.[28] Like Glissant's writing in the presence of the languages of the world, it uses flexible and inventive structures, and in addition, captures local sounds potentially unfamiliar to speakers of hegemonic, standardized English. Glissant too reflects on the blending of the oral and written languages, emphasizing for the most part the spontaneity and structural malleability of oral forms, yet Brathwaite's 'nation language' also further expands the consistency of language in its foregrounding of the grain of the voice, of nonverbal sounds accompanying the words. The 'nation language' of poetry incorporates the nonverbal as a form of expression, 'often it is English which is like a howl, or a shout, or a machine-gun or the wind or a wave'. In a discussion with Brathwaite, Glissant clearly distinguishes the former's 'nation language' from Martinican creole, and yet the theory of language invention implied by Brathwaite's model also adds to Glissant's championing of hybridization and dynamic invention a salutary attention to the expressiveness of vocal sound.[29]

In addition to this attention to the materiality of the voice, both Brathwaite and Glissant stress in their dialogue, as well as throughout their work, the active role of the physical landscape in Caribbean cultural expression. For both, the Caribbean landscape is not merely a décor or frame, but an active force whose materiality bears an expressiveness that also impacts on their conceptions of poetic language. As the Guadeloupian writer Daniel Maximin also elaborates in detail in *Les Fruits du cyclone: une géopoétique de la Caraïbe* (The Fruits of the Cyclone: A Geopoetics of the Caribbean), the poetics of Relation also names the connection between slave and island. Local geography and geology also contributed to the slave's dream of liberation and rerooting in a way that contests the colonial attempt to dominate and control the natural world.[30] A further dimension, then, to Glissant's writing in the presence of the languages of the world is this conception of world also as the nonhuman world, as if writing might also capture or at least dialogue with the language of the landscape that surrounds the writer and by which he is shaped. As J. Michael Dash has argued, Glissant's immersion in the language of landscape has been evident from the beginning, and Jana Evans Braziel has shown, in her contribution to Deloughrey, Gossan and Handley's volume on *Caribbean Literature and the Environment*, how *Le Discours antillais* already strove to give agency back to the Caribbean landscape.[31] In *La Cohée du Lamentin* (The Cohée of the Lamentin), published in 2005, moreover, the language of place was evidently foregrounded in part in the singular reference to Martinican geography in the title (which refers to a part of the beach in the Lamentin, the region of Martinique where Glissant was born), as well as through Glissant's evocations of natural phenomena, and through his commentaries on poetry, such as that of Césaire, giving voice and form to the material features of local territory. And in Glissant's own novels and poetry, the character of Marie Celat (Mycéa) represents a unique form of communication with the land. In *Pays rêvé, pays reel* (Dream country, real country), for example, she repeatedly figures the expressivity of the landscape as a form of textuality, at the same time as she imagines that her own language might somehow achieve a renewed bonding beyond the rupture caused by slave history.[32]

Glissant's late volume, *Une nouvelle région du monde* (A New Region of the World), however, offers a particularly rich and aesthetically complex theorization of the writer's immersion in the 'langages' of the physical world. This challenging text, with its subtitle 'Esthétique I' (Aesthetics I), promises a new genre of aesthetic thought in Glissant's oeuvre, hovering somewhere between philosophy and prose poetry, and provides a particularly compelling example of writing in the presence of the languages of the world in its attempt to converse with the Martinican landscape. This idea of the expressiveness of the nonhuman environment generates a renewed conceptualization of artistic representation and its invocation of the 'real'. Glissant's theory here rests on a rejection of a concept of representation reliant on the human creation of a form subsequently imposed upon the landscape. He explores a history of various forms of depiction, including the 'tableau', which fixes the movement of a scene, as well as the shift from a form of painting that claims to possess the real to one that seeks fusion with it. Yet in the face of this, Glissant asserts, 'chaque paysage s'obstine, tous coloriés et monotones et nuancés et nus et échevelés, vivants enfin, il ne suffit pas de les photographier ni de calculer à la fin leurs dispositions, il faudra exprimer aussi pourquoi leurs couleurs font un langage, qui révèle quoi?' (each landscape persists, all coloured and monotonous and nuanced and naked and dishevelled, finally alive, it is not enough to photograph them or in the end to calculate their position, it will be necessary to express also why their colours make a language, that reveals what?).[33] Rather than grafting a created form onto the landscape, then, Glissant suggests we should be aware of how the landscape itself creates its own art form and its own language; its shapes, colours, movements and forces are themselves a form of expression to which we need to attend. 'La Nature, quand elle est née, a fait ses propres installations' (when it was born, Nature made its own installations), argues Glissant, as the rocks of the shoreline, for example, punctuate the surface of the sand as if with exclamation and question marks.[34] Similarly, the sound of the sea, the flow of the rivers, the shapes of the mountains, can be conceived as actively contributing to the aesthetic sense we have of the landscapes around us. Glissant suggests that oral cultures have been better able to achieve this expressive dialogue, as they 'invoke' rather than 'represent' the world, and live alongside it rather than attempting to imitate it. This aesthetics that is able also to listen to and capture the expression of the world is the starting point, for Glissant, for a 'nouvelle région du monde'.

The opening pages of this treatise on aesthetics constitute a compelling performance of Glissant's conception of writing not only in the presence of multiple human languages, but also with the echo of those of land and sea. The conceptualization of representation and worldliness undertaken in *Une nouvelle région du monde* is prefaced with an extraordinary piece of evocative prose describing Diamond Rock, a steep, uninhabited basalt island situated to the south of Martinique's Fort-de-France and visible from Glissant's home. On the one hand, as Carine Mardorossian argues in her astute analysis of the passage, the rock is a figure for the ways in which history and geography mutually shape one another.[35] The rock is both the result of geological forces, a shape moulded by its volcanic composition and by the sea, and at the same time historically significant in that it played a crucial role in the Napoleonic wars. On the other hand, Glissant captures its vitality here by evoking both the expressiveness of its form, its shape, light and colours, and the ways in which the human eye, and his own description, reinterpret this aesthetics. Importantly, then, he is not so much seeking to capture a pure, untouched and unmediated natural landscape in this passage, but rather showing how our apprehension of the rock must be alive to the nonhuman forces and patterns that fashion and shape it even as we create our own aesthetic vision. His description weaves together elements of light and shade, the shaping and patterning of the rock, with references to its irreducibility and obscurity, as if to suggest that he can be sensitive to its aesthetic form without claiming to frame and possess it. Formerly attached to the mainland, for example, the rock is:

> à lui seul un vrai archipel, et tellement irréductible dans sa fragilité sculptée, les matins sourds et les nuits évaporées le creusent et le mangent sans tarir, et il maintient le lien, d'interrogation et d'exclamation, et il jette l'inquiétude et l'émerveillement au travers de toute la structure, qui vous saisissent comme un flot roulant.[36]

> (alone a veritable archipelago, and so irreducible in its carved fragility, the quiet mornings and evaporated nights dig it and eat it without drying up, and it keeps the link, interrogation and exclamation, and it throws worry and wonder through the whole structure, which seize you like a rolling stream.)

The imagery here at once conjures the expressiveness of the geological formation and betrays an awareness of the obscurity of its history, while also displaying the writer's own interpretation of its shape (using the figures, for example, of the question marks and exclamation marks). Glissant's proliferating sentences, moreover, again foreground incompletion, as if the passage can capture elements of the rock's form while showing that the text's own language will necessarily also be relative and partial.

Glissant's evocation foregrounds at the same time the ways in which we seek to translate and make sense of the shape of the rock as we try to attend to its hidden languages: 'nous observons que le corps de terre qui ainsi projette vers sa chute ou sa conclusion est d'une dame couchée, le menton très volontaire et le nez fort et relevé, le Rocher derrière est comme la tête d'un peigne accroché à quelque natte de cheveux sous-marins' (we see that the body of earth leaning towards its own fall or end is like a reclining woman, the chin very determined and nose strong and raised, the Rock behind is like a head with a comb attached to a plait on underwater hair).[37] Despite these anthropomorphic forms that the viewer might create out of the landscape, however, 'c'est la mer en vérité qui domine' (in truth it's the sea that dominates), as water continually reshapes the shoreline and muddles the 'text' that it simultaneously serves to create.[38] Glissant's aim is to remain open to this muddling, to the dynamic movement of the landscape, to its shifting expression at different moments and in the varying modulations of light and weather, and he seeks to eschew the fixity and completion he associated with the 'tableau' or painting. His own challenging, rich and evocative prose in this section points, then, to the language of the rock, of the geological environment, even as it necessarily weaves and translates that language into his own.

Glissant in this way stretches the boundaries of his writing so that it listens not only to other cultural idioms but also to the earth's own manifold, layered and interlocking forms of expression. This attentiveness to the aesthetics of the landscape can be conceived as a way to expand our understanding of language beyond the frameworks of monolingualism and multilingualism to include more fully the mutual shaping of human and nonhuman forms of expression. Glissant's arguments here can also be read in conjunction with those of Brian Massumi, who has asserted, through readings of Deleuze and Guattari, that we need to imagine expression not just as a message conveyed and determined by a speaker, but as part of a system involving nonverbal and material forces. Expression is not a process of transferring meaning but an event or a movement; it combines both linguistic and extralinguistic forces, and the subject is a conduit for it rather than its owner. The philosophical background to Massumi's argument is far broader than Glissant's focus on the landscape and physical environment, and yet his uncoupling of expression and human agency nevertheless sheds light on the latter's vision of nonhuman expressivity. Massumi insists:

> Expression is not in a language-using mind, or in a speaking subject *vis-à-vis* its objects. Nor is it rooted in an individual body. It is not even in a particular institution, because it is precisely the institutional system that is in flux. Expression is abroad in the world – where the potential is for what may become. It is non-local, scattered across a myriad struggles over what manner of life-defining nets will capture and contain that potential in reproducible articulations, or actual functions.[39]

Expression is not, therefore, the intended message created by any given subject, but a much more dynamic process weaving together subject and environment; it is 'always on the move, always engrossed in its own course, overspilling individual experience, nomadically evading responsibility'.[40] Glissant's attempt to conceptualize the expressiveness of the landscape similarly opens language up through this vision of its formation in and continual interaction with the world, with materiality and the structures within which it moves. Expression as Glissant conceptualizes it also specifically perceives in landscape and environment a set of forces, shapes and patterns, and constructs the material world as the producer of an aesthetics that moulds and impacts on what we conceive as our cultural, human languages.

Glissant's affirmation that he writes in the presence of the languages of the world offers in this way a refreshing challenge not only to narrow forms of association between language, culture and identity, but also to our conception of the interface between language and the world. No longer a series of systems divided up by the dominant concepts of monolingualism and multilingualism, 'langues' are seen rather as the backdrop for creative 'langages' immersed in and created out of the relational expressivity of both the cultural and the material world. Writing in the presence of the languages of the world, then, is a way both to foreground the creativity and ethical importance of 'langages' in relation to 'langues', and to show how our utterances are formed through our contacts not only with other peoples and cultures but also with the physical environment. Glissant's aesthetics, moreover, not only champions creativity in its call for innovation and unpredictability, but also recommends ethical respect for linguistic diversity in its preservation of opacity and calls for attentiveness to environmental forces as they too might escape our attempts at understanding and possession. The endeavour to gesture towards this relational expressivity in the writer's own oeuvre serves as a statement of resistance to the reductive exigencies of the dominant monolingual model of the globalized market. It also obliquely contests thoughtless forms of human imposition on the environment and constructs a poetics open to dialogue with the physical world as an active expressive force.

Notes

1 Édouard Glissant, *Traité du tout-monde* (Paris: Gallimard, 1997), 26.
2 Rebecca Walkowitz, *Born Translated: The Contemporary Novel in an Age of World Literature* (New York: Columbia University Press, 2015), 4.
3 Ibid., 24.
4 Brian Lennon, *In Babel's Shadow: Multilingual Literatures, Monolingual States* (Minneapolis: University of Minnesota Press, 2010), 9.
5 Paul Bandia, 'Postcolonial Literary Heteroglossia: A Challenge for Homogenizing Translation', *Perspectives: Studies in Translatology* 20.4 (2012): 419–31.
6 Ibid., 423.
7 Celia Britton, *Language and Literary Form in French Caribbean Writing* (Liverpool: Liverpool University Press, 2014).
8 Glissant, *Traité du tout-monde*, 86.
9 Ibid., 163. See also Mikhail Bakhtin, *The Dialogic Imagination: Four Essays*, trans. Caryl Emerson and Michael Holquist (Austin and London: University of Texas Press, 1981).
10 Ibid., 29. A number of critics have produced lucid commentaries on Glissant's concept of opacity. See for example Hédi Adlai Murdoch, 'Édouard Glissant's Creolized World Vision: From Resistance and Relation to *Opacité*', *Callaloo* 36.4 (2013): 875–90; Patrick Crowley, 'Édouard Glissant: Resistance and *Opacité*', *Romance Studies* 24.2 (2006): 105–15.
11 Glissant, *Traité du tout-monde*, 122.
12 Britton, *Language and Literary Form in French Caribbean Writing*, 152.
13 See Eric Prieto, 'Édouard Glissant: *littérature-monde* and *tout-monde*', *Small Axe* 14.3 (2010): 111–20.
14 'Le cri du monde' is the title of the first chapter of *Traité du tout-monde*. Critics such as Peter Hallward and Christopher Miller have criticized Glissant's thinking on the 'tout monde' for its abstract universalism and insufficient attention to specific struggles and conflicts. See Peter Hallward, *Absolutely Postcolonial: Writing between the Singular and the Specific* (Manchester: Manchester University Press, 2001) and Christopher Miller, *The French Atlantic Triangle: Literature and Culture of the Slave Trade* (Durham, NC: Duke University Press, 2008).
15 Glissant, *Traité du tout-monde*, 119.
16 Ibid., 121.
17 Ibid., 120.
18 Ibid., 26.
19 Ibid., 85.
20 Ibid., 119.
21 Ibid., 26.

22 Derek Attridge, *The Singularity of Literature* (London: Routledge, 2004).
23 Ibid., 19.
24 Ibid., 21.
25 Glissant, *Traité du tout-monde*, 127.
26 Ibid., 63.
27 See Hallward, *Absolutely Postcolonial*; Nick Nesbitt, *Caribbean Critique: Antillean Theory from Toussaint to Glissant* (Liverpool: Liverpool University Press, 2014).
28 Edward Kamau Brathwaite, *History of the Voice: The Development of Nation Language in Anglophone Caribbean Poetry* (London: New Beacon, 1984).
29 Edward Kamau Brathwaite and Édouard Glissant, 'A Dialogue: Nation Language and the Poetics of Creolization', in *Caribbean Cultural Thought: From Plantation to Diaspora*, ed. Yanique Hume and Aaron Kamugisha (Miami: Ian Roundle Publishers, 2013): 290–300.
30 Daniel Maximin, *Les Fruits du cyclone: une géopoétique de la Caraïbe* (Paris: Seuil, 2006).
31 J. Michael Dash, *Édouard Glissant* (Cambridge: Cambridge University Press, 1995); Jana Evans Braziel, 'Caribbean Genesis: Language, Gardens, Worlds (Jamaica Kincaid, Derek Walcott, Édouard Glissant)', in *Caribbean Literature and the Environment*, ed. Elizabeth Deloughrey, Renée K. Gossan and George B. Handley (Charlottesville and London: University Press of Virginia, 2005): 110–26.
32 For more on the place of landscape and environment in Glissant's poetry, see for example Mildred Mortimer, 'Conquest and Resistance in Édouard Glissant's Poetry', *Esprit Créateur* 32.2 (1992): 65–76; Carrie Noland, 'Édouard Glissant: A Poetics of the *Entour*', in *Poetry After Cultural Studies*, ed. Heidi R. Bean and Mike Chasar (Iowa City: University of Iowa Press, 2011): 143–72
33 Édouard Glissant, *Une nouvelle région du monde* (Paris: Gallimard, 2006), 33.
34 Ibid., 53.
35 See Carine Mardorossian, '"Poetics of Landscape": Édouard Glissant's Creolized Ecologies', *Callaloo* 36.4 (2013): 983–94.
36 Glissant, *Une nouvelle région du monde*, 13.
37 Ibid., 16.
38 Ibid.
39 Brian Massumi, *A Shock to Thought: Expression after Deleuze and Guattari* (London and New York: Routledge, 2002), xxi.
40 Ibid.

2

(Sino)graphs in Franco(n)texts: The multilingual and the multimodal in Franco-Chinese literature and visual arts

Shuangyi Li

François Cheng 程抱一 (1929–) and Shan Sa 山飒 (1972–) belong respectively to the older and younger generations of the group of established francophone Chinese migrant writers settled in France.[1] Cheng is the first French *académicien* of Asian origin, winner of the prestigious Prix Femina (1998) and the Grand Prix de la francophonie (2001) – the latter a prize awarded for a lifetime contribution to the French language. Shan was already a published and award-winning teenage poet in China before she left Beijing for Paris at the age of seventeen. Her subsequent French-language novels, too, won multiple awards, including the Prix Goncourt du premier roman (1998) and Goncourt des lycéens (2001). Her creative contribution is further affirmed by the French national honours, Chevalier de l'Ordre des Arts et des Lettres (2009) and Chevalier de l'Ordre national du Mérite (2011).

Like my somewhat playful title, Cheng and Shan wittingly play with words across languages and cultural contexts in their literary works, a creative manoeuvre that is often performed through dynamic translation and negotiation. Their intimate knowledge and embodied experiences of more than one culture and tradition inspire and empower them to create new positions in the literary field beyond the national framework. In Mads Rosendahl Thomsen's 'mapping' of world literature, Cheng and Shan may fall under the category of contemporary migrant writers who seek to articulate a cosmopolitanism in a globalized world and whose works '[bring] a certain strangeness to something familiar'.[2] What I would like to additionally highlight through this title is both writers' attempted renegotiation of the boundaries of text and image based on the linguistic and visual traits of Chinese and its difference from French, whereby multilingualism becomes inherently multimodal (hence the graphs in texts). In this respect, W. T. J. Mitchel's term 'imagetext', defined as 'composite, synthetic works (or concepts) that combine image and text',[3] becomes readily available for me to formally describe the works explored in this chapter. Indeed, while Cheng and Shan may be said to have become creative writers primarily of the acquired French language, their

---

The research of this chapter has been generously funded by the Swedish Research Council (*Vetenskapsrådet*) 2019–22.

calligraphic works and paintings have retained a decidedly Chinese visual aesthetic. The apparent cultural hybridity, multimodality and intermediality[4] of their creative works questions and challenges any monolithic sense of cultural belonging by exerting a high degree of aesthetic flexibility and transgressivity. Such works continuously test, expand, but also *rapprochent* (bring closer together) respective linguistic systems while embracing a rich semiotic approach to world literature that is conventionally bound by its textual medium and circulation.

As I have argued elsewhere, the particularity of the kind of Franco-Chinese translingual literature under scrutiny here may be more productively conceptualized as *exophone* writing, or even *exographic* writing for the subject matter of this chapter, not least because of its etymological association with exoticism – an unignorable quality of the Franco-Chinese literary and visual aesthetic that is conducive to the commercial success and rapid institutional integration of these writer-artists' works in France and beyond.[5] In addition to the somewhat trite definition of exophone writing as literature written in a language other than the author's native one, I draw on the more specific characterization of it, proposed by the German-Japanese writer Yoko Tawada, as literature 'born of an adventurous spirit to go outside [as indicated by the prefix "exo-"] the mother tongue'.[6] For Tawada, this 'adventurous spirit' is what may distinguish exophone literature from migrant and diasporic literature. In fact, my following analysis will demonstrate that Franco-Chinese literature continues to embody an equally 'adventurous spirit' for a *sinographic return* to the native tongue after a voluntary linguistic exile to the French phonetic script. Concretely, this chapter will examine the aesthetic and conceptual particularities of the works of calligraphy, both published in France: first, Cheng's *Et le souffle devient signe: Portrait d'une âme à l'encre de Chine* (2001; *And the Breath Becomes Sign: Portrait of a Soul in Chinese Ink*) and then Shan's *Le Miroir du calligraphe* (2002; *The Mirror of the Calligrapher*). I will suggest how they can be read into and seen through their respective novels, Cheng's *Le Dit de Tianyi* (1998; translated rather differently in English as *The River Below*, 2000) and Shan's *Impératrice* (2003; *Empress: A Novel*, 2006), whereby the sense of mediality, materiality and semioticity is significantly enhanced across the novelistic and calligraphic works.[7]

François Cheng

To begin with, both Cheng and Shan employ an essential metaphor of reflection in the titles of their works, i.e. 'portrait' and 'mirror'. Far from coincidental, both formulations echo a well-established tradition in Chinese poetics which often uses the mirror to symbolize not a work of art, as it tends to be the case in Western poetics, but the writer-artist's heart-mind (*xin* 心) – hence the '*soul*' of the 'calligrapher' – stressing 'vacancy and illusion, fairness, and honesty and empty quietude' as well as the understanding of 'the way of Heaven' fundamentally through 'reflections on the self'.[8] More specifically, the notion of self-reflexivity characterizes a distinctive nature of Chinese calligraphic practice, as Jean François Billeter authoritatively notes:

L'unique préoccupation du calligraphe chinois est de donner vie aux caractères, de les animer sans les forcer en rien. Il met sa sensibilité *au service de* l'écriture puis en vient, *par un renversement subtil*, à *se servir de* l'écriture pour exprimer sa sensibilité personnelle. C'est à la faveur de ce renversement que l'écriture chinoise devient un moyen d'expression d'une richesse et d'une finesse extrêmes.⁹

(The unique preoccupation of Chinese calligraphers is to give life to characters, to animate them, without stretching them to nothing. They *submit* their sensibility to writing, and then, *through a subtle reversal*, get to *make use of* the writing to express their personal sensibility. It is thanks to this reversal that Chinese writing becomes an extremely rich and fine medium of expression.)

Billeter's description pinpoints the dynamic of imitating and copying while expressing and sublimating personal and subjective differences. It is in this respect that calligraphy is appreciated on the same – if not higher – level as painting, poetry and music in the Chinese aesthetic tradition.

Cheng's calligraphic work 'Montagne-Eau' (Mountain-Water 山水) (Figure 2.1) perfectly exemplifies Billeter's observation. Figure 2.1 shows a typical page layout and presentation format of the book. At the centre is the calligraphic image of the two Chinese characters for 'mountain-water', which are surrounded by French texts

Figure 2.1 'Montagne – Eau' (Mountain – Water), in *Et le souffle* (2001 [2010], 90–1). @FrançoisCheng-Etlesouffledevientsigne-L'Iconoclaste.

marked in both black and red – black for Cheng's commentary, red for his translation of Chinese classical and canonical texts as well as the imprint of the calligrapher's personal seal. Cheng's 'disclosure' of his aesthetic intention in the commentary section does not simply reaffirm the general creative principle in Chinese calligraphy outlined by Billeter; as the following analysis will unfold, the French text and context of Cheng's calligraphic works also give a subtle, transcultural twist to the book as a whole.

The characters for 'mountain' and 'water' both have ancient pictographic origins, each supposedly mimetic of the respective natural phenomenon, and were therefore initially created and written according to direct human sensory perceptions. In fact, 'mountain' and 'water' belong to the small fraction of elementary Chinese characters whose pictographic forms have remained easily recognizable to this day.[10] Yet, Cheng's calligraphic take on the two characters visibly differs from both their primitive forms (e.g. those found on oracle bones) and their modern written forms (i.e. 山水), while still largely adhering to the conventional manoeuvre of strokes, such as the techniques of the beginning, flowing and ending strokes (起笔, 行笔, 收笔). The calligrapher does not make a mere copy of an existent writing which reflects a certain generic human vision, he invests his personal sensibility and subjectivity in such an act of copying, writing and making. This is best explained in Cheng's French text:

> Ainsi, ici, par la montagne qui est à la fois enracinée et élancée, je tente d'exprimer mon désir de contemplation et d'élévation; par l'eau qui est tout en méandres, en gestes d'épousailles, je montre mon besoin d'épanchement et de grâce.[11]

> (Thus, here, through the mountain, which is rooted and at the same time pointed, I attempt to express my desire for contemplation and elevation; through the water, which is all in meanders, in movements of joining together, I show my need for emotional effusion and the state of grace.)

The 'rootedness' is represented especially by the downward then right angle stroke and the sense of 'elevation' by repeated angular tops. By elaborating the pictographic trait of 'mountain-water', Cheng consciously brings the verbal text closer to the visual mode of painting. Mountains – rooted in earth, rigid, rock-solid, hermitic places for spiritual pursuit; water or rivers (sharing the same character in classical Chinese) – amorphous, moving, constantly joining in, like some intangible feelings; behind this self-proclaimed, apparently subjective personal sensibility lies Cheng's Daoist-informed aesthetic vision through a form of Chinese cultural conditioning, as he clarifies:

> Voilà rassemblées les deux grandes entités terrestres, duales et complémentaires, la montagne incarnant le principe Yang, et l'eau le principe Yin. Sans relief et dénivelé, l'eau ne pourrait pas s'écouler; sans l'eau qui la nourrit, la montagne s'assécherait. La montagne et l'eau sont viscéralement liées.[12]

> (Here are the two great earthly entities brought together, paired and complementary, the mountain incarnates the principle of yang, and the water the principle of

yin. Without relief and difference in altitude, water would not flow; without the nourishment of water, the mountain would dry out. The mountain and water are profoundly joined together.)

It is worth mentioning that 'mountain' and 'water' put together make the Chinese word for 'landscape' ('paysage' in French), as in 'landscape painting' (山水画). Cheng's Daoist underpinning of the mountain-water relation is then linked to the Chinese aesthetic concept *qingjing* 情景, which Cheng translates as 'sentiment-paysage' (sentiment-scenery). This concept explicitly puts mountain-water and the human agent in relation:

> À ces deux grandes entités, à leurs vertus respectives, les lettrés chinois aimaient à identifier les deux pôles de leur sensibilité. Cela est conforme à une notion importante de l'esthétique chinoise, à savoir, le *sentiment-paysage*. Cette notion désigne l'interprétation de l'esprit humain et de l'esprit de l'univers vivant, dont découle toute création artistique authentique. Le calligraphe se doit donc de traduire l'esprit que véhicule la forme graphique de chaque caractère, et par là de manifester son propre esprit.[13]

(Chinese literati liked to identify the two poles of their sensibility with these two great entities and with their respective qualities. This falls in line with another important Chinese aesthetic notion, namely, that of *sentiment-scenery*. This notion points to the interpretation of human spirit and the spirit of the living universe, through which all authentic artistic creations take place. Calligraphers have a duty to translate the spirit carried by the graphic form of each character, through which they also manifest their own spirit.)

This notion of sentiment-scenery applies to calligraphy as much as painting in the Chinese aesthetic tradition, as Cheng comments elsewhere in his theoretical writings, 'Tout comme dans la calligraphie, le réel qui apparaît [dans la peinture], sur papier ou sur soie, est à la fois une empreinte du dehors et un surgissement intérieur' (Exactly as in calligraphy, the real that appears [in the painting], whether on paper or on silk, is at the same time an impression of the outside and a sudden appearance from within).[14]

In Chinese calligraphy, red ink is almost exclusively used for the imprint of the artist's seal, which serves the function of a signature. However, in Cheng's book, red ink is additionally employed to mark passages and verses from Chinese canonical texts, which are translated into French by Cheng himself. In the example of 'Mountain-Water', Cheng inserts a Confucian saying that relates the quality of water to movement and human intelligence, and that of mountain to placidity and kindness. This consistent intertextual feature appears, in part, to intellectually 'validate' the calligraphic work including the calligrapher's own commentary, while enhancing a certain 'Chineseness' of the work as a whole.

What we witness on this page is a kind of deeply reflective writing and drawing that mediates between established philosophical and aesthetic notions and individual creative practice, and this results in the construction of personal theories about artistic creation. Cheng's theoretical observations become all the more 'personal' when he subsequently draws our attention to the cross-cultural resonance of the supposedly 'Chinese' aesthetic practice and vision:

> Le *sentiment-paysage* est une notion chère aussi aux grands artistes occidentaux. À propos de la Sainte-Victoire, Cézanne dit sensiblement la même chose que Shitao: 'La montagne pense en moi; je deviens sa conscience'.[15]

> (*Sentiment-scenery* is a notion also dear to great Western artists. About Mount Sainte-Victoire, Cézanne says more or less [*sensiblement*] the same thing as Shitao: 'The mountain thinks in me; I become its consciousness'.)

Cheng's choice of adverb 'sensiblement' deliberately echoes his earlier elaboration on Chinese literati's mountain-water 'sensibility'. The formulation that connects Cézanne to Shitao 石涛 (1642–1707) – a well-known seventeenth-century Chinese landscape painter – is intentionally ambiguous about the real source of the quoted remark (i.e. Cézanne's or Shitao's?). In fact, this reference to Cézanne at the end clarifies an earlier intriguing allusion in the passage to certain Old Masters' (les Anciens) conception and vision of the mountain as some 'frozen waves' (vagues figées) and 'fleecy hills' (moutonnement de collines),[16] which points to the dynamic between stillness and movement, between solidity and fluidity.

There is a curious amalgamation of linguistic, visual and philosophical traditions in this work, which evidently reflects Cheng's transcultural intellectual and artistic trajectory. This, in turn, may lead us to further investigate the kind of 'Chineseness' manifested on these pages, especiallycompared to the more traditional practice of Chinese calligraphy. Cheng himself states his position in the Introduction to the book:

> Je me nourris de la meilleure part de la tradition, mais je n'ai rien d'un 'traditionaliste'. Chaque calligraphie est pour moi l'occasion d'une recherche pour atteindre une réalisation vraie et personnelle. C'est dire que mon exercice est toujours inspiré, non par un esprit de convention, mais d'inventivité et de création.[17]

> (I live on the best part of the tradition, but I have nothing of a 'traditionalist'. Every piece of calligraphy is, for me, the occasion to try to reach a fulfilment that is real and personal. That is to say, my exercise is always inspired, not by a spirit of convention, but by that of inventiveness and creation.)

In other words, the notion of authenticity in Cheng's calligraphic works is not a generic and cultural one associated with traditional representation or 'faithful' translation, but fundamentally a personal, artistic and transcultural one of informed imagination and creation. The particular example of 'Mountain-Water' may not graphically demonstrate the most inventive or experimental aspects of Cheng's calligraphy. What follows are some other examples.

The work shown in Figure 2.2, entitled 'Entre source et nuage' (Between Source and Cloud), resembles the Chinese expression 'flowing water and moving cloud' (*liushui xingyun* 流水行云), which does not literally correspond to the French title. Not only are the characters considerably reformed to express the movements and transformations of water, the way they are spatially configured also offers other possibilities of character or radical combination (e.g. *dong* 动 as another word meaning 'to move or to act') and intentionally reveals the Daoist symbol of Taiji 太极in the middle, signalling the Way of mutual transformation.[18] The position of Taiji is effectively between the (flowing) 'water'/'source' on the left and the (moving) 'cloud' on the right, which directly echoes the title of the work. Cheng creates this work to express the movements of time as water, and explains how the final elongated stroke of the character rising at the end promises the unsuspected opening of another transformation ('vers la promesse d'une ouverture insoupçonnée').[19]

Meanwhile, 'Between Source and Cloud' (1990 [2002]) is also the title of a Chinese poetry anthology that Cheng selected and translated into French.[20] It derives from the following lines of the Tang poet Wang Wei 王维 (699–759), which are explicitly cited in red on the calligraphic page: 'Marcher jusqu'au lieu où tarit la *source*, / Et attendre, assis, que se lève le *nuage*' (行到水穷处/坐看云起时; 'Walk to where the *waters* narrow, / Sit, and wait, for the *clouds* to rise').[21] While the position of 'sit' clearly corresponds to that of 坐 in the Chinese original, but not to that of 'assis' in the French

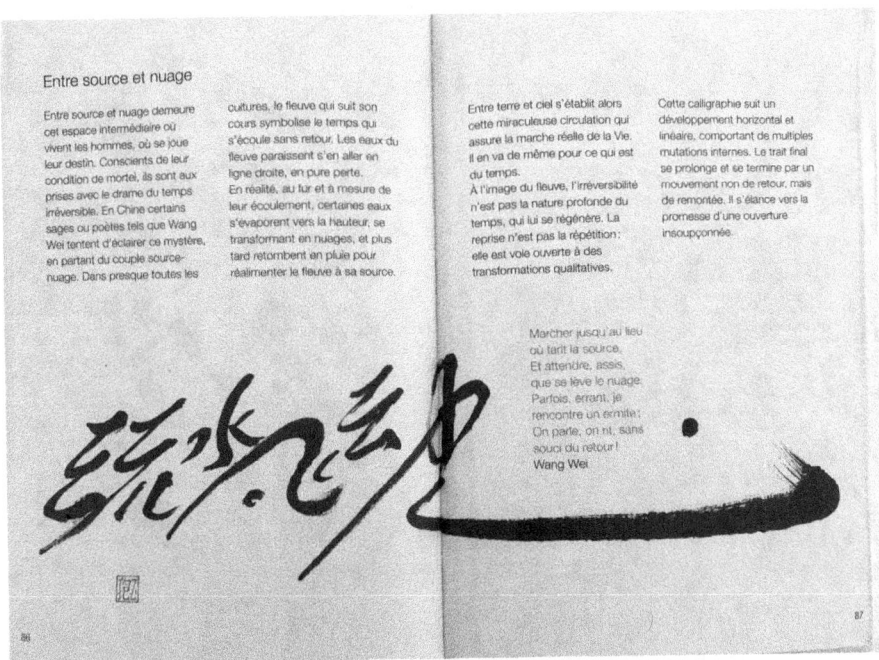

Figure 2.2 'Entre source et nuage' (Between Source and Cloud), in *Et le souffle* (2001 [2010], 86–7). @FrançoisCheng-Etlesouffledevientsigne-L'Iconoclaste.

version; the verb 'wait', which is not explicitly present in the Chinese version, is an evident retranslation from Cheng's 'attendre'. However, what the English translation fails to convey is the syntactical and lexical 'parallelism' of these two lines. To illustrate the 'profound spirit of parallelism',[22] Cheng offers a word-for-word French translation (duly included in the English translation): 'Marcher atteindre eau s'épuiser endroit / s'asseoir regarder nuage s'élever moment' (walk attain water narrow place / sit see cloud rise moment).[23] 'Source' (水) and 'cloud' (云) are thus placed in a symmetrical position. Cheng's calligraphic configuration of the two characters in the middle is informed by the two characters' median position in the two Chinese poetic lines. Resonating with his calligraphic work, Cheng comments on the two lines in the anthology thus: 'The true way of life is not to choose one or the other exclusively, but rather to embrace the Void between the two … and thus to participate in the universal transformation.'[24] It should be stressed that the title of this calligraphic work, 'entre source et nuage', is not a direct translation of any idiomatic Chinese expression per se; rather, it is a French-language creation based on Cheng's translation of a Tang poem. As I will elaborate later, this calligraphic image together with the classical Chinese poetic setting is directly transposed into the novelistic fabric of Cheng's *Le Dit de Tianyi*.

Likewise, the example of 'La quête' (The Quest) in Figure 2.3, which is supposed to convey the sinograph 寻 (*xun*, to search for), is drastically recomposed from its

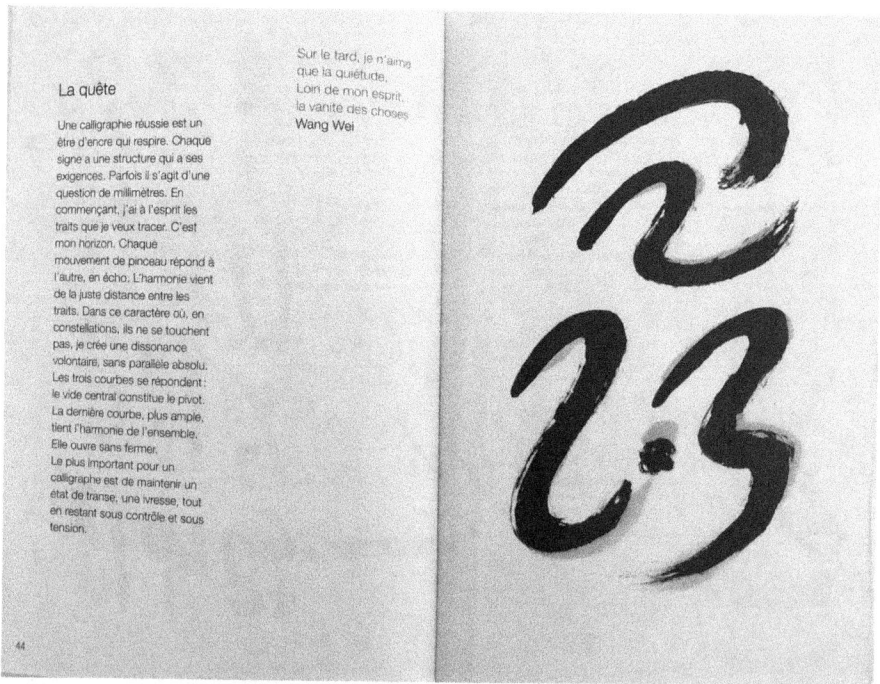

Figure 2.3 'La Quête' (The Quest), in *Et le souffle* (2001 [2010], 44–5). @FrançoisCheng-Etlesouffledevientsigne-L'Iconoclaste.

standard written form. This calligraphic work displays an aesthetic of asymmetrical parallel and, in Cheng's words, 'dissonance volontaire' (voluntary discordance), and expresses a sense of harmony through the sustainment of 'the right distance' (la juste distance).[25] The notion of quest is key to the understanding of the cross-cultural travel motif in Cheng's *Le Dit*, and this 'parallel' aesthetic is also particularly revealing of Cheng's 'open' and transformative approach to cultural translation between Western and Chinese heritages.[26]

The final example of 'La chute' (The Fall) in Figure 2.4 is even more inventive and intriguing. One additional feature in this work is Cheng's use of Chinese brush and ink to calligraph a short French poem composed by himself, in memory of a deceased alpinist. This invented sinograph is highly ambiguous. Most educated Chinese are able to quickly identify two or three character components of this piece, but it is practically impossible to decipher its holistic meaning without relying on the French text. In fact, there is still an issue of legibility even after reading the French text. Significantly, half of the French text recounts one of Cheng's own painful childhood experiences of falling while crossing the river, and this provides a narrative to each part of the sinograph we observe as well as to the poem we read. The lack of clear correspondences between the sinograph and the French-language narrative and poem on the same pages paradoxically entails a sense of semiotic and hermeneutic interdependence among

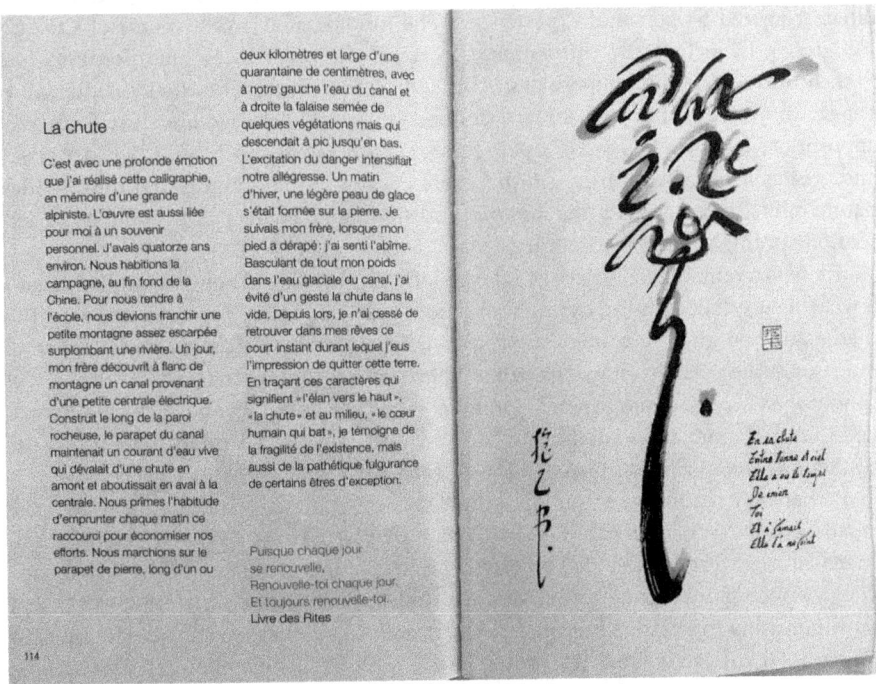

Figure 2.4 'La chute' (The Fall), in *Et le souffle* (2001 [2010], 114–15). @FrançoisCheng-Etlesouffledevientsigne-L'Iconoclaste.

them and calls for a constant movement of seeing, reading and understanding on the reader's part.

Each complete piece of Cheng's calligraphy in the book must therefore include both the sinograph *and* the surrounding French texts – be they translations, quotations, descriptions, commentaries, conceptual formulations or anecdotal narratives – as both the visual and the verbal are essential components of each signifying work of calligraphy. The order in which I have chosen to present Cheng's four calligraphic works is intended to illustrate a certain 'grativation away from representation and toward the symbolic'[27] – a process in which the intrinsically interdependent yet necessarily asymmetrical relationship between word and image is constantly readjusted.

Technically speaking, Cheng's imagetext presentation format per se is not unusual in the Chinese context. After all, there has been a long tradition of incorporating extensive inscriptions (by artists themselves) and colophons (by others) into Chinese paintings and calligraphic works since at least the Song dynasty (960–1279).[28] Traditional Chinese aesthetics rarely treats the visual and the verbal as separate entities in artworks, and it is a truism to state that 'Chinese poetry, calligraphy, and painting, known as *san-chüeh* [三绝 or *sanjue* in pinjin], or the three perfections, have been practiced together in single works of art'.[29] In a way, not even Cheng's graphic experiment may necessarily be seen as unusual in the Chinese context. Nakata Yūjirō remarks that Chinese calligraphy has always been 'roughly divided into two broad stylistic categories, traditional and innovative', and the formal change in the latter is often 'triggered by personal experience'.[30] The fundamental inventiveness of Cheng's calligraphy is, in fact, the *translational* creation of a space of communion between French and Chinese linguistic, aesthetic and philosophical traditions on the same pages. The documentary or literary connection between image and text forms, to appropriate John Hay's words, 'a perpetual relationship, a coexistence that demands and creates a space'[31] for *transcultural* experience. The multilingual and multimodal nature offers the respective francophone and sinophone readers and beholders varied semiotic points of entry into the artworks.

There is a remarkable degree of interpenetration between Cheng's calligraphic and novelistic aesthetics. In the example of 'The Quest' (Figure 2.3), I suggested how the theme and the graphic configuration of this work resonate strongly with the travel motif and the East–West comparative approach to Cheng's narrative style. I will continue to use the examples of 'Mountain-Water' (Figure 2.1) and 'Between Source and Cloud' (Figure 2.2) to demonstrate how calligraphy holds the key to revealing the aesthetic vision of Cheng's novel *Le Dit de Tianyi*.

Perhaps as a reading cue from the author himself, 'mountain-water' appears as a seal in red on the cover of one of the Livre de Poche editions of *Le Dit de Tianyi*. The novel can be read as a travel narrative that recounts the cross-cultural journey of the protagonist Tianyi, which spans through much of the turbulent twentieth century (1925–68), from wartime China to postwar Europe, and then back to a radically changed Communist China. At the diegetic level, the protagonist Tianyi *is* a calligrapher and painter, and the novel can also be read as a *Künstlerroman*: the physical and psychological growth of the protagonist goes conjointly with his artistic and spiritual pursuits as well as his quests for knowledge and love. It is at the foot of Mount Lu in Central China (Jiangxi Province) – made famous by the Song poet, painter and calligrapher Su Shi 苏轼 (1037–1101) – that the protagonist undergoes his artistic initiation, through his observation of the transformative relations between the mountain, the mist, the rain and the cloud, while practising calligraphy following in the footsteps of his father.[32] To echo Cheng's formulation of 'sentiment-scenery' earlier, the protagonist explicitly states: 'Pénétré de cette vision que nourrissait mon apprentissage de la calligraphie, je commençais à me sentir en communion charnelle avec le paysage' (Thus imbued with a vision nurtured by my apprenticeship in calligraphy, I began to experience a physical communion with the landscape).[33]

As he travels cross-culturally, the protagonist is frequently drawn to natural landscapes in both China and Europe – landscapes to be concretely understood as a series of mountains and rivers. Whereas mountains, such as Mount Lu, reflect cultural rootedness and origin, as well as spiritual exaltation, echoing Cheng's calligraphic configuration of the sinograph for 'mountain'; rivers in the novel, such as the Yangtze River, the Yellow River, the Seine and the Loire, establish a complex cross-cultural network subtly transforming cultural 'root' to 'route'. The protagonist describes himself as 'fils du fleuve' (child of the river).[34] His visit to the Loire in France transculturally echoes the aforementioned Chinese poetic setting associated with the work 'Between Source and Cloud' and the river as the symbol of time, and Cheng's remark on the 'unsuspected opening of another transformation' in the calligraphy now has a novelistic reincarnation. The protagonist reflects:

Remonter à la source. Serait-ce le commencement d'une nouvelle vie? Ou la fin d'une autre? Que le temps soit cyclique et que tout nouveau cycle entraîne un changement à la fois pressenti et inattendu, c'était un vieux thème parfaitement intégré dans ma vision, dont je ne mettais plus en doute la validité. ... En cette contrée étrangère, nouveau à ce point, ne pourrais-je par un acte volontaire couper les racines du passé, dénouer les nœuds les inextricables? Couper les racines? Peut-être. L'homme n'étant que cet animal qui glisse sur la surface de la terre, auquel la culture se contente de fournir quelques vieilles recettes d'usage, est-il réellement si profondément enraciné qu'il ne puisse pas envisager sa transplantation?[35]

(Upriver to the source. Would it be the beginning of a new life? Or the end of another? That time is cyclical and that each new cycle brings changes both foreseen and unexpected was an old theme, an integral part of my vision, and I no longer doubted its validity. ...In this foreign country, now a new person, by an act of will couldn't I cut the roots of the past, untie the most inextricable knots? Cut the roots? Maybe. Since man is merely a creature gliding over the surface of the earth, an animal the culture hands a few tried and true ways, is he really so deeply rooted that he can't imagine being transplanted?)

Indeed, even the tripartite structure of the novel may be said to mirror the landscape dynamics of the mountain-water and source-cloud: departure (the 'source'), journey (the 'route') and return (the water returning to the mountain source and route). This visual, calligraphy-informed landscape reflection and aesthetic conception can be seen as a distinctively Chinese element Cheng brings to French travel narratives.

Shan Sa

The idea of 'mountain' takes us directly to the francophone Chinese writer, painter and calligrapher Shan Sa, because this pen name of hers literally means 'the rustling of wind in the mountain' and the imagetext of a three-peak mountain is clearly visible in the artist's seal.

Le Miroir du calligraphe (2002) was published in France one year after Cheng's *Le Souffle* in France, but the book shows a significantly different approach to 'Chinese' calligraphy. Many of the visual works presented in *Le Miroir* may be more accurately described as calligraphy inspired colourful ink wash paintings, which are also frequently accompanied by French texts – Shan's own poems, personal accounts of her relationship with calligraphy and painting, and her reformulation of classical Chinese fables. Compared to Cheng's volume, Shan's texts are much less explanatory or commentarial in relation to individual images, and the kind of philosophical and, to some extent, pedagogical discourses are almost completely absent. The highly abstract forms of Shan's visual works make the intermedial relation between image and text in *Le Miroir* look rather arbitrary. If we return to Billeter's earlier characterization of Chinese calligraphy as the calligrapher's animation of characters 'without stretching them to nothing' – and if 'nothing' refers to their verbal mode – some of Shan's works in *Le Miroir* may not be seen or read as calligraphy. In many ways, they appear to be closer to the kind of 'decorative art' that Cheng is explicitly against, as he warns in *Et le souffle*: 'Toute enflure ou exagération, toute recherche d'effets voyants ou tapageurs, au mépris des lois fondamentales, ne font que ramener la calligraphie à un art décoratif' (All the exaggerations and all the attempts at showy and ostentatious effects, which ignore the fundamental laws [of Chinese calligraphy], will only reduce calligraphy to a form of decorative art).[36] Curiously, also on page 24 but in her own volume, Shan mounts a strong argument precisely against the kind of 'fundamental laws' on Cheng's mind by highlighting the limit of verbal entity:

> Comme l'écriture, l'art est d'une quête perpétuelle de liberté. Il n'y a pas de roman ni de calligraphie sans langage. Mais le langage est le geôlier de l'esprit. Je ne savais comment briser les signes, comment transgresser un art millénaire codifié dans ses moindre [*sic*] gestes.[37]

> (Like writing, art is a perpetual quest for liberty. There is no novel or calligraphy without language. But language is the prison house of the mind. I didn't know how to break the signs, how to transgress an ancient art that has been codified in its slightest movements.)

As we will see, between Chinese and French, Shan's artistic response to the issue of language is a translingual one and she seeks intuitively to create an aesthetic hybrid in visual art in its 'perpetual quest for freedom'. Compared to the traditional emphasis on rigid control and repetition in the practice of Chinese calligraphy historically dominated by male masters, Shan can be said to strive for a more fluid, 'feminine' and translingual perspective to this art.[38]

In the title of this chapter, I deliberately bracket the prefix 'sino-' in the word 'sinograph', and this, in Shan's case, is because her calligraphic experimentation is not confined to the *Chinese* script. The example in Figure 2.5,[39] which appears to be a Chinese character or word written in the 'cursive form' 草书, displays in fact the vertically spelt French word 'falaise' (cliff). Not only is the up-to-down vertical arrangement in line with the writing and reading order in traditional Chinese calligraphy, it also adheres to the up-down structure of the corresponding Chinese character 崖, with 山 (mountain) on top and 厓 (indicating a kind of 'higher edge') at the bottom.[40] Shan clearly employs different depths of intensity of the black ink to discriminate the two parts of the French 'character', and the prominent stroke of 'L' in the middle is redolent of the corresponding Chinese radical 厂 in 崖, especially in its cursive form(s). Only part of this sinograph may be said to reflect a certain pictographic origin. For instance, the second-century Chinese dictionary *shuowen jiezi* 说文解字 (literally 'explaining graphs and analysing characters') considers 厂 to be a pictographic radical that suggests a kind of 'shelter' or 'cavern' in the mountain inhabitable by humans; the vertical construction of two 土 (soil, earth) in 圭 may indicate 'higher ground'. However, the radical 山 was added to the character 厓 much later in time mainly out of *semantic* precision rather than pictographic values so that 崖 now refers specifically to 'mountain edge' (i.e. cliff) as distinct from 'water edge' (e.g. river bank), which we can see in another character 涯, with the component 氵 (water) on the left. Yet, calligraphers would generally endeavour to recuperate or sometimes even reinvent characters' pictographic significance by approximating sinographic forms to their meanings. Here, Shan even tries to convey a sense of 'rustling wind' through the vigour and swift movement of her strokes. Thus, the meaning of the French word 'falaise' (cliff) is visually conveyed in this calligraphic rendition, and the alphabetic script – primarily used to indicate sound – is given a Chinese calligraphic makeover with a visual representation that formally matches its meaning through a kind of isomorphic operation. As a result, there is a much-enhanced sense of materiality, as though this phonetic script, too, had a pictographic origin.

Shan's visual translingualism is further highlighted in two contrastive calligraphic works on the moon. Figure 2.6, entitled 'La lune auréolée' (The Glowing Moon),[41] is a basic sinograph for 'the moon', with a clear pictographic origin. On the other hand, Figure 2.7, entitled 'La lune' (The Moon),[42] shows again the vertically spelt French word 'lune'. Seeing these two calligraphic works comparatively and knowing their shared lunar denotation encourage us to perceive their structural similarity, and we are most likely to appreciate the unusual aesthetic layout of the French 'lune' through its sinographic counterpart. For once, the alphabetic script appears to have more complicated strokes than its Chinese 'original' (with only four strokes).

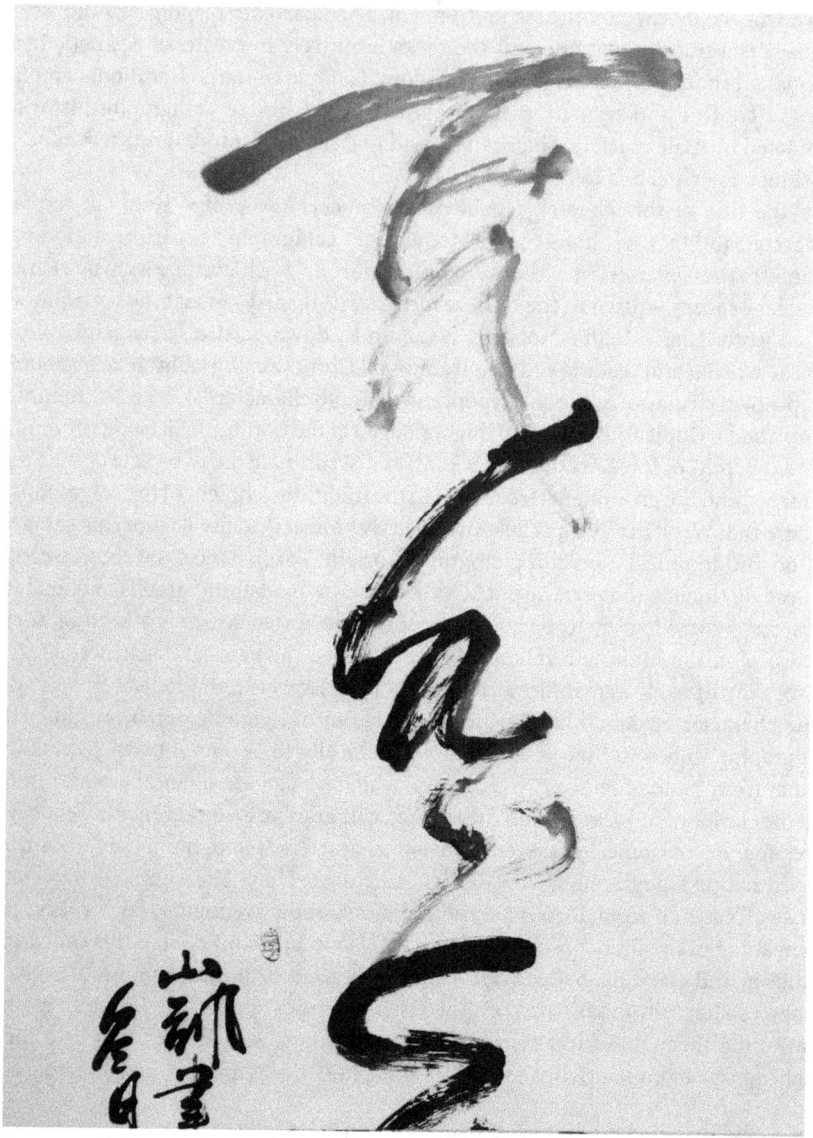

Figure 2.5 Shan Sa, 'La Falaise' (The Cliff), in *Le Miroir du calligraphe* (Paris: Albin Michel 2002, 27).

There is more to this example in Figure 2.7. A lightly inked circle appears on the top left, which resembles the sun (or a full moon, for that matter). The circle gives the pictographic origin of the sinograph for 'sun' or 'day' 日, usually seen with a dot written in the middle to mark the sunlight in ancient scripts. Indeed, the sinographs for the sun 日 and the moon 月 can look quite similar, especially when written in a cursive way. Moreover, when 'sun' is placed next to 'moon', they form the character

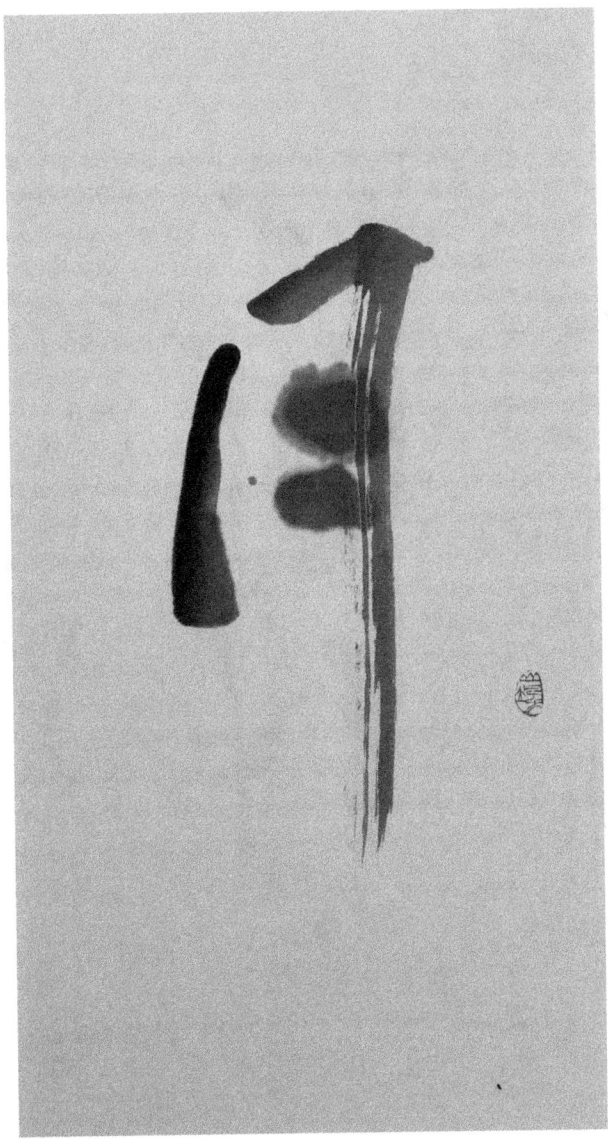

Figure 2.6 Shan Sa, 'La lune auréolée' (The Glowing Moon), in *Le Miroir du calligraphe* (Paris: Albin Michel 2002, 75).

明, meaning 'bright light' or 'luminous'. In a way, Figure 2.7 can be seen as a French word for 'moon' combined with an elementary sinograph for 'sun'. As we will see, this sun-moon-bright light configuration will play a pivotal role in my proposed reading of Shan's novel *Impératrice* (*Empress*).

Structurally speaking, this calligraphic work as a whole is redolent of a well-established tradition in classical Chinese paintings, known as 'moon appreciation

Figure 2.7 Shan Sa, 'La lune' (The Moon), in *Le Miroir du calligraphe* (Paris: Albin Michel 2002, 120).

paintings'赏月画. These paintings sometimes depict a scene during the Chinese Mid-Autumn Festival, with family members gathering together enjoying the moon. But more often in landscape paintings, the moon appears as a 'solitary symbol that transcends time and space',[43] with or without a human agent observing it. Through such a prism, the circle may represent the full moon and the piling letters of 'lune' may be visually evocative of a lofty mountain landscape (e.g. cliff) or moon appreciation tower. The final long stroke at the bottom is indicative of the horizon, and its finite, earthly rootedness is contrasted with the sense of eternity and solitude symbolized by the moon in an infinite sky above.[44]

It is Shan herself who gives us cue to read her calligraphic works into *Impératrice*, which rewrites in French the legend of Empress Wu Zetian 武则天 (624–705) in seventh-century China during the Tang dynasty. The novel has all the features of a historical biography. It textually and translingually engages with the visual and semiotic qualities of the above-mentioned lunar series of sinographs. Not only does Shan reveal in *Le Miroir* that Empress Wu's calligraphy is a vital source of inspiration for her,[45] Shan explicitly calligraphs 曌 *zhao* – a new character famously invented or adopted by Wu to replace her own original homophonic name 照 *zhao* – for the cover of her novel (Figure 2.8). This sinograph consists of 'bright light' 明 on top, which can be further divided into 'sun' 日 and 'moon' 月, and 'sky' 空 at the bottom.[46] It conveys the idea that the sun and the moon together appear and shine over the land under heaven 天下, implying the absolute domination of the world. Indeed, according to the aforementioned second-century Chinese dictionary *shuowen jiezi*, 明 is a direct synonym for 照 (i.e. 照, 明也). Once we are acquainted with such imagetext relations, the central leitmotif of the novel becomes much clearer. In the following passage near the beginning of the novel, the first-person narrator, aged five then, describes her perception of the evening, as she has been asked to represent the family at a Buddhist mourning ritual in the mountain and pray for the recently deceased grandmother:

La montagne respirait. La montagne était triste, la montagne était contente. … Le ciel s'ouvrait à la verticale quand descendait le crépuscule ocre, jaune, noir. Quand le soir montait des vallées, les astres se dévoilaient. …chaque étoile était une écriture mystérieuse et le ciel un livre sacré. …

La lune croissait et décroissait. Les jours, points, cercles se transformaient en caractères cursifs dont on ne distinguait plus le sens. J'appréhendais le temps en regardant le Bouddha qui, sous les pics de fer, se matérialisait. Regard tendre, sourire mystérieux, …. J'étais muette de stupeur: la divinité a surgi du néant![47]

(The mountains seemed to breathe. The mountains were sad; the mountains were happy. …The sky opened up vertically when dusk fell, all ochre, yellow and black. When evening came up from the valleys, the heavenly bodies revealed themselves. …Every star was a mysterious writing on the sacred book of the sky. …

The moon waxed and waned. The days, those tiny dots and circles, changed into a flowing script whose meaning was now lost. I understood the passage of time by watching the Buddha gradually materializing under those iron picks. Gentle eyes, a mysterious smile, …I was mute with awe: Dinivity had risen from nothingness.)

At first glance, this passage depicts the passing of time in a classic Chinese setting. 'The moon waxed and waned' echoes the Chinese expression *yin-qing-yuan-que* 阴晴圆缺 describing the various states of the moon and, by analogy, the fugacity and unpredictability of human lives. As can be seen, Shan's novelistic mise en scène

Figure 2.8 The book cover of the French version of *Impératrice* ((Paris: Le Livre de Poche) 2003), the Chinese character 瞾 *zhao* is composed by Shan herself. © Le Livre de Poche.

is effectively based on the calligraphic configuration of the protagonist's name, e.g. 'day'/'sun', 'moon', 'sky', 'dots', 'circles', 'flowing script' and 'mysterious writing'. Shan even specifically emphasizes the vertical arrangement of this scene, just as in classical Chinese calligraphy. Furthermore, the image of the sun and the moon appearing together in the sky – generally thought to achieve perfect balance and harmony between yin and yang – takes on an auspicious significance according to Chinese astrology, the corresponding Chinese idiom being *ri-yue-jiao-hui* 日月交辉. This then ties in with the divine presence of the smiling Buddha. Incidentally, the historical Empress Wu is famous for commissioning the construction of gigantic Buddha statues in her own image. Finally, the background setting of a 'breathing mountain' in this passage is also well intended, if we remind ourselves that the author's name means 'the rustling of wind in the mountain' in Chinese.

The calligraphy-informed imagery, together with the presence of the mountain and the image of a mysteriously smiling Buddha, plays a fundamental structural role in the novel: it begins with 'Lunes interminables, univers opaque' (Endless moons, an opaque universe)[48] and ends with a series of self-affirmations: 'Je suis …ce vent qui murmure. …Je brille comme une étoile. …Je suis le sourire indulgent de la Montagne. Je suis le sourire énigmatique de Celui qui fait tourner la Roue de l'Éternité' (I am … the whispering wind. …I shine like a star. …I am the Mountain's indulgent smile. I am the enigmatic smile of He who turns the Wheel of Eternity).[49] In many ways, this recurrent mise en scène echoes the classical Chinese aesthetic notion of 'sentiment-scenery' introduced by Cheng in *Le Souffle*. In this case, the calligrapher-novelist has a duty to translate the spirit of the historical character as well as her sinographic work, through which she manifests her own spirit. Shan evidently identifies and develops an emotional relationship with the subject of her research.

Francophone readers are likely to experience an aesthetic of *étrangeté* (in the sense of both 'strange' and 'foreign'), which is brought about by the traits of sinographic writing that has conditioned the author's vision.[50] Such an effect is fully intended by Shan: 'Et j'espère que cette langue française est écrite de telle manière qu'à travers elle, on aperçoit ce qu'est la langue chinoise. C'est peut-être là ce qui fait le style de tous mes livres' (I hope that this French language is written in such a way that through this language, we perceive the Chinese language. And this is perhaps what characterizes the style of all my books).[51] It looks as if what has set out to be a 'perpetual quest for freedom' becomes an opportunity for Shan to flaunt a kind of linguistic exoticism, but as Xiaofan Amy Li remarks: 'something becomes exotic not because it is inherently so but because its audience and their perspective make it so'.[52] If Cheng's and Shan's decisions to create multimodal works primarily in French and for a francophone readership are understood as an exophone adventure to go outside their native language, their aethetic experiments with the French texts and contexts may be said to exhibit a palpable sense of an exographic return to Chinese writing and traditional artistic conception.

Franco-Chinese literature as world literature

From the perspective of world literature – whether understood as different modes of circulation or reading across languages, media and cultures – it may seem obvious to relate Cheng and Shan's multilingual and multimodal works to early-twentieth-century French canonical works, such as Guillaume Apollinaire's *Calligrammes* (1918) and Victor Segalen's *Stèle* (1912). In fact, Cheng had translated some of Apollinaire's poems from *Calligrammes* into Chinese in 1984,[53] long before the publication of his calligraphic and novelistic works in France; and he has also written texts on Segalen since 1978, which have been published collectively as a volume titled *L'Un vers l'autre. En voyage avec Victor Segalen*.[54]

However, the fundamental aesthetic intentions are radically different. Both Apollinaire's and Segalen's works are primarily preoccupied with *poetic* forms. Apollinaire's visual poetry is generally seen as an avant-garde phenomenon that sets out to '[break] decisively with the past and [devote] to exploring new territory',[55] through a new consciousness of the materiality of the signifier that soon came to mark *European* literary modernity. Interestingly, the word 'calligramme', derived from the Greek 'kalos' and 'gramma' meaning 'beautiful letter', a pedantic word for *belles-lettres*,[56] refers to an art form that may *not* even be considered as calligraphy in the Chinese context.[57] As for Segalen, despite his extensive sinological experience, the author 'explicitly sets out to use China as a set of dehistoricized formal possibilities, deploying elements of traditional Chinese culture as "forms" with which to compose his own poetic language',[58] importantly, in his native French. Segalen's formulation of the 'aesthetic of the diverse' in his 'Essay on Exoticism' notably advocates a 'programmatic commitment to preserving rather than appropriating Chinese cultural difference'[59] and conceptualizes – somewhat contradictorily – China and Chineseness as mere forms.

Yet, Cheng is determined to construct a relational understanding of Segalenian poetics beyond mere 'Chinese forms', as he sees in Segalen 'un effort non moins intense d'ouverture, de bouleversement, d'assimilation et de transformation' (no less intense an effort at opening up, dramatic change, assimilation and transformation), and he describes the 'style segalénien' (Segalenian style) as coming from 'cet espacement de soi au travers de l'autre' (this distancing from self through the other).[60] Cheng's reading and intellectual 'voyage avec Segalen' (journey with Segalen) is infused with a relational and planetarian thinking that is often characteristic of the world literature mode of reading: 'En [le] sein [de la Terre], devenus des êtres de langage, nous avons entrepris un dialogue de fond avec nos semblables, avec l'univers des vivants et, comme irrésistiblement, avec une forme de transcendance' (In Mother Earth's breast, becoming beings of language, we've taken part in a fundamental dialogue with our own kind, with the universe of the living and, quite irresistibly, with a form of transcendence).[61]

Cheng and Shan's point of departure is the exophone as well as exographic representation of Chinese culture in both content and form, across media and genres. Their visual and literary aesthetic destination is decidedly transcultural, which turns problems of cultural authenticity and linguistic representability into a productive form of creative tension. Their multilingual and multimodal agenda aims to reconnect rather than to break with the past in culturally displaced conditions. Such an agenda is not exactly preoccupied with poetic forms but forms of poetics, visual and literary, across calligraphic and novelistic works.

In contemporary global cultural productions about China, the sinograph, including Chinese ideograms and calligraphy, is often reductively essentialized as the hallmark of Chineseness. This is a central component of Tu Wei-ming's formulation of Cultural China, as the critic provocatively asserts that 'written Chinese (*hanzi*, *kanji* in Japanese), as a distinct cultural symbol significantly different from an alphabet, gives literate Chinese a strong sense of membership in a unique discourse community'.[62] Cheng and Shan seem to have rather complex, and at times, paradoxical attitudes and relations to the Chinese script. Instead of demystifying the Chinese script for their predominantly Western readership, they often play with Western fantasy about the Chinese script, by, for example, only engaging with its pictographic quality. At the same time, they are seen to knowingly re-mystify the Chinese script, often out of aesthetic and stylistic strategies or translingual and intermedial experiments. Cheng remarks on living 'on the best part of the tradition' but being always inspired by a spirit of 'inventiveness and creativeness'.[63] Shan, at the beginning of *Le Miroir*, reiterates the clichéd kind of 'eternal China' through calligraphy: 'Éternité ... Éternité ... Éternité. Les dynasties ont disparu mais l'art des idéogrammes se perpétue. La Chine renaît à chaque instant où un enfant devient calligraphe' (Eternity ... Eternity ... Eternity. Dynasties are gone but the art of the ideogram perpetuates. China is reborn every time a child becomes a calligrapher).[64] Meanwhile, Shan also expresses her constant urge and struggle to break the sinograph, to transgress this ancient, rigidly codified art, and to reapply it to the alphabetic script, in order to suit her hybrid cultural identity. Profoundly nostalgic though they may appear – especially 'nostalgic' in its Greek etymological sense of 'home-returning' (*nostos*) and 'pain' (*algos*) – these works also creatively translate and aesthetically transform Franco-Chinese writer-artists' own experiences of *migrance*: 'migration' and 'errance' (wandering), often 'souffrance' (suffering), but in the end, 'renaissance' in the 'jouissance'.[65] Migrant writers and artists are often criticized for deliberately seeking and creating hybridity at the expense of authenticity.[66] In effect, rather than aiming to conserve authentic notions of Chinese and French tradition, Cheng and Shan are seen to turn their geographically, linguistically and culturally displaced conditions into a cosmopolitan consciousness and a privileged vantage point, which allow them to (re)connect with and (re)invent traditions, and to embrace the large context of world literature beyond the national framework while trying to stay true to their individual selves instead of cultural roots. In turn, one could argue that it is also the critical framework of world literature that is best suited to bring out the aesthetic values of such multilingual and multimodal hybrids of literature.

Notes

1   Other notable figures of this group may include the Nobel Prize laureate Gao Xingjian (1940–) and the writer-filmmaker Dai Sijie (1954–). The perception of such a 'group' is conveniently based on their cultural origin and the shared sense of Franco-Chinese cross-cultural mobility reflected in their intellectual thinking and artistic creation. However, this does not imply that they have actively gathered together and consciously created a uniform literary and artistic movement.

2 Mads Rosendahl Thomsen, *Mapping World Literature: International Canonization and Transnational Literatures* (London: Continuum, 2008), 99.
3 W. J. T. Mitchell, *Picture Theory: Essays on Verbal and Visual Representation* (Chicago: University of Chicago Press, 1994), 89.
4 I employ both 'multimodality' and 'intermediality' as umbrella terms to cover a variety of modal and medial relations. Fully aware of the overlap between mode and media, my use of 'multimodality' describes the simultaneous engagement of more than one sense faculty in textual production, that is, referring 'mode' to semiotic forms (verbal, visual, etc.) while 'media' refers to material platforms (books, paintings, art installations, etc.) and 'intermediality' stresses the interaction between those different material platforms. See Klaus Kaindl, 'Multimodality and Translation', in *The Routledge Handbook of Multimodal Analysis*, ed. Carmen Millán and Francesca Bartrina (London: Routledge, 2013): 257–69, 261; Tong King Lee, *Experimental Chinese Literature: Translation, Technology, Poetics* (Leiden: Brill, 2015), 11.
5 For discussions on the linguistic and visual exoticism in Shan Sa's and Dai Sijie's literary and cinematic works, see Shuangyi Li, 'Translingualism and Autoexotic Translation in Shan Sa's Franco-Chinese Historical Novels', *Essays in French Literature and Culture* 55 (2018): 115–31; 'Novel, Film, and the Art of Translational Storytelling: Dai Sijie's *Balzac et la Petite Tailleuse chinoise*', *Forum for Modern Language Studies* 51.4 (2019): 359–79.
6 Angela Yiu, 'National Literature and Beyond: Mizumura Minae and Hideo Levy', in *Routledge Handbook of Modern Japanese Literature*, ed. Rachael Hutchinson and Leith Morton (New York: Routledge, 2016): 227–40, 234.
7 François Cheng, *Et le souffle devient signe: Portrait d'une âme à l'encre de Chine* (Paris: L'Iconoclaste, 2001 [2010]); *Le Dit de Tianyi* (Paris: Albin Michel, 1998); *The River Below*, trans. Julia Shirek Smith (New York: Welcome Rain, 2000); Shan Sa, *Impératrice* (Paris: Le Livre de Poche, 2003); *Empress: A Novel*, Kindle eBook, trans. Adriana Hunter (London: HarperCollins, 2006); *Le Miroir du calligraphe* (Paris: Albin Michel, 2002).
8 Yue Daiyun, *China and the West at the Crossroads: Essays on Comparative Literature and Culture*, trans. Geng Song and Darrell Dorrington (Singapore: Springer, 2016), 222, 225.
9 Jean François Billeter, *Essai sur l'art chinois de l'écriture et ses fondements* (Paris: Éditions Allia, 2010), 11–12,; my italics and translation.
10 Ever since the famous standardization of the sinograph during the Han dynasty (206 BCE–220 CE), known as *libian* 隸變 or *liding* 隸定, most Chinese characters have formally evolved much beyond their original pictographic roots.
11 Cheng, *Et le souffle*, 90–1; my translation.
12 Ibid.
13 Ibid.
14 François Cheng, *Souffle-Esprit: Textes théoriques chinois sur l'art pictural* (Paris: Seuil, 1989 [2006]), 166; my translation.
15 Cheng, *Et le souffle*, 91.
16 Ibid.
17 Ibid., 24.
18 For Cheng's more detailed explanation of the Daoist symbol, see François Cheng, *The Way of Beauty: Five Meditations for Spiritual Transformation*, trans. Jody Gladding (Rochester: Inner Traditions, 2009), 66.

19 Cheng, *Et le souffle*, 87.
20 François Cheng, *Entre Source and Nuage. Voix de poètes dans la Chine d'hier et d'aujourd'hui* (Paris: Albin Michel, 1990).
21 Cheng, *Et le souffle*, 87; *Chinese Poetic Writing: With an Anthology of T'ang Poetry*, trans. Donald A. Riggs and Jerome P. Seaton (Bloomington: Indiana University Press), 206–7; my emphasis.
22 Cheng, *Chinese Poetic Writing*, 207.
23 François Cheng, *L'écriture poétique chinoise. Suivi d'une anthologie des poèmes des Tang* (Paris: Seuil, [1977] 1996), 69; *Chinese Poetic Writing*, 207.
24 Ibid.
25 Cheng, *Et le souffle*, 44–5.
26 For a thorough discussion of Cheng's idea of cultural translation as constructions of artistic and mythical 'parallels' and 'equivalents' between the West and China, see Shuangyi Li, *Proust, China and Intertextual Engagement: Translation and Transcultural Dialogue* (Singapore: Palgrave Macmillan, 2017), 176–232.
27 Wen C. Fong and Alfreda Murck, 'The Three Perfections: Poetry, Calligraphy, and Painting', in *Words and Images: Chinese Poetry, Calligraphy, and Painting*, ed. Murck and Wen C. Fong (Princeton: Princeton University Press, 1991): xv–xxii, xviii.
28 De-nin D. Lee, 'Colophons, Reception, and Chinese Painting', *Word & Image* 28.1 (2012): 84–99, 84.
29 Fong and Murck, *Words and Images*, xv.
30 Nakata Yūjirō, 'Calligraphic Style and Poetry Handscrolls: On Mi Fu's Sailing on the Wu River', in *Words and Images* ed. Murck and Fong: 91–106, 91.
31 John Hay, 'Poetic Space: Ch'en Hsüan and the Association of Painting and Poetry', in *Words and Images*, ed. Murck and Fong: 173–98, 184.
32 For a detailed analysis of this scene, see Li, *Proust, China and Intertextual Engaegment*, 154–66.
33 Cheng, *Le Dit*, 19; *River Below*, 6.
34 Ibid., 268; 185.
35 Ibid., 271; 187–8.
36 Cheng, *Et le souffle*, 24.
37 Shan, *Le Miroir*, 24; my translation.
38 However, it would be wrong to assume that women are historically excluded from practising poetry, calligraphy and painting in China; see Marsha Weidner, *Views from Jade Terrace: Chinese Women Artists 1300-1912* (Indianapolis: Indianapolis Museum of Art, 1988); Kang-i Sun Chang and Haun Saussy, *Women Writers of Traditional China: An Anthology of Poetry and Criticism* (Stanford: Stanford University Press, 1999).
39 Shan, *Le Miroir*, 27.
40 Note, however, that the bottom part also serves to mark the pronunciation of 崖 *yá* as a whole.
41 Shan, *Le Miroir*, 75.
42 Ibid., 120.
43 Yue, *China and the West*, 227.
44 This is also a recurrent imagery in classical Chinese poetry. The Tang poet Li Bai (701-61) is so famous for his fondness for lunar appreciation that the folk legend 太白捞月 had it that he died drunk trying to fetch the reflection of the moon from the water. See Yue, *China and the West*, 227–31.

45   Shan, *Le Miroir*, 24.
46   Furthermore, 空 also means 'emptiness', 'voidness' or even 'nothingness', which is a central tenet in Buddhism. Wu's pursuit and elevation of Buddhism is well known.
47   Shan, *Impératrice*, 21; *Empress*, 9.
48   Ibid., 9; 1.
49   Ibid., 443–4; 318.
50   Sophie Croiset, 'Passeurs de langues, de cultures et de frontières: la transidentité de Dai Sijie et Shan Sa, auteurs chinois d'expression française', *Trans-* 8 (2009). Available online: http://trans.revues.org/336, para. 22 (accessed 27 August 2019).
51   Cited in Croiset, 'Passeurs de langues', para. 19; my translation.
52   Xiaofan Amy Li, 'Introduction: From the Exotic to the Autoexotic', *PMLA* 132.2 (2017): 392–6, 393.
53   Cheng Baoyi, trans., *Faguo qiren shiyuan* (法国七人诗选 *A Selection of Seven French Poets' Works*) (Changsha: Hunan renmin chubanshe, 1984), 70–80.
54   François Cheng, *L'Un vers l'autre. En voyage avec Victor Segalen* (Paris: Albin Michel, 2008 [2019]).
55   Willard Bohn, *Modern Visual Poetry* (Newark: University of Delaware Press, 2001), 17.
56   Ibid., 38.
57   The Chinese word referring to this non-calligraphic art category is *meishuzi* 美术字 developed since the twentieth century, which Billeter translates as 'caractères artistique' in French and Gao Jianping translates as 'art lettering' in English. See Billeter, *L'art chinois de l'écriture*, 13. For a helpful distinction between calligraphy and art lettering, see Jianping Gao, *Aesthetics and Art: Traditional and Contemporary China in a Comparative Perspective* (Berlin: Springer, 2018), 8–10.
58   Christopher Bush, *Ideographic Modernism: China, Writing, Media* (Oxford: Oxford University Press, 2010), 74.
59   Ibid., 73.
60   Cheng, *L'Un vers l'autre*, 65; my translation.
61   Ibid., 104.
62   Weiming Tu, *The Living Tree: The Changing Meaning of Being Chinese Today* (Stanford: Stanford University Press, 1994), vi.
63   Cheng, *Et le souffle*, 24.
64   Shan, *Le Miroir*, 1.
65   Caroline Quignolot-Eysel, 'De la migration à la migrance, ou de l'intérêt de la psychanalyse pour les écritures féminines', *Littératures du Maghreb (Algérie, Maroc, Tunésie, 1806–2015)* (1999), my translation. Available online: http://www.limag.com/Textes/Iti27/Quignolot.htm (accessed 3 September 2019).
66   Elleke Boehmer, *Colonial and Postcolonial Literature* (Oxford: Oxford University Press, 1996), 233–43.

3

A 'boundless creative ferocity': The *Souffles* generation, Moroccan poetry and visual art in dialogue

Khalid Lyamlahy

Reading between words and images

In March 2016, Morocco celebrated the fiftieth anniversary of *Souffles-Anfas*, a leading avant-garde journal of culture and politics founded in March 1966 by a group of Moroccan poets and artists. The commemoration, held at the Moroccan National Library in Rabat, featured a series of events, including an international conference with academics and writers, reading sessions, a musical concert and the republication of all the past issues of *Souffles-Anfas* as well as an exhibition by the painters who contributed to the journal. In a booklet presenting the events, the exhibition was described as 'mettant en valeur la grande originalité de la conception graphique de la revue' (highlighting the great originality of the journal's graphic conception).[1] Launched initially in French (*Souffles*) and published also in Arabic (*Anfas*) starting from 1971, the journal served not only as a bilingual platform for experimental writing and postcolonial thought, and a tribune to the Moroccan far left, but also as a window on creative and abstract artwork from Morocco and beyond. Until its ban in 1972, *Souffles-Anfas* embodied a sense of creative multilingualism in the sense that it combined literary and artistic content while promoting translation, linguistic blending and the inclusion of popular and visual culture in innovative ways. The '*Souffles* generation' has come to designate the writers and artists who sought, through their contribution to the journal and in their later works, to renew Moroccan literary and artistic forms, and, in doing so, to lay the foundations for a broad cultural revolution.

This chapter argues that the multigeneric production of *Souffles-Anfas* and its legacy can be construed as 'world literature' because it transcends national and cultural boundaries while performing the dynamism of language through the creative blending of literary and visual art. This blending is at the core of the idea of 'worldliness', which implies the dissemination of cultural production to a global audience. This chapter builds upon David Damrosch's assumption that 'world literature' as 'a mode of circulation and of reading' is 'applicable to individual works as to bodies of material'.[2] The publication of the first Anglophone anthology from

Souffles-Anfas in 2016 and the growing interest in the individual works of the *Souffles* generation have certainly reinforced the image of the journal as a rich and multilayered body of material that can be approached from a global and multilingual perspective. The combined exploration of verbal and visual languages here serves to promote a redefinition of 'world literature' as, in Lorna Burns's words, 'an assemblage open to dissident acts of readings which imagine alternative forms of relation'.[3] In doing so, this chapter develops a new dialogic approach that casts further light on the relationship between Maghrebian postcolonial literary production and the idea of world literature.[4] I define the multilingualism of *Souffles-Anfas* not only as the combination of French and Arabic content starting from the double issue 10–11 of *Souffles* published in 1968 but also as the multiple innovative ways in which the journal redefines, destabilizes and performs its creative content through linguistic blending as well as literary and visual dialogue. A multilingual platform that challenges generic and thematic boundaries, the journal exhibits a 'worldly' understanding of the act of creation, at once attentive to cultural and linguistic challenges in postcolonial Morocco and open to transnational dialogue and cultural interaction.

Thinking the relationship between multilingualism and world literature through the experience of *Souffles-Anfas* and its contributors needs to take into consideration the close relationship between and interaction of literary and visual modes of expression. As rightly noted by Jan Baetens, 'the globalization of world cultures and the subsequent encounter of world literature and popular literature have reinforced the "word and image" debates about writing'.[5] The dialogue between texts and images provides a space to discuss the porosity and dynamism of language, and constitutes one possible configuration of world literature. Debates about the concept of 'world literature' have often drawn parallels between verbal and visual modes of expression. In 1900, Richard Meyer's early attempt to define 'world literature' was by 'using a range of metaphors, in particular, vitalistic imagery (like the "hibernation" and new awakening of texts of world literature)' and 'landscape metaphors' which 'have a suggestive effect and are used to describe the historical dimension of world literature'.[6] The use of such metaphors, I would argue, is not only a rhetorical or stylistic device but also a way to outline the visual richness of world literature and emphasize the act of reading as a creative navigation between words and images rather than an exclusive focus on verbal content.

One century after Meyer's essay, Franco Moretti borrows two metaphors from cultural history to describe the difference between national and world literature:

> Trees need geographical *discontinuity* (in order to branch off from each other, languages must first be separated in space, just like animal species); waves dislike barriers, and thrive on geographical *continuity* (from the viewpoint of a wave, the ideal world is a pond). Trees and branches are what nation-states cling to; waves are what markets do [...] This, then, is the basis for the division of labour between national and world literature: national literature, for people who see trees; world literature, for people who see waves.[7]

World literature is as much about reading and discussing literary texts from a global perspective as it is about 'seeing' the aspects of continuity and discontinuity between the local and the universal, the verbal and the visual, the monolingual and the multilingual. In *Graphs, Maps, Trees*, Moretti similarly explains that the use of models borrowed from the natural and social sciences allows us to 'place the literary field literally in front of our eyes' and 'to widen the domain of the literary historian, and enrich its internal problematic'.[8] Although Moretti's work has been criticized for the limitations of distant reading, his models still serve as visual devices that help readers engage with meanings and interpretations in a dynamic manner. If the 'worldliness' of literary texts has to do, according to Edward Said, with the ways in which they exist as 'always enmeshed in circumstance, time, space, and society',[9] the same can be said of artistic and other creative works. In *How to Read World Literature*, Damrosch argues that 'works of art refract their cultures rather than simply reflecting them, and even the most "realistic" painting or story is a stylized and selective representation'.[10] When it comes to discussing the 'worldliness' of creation and the circulation of creative practices, representations and meanings, the artistic and the literary are often brought together, including from a pedagogical perspective. John Pizer, for instance, explains that, in his attempt 'to teach world literature *as* literature', he was still 'paying close attention to artistic elements in the works, but also examining how these elements were informed by the distinct cultural/linguistic nuances grounding their production'.[11] In other words, linguistic, artistic and literary patterns are inextricably intertwined. Texts and images are multilingual not only in their mutual interaction and simultaneous presence in the world but also in their openness to dissemination and interpretation. An engagement with multilingualism as a mode of reading benefits from the circulation of aesthetic idioms between the verbal and the visual. Therefore, I use 'worldliness' hereafter as a notion that includes the interrelated and globalized ways in which the creative experience, be it textual, visual or both, is described, performed and understood in a specific multilingual context.

With this in mind, this chapter examines the way in which Moroccan writing, from the journal *Souffles* to the later works of two of its cofounders, displays a 'worldly' understanding of language by revealing the interpenetration of art and poetry and revisiting the act of literary and visual creation beyond cultural, linguistic and generic boundaries. In doing so, the *Souffles* generation redefines the language of creation as inherently multilingual in the sense of an intensified, permeable and boundless idiom that encourages in turn a creative mode of reading between literature and artwork.

Multilingual creativity beyond boundaries

In his essay on the work of Belgian artist Magritte, Foucault comments on the subordinate yet unstable relationship that exists between plastic representation and linguistic reference, adding that 'what is essential is that verbal signs and visual representations are never given at once. An order always hierarchizes them, running from the figure to discourse or from discourse to the figure'.[12] This hierarchical order reinforces the boundary usually set between word and image, literature and art. As a result, creative works are often not only separated by national and territorial boundaries but also shaped by the organizing principles and hierarchical barriers that stand between the verbal and the visual, the literary and the artistic.

In their introduction to the Anglophone anthology from *Souffles-Anfas*, editors Olivia C. Harrison and Teresa Villa-Ignacio evoke the 'boundless creative ferocity'[13] at play in the journal's impressive combination of texts and illustrations. Throughout its six years of publication, *Souffles-Anfas* featured contemporary artwork, striking cartoons, visual poems and original posters commissioned for special issues. This notion of 'boundless creative ferocity', I would argue, is particularly relevant to describe the multilingual identity of the journal. In the following sections, I provide a brief analysis of each term ('boundless', 'creative' and 'ferocity') in relation to the content of the journal as a worldly body of verbal and visual material.

The word 'boundless', to start with, refers to the journal's persistent call to challenge national borders and foster transcultural and transdisciplinary dialogue in creation. In his famous prologue to the first issue, Moroccan poet and editor-in-chief Abdellatif Laâbi writes that '*Souffles* ne se reconnaît d'aucune niche ni d'aucun minaret. Nos amis écrivains maghrébins, africains, européens ou autres sont invités fraternellement à participer à notre modeste entreprise' (*Souffles* is not sponsored by any niche nor any minaret and does not recognize any frontiers. Our Maghrebi, African, European, and other writer friends are fraternally invited to participate in our modest enterprise).[14] The journal featured contributions by renowned figures from all over the world including, for instance, Tunisian author Albert Memmi, Haïtian poet and novelist René Depestre, Lebanese-American poet Etel Adnan and Senegalese novelist and filmmaker Ousmane Sembène.

This overt rejection of boundaries is also manifest in the journal's choice to investigate and draw inspiration as well as visual and symbolic power from popular culture. In the third issue, Moroccan writer and filmmaker Ahmed Bouanani celebrates oral tradition and popular poets, while railing against those who 'jettent un discrédit sur tout ce qui n'est pas composé en arabe classique littéraire et relèguent dans l'oubli ces "poètes vulgaires et illettrés" qui, pourtant, ont exprimé les sentiments les plus profonds de la vie de notre peuple' (dismiss anything not composed in literary Arabic, casting into oblivion these 'vulgar and illiterate poets' who nevertheless have expressed the deepest sentiments of our people).[15] Bouanani's rehabilitation of popular poetry relies on an implicit call to challenge the linguistic hierarchical structure of Moroccan society and to acknowledge the ability of the vernacular language to convey cultural and emotional experiences. The same effort is developed by Abdelkébir Khatibi, another early contributor to *Souffles*. In *La Blessure du nom propre* (The Wound of the Proper Name), a combined study of tattoos, calligraphy and popular proverbs and narratives, Khatibi at once problematizes and dismantles the traditional boundaries between popular and high cultural forms. In his preface, Khatibi contends that 'se mettre à l'écoute de la culture populaire est une forte intervention idéologique qui traverse et contamine toute décision de parole' (to listen to popular culture is a strong ideological intervention that suffuses and contaminates every decision of speech).[16] By investigating popular culture from an analytical and multidimensional perspective, and by pushing this investigation beyond dogmatic closure and folkloric appropriations, Khatibi redefines cultural production as a site of diversity, plurality and inclusion.

Besides being the space of a 'boundless' movement of thought and creation, *Souffles-Anfas* championed the power of creativity and innovation over stagnation. This dynamic creativity, of which the blending of languages, texts and images is one manifestation, circulates not only across artistic forms and disciplines, but also between the artist and the audience. Italian art critic Toni Maraini notes, for instance, that Moroccan modern art does not seek to represent nor to commemorate but rather to engage with the sensibilities of the viewer. This connection is made possible through, in her words, 'un langage non finalisé sur le plan de l'utilité matérielle' (an unfinished language in terms of material usefulness),[17] which encourages the viewer to take part in the creative process. As a result, the Moroccan artwork becomes a space of productive dialogue between artists, viewers and critics. The poems published in the journal and often accompanied by artwork extend this dialogue to the literary sphere. By combining varied structures, geometric layouts and interrupted lines, these poems turn the page into a living canvas. They are, in Rebecca Walkowitz's words, 'translatable because they consist of visual images [...] The lines of the poem, as literal lines on the page, deflate poetry's usual emphasis on words while at the same time drawing attention to metaphor'.[18] This multilingual creative gesture produces original and visually striking works which encourage the involvement of the reader. In this respect, Laâbi denounces in his prologue the incapacity of national literature 'à "toucher" le lecteur, à obtenir son adhésion ou à provoquer en lui une réflexion quelconque, un arrachement de son conditionnement social ou politique' (to 'touch' the reader, to gain his adherence, or to provoke in him some kind of reflection, a wrenching away of his social or political conditioning).[19] For the *Souffles* generation, the value of cultural production remains closely tied to its ability to open up a space for audiences to take part in the creative process. As Moroccan poet and cofounder of *Souffles-Anfas* Mohammed Khaïr-Eddine mentions in one of his interviews, the reader is expected to demonstrate 'une collaboration active' (an active collaboration)[20] based on a continuous and repeated effort. Visual poetry and the creative blending of languages, texts and images are one way to arouse the interest of the reader and facilitate his active immersion.

The third word, 'ferocity', captures both the transgressive discourse developed in the journal and the strategy of linguistic violence promoted by its contributors. Khaïr-Eddine, whose poetics owes a lot to Rimbaud and Lautréamont, is well known for his theory and practice of 'guérilla linguistique' (linguistic guerrilla warfare),[21] which consists in distorting the French language by using subversive images, striking metaphors and unusual words. In one of his articles, Laâbi similarly praises the creator 'qui fait un usage singulier et irremplaçable de la langue [...], propose et impose un nouveau langage, marqué du sceau de son univers créateur' (who makes a singular and irreplaceable use of language, who proposes and imposes a new language, marked with the seal of his creative universe), adding that the Moroccan writer must 'désarticuler cette langue qui est sienne, [...] la violenter pour lui extirper toutes ses possibilités' (disarticulate his language, do violence to it, in order to extract all its possibilities).[22] For the *Souffles* generation, linguistic creativity is an act both of violence and renewal, a technical deconstruction to regenerate and enrich literary works. Ferocity is required in order to appropriate and make use of all linguistic possibilities. Multilingualism becomes therefore the result of a provocative and powerful intervention on language. Unsurprisingly, this creative ferocity is also manifest in the work of Moroccan painters through their use of innovative and often radical techniques. In Maraini's words, Jilali Gharbaoui focuses on 'le geste et les traits nerveux' (movement and nervous brush-strokes), Mohamed Chebaa and Mohamed Melehi use 'la vibration des couleurs et des espaces' (the vibration of colours and spaces), while in Mohamed Hamidi's work, 'c'est au moyen de la construction chromatique que la toile s'ouvre aux différentes dimensions' (the chromatic construction opens up the canvas to different dimensions).[23] The creativity of the *Souffles* generation is ferocious in the sense that it not only embodies linguistic violence and visual disruption but also regenerates the techniques, structures and tools of creation. At the same time, this process of regeneration is in itself dynamic and open to the world, since the aim of Moroccan avant-garde painters, mostly trained in Western academies, was precisely to redefine modernism 'beyond its western/colonial boundaries, so that it could achieve a new historical validity in universal terms'.[24]

The climax of this 'boundless creative ferocity' is probably the substantial shift operated by the journal in 1969, starting with the special issue dedicated to the Palestinian revolution. Moroccan journalist and literary critic Kenza Sefrioui, while acknowledging the 'esthétique de choc' (aesthetics of shock)[25] developed since the creation of the journal, notes that 'l'abstraction, qui était le fil conducteur esthétique de la première période, cède la place à la représentation figurative de foules en armes et de manifestations; la revue affiche sa volonté d'être une avant-garde révolutionnaire' (abstraction, which used to be the aesthetic common thread of the first period, is replaced by the figurative representation of armed crowds and protests; the journal displays its desire to be a revolutionary avant-garde).[26] Starting with the issue 16–17, and in line with the turn from abstract art to political representation, the journal regularly featured reproductions of geographic maps, portraits and photographs from festivals in Africa or camps of Palestinian refugees in Lebanon. The idea of revolution becomes embodied in the dialogue, once again, between analytical, and often incendiary, texts by political activists such as Abraham Serfaty, and striking images of armed combatants, popular workers and leading anticolonial figures such as Patrice Lumumba. In this period, Sefrioui aptly observes, 'l'image prend de plus en plus le statut de document. Elle est explicitement liée au texte, alors que ce n'était pas systématiquement le cas auparavant' (the image becomes increasingly a document. It is explicitly related to the text, whereas this was not systematically the case in the previous period).[27] Simultaneously, the journal finds in the combination of political discourse, figurative representation and photographic reports from all over the world a way to regenerate its ferocious aesthetics and to serve the revolutionary agenda of the Moroccan far left.

If the idea of crossing linguistic boundaries became more concrete in 1971 with the launch of *Anfas*, the Arabic counterpart of *Souffles*, the journal's bilingual turn, I would argue, was only one step in the process of rethinking the relationship between language and cultural production. Since its launch, *Souffles-Anfas* sought to overcome the traditional debates on linguistic identity and go beyond the usual question of language choice by highlighting the relationship between the verbal and the visual. In a particularly evocative article published in 1970, Laâbi writes that 'notre littérature de demain devra surmonter définitivement le bilinguisme pour son action, sa cohérence et sa beauté futures' (literature we envisage for tomorrow must definitively overcome bilingualism for the sake of its future effectiveness, coherence, and aesthetic appeal), adding a few lines later that:

> le problème de la nationalité littéraire n'est une affaire ni d'identité ni de passeport. Il ne peut non plus être résolu du seul fait de l'usage de la langue nationale. Le contenu de l'œuvre ... est là encore le critère décisif.[28]

> (the problem of literary nationality is not a question of identity or passport. Nor can it be resolved by the sole use of a national language. The content of a work ... is once again the decisive criterion.)

Focusing on the fruitful dialogue between textual and visual forms was, for the *Souffles* generation, one way to overcome bilingualism and embody a multilingual aesthetics. The creative potential of the journal lies at the intersection of the need to challenge linguistic forms and boundaries and the quest for other means to convey political and revolutionary discourses. In this respect, it is revealing that a number of contributors to the journal explored other forms of creative expression, including, for instance, Khaïr-Eddine, Laâbi and Tahar ben Jelloun who all tried their hands at drawing or painting.[29] In the following sections, I focus on Laâbi's and Khaïr-Eddine's interaction with Moroccan artists as a way to explore the multiple ways in which the multilingual ethos of the journal was continued and revisited in their later works.

Abdellatif Laâbi: Mobility and multilingual aesthetics

Laâbi can certainly be considered as a multilingual creator. Besides his activity as a poet, he translated Arabic poetry and fiction into French, wrote several political and cultural essays and contributed to children's literature, a genre that can be described, following Jacqueline Rose, as 'the central means through which we regulate our relationship to language and images as such'.[30] This transdisciplinary and translingual activity at once informs Laâbi's work as a whole and enriches his own conception of language. Laâbi's multilingualism is manifest not only in his creative intermingling of literary genres and crossing over from one language to another but also in his ability to put poetic creation in dialogue with visual art in what can be read as a continuation of the legacy of *Souffles-Anfas*.

In 2000, Laâbi's short text *L'écriture au tournant* was published alongside a painting by Moroccan artist and novelist Mahi Binebine. The painting, which represents a yellow strip running through a human head with an open mouth, can be interpreted as a reference both to the prison where Laâbi spent eight years and to shouting as a metaphor for poetic creation. The discontinuity created by the horizontal strip and the disjointed head carries the dual meanings of torture and screaming, suffering and resistance, silence and speech. In his text, Laâbi writes that 'écrire revient à violer la loi du silence imposée par les tyrannies au pouvoir et le consensus social, qu'il soit d'ordre moral, religieux ou patriotique' (It [writing] amounts to a violation of the law of silence imposed by the tyrannies in power and by the social consensus, be it moral, religious, or patriotic in nature).[31] Binebine's painting serves at once to document Laâbi's experience as a political prisoner during the Moroccan 'Years of Lead' and to redefine the act of creation as a physical process, a bodily struggle against silence and oppression.

The same productive dialogue between Laâbi's texts and Binebine's artwork is continued in the collection of prose poetry *Pourquoi cours-tu après la goutte d'eau?* (Why Do You Chase After the Water Drop?) published in 2006. Laâbi's texts include an imaginary conversation with Dostoevsky at the prison of Salé, a letter to Turkish poet Nazim Hikmet and a fictional testamentary text by Russian poet Mayakovski. The last two texts take the form of imagined dialogues between the poet and his late parents. Laâbi not only invokes international literary figures to reflect on the relationship between writing and freedom but also transcends the conventional boundaries between prose and poetry, the local and the universal, the intimate and the public. The silent language of his father's hands and the wise words of his mother are intermingled with the fictional voices of international writers to create a multilingual space of remembering and celebration. This conversational aspect is reflected in Binebine's drawings, two of which represent respectively a man leaning towards a second one imprisoned in a box, and a third man carrying a fourth one on his shoulders. Here again, the bodily language serves to extend and support Laâbi's multilingual aesthetics. The ideas of dialogue and solidarity are embedded in the connection between the verbal and the visual. Multilingualism provides a way to figure the poet's quest as universal, as suggested by the fictional will of Mayakovski: 'Moi le Bagdadien (aurais-je des origines arabes?), je termine en vous renvoyant à ces paroles de Fariduddine al-Attar: 'Pourquoi cours-tu après la goutte d'eau alors que tu te diriges vers la mer ?' (Me the Baghdadi (am I of Arab origin?), I conclude by referring you to the words of Farid ad-Din Attar: 'Why do you chase after the water drop while you're heading towards the sea?').[32] The unexpected evocation by the Russian poet of his twelfth-century Persian fellow and the playful confusion of Mayakovski's hometown Baghdati in current Georgia with the city of Bagdad in Iraq serve to reinforce the multilingual ethos through spatial connection, temporal variation and transcultural dialogue.

Laâbi's multilingual aesthetics thrives on the continuing presence of and exchange with the other. In his preface to *Ruses de vivant*, a collaborative work with Moroccan painter Mohamed Kacimi, Laâbi describes writing as the transformation of 'le désir réciproque de réaliser un ouvrage commun où peinture et poésie mettraient dans la balance leur pesant d'âme et de chair' (a mutual desire to produce a joint book in which painting and poetry would weigh in with their spirit and flesh).[33] The process of writing is a physical impulse triggered by the inspiring presence of the other: 'J'ai rarement autant ressenti, en écrivant, que quelqu'un d'autre poussait ma main, la retenait et reposait délicatement sur la page' (rarely have I felt, while writing, that someone else was pushing my hand, holding it and delicately putting it down on the page).[34] Multilingualism is not only reflected in the connection between the verbal and the visual but also integrated as a mode of writing based on creative interaction and mutual influence.

In *Petit Musée portatif* (2002), another collaborative work with Moroccan artist Abdallah Sadouk, the combination of poems and images creates a new model of conceptual blending around the representation of everyday material objects and the themes of exile, belonging and poetic influence. The collection is structured as a series of brief poems about pieces of furniture, writers, artists and other people which all constitute, as suggested by the title, the personal museum of Abdellatif Laâbi. The word 'portatif' (portable) in the title suggests a sense of mobility and variation. Laâbi's travelling fragments form what Françoise Ascal defines in her preface as 'un paysage intérieur' (an inner landscape) at once 'incarné, recomposé, métissé, à l'image du brassage qu'affectionne son habitant' (embodied, reconstructed and mixed just like the intermingling appreciated by its inhabitant).[35] This work of embodiment, reconstruction and hybridization is made possible through a substantial effort to match each poem with its corresponding visual representation.

Poems about Laâbi's parents, to start with, are presented alongside black-and-white and slightly blurred photographs. The poem dedicated to the father, for instance, is a moving text in which Laâbi starts by describing the paternal body:

Assis devant son établi
la cinquantaine
les sourcils noirs fournis
les lèvres gourmandes
rasé de près
retenant son souffle
devant l'objectif.[36]

(Seated beside his workbench
in his fifties
black and thick eyebrows
fleshy lips
clean shaven
holding his breath
as he faces the camera.)

The detailed restitution of the father's body, closely associated with his workspace, is interrupted at the moment when the photograph is taken. The following verses capture simultaneously the loss of the father and the poet's impossible return to childhood:

le temps s'arrête
Les années forment
une haie d'honneur
pour laisser passer
l'ombre lumineuse
De son lointain exil
l'enfant se détache
pour le suivre.[37]

(time stops
The years form
a guard of honour
to let his
illuminated shadow through
From his remote exile
the child breaks away
to follow him.)

The oxymoronic 'ombre lumineuse' (illuminated shadow) reveals the contradictory aspect of writing loss and grief. While the shadow circulates between the poem and the photograph, the father, like childhood, remains out of reach. His photograph is at once what triggers the poem and pinpoints its limitations. Only a dialogue between the poetic and the photographic can reproduce the paradoxical process of writing as an act of mourning and remembering.

This multilingual aesthetics is further developed in the poems dedicated to fellow artists and presented alongside reproductions of their respective works. In a poem dedicated to Moroccan painter Abbes Saladi, for instance, Laâbi writes:

L'arbre est féminin
au grand dam
de la langue française
Elle arbore ses seins nus
au grand dam des barbus
musulmans de la dernière heure.[38]

(The tree is feminine
to the great displeasure
of French language
She displays her naked breasts
to the great displeasure of bearded men
eleventh-hour Muslims.)

Here, Laâbi astutely uses Saladi's painting, a visual representation of a tree as a woman, to formulate an implicit critique of both French language and religious extremism. Laâbi's poem not only comments on Saladi's artwork but also uses it to challenge linguistic determinism, reject gender discrimination and convey a resolutely political and critical discourse.

In a different but equally original gesture, poems accompanied by Sadouk's drawings describe the multiple ways in which everyday objects are used, transformed, and often forgotten or dismissed. Remembering a pair of stirrups made by his late father, Laâbi writes:

> Ils ont rapetissé
> depuis la mort
> du maître sellier
> Mais ils s'étreignent
> en souvenir du cheval triste
> qui galope encore
> vers l'enfance.[39]

> (They have shrunk
> since the passing
> of the saddler
> But they embrace each other
> in remembrance of the sad horse
> who still gallops
> towards childhood.)

Laâbi's description emphasizes the relationship between the artist (his father) and his creation. Artwork is located at the crossroads of the nostalgia for childhood and the interlacing of painting and poetry as an attempt to recover the fragments of a lost past. While Laâbi's poetry is embedded in memory, Sadouk's drawings are concerned with the fleeting aspect of furniture which is depicted in hazy settings echoing the universal experiences of loss and oblivion. The contrast between poetry and visual representation is compelling. For instance, Laâbi writes about a dining table:

> A force de manger dessus
> on oublie sa fêlure
> ses gravures cunéiformes
> ses senteurs d'huile vierge
> de Meknès
> On la nettoie
> sans la moindre caresse.[40]

> (By dint of eating on it
> we forget its crack

its cuneiform engraving
its fragrance of virgin oil
from Meknes
We clean it
without the slightest caress.)

Laâbi's sensorial description turns a mere piece of furniture into a living body that needs attention and care. In contrast, Sadouk's depiction of the dining table, with its hazy shape and approximate decoration, is less an illustration of Laâbi's poem than a symbolic object, a dematerialized representation of the very act of remembering. Here again, the poet's intimate space, once appropriated and reconfigured by the artist, opens up to the reader an extensive world of emotions and reflections about everyday life. In this context, the act of reading becomes a multilingual quest for signs and meanings conducted through both the back-and-forth movement and the discrepancy between poetry and artwork. Sadouk's drawing serves as the directing image in the passage from individual experience to collective understanding, thus materializing the 'worldliness' of Laâbi's poem. Throughout its dialogue with personal memories, everyday objects and art pieces, *Petit musée portatif* includes an invitation to redefine the language of creation beyond literary, artistic and social boundaries. The relationship between art and poetry is driven by the principle of mobility as it constantly shifts from loose interpretation to creative rewriting. As a representation of the multilingual identity of collaborative work, the collection performs a 'boundless creativity' in the sense that it rejects standardization and regularity, and fosters instead the unpredictable impulse of memory, dialogue and displacement.

Mohammed Khaïr-Eddine: A mirror game of languages

Another form of this 'boundless creativity' can be traced in the poet's attempt to explore and think about other creative forms. In *M'seffer vu par Khaïr-Eddine* (1995), Khaïr-Eddine tries his hand at art criticism by reflecting on the work of Moroccan artist Lahbib M'seffer. The book is published as part of a collection entitled 'Silhouettes' and aimed to celebrate 'la rencontre des mots et des images, à travers la dualité du peintre et de l'écrivain' (the encounter of words and images through the duality of the painter and the writer).[41] This duality is manifest in the form of the volume itself, composed of two separate booklets facing each other and opening with the respective portraits of Khaïr-Eddine and M'seffer, executed by Moroccan artist Abdelkébir Rabi. In his preface, Moroccan art critic Moulim El Aroussi reveals that Rabi played a major role in bringing M'seffer back to painting after a career in banking and administration. The duality of the book is symbolically opened to a third party as Rabi's introductory portraits serve to highlight the ideas of representation, exchange and transmission. The dialogue between the poet and the artist is reflected in Rabi's portraits of both, which invite the reader to move from Khaïr-Eddine's words to M'seffer's artwork and vice versa. El Aroussi describes the dialogue between the two Moroccan creators as a 'jeu de miroir' (mirror game)[42] in the sense that Khaïr-Eddine's once explosive poetics and subversive language are contrasted with M'seffer's romantic paintings and peaceful landscapes. The creative gesture at the core of the volume thrives on this interstitial and contrasting space in which Khaïr-Eddine seems to find peace and stillness after his early years of linguistic guerrilla and radical aesthetics.

In his reading of M'seffer's works, Khaïr-Eddine seems to search for the echoes of his own experience, as if his friend's paintings served as mirrors reflecting back his own conception of creation and opening a dialogic space in which he could see himself in new light. Khaïr-Eddine writes for instance that 'M'seffer exécute le travail de la toile par touches rapides et quasi imperceptibles tel un poète égrenant des mots rares ou familiers' (M'seffer paints with rapid and almost imperceptible brush-strokes as a poet reeling off rare or unfamiliar words), and he adds: 'Il y a chez lui beaucoup de poésie et cette poésie est davantage vécue que réfléchie' (there is a lot of poetry in his works and it is based more on lived experience than on reflection).[43] Khaïr-Eddine's reference to lexical innovation and to lived experience as an impulse for artistic creation hints at his own practice of poetry. M'seffer's rapid and vigorous brush-strokes echo Khaïr-Eddine's oral performances when he used to read loud or recite long fragments of his poetry. Similarly, M'seffer's active connection with the landscapes he paints deeply resonates with Khaïr-Eddine's unwavering attachment to his southern homeland.

By revisiting M'seffer's works from a personal and literary perspective, Khaïr-Eddine develops a bilingual mode of reading art. Throughout the volume, he draws parallels between the Moroccan painter and a number of literary figures. He writes, for instance, that 'M'seffer sait rendre au détail, comme Kafka, toute sa charge intentionnelle' (M'seffer, like Kafka, knows how to restore the intentional power of details),[44] and praises him as 'un créateur responsable. Responsable au sens rimbaldien' (a responsible creator. Responsible in a Rimbaldian sense)[45] in reference to Rimbaud's call in his *Lettres du voyant* to make oneself a seer and regenerate the language of creation. This constant effort to connect M'seffer with the realm of literary and poetic creation can be read as an attempt to merge the textual and the visual, to cast light on the quest for a common language of creation. The reference to both Rimbaud and Kafka suggests that this common language needs to be at once revealing and transgressive, precise and disturbing, all-encompassing and thought-provoking. The universality of such language is grounded, as in Rimbaud's and Kafka's poetics, in its structural and stylistic specificities. Significantly, Khaïr-Eddine writes that 'chez M'seffer, la toile peinte est d'abord un texte … mais un texte complexe; il a sa syntaxe et sa prosodie; sa rythmique et sa sémantique particulière' (M'seffer's painting is firstly a text … but a complex text; it has its syntax and prosody; its rhythm and specific semantics).[46] Khaïr-Eddine's reading seeks not only to connect art to literature but also to bridge the gap between the particular and the universal in creation.

Khaïr-Eddine's reading goes further and develops a multilingual approach to the act of creation by drawing a significant parallel between art and music. Khaïr-Eddine's interest in music builds on the original idea that 'la musique est la véritable vibration du monde, le langage premier – et non primitif – qui génère d'autres langages; c'est la voix des atomes et des particules invisibles dont toute matière est constituée' (music is the real vibration of the world, the first – and not primitive – language that generates other languages; it is the voice of atoms and invisible particles of which every substance is made).[47] By considering music as the worldly idiom from which other languages originate, Khaïr-Eddine emphasizes the universal scope of his discourse. For him, M'seffer captures the music of the universe, namely the energy of the cosmos, which he then reinterprets and reproduces as a 'musicalité chromatique' (chromatic musicality).[48] This composed term, which recalls Baudelaire's synaesthesia, refers to the way in which the distribution and variation of colours can reproduce natural movements as perceived and experienced by the artist. In this context, reading artwork from a multilingual and universal perspective amounts to engaging with the sounds, the vibrations and the colours which all constitute the language of the painter. Khaïr-Eddine's approach to M'seffer's works is both creative and multilingual for it regenerates the meaning of the artwork while uncovering its various connections and levels of representation in relation to textual, visual and even musical elements.

Furthermore, Khaïr-Eddine's multilingual dialogue with M'seffer's work promotes the idea that artwork, like poetry, is constantly in motion and particularly sensitive to contradictions and tensions. Thus, Khaïr-Eddine compares M'seffer's work to 'une sorte de laboratoire de l'image vivante, du trait frémissant' (a kind of laboratory of the living image, of the trembling stroke) that creates '[un] paysage non figé, toujours en évolution, car il est savamment rythmé par la dynamique générale' (a non-static landscape, always evolving, for its cadence is skilfully set by global dynamics).[49] This dynamism, which opens artwork to interpretation, is also what allows the painter to conceive of Moroccan landscapes as paradoxical spaces. In the opening lines, Khaïr-Eddine describes the homeland as 'cette terre marocaine à la fois tourmentée et sereine' (this Moroccan land at once tormented and serene), and celebrates M'seffer's 'communication complète avec le sol natal, avec tout ce que celui-là et celle-ci comportent d'impondérables et d'éraflures' (complete communication with the homeland, including imponderables and scratches).[50] Khaïr-Eddine's relationship with Morocco, which he voluntarily left in 1965 to spend fourteen years in France, can be described, in Edward Said's words, as an 'unhealable rift forced between a human being and a native place, between a self and its true home'.[51] Khaïr-Eddine seems to find in M'seffer's romantic landscapes a healing echo to his own nostalgia for a lost homeland. As a result, his multilingual approach not only connects art and literature but also allows him to measure the distance between the past and the present and get a sense of lost spaces and temporalities. Khaïr-Eddine considers that M'Seffer recounts 'l'Histoire d'un pays vu et vécu à travers toutes ses parcelles terriennes, ses cieux, ses côtes houleuses, ses arbres serrés ou distants les uns des autres, ses maisons blanches, ses coteaux, collines, mares, herbes folles, etc …' (the History of a country seen and experienced through its parcels of land, its skies, its stormy coasts, its tight or distant trees, its white houses, its hillsides, hills, ponds and wild grass, etc.).[52] This incomplete list reveals at once the visual scope of M'seffer's work and its attempt to encompass the complete geography and history of the Moroccan homeland. As a result, Khaïr-Eddine's multilingual reading is confronted with the resurgence of spatial and temporal boundaries, which carry an underlying degree of doubt and uncertainty about artistic practice.

Multilingualism, loss and reconstruction

One reason behind this doubt is the fact that while the experience of *Souffles-Anfas* was concerned with promoting a 'boundless creative ferocity', notably through the blending of literary and visual art and the reinvention of new cultural forms, the multilingual identity of the journal and its legacy of 'worldliness' were faced with a deep sense of frustration and failed expectations. The origins of this frustration lie not only in the political disillusionment of the Moroccan left, of which *Souffles-Anfas* was one leading platform, but also in the cultural challenges experienced from the outset by the journal and its contributors.

When reconsidering the experience of *Souffles-Anfas*, it appears that multilingualism was at once a practical achievement, embodied in both linguistic blending and the creative intermingling of verbal and visual material, and an elusive, almost unattainable goal, hindered by the problems of cultural distribution and assimilation. In other words, while *Souffles-Anfas* 'began practising a politics of bilingualism and translation from the ninth issue which includes a French translation of a manifesto by Syrian poet Adonis' and then started 'featuring new Maghrebi literature in both French and Arabic',[53] the contributors were from the beginning, and remained, concerned about their ability to reach and engage with broader audiences. In his prologue to the first issue, Laâbi recognizes 'le problème de la communication de cette poésie' (the issue of communicating this poetry) to Moroccan audiences, especially as translation is 'étrangement jamais pris[e] au sérieux' (strangely never taken seriously) while illiteracy reduces the potential readership to 'un résidu presque dérisoire' (a nearly derisory residue).[54] In the double issue 10–11, which featured a number of contributions in Arabic, Moroccan novelist Mohammed Berrada notes that Maghrebi literature, in drawing inspiration from both Eastern and Western sources, runs the risk of becoming 'a "hybrid" literature that has lost its national grounding and historical authenticity'.[55] At the same time, while calling to fight against underdevelopment and stagnation, he warns against the danger of implementing cultural changes that 'will be limited to the infrastructure without affecting the surface, allowing intermingling, confusion, accumulation, and "modernization" to continue without comprehension or assimilation'.[56] Laâbi's and Berrada's reflections pinpoint the sociocultural limitations of the discourse developed by *Souffles-Anfas*. The universal ambition of the journal and the multilingual practice of its contributors were constantly hampered by the local realities of cultural production, dissemination and assimilation.

As the years passed, the ferocity of the *Souffles* generation seems to have waned while the hopes for a socio-cultural awakening remained mostly unfulfilled. The experience of the journal is now remembered as a unique moment of creative and boundless energy, a fleeting light in the period of postcolonial political disillusionment and cultural self-reconstruction. It is no coincidence that Laâbi opens his foreword to the booklet of the commemorative exhibition by the *Souffles* painters in 2016 with this call: 'Laissons de côté la nostalgie!' (Let's put nostalgia aside!).[57] In the same document, Moroccan painter and cofounder of *Souffles* Mohammed Melehi recollects the circumstances of his first meeting with Laâbi in 'une anecdote, certes empreinte de nostalgie, mais d'une portée symbolique importante' (an anecdote, which, while nostalgic, holds an important symbolic significance).[58] Voicing or resisting nostalgia for both the beginnings of the journal and the cultural effervescence it represented at the time forms another language that needs to be considered and translated.

Reading world literature from a multilingual perspective is also about acknowledging the discrepancy between the experience of boundless creativity and that of loss and disenchantment. In a revealing reflection, Khaïr-Eddine suggests that 'peut-être qu'un jour, après nous, d'autres analystes à la sensibilité différente et qui auront découvert un monde que nous ne connaîtrons pas, diront des toiles de M'seffer ce chagrin vorace qui n'est pas loin des grandes nostalgies' (maybe someday, once we're gone, other analysts with different sensibilities, who would have discovered a world unknown to us, would identify in M'seffer's paintings this voracious sorrow that resembles great nostalgias).[59] In a rapidly changing environment, in which spatial and temporal boundaries are constantly negotiated and displaced, the experience of reading through the lens of multilingualism involves an inevitable confrontation with the experience of loss. This is probably one of the lessons from the *Souffles* generation: in global art as in world literature, the creative fabric of multilingualism is where representations, meanings and modes of reading are subject to endless construction and reconstruction.

Notes

1 Fondation Laâbi pour la Culture, 'Commémoration du Cinquantenaire de la création de la revue Souffles' (2016), 5. Unless otherwise indicated, all translations are mine.
2 David Damrosch, *What Is World Literature?* (Princeton: Princeton University Press, 2003), 5.
3 Lorna Burns, *Postcolonialism after World Literature: Relation, Equality, Dissent* (London: Bloomsbury, 2019), 23.
4 See Charles Bonn and Arnold Rothe, eds., *Littérature maghrébine et littérature mondiale* (Würzburg: Verlag Königshausen & Neumann, 1995) and Jane Hiddleston, 'Writing World Literature: Approaches from the Maghreb', *PMLA* 131.5 (2016): 1386-95.
5 Jan Baetens, 'World Literature and Popular Literature: Toward a Wordless Literature?', in Theo D'haen, David Damrosch and Djelal Kadir (eds.), *The Routledge Companion to World Literature* (Oxford: Routledge, 2012) 336-344, 342.
6 Monica Schmitz-Emans, 'Richard Meyer's Concept of World Literature', in *The Routledge Companion to World Literature*, 49-61, 50.
7 Franco Moretti, 'Conjectures on World Literature', *New Left Review* 1 (2000): 54-68, 67-8.
8 Franco Moretti, *Graphs, Maps, Trees: Abstract Models for A Literary Theory* (London and New York: Verso, 2005), 2.
9 Edward Said, *The World, the Text, and the Critic* (London: Faber and Faber, 1984), 35.
10 David Damrosch, *How to Read World Literature* (Malden: Wiley-Blackwell, 2009), 2.
11 John D. Pizer, *The Idea of World Literature: History and Pedagogical Practice* (Baton Rouge: Louisiana State University Press, 2006), 17.

12 Michel Foucault, *This Is Not a Pipe*, trans. James Harkness (Berkeley and Los Angeles: University of California Press, 1983), 32–3.
13 Olivia C. Harrison and Teresa Villa-Ignacio, 'Introduction: *Souffles-Anfas* for the New Millenium', *Souffles-Anfas: A Critical Anthology from the Moroccan Journal of Culture and Politics* (Stanford: Stanford University Press, 2016) 1–12, 8.
14 Abdellatif Laâbi, 'Prologue', *Souffles* 1 (1966): 3–6, 6; 'Prologue', trans. from the French by Teresa Villa-Ignacio, in *Souffles-Anfas: A Critical Anthology*, 17–21, 21.
15 Ahmed Bouanani, 'Introduction à la poésie populaire marocaine', *Souffles* 3 (1966): 3–9, 4; 'An Introduction to Popular Moroccan Poetry', trans. from the French by Robyn Creswell, in *Souffles-Anfas: A Critical Anthology*, 46–55, 47.
16 Abdelkebir Khatibi, *La Blessure du nom propre* (Paris: Denoël, 1974), 22; trans. by Matt Reeck.
17 Toni Maraini, 'Situation de la peinture marocaine', *Souffles* 7–8 (1967), 15–19, 16; 'Moroccan Painting Today', trans. from the French by Addie Leak, in *Souffles-Anfas: A Critical Anthology,*, 105–9, 106.
18 Rebecca L. Walkowitz, *Born Translated: the Contemporary Novel in an Age of World Literature* (New York: Columbia University Press, 2015), 19.
19 Laâbi, 'Prologue', 3; 'Prologue', 18.
20 Abdellatif Abboubi, *Mohammed Khaïr-Eddine: Le temps des refus: Entretiens 1966–1995* (Paris: L'Harmattan, 1998), 27.
21 Mohammed Khaïr-Eddine, *Moi l'Aigre* (Paris: Éditions du Seuil, 1970), 24.
22 Abdellatif Laâbi, 'Réalités et dilemmes de la culture nationale', in *Souffles* 4 (1966), 4–12, 12; 'Realities and Dilemmas of National Culture', trans. from the French by Olivia C. Harrison and Teresa Villa-Ignacio, in *Souffles-Anfas: A Critical Anthology*, 61–73, 72.
23 Maraini, 'Situation de la peinture marocaine', 16–17; 'Moroccan Painting Today', 106–7.
24 Rasheed Araeen, 'Art and Postcolonial Society', in Jonathan Harris (ed.), *Globalization and Contemporary Art* (Chichester: Wiley-Blackwell, 2011), 365–74, 370.
25 Kenza Sefrioui, *La Revue Souffles (1966–1973): Espoirs de révolution culturelle au Maroc* (Casablanca: Editions du Sirocco, 2013), 66.
26 Ibid., 100.
27 Ibid., 103.
28 Abdellatif Laâbi, 'Littérature maghrébine actuelle et francophonie', in *Souffles* 18 (1970), 35–8, 37; 'Contemporary Maghrebi Literature and Francophonie', trans. from the French by Lucy R. McNair, in *Souffles-Anfas: A Critical Anthology*, 226–32, 229–30.
29 Some of Khaïr-Eddine's drawings were published in *Lettres et poèmes à sa femme Zhor Jendi et autres écrits épistolaires et littéraires* (Rabat: Marsam, 2012); Ben Jelloun and Laâbi exhibited their paintings respectively at the Institut du Monde Arabe in Paris (October 2017–January 2018) and the Matisse Art Gallery in Marrakesh (November–December 2018).
30 Jacqueline Rose, *The Case of Peter Pan or the Impossibility of Children's Literature* (Philadelphia: University of Pennsylvania Press, 1984), 138–9.
31 Abdellatif Laâbi, *L'Ecriture au tournant* (Neuilly-sur-Seine: Al Manar, 2006), 54; *In Praise of Defeat*, trans. Donald Nicholson-Smith (New York: Archipelago Books, 2016), 815–16.
32 Abdellatif Laâbi, *Pourquoi cours-tu après la goutte d'eau?* (Neuilly-sur-Seine: Al Manar, 2006), 54.

33 Abdellatif Laâbi, *Ruses de vivant* (Neuilly-sur-Seine: Al Manar, 2004), 7.
34 Ibid., 8.
35 Françoise Ascal, 'Avant-dire', in Abdellatif Laâbi, *Petit musée portatif* (Neuilly-sur-Seine: Al Manar, 2002), 7–8, 7.
36 Laâbi, *Petit musée portatif*, 26.
37 Ibid.
38 Ibid., 33.
39 Ibid., 16.
40 Ibid., 9.
41 Mohammed Khaïr-Eddine and Lahbib M'seffer, *M'seffer vu par Khaïr-Eddine* (Casablanca: Arrabeta Editions, 1992), 1.
42 Moulim El Aroussi, 'Préface', in *M'seffer vu par Khaïr-Eddine*, 3–5, 3.
43 Khaïr-Eddine, *M'seffer vu par Khaïr-Eddine*, 7.
44 Ibid., 11.
45 Ibid., 15.
46 Ibid., 17.
47 Ibid., 2.
48 Ibid., 22.
49 Ibid., 13.
50 Ibid., 7.
51 Edward Said, *Reflections on Exile and Other Essays* (Cambridge, MA: Harvard University Press, 2000), 173.
52 Khaïr-Eddine, *M'seffer vu par Khaïr-Eddine*, 11.
53 Harrison and Villa-Ignacio, 'Introduction: Souffles-Anfas for the New Millenium', 1–12, 4.
54 Laâbi, 'Prologue', 5; 'Prologue', 20.
55 Mohammed Berrada, 'Generation Drive', trans. from the Arabic by Maya Boutaghou and Holda El Shakry, in *Souffles-Anfas: A Critical Anthology*, 138–41, 139.
56 Ibid., 140.
57 Abdellatif Laâbi, 'De *Souffles*, les mains heureuses', in *Les Peintres de Souffles: Exposition*, Fondation Laâbi pour la Culture (2016), 6; trans. Touria Binebine, 7.
58 Mohamed Melehi, 'Souffles, pour la mémoire' in *Les Peintres de Souffles: Exposition* (2016), 8–13, 8; trans. Touria Binebine, 9.
59 Khaïr-Eddine, *M'seffer vu par Khaïr-Eddine*, 17.

4

The heterolingual zone: Arabic, English and the practice of worldliness

Claire Gallien

At this juncture in time, English is still the dominant language that many authors aspiring to world recognition write in, or into which they should at least be translated. Yet, there are two ways for English to circulate in the world – one is by being global, the other is by becoming worldly. English as a global language is modelled on the colonial paradigm of centre/periphery, where English expands outward and where the periphery must connect to the centre, be articulated or at least adapted to its terms, validated by it and translated into it, in order to be circulated worldwide. I am not claiming this paradigm does not exist, nor am I undermining its force. It is still the case that literatures must be relevant to the English-speaking Global North in order to become global. However, there are numerous excellent volumes and articles already published on this issue and my chapter therefore does not focus on this aspect.[1] I am interested here in how English becomes worldly. We will see that contrary to the *global paradigm*, which has a blunting effect on literature, the *worldly paradigm* has an enhancing potential through greater complexity and creativity. By becoming worldly, I mean works in English that would attach themselves to other languages, scripts, forms, genres, literary traditions, perspectives and cosmovisions, and through this type of literary attachment (or what Edward Said beautifully conceptualized as 'affiliation' in opposition to the 'filiation' of the tribe)[2] turn into enmeshed formations. Obviously these witting and unwitting gestures of linking are not something new or specific to English. After all, it would be hard to find one type of literature that is not intertextual. Yet, imperial ideology, as applied to linguistic and literature, has created an amnesia concerning the relations between English and the world.

In this chapter, I place Anglophone-Arabic[3] writing within the larger debate on world literature and multilingualism. Indeed, the novelists and poets I have selected possess and are possessed by multiple languages, i.e. Arabic, in its classical form and its various vernaculars (Iraqi, Palestinian, Syro-Lebanese …), English and other European languages and minority languages such as Kurdish. For some, English is the language they have always written in, and they reserve Arabic vernaculars for home and private exchanges. For others, English and Arabic are alternatively used, and for others still, Arabic is the language of writing, whether due to a lesser command of English or due to a positive and militant 'politics of language'. Hanan al-Shaykh has made her career as a writer in Arabic, 'refusing' to write directly in English, while recognizing the influences of Russian, French, English, Arabic classical and contemporary Egyptian literatures on her prose.[4]

My chapter includes a selection of contemporary poetry and prose published by Arab writers in Arabic, English or both, who practise self-translation and/or navigate between the two languages. I start with a reflection on heterolingualism, as distinct from multilingualism, in the case of Anglophone-Arabic literature. Then my chapter proposes to question the apparent belonging of these texts to one language only (either Arabic or English) and to define them as 'born-translated' instead. The last sections offer close readings of excerpts from the texts that showcase their engagements in heterolingual practices by breaking scripts (Dunya Mikhail, Zeina Hashem Beck), language boundaries and unity (Suheir Hammad), and Orientalist projections (Sinan Antoon). The production of Arab writers in English has been well researched.[5] The authors I selected for this chapter navigate between both languages or write in Arabic but are known in the Anglosphere through (self-)translation. In all cases, my selection does not presume to be representative of the Anglo-Arab literary tradition in its entirety.

Mikhail's *The Iraqi Nights* (2014) is a collection of poems, with drawings resembling ancient Sumerian tablets and with the poet's handwriting added to the printed pages. The collection is initially written in Arabic and then translated into English, but in the English translation the ancient Sumerian tablets and the poet's handwriting in Arabic remain and are essential to the creation of meaning. Hashem Beck's bilingual duet poems entwine scripts and languages that sometimes translate into one another and sometimes diverge from each other. Non-Arabic speakers only get at best one half of the poem, but they in reality get the full story, in the sense that they keep us aware of what we might not understand. Conversely, bilingual readers in Arabic and English may understand the full poem but the reality is that the two versions do not compare. The two partners are neither equal nor identical. Hammad's *breaking poems* (2008) are written in English but in a syntax that breaks with linguistic norms and unearths the violence of normative language and consensual representations. Her breaking poems in English open a space where Arabic comes in and where both languages lodge and dislodge each other, through what I have analysed elsewhere as the 'minorization' of English.[6] As I argue with Hammad and in my additional reflections on Ashraf Fayadh's *Instructions Within* (2017), the disruption of forms, contents, expectations and policed morality does not lead to chaos and atomization but on the contrary to the formation of intense and committed collectives. Finally, I offer comparative micro-readings of Antoon's *Ya Maryam* (2012)/*The Baghdad Eucharist* (2017) that question the dominant discourse on Iraqi sectarian violence and war but do not produce the same effect whether directed inside or outside what Emily Apter referred to as the 'translation zone' – in other words, for its English or Arabic readers.[7] The close readings indicate that a text is not heterolingual *by nature*, and in that regard it differs greatly from texts that would just be published in a bilingual format. It becomes heterolingual *by practice* and to highlight the political dimension of literature.

ἕτερος/*heteros*

The first meaning of 'multilingual' refers to texts written in or containing more than one language – in this case Arabic and English – with interactions ranging from 'hard' to 'soft' multilingualism,[8] from an emphasis on incommensurability to one on translatability. This is the case here for instance in the bilingual edition of Ashraf Fayadh's prison poems or Zeina Hashem Beck's bilingual duet verses. Dunya Mikhail's Arabic poetry involves bilingualism, when translated, since the verses are in English but Mikhail's handwriting interwoven with her drawings stays in Arabic. Yet, these bilingual texts (though they could also be multilingual and the conclusion would be the same) do not necessarily disrupt the monolingual paradigm, or what Jacques Derrida called the 'fiction' of speaking in *a* tongue.[9]

There is, however, a second understanding of multilingualism at play in the poetry and prose I study for this chapter. This second form of multilingualism may work in combination with the first. It refers not to the co-presence but to what I would call the 'sub-presence' of a language or multiple languages in another, de facto positing diglossia as starting point. This reflection echoes Samia Mehrez and Rey Chow's works on the presence of multiple languages in ostensibly monolingual tongues in postcolonial contexts. Mehrez exposed in 'Translation and the Postcolonial Experience' the counter-hegemonic force of multilingualism, and Chow in *Not Like a Native Speaker*, linguistic estrangement and unequal power relations between languages.[10] Here, Mikhail and Beck's multilingualisms mean not just a capacity to think and write in more than one language. Both poets also foreground the co-presence and sub-presence of languages and literary traditions. Their poetry vibrates with interlingual and intertextual resonances that foster new perceptions, new imaginaries and new cognitions (as opposed to mere *recognitions*) of the world.

The authors of Anglophone-Arabic writings I am working on are at least bilingual due to their ancestry, family, education and the fact that they received at least part of their formation in the USA, have lived there or migrated there. Dunya Mikhail grew up in Iraq but is now based in the USA and has received US nationality; Zeina Hashem Beck is Lebanese, did her BA in English at the American University of Beirut and now lives in Dubai; Suheir Hammad is American of Palestinian origin from Jordan and moved to the USA when she was just a child; Sinan Antoon is Iraqi and moved to the USA to do a PhD at Harvard and is now based there and in Germany.

These authors are not the only one to have been born and raised or educated in a multilingual diasporic environment. The question I am asking then is do they have a specific way to be multilingual? My essay is arguing that, given the context in which they write and in which they are read, their multilingualism possesses a specific inflection. They are writing or are translated in a dominant language (i.e. English) from the perspective of a language that is transnational and considered sacred by many. To a certain extent, because Arabic is the language of the Qur'ān, because it bears 'classical' (*fuṣḥā*) status, and has a 'standard' version used in education and publishing throughout the Arab world, it also holds a relationship of power over its multiple dialects (*'ammiyyah*) and the other local languages, which it sometimes violently dominated – a well-known example is Tamazight in Morocco. Therefore, recourse to a binary grid of dominating/dominated when analysing the English/Arabic relation is problematic, because it also implies erasing a long history of linguistic and cultural hegemony in Arabic, with consequences to this day. Suheir Hammad breaks her poetry in English not with the insertion of standard Arabic but precisely with Palestinian Arabic.

Yet, when standard and vernacular forms of Arabic travel to the Anglosphere their symbolic meanings change too. From being state-sponsored or state-enforced (as French for instance was when it crushed regional languages in the metropole and demoted indigenous languages in its former colonies), Arabic is turned into a language spoken by an ethnic minority and becomes even the 'language of the enemy' as it crosses to the USA and is associated with war and terrorism.[11] This association is not just the effect of individual statements by alt-Right people declaring Arabic as the language of the enemy; it takes place within what Foucault categorizes as a 'discursive formation'.[12] Therefore, in the context of the Global North, largely governed by neo-conservative and neo-liberal US rhetoric, and where Arabic evokes anxiety, fear and suspicion, creating multilingually in Anglo-Arabic is in itself an act of resistance.

Borrowing from Suheir Hammad's collection *breaking poems*, Michelle Hartman conceptualizes 'breaking English' in opposition to the weakened and defeated version of what is known in postcolonial writing as 'broken English':

> My use of the concept of the break in this study focuses on the generative possibilities – it allows us to 'break into' the texts and let them 'break things down.' Writing and language that may on the surface look 'broken' – according to mainstream conceptualizations of what the English language should be – are conceived here as strategically engaged in 'breaking' to open up critical and creative spaces to develop new and challenging soundscapes in texts ... positive generative sources for manifesting other kinds of breaks that reimagine society, liberation, and freedom.[13]

By intentionally interrupting scripts, languages and representations, the authors of Anglophone-Arabic writings not only break hegemonic structures of discourse, they also induce a shift of attention from signified to signifier, from representation to the materiality of words, grammars and forms, which serve as support for these representations. This shift is particularly crucial in the case of post-9/11 Anglo-Arab and translated Arabic literature in the West, which has been persistently called to 'represent' 'Arab' and 'Muslim' identities, to 'witness' and 'respond' to contemporary geopolitical crises and to abide by what Gana and Härting called the 'imperative' to narrate violent events, to make them speak and speak coherently, to an order of credibility imposed from outside.[14] In our case, it means that the publishing industry demands of Arabic writers that they write about terrorism, wars in the Middle-East, Islamophobia, Arab sexuality and Arab woman oppression, to comply with readers' expectations in the Global North. To be clear, cultural productions do not have to be caricatural to repeat stereotypes. For instance, the number of films set in the Middle East or North Africa, produced by Arab film directors, and often women, focusing on the topic of female social, familial and religious oppression is alarmingly high. This is not of course to deny the reality and violence of the issue but to repeat that it is crucial to take into account the places of reception. When circulated in Western states self-described as secular liberal democracies, the films repeat a monolithic representation of the Arab woman (which in itself is a very problematic category), with the heroine as either oppressed or resisting. Therefore, the displacements from signified to signifier, content to form, constitute an option that the writers I discuss have chosen in order to militate against the testimonial imperative and also to bring forward the issue of the frames and props delineating the contours of representation. Therefore, I argue that the concept of 'heterolingualism' – with *heteros* derived from the ancient Greek ἕτερος, meaning 'other', 'another', 'different' – is more relevant to analyse the action and effect of Anglophone-Arabic prose and poetry than 'multilingualism'.

I borrow the concept from Rainier Grutman and Myriam Suchet, who defined it as the 'dramatization of a language as more or less alien across a continuum of alterity constructed in and through a given discourse (or text)'.[15] Contrary to the common use of the term 'multilingualism', which relates to 'multiculturalism' and therefore to the idea of the presence of integrated 'multiple' cultures or languages in a larger body (be it a person or a group), 'heterolingualism' places the emphasis on the principle of entangled alterity. Otherness does not lie outside but inside, hence the idea of entanglement, and the deployment of creative principles such as creolization, archaism, linguistic palimpsest and invention.

I argue that Anglophone-Arabic writing's heterolingual creativity is two-fold. On the one hand it results in the breaking of text, language and regimes of truth (stereotypical narratives, tropes, representations), using the manifest presence of Arabic as initiating the break. On the other, it is based on a latent or palimpsestic presence of Arabic in English, creates contrapuntal effects that redirect meaning, modify soundscapes and readers' affects towards their languages. The second conception of creative heterolingualism implies that we move away from a conception of language as transparent and of the speaker's/reader's relation to language as a-perspectival. Suchet's understanding of heterolingualism returns to a conception of language as opaque and of the speaker's/reader's relation to it as anamorphic. Indeed, the form the language takes varies according to the position one holds and a new image may surface and replace a previous one when viewed from a different perspective. The anamorphic presence of Arabic in English does not create a single effect, i.e. that of breaking English, which has been by and large the only paradigm retained to analyse their interactions (and again, given the international context governing relations between the USA and the Middle-East, the choice of the paradigm of the 'break' is understandable). I contend that Arabic is not 'inserted' or 'injected' in the English text to break it. Rather, it is already present, in anamorphosis, and it allows for all sorts of transformation, combination, play, discontinuity, friction.

What I am trying to achieve here is a translation of the work on 'friction' by Tim Cresswell,[16] who uses geography and geographical concepts in his analysis of social and cultural phenomena, into literary theory. Cresswell states that mobility never occurs in a frictionless world and that it is the result of a political distribution of who may travel and who has to stop. But Cresswell also indicated that friction – in mechanical terms – is the precondition of mobility; that it is through the friction of particles and matter that we move. Translated into literary theory, heterolingualism produces this friction that is essential to any creative and critical process in the sense of dislodging and moving our preconditioned cognitive categories, including how we hold a book in our hands and read it. In *Instructions Within*, the editor Lynne DeSilva-Johnson wrote at the end:

> The westerner might ... [be] feeling vaguely uncomfortable holding the book and/or turning pages 'backwards' but this is precisely the point: to disrupt the proprioceptic modeling that tells you that the way you do things, your patterning, is not only yours but 'right' or 'normal', when in fact hundreds of millions of people – billions of people – experience books and texts in directions different from your own.[17]

This function of heterolingualism relates to what John Solomon conceptualized as 'the ethics of heterolingual address', namely a recognition that 'the plurality of languages in a given situation does not in itself guarantee access to the heterolingual mode of address' and consequent 'commitment to heterogeneity in all situations'.[18]

Born translated

The notion of heterolingual literature is related to Rebecca Walkowitz's notion of 'born translated' texts. According to Walkowitz, there are two ways to be 'born translated' and these two ways map on the initial distinction I was proposing between 'global' and 'worldly' Englishes. The first meaning she adduces is related to books that have been written from the start in view of translation and the structure as well as contents of which are shaped for and by translation.[19] Similarly to works pre-emptively written in English, so as to secure a global market from the start, these are books that are seemingly monocultural and monolingual, written in a very simple style, so as be translated and circulated easily. Yet, 'born translated' also encompasses the view of literature written as a form of translation. They are books that 'block readers from being "native readers", those who assume the book they are holding was written for them or that the language they are encountering is, in some proprietary and intrinsic way, theirs'.[20] They resist 'the unique assignment of languages, geographies, and states', ask the reader to consider that literatures, as we have known them, are 'already combined' and therefore invite what Walkowitz calls 'new ontologies' of literature.[21]

The Anglophone-Arabic poetry and novels explored in this chapter are preoccupied with the ongoing worldly (as opposed to global) history of English language and literature. Cutting across the national frames given to languages and literary traditions in the West, their works represent acts of un-blanking the fact that this history has been infused by a variety of linguistic formations and literary traditions, which constitute the layers of its literary time. Their works also feature as acts of worlding English literature through their engagements with creative heterolingualism.

The fiction of monolingualism also has a history, which is both personal, having to do with the experience of being born in *a* language, and global, related with the rise of nationalism and colonialism.²² Indeed, print, the rise of vernacular literatures and the idea of regulating languages through the use of grammars are combined phenomena marking the Renaissance period in Europe. These phenomena intensified in England in the late seventeenth and early eighteenth centuries with the development of the book market and, with larger audiences gaining access to literacy, it became incumbent upon the literary elite of the day to police the practice of both the spoken and written word. The interventions of Daniel Defoe in *An Essay Upon Projects* (1697), of the Earl of Shaftesbury in *Characteristics of Men, Manners, Opinions, Times* (1711) and then of Joseph Addison and Richard Steele in the periodicals of *The Spectator* (1711–12) and *The Tatler* (1709–11), were all directed towards the codification of a proper grammar of the English language and contributing to the elaboration of the aristocratic myth of a polite language (later morphing into 'Standard English').²³ This approach to language through codification, purification and homogenization was transferred to the colonies when British orientalists studied Indian languages and started to translate Indian literatures. Indian vernacular languages were disqualified because of their hybrid natures. The attention of orientalists shifted to Sanskrit and the Sanskritization of Indian literature by way of purifying the vernaculars of their Persian and Arabic influences, as Nathaniel Halhed advocated in his Bengali grammar of 1778.²⁴

Therefore, making English worldly again, through heterolingual practices, constitutes an attempt to supersede elite, national and colonial histories of language and literature formations. As Clare Pollard insightfully reminds us in her editorial of the issue of *Modern Poetry in Translation* devoted to the multiple languages of the United Kingdom: 'to suggest these islands have ever been monocultural or monolingual is a brazen falsehood'.²⁵ Therefore, while multilingual creativity is certainly not restricted to English literature or to the sole presence of Arabic in English, one must recognize a disruptive heterolingual specificity to Anglophone-Arabic writing, which has largely to do with the post-9/11 and the 'War on Terror' climate, even if and when writers in these languages do not, or refuse to, respond to this context directly and explain why Arabs or Muslims are not 'terrorists' and why Arabic is not 'the language of the enemy'.

Breaking script

In order to explore this disruptive heterolingual specificity of Anglophone-Arabic writings, I focus on the literary and political implications of multiscriptual writing in Dunya Mikhail's *The Iraqi Nights* (2014) and Zeina Hashem Beck's poem 'Estranged' published in *MTP* (no. 1, 2019). Their multiscriptual practices recall Peter D. MacDonald's fourth proposition in *Artefacts of Writing*. I reformulate the proposition (which initially reads: 'some forms of literature interfere with the workings of the literate brain, posing a challenge to readers of all kinds'[26]) to apply it to my corpus and argue that 'heteroscriptual play in Anglo-Arabic literature interferes with the workings of the literate brain, posing a challenge to English-speaking readers of all kinds'. Indeed, I read Mikhail's Arabic handwriting weft around and into the illustrations of her poems and Hashem Beck's duet poetry not as a mere puzzle to an English-speaking literate brain but as real action to frustrate any claims to privilege access to reality, to experience or to expertise.

On the page of 'Estranged', English and Arabic scripts exist separately yet in an active relationship with each other. Visually, the scripts are separated by a transparent line – or shall we say a mirror – running in the middle of the page, aligned on the left for English and on the right for Arabic, to respect the directions in which the languages are normally read. Yet the idea of a mirror image between the two languages and two versions of the poem is already frustrated by the fact that the English script on the left is not aligned with the Arabic on the right; rather, as partners in a duet, they dance or sing separately, one after the other. For those with access to Arabic, it also clear that the poems, while approaching the same topic, namely estrangement, do so differently. Arabic is not a translation of English or English of Arabic in any strict sense of the term. Both poems are reformulations of one another and have different ways to present how estrangement feels.

The English poem, alignment left, reads like a casual conversation, thoughts scattered for a departed friend about life in a city when dear ones have left or are leaving. It peruses death and being ready to leave, it reflects on destruction of cities and the many ways to prostitute a city, which has already degraded many. The Arabic poem, alignment right, reads like a monologue to the self, where the voice of the poet returns to days past with nostalgia, before departure, and then to a life of departures from West to further West and separations, where the poet leaves to oil countries and her friend to the First World. In other words, the Arabic part of the poem represents a conversation that does not take place in the English part, which is about trying to reconnect with the friend left behind and keeping in touch. The Arabic part, the one which is out of reach for readers in English, delves into the deeper past, memories of war and separation.

And then come the bilingual stanzas in the poem quatrains formed of two lines in English and two in Arabic, or the opposite, two in Arabic and two in English. Therefore despite the different entry points on reality, there are moments both visually and cognitively where the experiences meet and then a common ground is shared in the centre of the page. The space of the common ground is also interesting in that it posits no necessary blending into a single unit. English and Arabic meet in the stanza aligned at the centre of the page, not in a word-for-word translation but more as echoes and sometimes in contradiction to one another. For instance the 'summer' becomes a 'night' in Arabic, or the 'future self' in Arabic is turned into 'the self in the past' in English.

أفضل نفسي الآن على نفسي المستقبلية
though I like the me I am now more than the me back then.²⁷
(transliteration: üfaḍḍilu nafsī al-ān ʿalā nafsī al-mustaqbaliyah)
[literal translation: I prefer myself now than my future self]

The political implications of such scriptural and poetical gestures are critical in that they mean that shared space is open despite difference or rather precisely open because of difference. Hashem Beck comments on the duet form stating that 'it allows for a layering of meanings' and makes room for 'questions like: would I think of or speak to this place, person, memory, etc. the same in different languages?'²⁸

Dunya Mikhail is from the Assyrian-Christian community of Iraq and an exiled poet who left her country in 1996 in the aftermath of the Gulf War and mounting harassment under Saddam Hussein's dictatorship. In *The Iraqi Nights* she reflects on the power of poetry to confront and ward off death, reopening the wounds of war and using poems to face and remember the violence while at the same time restating the richness of Iraqi culture. Mikhail uses the brevity of poetry and the play with form that it allows in order to highlight both topics. For instance, in a very evocative designing for her poem 'A Half-Burned Page on al-Mutanabbi Street', Mikhail adds large blank space in the line of the verses and between words so as to create a visual representation of pages of books blown off by a bomb detonated on this most famous book market street in Baghdad. The first four lines of the poem go:

Is	this	a sign	then?		
This page	floating		in the		air?
This	floating page	from	a	half-burned	book?
This	half-burned	book	on	al-Muttanabi	Street?²⁹

Her visual poetry also evocatively underlines the multilingual and multicultural richness of Iraq. Indeed, the reader of *Al-Layalī al-ʿirāqīyah* (Iraqi Nights) is informed in the prelude that the poems she is going to read are inscriptions left by Ishtar on the gates of her Sumerian city after she was kidnapped by a gang of masked men. The embedding gesture structuring the paratext is absolutely crucial to an understanding of the politics of her poetry, where Arabic language belongs to 'the land of Sumer', and where Ishtar, who is both the female voice articulating the poems and also obviously a reference to the Mesopotamian goddess associated with love and war, repeats the gesture of Shahrazad in the *Thousand and One Nights* and confronts violence and death with her poetry.

Visually, the poems of *Al-Layalī al-ʿirāqīyah* repeat this opening resistant gesture in presenting Mikhail's Arabic handwritten verses woven in and around the drawings recalling Sumerian tablets. What is interesting with the English translation is that it is there on the page but placed in the top-left corner, set aside from the Arabic-Sumerian dialogue that is going on in the visuals. In other words, English may be used for the poems to globalize, that is, to circulate beyond the original language in which they were written, namely Arabic, but the poem becomes worldly in the interweaving of untranslated handwritten words in Arabic and the drawings resembling Sumerian-like tablets. The page of the poem becomes a 'translation site'[30] where the interactions between different signs bears meaning. For instance, Arabic script fuses in the form of the shell and becomes the shell in Tablet 1 (Figure 4.1). The poet may also place Arabic in the image and tell the same story twice through two different media as in Tablet 10 (Figure 4.2). Language may be placed below the drawing, as a form of translation

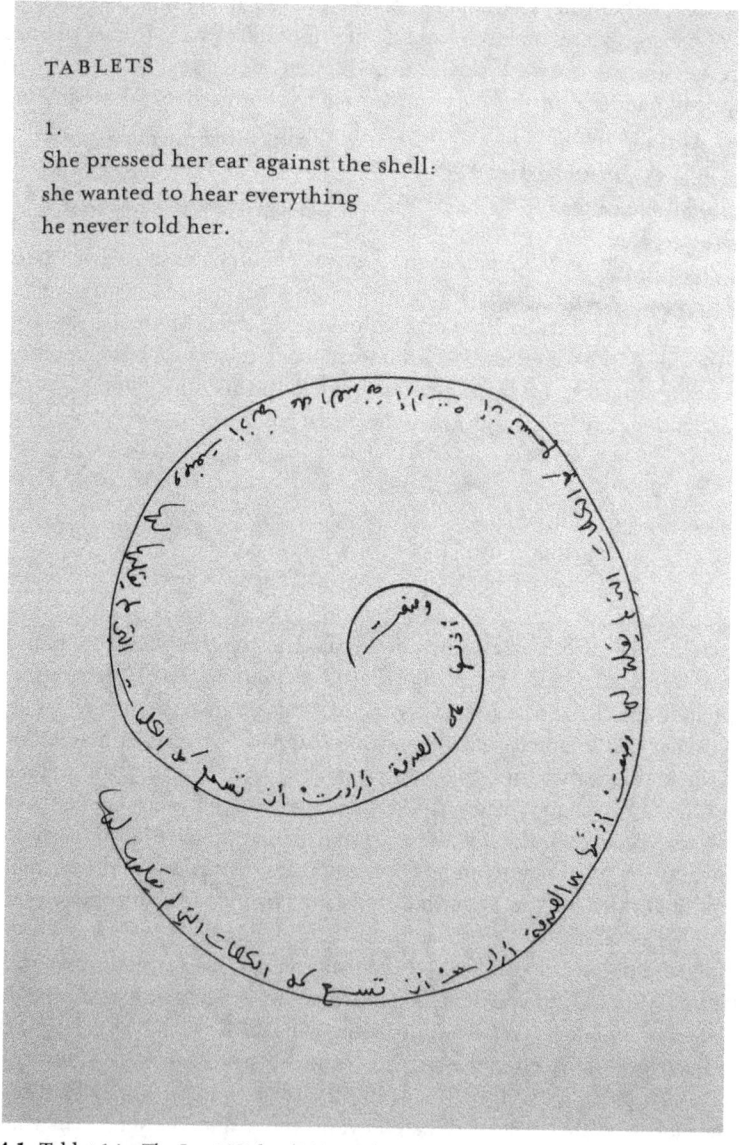

Figure 4.1 Tablet 1 in *The Iraqi Nights* (2014, 13).

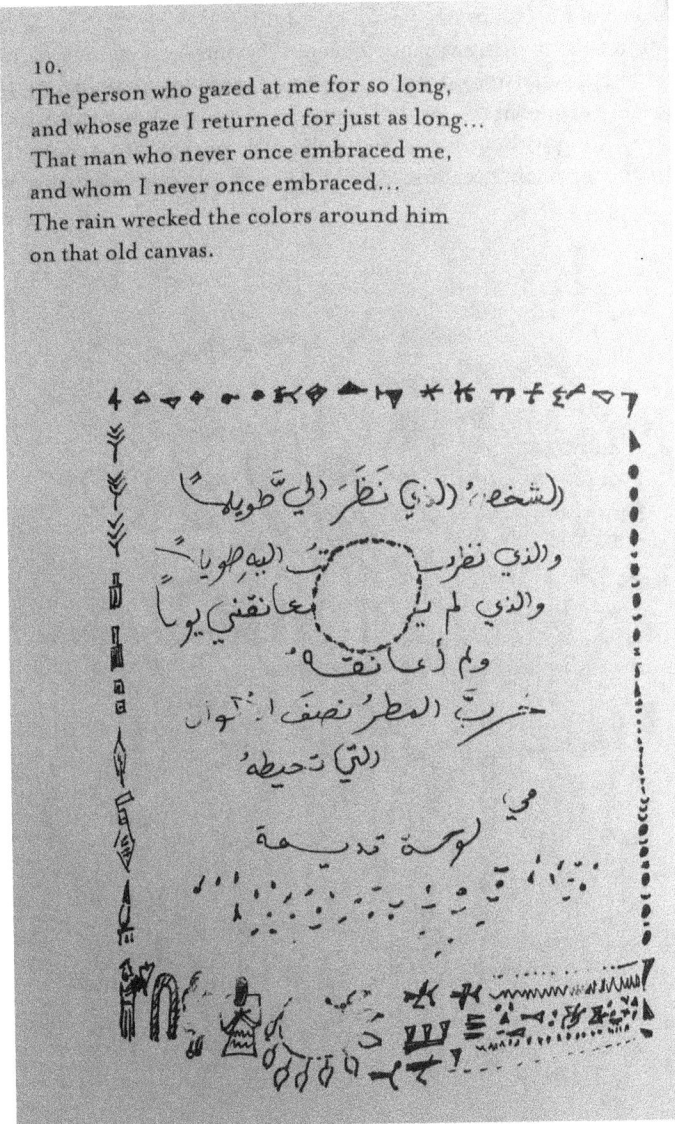

Figure 4.2 Tablet 10 in *The Iraqi Nights* (2014, 22).

for an image that cannot be cracked. Language may also disappear from the picture altogether, as in Tablet 20 (Figure 4.4). What all these configurations reveal is that language and image, Arabic and Sumer, interact in various ways, ranging from intensification to deflection of meaning, and very crucially that these connections are not natural but they are the result of a design, in other words of a choice of where to place which of the two and what relation to privilege between the two.

The presence of English in the corner highlights for non-Arabic speakers how the Arabic script in spite of being visually (deceptively) interlaced with the drawing may tell a very different story from it, and conversely how when absent from the drawing and just present outside, in the top-left corner of the page, it in fact mirrors what the tablet is representing without words, as in the case of Tablet 11 and 20 (Figures 4.3 and 4.4). In this last configuration, Arabic deploys the story, or rather *a* potential

Figure 4.3 Tablet 11 in *The Iraqi Nights* (2014, 23).

20.
Cinderella left her slipper in Iraq
along with the smell of cardamom
wafting from the teapot,
and that huge flower,
its mouth gaping like death.

Figure 4.4 Tablet 20 in *The Iraqi Nights* (2014, 32).

story, contained in the drawing, because readers are free to wonder if that is really the only story contained in the tablet, the only way to 'interpret'. Arabic poetry offers one potential translation of graph into language, a translation that makes sense, but that obviously does not cover the image in its entirety. Indeed, when we look at Table 11 (Figure 4.3) for instance, 'the husbands that were lost and then found' and 'the prisoners of war' may be linked with the images drawn in the third and fourth rectangles, 'the kite that took her' with the second rectangle, but then the rest of the poem in Arabic 'in her dream, / to some other place, / while she stood before the camera / to have her smile / glued into the passport' does not relate to the visual, nor do the other three rectangles find their language equivalents in the poem. What is eloquently dramatized here is the act of translation itself, as a form of drawing closer to another language and imaginary, while recognizing the holes, distances, approximations, in other words the absence of transparency.

Breaking language

Just as they break with any casual relation to default scripts and bring to light the erasures that come along with the imposition of one script over other scripts or other sign systems, Anglophone-Arabic writings also engage with the practice and politics of breaking dominant languages. Suheir Hammad is a very interesting poet in the study of this commitment to breaking the *hegemon* in greater detail. Indeed, Hammad, in solidarity with African-American literature and music,[31] especially jazz and hip hop, devised a poetic technique she called 'break'.

Her collection *breaking poems* includes (but is not restricted to) the topics of the violence of displacement and war. Obviously, the various ways in which she breaks the English grammar and language recall the postcolonial literary experimentation of creole and hybrid English. It would be absurd to negate this postcolonial affiliation, which may not be intended by the poet, but certainly reflects a valid mode of reading her poetry given the colonial context of Palestine, to which she is historically, culturally, linguistically and emotionally connected. Yet, her breaking English achieves something more than broken English and the reflection of patois in English. It permits the materialization of violence in language. Gana and Härting discussed the assignation of Arab writers in English to talk about the wreckage of war in the Middle East for the Global North in a language that is clear and coherent and reflected further on the violence both of the assignation (to write about one topic only) and of the injunction (to write about it coherently and make sense of the horror).[32] Gana and Härting emphasized the deeply problematic posture that Anglophone-Arab writers are expected to endorse for the global book market. In this context, Hammad's *breaking poems* are an important gesture of poetic refusal to approach global violence and Palestine with a colonial language and posture that would remain safe, unaffected, untainted, unbroken by the violence.

'– break (face) –' is a poem composed at Qalandia after the poet had the experience of going through the checkpoint to reach Jerusalem while the Palestinian families waiting in the queue were denied entry and returned to the West Bank. From that experience, Hammad remembers the silent tears that had left two lines across her face, her – break (face) –, and a poem shorn of its punctuation marks and of its conjugated verbs:

qalandia a head a family four so quiet their absence alert walk forward away permission denied hospital slip a father blind thigh iv hand son's shoulder boy what 4 who 5 the mother holds a baby low whimper in blanket nonviolence is another's dream a haunting map projected onto body memory where men done what they been a blueprint of flight sun of spare parts of wet lands open women sea loss waves voices bass mirror my face the road map the pieces plan the partition through.[33]

This scene of routine violence refuses to be turned into a fluid sentences. Instead, her poem destabilizes grammatical categories (words read simultaneously as nouns and verbs) and readers' expectations. For instance, 'road map' may be heard as a compound noun but then most likely read as a noun followed by a verb (unconjugated though). In other words, the reader is left with either of two unsatisfactory options: read 'road map' as a compound noun but then misspelt (instead of being written in one block the noun 'roadmap' is divided into two lexemes) or respect the syntax, read two words, a noun (road) and a verb (to map), but then recognize the grammatical error ('map' should have been written as 'maps' in the present tense or 'mapped' in the past tense). The role of poetry here is to leave the language and the discourse that 'represent' in a state of indeterminacy and readers in a zone of insecurity. Language is turned into a checkpoint and poetry symbolically duplicates the contingency and insecurity of those who live on the checkpoints and have to cross them. The repetition of the plosive 'p' at the end translates into sound the violence of partition. The adverb 'through' placed at the very end of the poem denotes a movement across, which contrasts with the stops produced by the series of plosive ('map the pieces plan the partition'), and indicates the cut that history, partition, militarized space have imposed on people's lives.

Therefore, Hammad challenges our modes of reading. This is not to imply that the disruption can in any way compare with the violence of Palestinian life under Israeli colonization and apartheid; but to insist on the fact that poetry and its readers cannot feed on the misery of others without going through some form of trouble. In this case, the poetics of the break serves this purpose. Promises of peace, roadmaps, the loss of a land and the wounds inflicted on bodies break the poem. This is not to the point of unspeakability, because the bodies and movements of the woman, children and father are visible, and it is crucial not to lose them, not to unsee them, behind the haze of a constructed chaos. But it is to the point that language returns maimed.

Hammad breaks language with language – that is, she not only breaks syntax, but she also interjects Arabic into English and English into her transliterated Arabic poems. The Arabic introduced does not create exoticism. They are words related to her Palestinian ancestry but also reproduce a natural way to talk between languages, swapping to Arabic for coordination conjunctions such as 'and' consistently presented in its translated form 'wa' and 'I' into 'ana'. For instance, the last stanza in '– break (naher al-bared) –' goes:

Poem is my body my language my country
Wa bas ana closed to tourism
Ana closed to journalists wa bas
Ana closed to translation.[34]

The poet plays with the paradox of refusing translation while locating herself already in translation. Similarly, English breaks her Palestinian-Arabic in 'Ma ba3rif aktob bil arabi', which ironically translates in English as 'I do not know how to write in Arabic'. Her 'text-English Arabic' poem is written with the letters *ḥa* as 7 and *'ayn* as 3. The use of the 7 and 3 and the Romanized alphabet is not mere language play but underlines dislocation and estrangement. It is heterolingualism performed. Written during PalFest, the poem contains segments of the Palestinian voices she heard, not necessarily connected together, but voices of what they said to each other, to her, or about her. The poem holds together the intimate, because it is written in the way Arabic 'feels' to her, and the collective; it makes room both for the collective, as fragmented in a myriad of voices, and the individual voices remembered in the space of a poem and travelling with it.[35]

Breaking projections

The last heterolingual practice I discuss in this essay is one that attempts to disrupt default/Orientalist narratives about Arab and Muslim countries in the West. I choose to focus on Sinan Antoon who is an academic, poet, novelist and (self)-translator working in Arabic and English and who has been quite vocal in denouncing the Western perpetuation of Orientalist and imperialist views in the Middle East. As a critic, he has repeatedly warned against the embargo on Arabic literature and, in the post-9/11 context, lambasted the forensic interest for Arabic in the West.[36] Given the aversion, it is striking that Antoon should systematically locate his novels in post-2003 war-torn Iraq, and all the more so in his third novel, *Ya Maryam* (2012), translated into English as *The Baghdad Eucharist* (2017) by Maia Tabet. Indeed, Antoon explained that the personal and the horrific were so much intertwined in this novel that he could not bring himself to translate it.[37] Yet, the paradox is only apparent since his publications derail the dominant narrative in the West framing the fall of Saddam Hussein's dictatorship and the War on Terror.

In *The Baghdad Eucharist*, Antoon returns to Iraq, not to depict the horrors of war through sensationalism and voyeurism; rather, he has members of an Iraqi-Christian family confronted with collisions within and between themselves, coming from both inside and outside, from the present and the past. Antoon's novels contribute to the production of urgent counter-narratives to American mainstream representations of the conflict, where the vision of Iraq is tragically reduced to battlefields in the desert, where the focus is placed on US war veterans, as in 'In the Valley of Elah' (2007), and US war heroes. The local population is either totally obliterated or represented as barbarians, as in the movies *American Sniper* (2014) or *The Wall* (2017). It is crucial to keep this US cultural context in view to understand Antoon's literary intervention and the urgency of his counter-narratives that retell the story of Iraq in English from the perspective of Iraqis.

Amongst Antoon's numerous works, *The Baghdad Eucharist* in particular triggered my interest as a result of the presence of several (picture) frames in the diegesis and what these may entail in my reflection on heterolingualism and anamorphism. Indeed, the diegesis is built on embedded stories, which emerge from pictures or footages that the narrator sees or in which he takes part. The presence of frames and the framing of stories draws the reader's attention on the question of anamorphic vision, i.e. how a new picture emerges by changing her/his position in front of the painting. This in turn invites further reflection on historical memory, selection and the language of the archive. The novel, by being translated, addresses multiple and different audiences. But it does more than just expanding the number of readers. Translated novels imply what I would call a heterolingual form of address that resonates differently depending on the contexts of reception and horizons of expectation.

The novel tells of stories of the members of the Iraqi-Christian family emerging from picture frames. Part 2 of the novel is indeed entitled 'Family Photographs' (simply 'ṣuwar' in Arabic, namely 'photographs') and section 10 for instance opens on a description of the picture of a family table gathering and then unravels the threads of the characters' stories present on that day for this gathering and this picture. With these various threads, Antoon is able to weave a tapestry of Iraq where sectarianism appears as the result of global geopolitical decisions, as something directed from top down, not from bottom up. The parts of the novel dealing with this topic of imported sectarianism are present in both the Arabic and English versions. Yet, it appears as much more dissenting for English readers who have had no experience of life in Iraq precisely because it goes against default narratives and pictures of internecine hatred, intolerance and violence circulated in global mass media.

Saadoun sighed and said,

> By the time the turbans unravel, we will be dead and buried. That is, if they do. Between Iranians, Arabs, and Americans, our country has been decimated. Honestly, it's still a mystery to me. Has there been sectarianism all along and we simply weren't aware of it? Is it even possible? Where was it lurking all that time? Or is it all a result of foreign interference and this hatred for us, and all those people returning from abroad who brought all their filth with them? Take Sundus, for example, isn't she married to a Shiite? Was that a problem fifteenth years ago?[38]

The novel in English does not resonate with bombs only but also with the sound of Youssef Omar's *maqāmāt*.[39] The other counter-narrative offered by the fiction is one that undermines the depiction of Iraq as monolingual, mono-religious and monocultural. This narrative is addressed primarily to Arabic speakers in Iraq and in exile who are either supporters or victims of the global Islamic State propaganda defacing Islamic diversity and dignity. Section 6 in the third part of the novel is remarkable for its bringing together of religious soundscapes across different timelines. When characters would oppose the co-presence of the Islamic, the Christian, and the Aramaic and Syriac traditions, this section of the novel interweaves them contrapuntally, showing how they respond to each other in mutual enhancement and constitute the very fabric of the space they live in.

The scene starts with Youssef walking towards a little grotto enclosing a statue of the Virgin Mary in a Church in Baghdad. The protagonist notices the palm tree and how it grew since his last visit. This vision brings happiness to his heart as it feels to him the tree is protecting Mary. His Christian ancestry does not prevent him from appreciating Qur'ānic verses, especially those related to Maryam/Mary. Indeed, visiting the grotto with the palm tree brings to his memory the recitation of surah Mariam by the world-renown Egyptian *qāriʾ* (Qurʾān reciter) ʿAbd al-Bāsiṭ ʿAbd al-Ṣamad, and the conflictual conversation he had had with his sister Hinna when he was endorsing the legitimacy of the Qurʾānic version of Maryam/Mary's parturition below the palm tree. The narration flashes forwards to the present again and Youssef enters the Church. There, in gold Kufic script, are inscribed the words of the Credo, which is quoted in its entirety as interlude in the diegesis. Youssef then lingers on in the Church, moved by the chants in Aramaic and Syriac intoned by the priest.[40] It seems that, with this scene, the fiction does not invent a post-sectarian multilingual Iraq. It restates what has always been there, with all the tensions of what mutual and contrapuntal presence implies, but also with all its richness.

Coda

Because Kurdish was a banned language under the al-Assad father and son's dictatorships, the Kurdish Syrian poet and translator Golan Haji has always written his poetry in Arabic, while letting it be haunted with Kurdish language and oral literature. Precisely because of the repressive regime in which Haji began his career as a poet – he now lives in exile in France – he emphasizes how a language and a literature are never alone and self-enclosed, but they live in the haze of others, and let others live in their midst. Translation is 'not just moving the words from language to language' but it is conveying what he calls 'the shadow of meaning', i.e. the sensations and images that come with the text one translates,[41] and the other languages that are implied in the text and reappear in anamorphosis. Therefore, as Haji points out, it is pointless to seek perfect translation. Texts and languages always exceed what is on the page and are always already elsewhere.

To repeat the phrase of the poet Stephen Watts, who is also Haji's translator for *A Tree Whose Name I Don't Know* (2017), poetry performs as a 'journey across breath'.[42] Defining poetry and language as such constitutes a radical break from the national and/or regional frames ascribed to literature and a departure from what Jon Solomon called the 'apparatus of area'. Solomon's critique of area studies is related to translation theory as 'transfer' or 'bridge', which presupposes the compartmentalization of languages, cultures, literary traditions in discrete units, and the creation of hierarchies between them. If one starts thinking of poetry as a journey across breath, looking for meaning not only in language but also in its shadow and haze, and if one becomes attentive to the heterolingual practices of novelists and poets pushing against the monolingual construction of literature, then one has already started to write in a critical language that is at one remove from the default national and monolingual modes, and to conceive of linguistic and literary belongings in ways that are unstable, attentive, open and creative. Only then may English shift from 'global' to 'worldly' status, which implies considering that it exists through the other languages that people it, that it interacts with the world not through cosmopolitan travel, easy access and the false security that it will ultimately be translated and understood, but through the humble perception that it is ever relying on other voices to articulate its own.

Notes

1. Amongst other sources, I would refer my readers to Emily Apter, *Against World Literature: On the Politics of Untranslatability* (New York: Verso, 2013); Timothy Brennan, *At Home in the World: Cosmopolitanism Now* (Cambridge, MA: Harvard University Press, 1997); Sarah Brouillette, *Literature and the Creative Economy* (Stanford: Stanford University Press, 2014); Sarah Brouillette, *Postcolonial Writers in the Global Literary Marketplace* (Basingstoke: Palgrave Macmillan, 2007); Pascale Casanova, *La République mondiale des lettres* (Paris: Editions du Seuil, 1999); Pheng Cheah, *What Is a World? On Postcolonial Literature as World Literature* (Durham, NC: Duke University Press, 2016); David Damrosch, *What Is World Literature?* (Princeton: Princeton University Press, 2003); Ben Etherington, and Jarad Zimbler, eds., *Cambridge Companion to World Literature* (Cambridge: Cambridge University Press, 2018); May Hawas, ed., *The Routledge Companion to World Literature and World History* (New York: Routledge, 2018); Graham Huggan, *The Postcolonial Exotic: Marketing the Margins* (London: Routledge, 2001); Franco Moretti, *Graphs, Maps, Trees: Abstract Models for a Literary History* (London: Verso, 2005); Franco Moretti, *Distant Reading* (London: Verso, 2013); Aamir Mufti, *Forget English! Orientalisms and World Literatures* (Cambridge, MA: Harvard University Press, 2016); Warwick Research Collective, *Combined and Uneven Development: Towards a New Theory of World-Literature* (Liverpool: Liverpool University Press, 2015).
2. '"Worldliness" was meant to be a rather bludgeon-like term to enforce the location of a cultural practices back in the mundane, the quotidian, and the secular. Affiliation is a rather more subtle term that has to do with mapping and drawing connections in the world between practices, individuals, classes, formations – that whole range of structures that Raymond Williams has studied so well in books like *The Long Revolution* and *The Country and the City*. Above all, affiliation is a dynamic concept; it is not meant to circumscribe but rather to make explicit all kinds of connections that we tend to forget and that have to be made explicit and even dramatic in order for political change to take place' (Edward Said, *Power, Politics and Culture* (New York: Vintage Books, 2001), 336).
3. I use the term 'Anglophone-Arabic' to refer to works by authors who write, think and live between these two languages. I use Anglophone-Arabic instead of the more common designation of Anglo-Arab in order to produce a shift in emphasis from ethnicity to language, and stand closer to my authors' concerns here which are linguistic and literary and not ethnic per se.
4. Hanan al-Shaykh, 'My Travels Through Cultures, Languages and Writing: From Abu Nuwas to Bint Al-Shaykh', presented at the Talks and Discussions series,

British Library, London, 7 November 2019. Available online: www.youtube.com/watch?v=M_etRG1o-k8 (accessed 10 December 2020).
5 The critical literature on Anglo-Arab writing is vast. Gana and Hassan actually do provide in their books substantial bibliographies. Additionally, I would like to point to Anna Ball and Nabil Matar's edition of *The Edinburgh Companion to the Postcolonial Middle East* (2018) and also to the special issue I edited for *Commonwealth Essays and Studies* entitled 'Anglo-Arab Literatures' in 2017 with articles by Jumana Bayeh, Geoffrey Nash, Sarah Irving, Nora Parr, Tahia Abdel Nasser, Sophia Brown, Irene Fernandez Ramos and Valeria Anishchenkova. Available online: www.univ-paris3.fr/39-2-spring-2017-anglo-arab-literatures-460176.kjsp?RH=1226586296353 (accessed 10 December 2020).
6 Claire Gallien, 'Anglo-Arab Literatures – Enmeshing Form, Subverting Assignation, Minorizing Language', *Commonwealth Essays and Studies* 39.2 (2017): 5–12.
7 Emily Apter, *The Translation Zone: A New Comparative Literature* (Princeton: Princeton University Press, 2006). Her concept of 'translation zone' is useful as a way of thinking about the (geo)political use and impact of translation practices and studies in a post 9/11 world order.
8 Yaseen Noorani, 'Hard and Soft Multilingualism', *Critical Multilingualism Studies* 1.2 (2013): 7–28, 9.
9 Jacques Derrida, *Le Monolinguisme de l'autre. Ou, la prothèse d'origine* (Paris: Galilée, 1996).
10 Samia Mehrez, 'Translation and the Postcolonial Experience: The Francophone North African Text' in *Rethinking Translation: Discourse, Subjectivity, Ideology*, ed. Lawrence Venuti (New York: Routledge, 1992): 120–38; Rey Chow, *Not Like a Native Speaker: On Languaging as a Postcolonial Experience* (New York: Columbia University Press, 2014).
11 Claire Gallien, 'When Literature Becomes an "Enhanced National Security Threat" – Literary Interventions of the "Terrorist" and "Terrorist" Interventions of Literature', *The Journal of Commonwealth Literature* (OnlineFirst 26 February 2019). Available online: https://journals.sagepub.com/doi/abs/10.1177/0021989419826366?journalCode=jcla (accessed 10 December 2020).
12 Michel Foucault, *L'Ordre du discours* (Paris: Gallimard, 1971).
13 Michelle Hartman, *Breaking Broken English: Black-Arab Literary Solidarities and the Politics of Language* (New York: Syracuse University Press, 2019), 53.
14 Nouri Gana and Heike Härting, 'Introduction: Narrative Violence: Africa and the Middle East', *Comparatives Studies of South Asia, Africa and the Middle East* 28.1 (2008): 1–10.
15 Myriam Suchet defines heterolingualism as the 'mise en scène d'une langue comme plus ou moins étrangère le long d'un continuum d'altérité construit dans et par un discours (ou un texte) donné' in Myriam Suchet *L'imaginaire hétérolingue* (Paris: Classiques Garnier, 2014): 18.
16 See in particular Tim Cresswell, *On the Move: Mobility in the Modern Western World* (London: Routledge, 2011).
17 Lynne DeSilva-Johnson, 'This Book is Not Backwards', in Ashraf Fayadh, *Instructions Within* (London: English Pen, 2017), 290.
18 Jon Solomon, 'Translation, Violence, and the Heterolingual Intimacy', *Transversal Texts* (July 2007). Available online: http://eipcp.net/transversal/1107/solomon/en (accessed 10 December 2020).

19 Rebecca Walkowitz, *Born Translated: The Contemporary Novel in an Age of World Literature* (New York: Columbia University Press, 2015), 3.
20 Ibid., 6.
21 Ibid., 22.
22 Benedict Anderson in *Imagined Communities* (1983) and *The Spectre of Comparisons* (1998) are fundamental entry points in the debate. See also Sandra Bermann and Michael Wood, eds., *Nation, Language, and the Ethics of Translation* (Princeton: Princeton University Press, 2005); Paul Jay, *Global Matters: The Transnational Turn In Literary Studies* (Ithaca: Cornell University Press, 2010); Naoki Sakai and Yukiko Hanawa, eds., *Specters of the West and the Politics of Translation* (Ithaca: Cornell University Press, 2001), Jon Solomon, 'Translation, Violence, and the Heterolingual Intimacy'.
23 On Shaftesbury, see Lawrence Klein, *Shaftesbury and the Culture Of Politeness: Moral Discourse and Cultural Politics in Early Eighteenth-Century England* (Cambridge: Cambridge University Press, 1994). On language and the culture of politeness, see Susan Fitzmaurice, 'The Commerce of Language in the Pursuit of Politeness in Eighteenth-Century England', *English Studies* 79 (1998): 309–28; Richard Watts, *Politeness* (Cambridge: Cambridge University Press, 2003); *Language Myths and the History of English* (Oxford: Oxford University Press, 2011), 'Language Myths', in *The Handbook of Historical Sociolinguistics*, ed. Juan Manuel Hernández-Campoy and Juan Camilo Conde-Silvestre (Oxford: Wiley Blackwell, 2012), 585–606; Ingrid Ticken-boon van Ostade, ed., *Grammars, Grammarians and Grammar-Writing in Eighteenth-Century England* (Berlin: Mouton de Gruyter, 2008); Carey McIntosh, *The Evolution Of English Prose 1700–1800: Style, Politeness, and Print Culture* (Cambridge: Cambridge University Press, 1998).
24 Claire Gallien, 'From One Empire To the Next: The Reconfigurations Of "Indian" Literatures From Persian To English Translations', *Translation Studies* (OnlineFirst, 24 October 2019). Available online: www.tandfonline.com/doi/abs/10.1080/14781700.2019.1678069?journalCode=rtrs20 (accessed 10 December 2020).
25 Clare Pollard, 'Editorial', *MPT* 'Our Small Universe' 1 (2019): 1–2.
26 Peter D. McDonald, '*Artefacts of Writing*. Fourth Proposition'. Available online: https://artefactsofwriting.com/first-proposition/fourth-proposition/ (accessed 10 December 2020).
27 Zeina Hashem Beck, 'Estranged/غربة', *MPT* 'Our Small Universe' 1 (2019): 33–8, 37.
28 Ibid., 33.
29 Dunya Mikhail, *The Iraqi Nights*, trans. Kareem James Abu-Zeid (New York: A New Directions Books), 60.
30 'Translation sites argue against multilingualism as a simple juxtaposition of languages […] they crystallize language relations in time and space, defining specific moments of exchange or confrontation. They focus attention not on the multiplicity of languages but on their interactions and their rival claims'. Sherry Simon, *Translation Sites* (Abingdon: Routledge, 2019), 3.
31 Michelle Hartman in *Breaking Broken English* studies in greater details the influence of jazz and hip hop in Hammad's poetry. In particular, Hartman reads Hammad's use of break as rhythmic technique in relation with what Fred Moten conceptualized as the breaking aesthetics of Black radical literature in *In the Break* (2011). This shared technique of 'breaking' English, a counter to writing or performing in 'broken' English, which still implies defectivity and lack, creates what Hartman analyses as

literary solidarity between Arab-American and Black-American writing. See Michelle Hartman, *Breaking Broken English: Black-Arab Literary Solidarities and the Politics of Language* (Syracuse: Syracuse University Press, 2019), esp. 51–3 and 63–78.
32 Gana and Härting, 'Introduction', *CSSAAME*.
33 Hammad, Suheir, *breaking poems* (New York: Cypher Books, 2008), 58.
34 Ibid., 49.
35 'breaking poems', *body on the line* (26 May 2009). Available online: https://bodyontheline.wordpress.com/tag/breaking-poems/ (accessed 10 December 2020).
36 See for instance in Malcolm Forbes, 'Iraqi writer Sinan Antoon on his novels about his embattled homeland', *The National* (14 May 2015). Available online: www.thenational.ae/arts-culture/iraqi-writer-sinan-antoon-on-his-novels-about-his-embattled-homeland-1.116492(accessed 30 August 2020).
37 Ibid.
38 Sinan Antoon, *The Baghdad Eucharist* (Cairo: Hoopoe, 2017), 62/*Ya Maryam* (Beirut: Dar al-Jamal, 2012), 71.
39 Ibid., 73/93. Note: *Maqāmāt* is an Arabic literary genre that alternates rhymed prose with intervals of poetry.
40 Ibid., 77–82/97–102.
41 Ryan van Winkle, 'Golan Haji – Every Writing is a Translation. An Interview with Kurdish Poet, Golan Haji', in *Prairie Schooner* (16 May 2013). Available online: https://prairieschooner.unl.edu/blog/golan-haji-every-writing-translation (accessed 10 December 2020).
42 Stephen Watts, *Journey Across Breath/Tragitto nel respire*, trans. Cristina Viti (London: Hearing Eye, 2011).

Part II

A multilingual ecology of world literature and modes of circulation

5

'O local sen paredes': The multilingual ecology of Manuel Rivas's *A desaparición da neve* (*The Disappearance of Snow*)

Laura Lonsdale

Manuel Rivas is not only Galicia's most internationally renowned contemporary author, but also a journalist, activist and founding member of Greenpeace Spain whose long-standing dedication to environmental causes earned him a major award in 2009. This was an important year for the writer, bringing in addition his election to the Galician Academy or Real Academia Galega – which he marked with an inaugural speech on memory, ecology and language – as well as the publication of his only multilingual collection of poetry to date, *A desaparición da neve* (*The Disappearance of Snow*).[1] Published simultaneously in Spain's four most widely spoken languages (Castilian, Catalan, Galician and Basque) and described by Rivas as an island or forest of biodiversity, a celebration of 'the richness generated by linguistic variety'[2] (la riqueza que genera la pluralidad lingüística) as well as 'an ecological protest against the destruction of the planet' (un grito ecológico en contra de la destrucción del planeta),[3] the collection was well received in the national press as a timely intervention in the typically febrile politics of language in Spain. Yet despite the positive fanfare surrounding its publication it has generated surprisingly little in the way of a response among critics, as if the metaphor of biodiversity had already exhausted all the collection's interpretative possibilities. I would like to suggest that these remain largely to be explored, however, particularly if we move beyond the idea of 'biodiversity' towards the richer idea of 'ecology', which in biology is concerned not just with variety but with 'the interaction between organisms and their environment, and [the] structure and function of ecosystems'.[4] This metaphorical shift allows us to think of the collection's multilingualism not simply as a celebration of diversity, but as a linguistic ecosystem within which an ecological poetics can be articulated.

Ecological metaphors have become popular in recent years, applied to everything from business and politics to world literature. Ecology offers not only a structural metaphor for complex systems of interaction, but also 'lies tantalizingly close to important ethical issues',[5] quickly becoming enmeshed with philosophical, political and even poetic concerns, though not always environmental ones. Rivas himself has identified a 'Copernican turn' (xiro copernicano) in our understanding of ecology not just as an area of scientific study, but as a renewed way of both seeing and living intimately bound up with co-existence and with an idea of the local as an expression of the universal.[6] This speaks to debates in world literature about the place of the local within the realm of the global, resonating not only with the ecological metaphor as it has been employed by Alexander Beecroft – whose *An Ecology of World Literature* (2015)[7] is 'not ecocriticism in the conventional sense' but aims rather to 'facilitate the comparative study of the interactions between literatures and their environments'[8] – but also with Neil Lazarus's idea that the universal is always localized (there are '*only local universalisms*').[9]

The extension of ecology beyond environmentalism – for all that Rivas is an environmentalist – is reminiscent of Timothy Morton's *The Ecological Thought* (2010), which also conceives of ecology as a way of thinking connections rather than as a specific set of environmental concerns. Both Morton's ecological thought and Rivas's ecological poetics are founded on a notion of ecology as the interconnectedness of all things, figured in the image of a 'mesh' by Morton[10] and concentric circles by Rivas.[11] Morton's ecological thought is unashamedly concerned with enormity and everything, in direct opposition to both 'humanist refusals to see the big picture'[12] and environmentalist preferences for the local and the organic; similarly, Rivas's concern with 'the preservation of biodiversity in nature, language and culture' has been described as 'an ecological form of globalization'.[13] But whereas Morton is entirely dismissive of any localized or located concept of the environment, proclaiming the slogan of ecological thought to be 'dislocation, dislocation, dislocation',[14] Rivas retains in his conception of ecology a very significant space for the local and the located. Indeed, if Morton's image of the ecological thought is of a 'vast, sprawling mesh of interconnectedness without a definitive centre or edge',[15] Rivas's concentric circles suggest on the other hand a series of bounded, interlinked unities, an image we might well consider relevant to the linguistic organization of *A desaparición da neve*, and the political context from which it emerges.

Of the four languages represented in the collection, Castilian is the only one to have official status throughout Spain, while the other three – Catalan, Galician and Basque – have been co-official in their respective autonomous communities since 1981, having been suppressed and excluded from the public realm during the nearly forty years of Franco's dictatorship (1939–75). Rivas, who writes in Galician but translates his own poetry into Castilian, has claimed the Galician language is today at risk of extinction due to a politics of 'bioperversity' (bioperversidad), and has called for Galicians of all political hues to come together to create 'a habitat in which the language can grow happily, a space that will be congenial to it …, a breeding ground that can also be a space of liberty and solidarity, and so I celebrate the local which is also universal' (un hábitat en el que la lengua crezca feliz, un espacio de simpatía para ella … [un] vivero y para que sea espacio de libertad y solidaridad, brindo por lo local que es universal).[16] That this political context is relevant to the collection is apparent not only from what Rivas has said in interviews, in which he has bemoaned the emphasis on linguistic conflict,[17] but also from his choice of languages, which are those most persistently associated with nationalist claims within

Spain. Organized into discrete language units with only occasional language mixing in individual poems (and then usually with English or French rather than between the four Iberian languages), Rivas's collection connects rather than blends the languages it brings together, creating an ecosystem of associated languages while maintaining the autonomy of each one, in a political context in which language is at the forefront of both centralist and secessionist discourses. The idea of a linguistic ecosystem, an image Rivas does not directly employ but which resonates with his many other ecological metaphors, implies both the co-existence of particular languages and their individual claim to participation and preservation, while suggesting also that they are living things whose existence may be fragile. Rivas's focus both on the individual life form and its ecological participation in a wider system of connections seems to be at the heart of what he has described, quoting the Portuguese writer Miguel Torga, as 'o local sen paredes'[18] (the local without walls), a nuanced version of universalism that opens up the local to new configurations, while preserving a space within which the voice of a minority culture and language can be heard.

The title of the collection is given in the order Galician, Catalan, Basque, Castilian; the sections following the order Galician, Castilian, Catalan, Basque – a small but meaningful difference that seems to refuse any particular linguistic hierarchy while maintaining Galician, the language of the poems' original composition and traditionally a language of the rural poor, as first among equals. While the most immediate context is therefore the nation – both the stateless nation and the nation-state – the implications of the linguistic ecosystem also extend to the relationship between the local and the global, not least because all four languages in the collection are spoken outside their regional or national boundaries.[19] Dolores Vilavedra, translator of Rivas's Galician fiction into Spanish, observes that the multilingualism of *A desparición da neve* achieves linguistic visibility in two senses, bringing to light the original language of composition while exposing also the act of translation that brings the work into circulation.[20] Like other writers concerned with the visibility of minority languages, not only in Spain but in the context of globalization and a largely Anglophone world literature, Rivas seeks both to make his own linguistic community visible while placing it within a network of relations through an equally visible process of translation. Rivas's concentric circles capture the overlap and interlinking of individual entities that nonetheless retain a degree of autonomy and separateness, an ecological vision that lacks some of Morton's (Anglophone?) confidence in the unbounded, though it clearly aspires to an idea of 'o local sen paredes'.

This idea is thrown into greater relief when we consider that, to a reader of romance languages, three of the collection's four language sections are largely intelligible, while the fourth, Basque, is largely unintelligible: the Iberian linguistic context provides a set of concentric circles that will, to the majority of the collection's readers, offer a graduated experience of strangeness, of the unfamiliar within the realm of the familiar, highlighting linguistic overlap while leaving space for the unintelligible or the not yet understood. It is interesting to consider, in this light, the account Kirsty Hooper gives of her attempts to navigate Rivas's *A desparición da neve*, and I quote her at length because she so effectively captures the challenges Rivas's multilingual collection presents to the reader:

¿Cómo, precisamente, se lee un poemario en cuatro lenguas paralelas? Cuando yo comencé a leer el poemario, empecé con la sección en gallego, que es la primera: empecé así por dos razones. Primero, porque de las cuatro lenguas representadas, el gallego es el que leo con más facilidad, pero también, porque tenía el sentido de que aquella era la versión 'original', 'auténtica', y para una razón que no sabría explicar hoy, esto me parecía importante. Sin embargo, después de leer los primeros poemas, me asaltó una sensación de preocupación y empecé avanzando más rápido, primero a la sección en castellano, luego a las de catalán y vasco. Según avanzaba, me sentía progresivamente menos cómoda con la lengua (sé poco del catalán, y menos del vasco) y a la vez, progresivamente más intrigada. Si el poemario parecía seguir (hasta enfatizar) las limitaciones de mis conocimientos lingüísticos, ¿cómo sería para un lector vasco, que tendrá que empezar al final, como un lector japonés o árabe? ¿O para un catalán, empezando en pleno libro? Me venía el impulso de leer las cuatro versiones simultáneamente, avanzando y retrocediendo según distintos criterios, leyendo múltiples versiones de este poema, o sólo la versión gallega de aquella, algunas veces reconociendo inmediatamente el corazón del poema, otras veces quedando perpleja ante las formas desconocidas de las palabras. No he leído el libro de principio al final, sino he seguido un camino menos directo que a veces desaparece en las grietas, los espacios de entre de las cuatro lenguas. Todavía no me gustaría decir que he 'leído' el poemario, únicamente que he explorado algunos de los senderos más bonitos.[21]

(How exactly are we supposed to read a collection in four parallel languages? When I started reading the poems I began with the section in Galician, which comes first, and I began there for two reasons. Firstly, because of the four languages present in the book Galician is the one I read most easily, but also because I felt this was the 'original', 'authentic' version, and for some reason I can't now explain this seemed important to me. But after reading the first few poems I was suddenly seized with anxiety and started moving through the collection more quickly, first to the section in Castilian, then to the ones in Catalan and Basque. As I advanced I felt less and less comfortable in the language (I speak very little Catalan and even less Basque) and, at the same time, more and more intrigued. If the collection seemed to follow (and even emphasize) the limits of my linguistic knowledge, what must it be like for a reader in Basque, who would have to start at the back of the book, like a reader in Japanese or Arabic? Or a reader in Catalan, who would have to start in the middle? Suddenly I got the impulse to read the four versions simultaneously, moving forward and back depending on what I was looking for, reading multiple versions of one poem or only the Galician version of another, sometimes going straight to the heart of the poem, at other times left feeling perplexed by the unfamiliar forms of the words. I haven't read the book from beginning to end, but have instead followed a less direct route that sometimes disappears between the cracks, into the spaces between the four languages. I still couldn't say that I've 'read' the collection, only that I've explored some of its prettiest byways.)

Hooper's images are of navigation, of negotiating changing linguistic terrain and exploring the 'prettiest byways' of a landscape that otherwise is disorientating. And this disorientation, this sense of strangeness, is inextricably also an experience of connection, not only between the four languages themselves (as she begins to feel the urge to read them simultaneously), but also to other languages and to the readers of other languages, such as Japanese and Arabic, whose navigation of the terrain is evoked empathetically. In this sense, then, the disorientating, non-linear reading experience, the navigable landscape of the book with its bridges as well as its areas of inaccessibility, provides the affective and conceptual space within which an ecological poetics – a poetics of connection and estrangement – can be elaborated.

This brings us back to Morton, whose ecological thought is about being connected to strangeness while feeling estranged from oneself, thanks to an awareness of the sheer immensity of the ecosystem to which we belong (an awareness derived, for example, from the Apollo 8 Earthrise pictures, which altered forever our perspective on the earth). For Morton it is this ecological awareness that lies at the heart of ecological thinking, and consequently 'Ecological art, and the ecological-ness of all art, isn't just *about* something (trees, mountains, animals, pollution, and so forth). Ecological art *is* something, or maybe it *does* something.'[22] This idea marks a riposte to the realist or mimetic strand of ecocriticism that seeks to 'keep faith' with the natural environment through the 'accurate representation' of the natural world,[23] a literalist approach to the relationship between ecology and art that 'overlook[s] the way in which all art – not just explicitly ecological art – hardwires the environment into its form':[24]

> Art is ecological insofar as it is made from materials and exists in the world. It exists, for instance, as a poem on a page made of paper from trees, which you hold in your hand while sitting in a chair in a certain room of a house that rests on a hill in the suburbs of a polluted city. But there is more to its ecological quality than that. The shape of the stanzas and the length of the lines determine the way you appreciate the blank paper around them. Reading the poem aloud makes you aware of the shape and size of the space around you … The poem organizes space. Seen like this, all texts – all artworks, indeed – have an irreducibly ecological form.[25]

The notion that the material and formal dimensions of the work inform our reading of the text is of course not new, particularly where poetry is concerned, though the conception of this process as 'ecological' does somewhat alter our sense of what its implications might be. Texts and artworks may have an irreducibly and therefore unavoidably ecological form, but we might extrapolate from this idea that 'explicitly ecological art' will strive to make readers aware of their participation in the ecosystem in a way that will – or at least could – generate in turn a sense of both connection and estrangement. The multilingualism of Rivas's collection therefore '*is* something' or '*does* something' ecological, creating a linguistic ecosystem that points to both the integrity of the individual unit, to the local, while also its participation in a network of connections both familiar and strange.

Of course the image of a linguistic ecosystem implies not only a circuit of connection between languages, but also between language itself and the natural world. And in the context of a concern with localism this circuit of connection is highly relevant to the Galician poetic tradition, which has at its root (and possibly at its heart) a close relationship between nature, land and language. In the mid- to late nineteenth century, Galicia's most outstanding poet and leading figure of its cultural and linguistic resurgence or *Rexurdimento*, Rosalía de Castro, wrote lovingly in her *Cantares gallegos* (Galician Songs) (1863) of the landscape, folklore and rural traditions of her homeland, themes which have exerted an enduringly shaping influence on what Helena Miguélez-Carballeira has described as Galicia's 'sentimental' national consciousness:

> [In] Galicia ... the conjunction between the national and the sentimental has had particular historical significance ... the trope of Galician sentimentality as a marker of national identity has appeared repeatedly in modern representations of the region, its language and its people, forming a continuum that extends throughout the textual and visual corpus on Galician history and culture from the late nineteenth century up until present times. Its manifestations are ... varied ... but they concentrate on the assumption that Galicians are a nostalgic people, living in harmonious communion with their landscape or yearning for its beauty if away from it.[26]

This sentimentality is so rooted in Galician nationalism that one of its 'central metaphors' is that of the 'revered *terra nai*', or Mother Land, 'symbol of a femininely connoted hearth, home and landscape';[27] an idea complemented on both sides of the nationalist debate by a perception of the Galician language as 'sweet and poetic', 'best suited to lyrical writing'[28] and the elaboration of rural themes. This symbolic, mythologized union between nature, land and language perfectly illustrates why Morton is nervous of concepts such as 'the environment', which too easily turn localism into parochialism and become puritanical about 'nature'. For Morton, 'the ecological thought' relies fundamentally on undermining the Romantic idea of Nature (with a capital N) that in his view underpins much ecocritical and environmentalist thinking, because this reified Nature is too invested with the 'unnatural' and undemocratic qualities of 'hierarchy, authority, harmony, purity, neutrality, and mystery' to be useful to ecology.[29] 'Ecology without Nature' becomes necessary, he argues, when we understand that not only is our conception of Nature constructed, but that it feeds into the ideologies of both capitalism (because we regard nature as exploitable) and nationalism (because we focus too much on particular environments and too little on ecological connection). He therefore rejects the 'environment' as too localized a concept to be useful to ecological thinking, preferring instead the image of the 'mesh' that we have already encountered.

If Morton, as a scholar of English Romanticism, conceives his ecological thought in the shadow of that movement, so must Rivas, as a Galician poet, conceive his poetic project in relation to a cultural tradition heavily inflected with Romantic and nationalist conceptions of both land and language. Rivas has sought to underplay the bucolic sentimentalism of Rosalía and her contemporaries by describing their Galician landscape as a 'paraíso inquieto' or 'troubled paradise';[30] though as Miguélez-Carballeira points out he is himself deeply indebted to a myth that has been 'integral to Galician cultural history' since the nineteenth century.[31] It is certainly true that his work is deeply rooted in Galicia's cultural and physical landscape and notable, at least in his fiction, for its 'tenderness and lyricism';[32] and it is also true that the myth of the maternal earth – and of woman as earth mother – persists in both his literature and his journalism, as made plain by the earthy, bare-breasted women gracing the covers of both his poetry collection *A boca da terra* (Mouth of the Earth) (Visor 2015), and his book of essays on environmental and other themes, *A cuerpo abierto* (Sensitive Bodies) (Alfaguara 2008).[33] Yet though this culturalist and maternalist strain is undoubtedly present in his work, there seems also to be an attempt in *A desaparición* to overcome the limitations of Galicia's sentimental attachment to the *terra nai*, and perhaps to mitigate the 'sweetness' of its language, through irony, humour, ugliness and impoverishment. In fact, as Vilavedra notes, this has been a preoccupation in Rivas's poetry for some time: she describes the poems of his much earlier collection *Ningún cisne* (No Swans) (1989) as 'brief flashes of reality in which sentimentality is counteracted by touches of irony or humour that introduce an element of rupture. Galicia and its contradictions are at the heart of the poet's concerns' (breves flases sobre la realidad en los que la sentimentalidad se compensa siempre con un apunte irónico o humorístico que introduce un elemento de ruptura.[34] Galicia y sus contradicciones aparecen como el centro de las preocupaciones del poeta). The same could be said of much of his journalistic and non-fictional work, including *Galicia, el bonsái atlántico* (Galicia, the Atlantic Bonsai) (1989) and *Unha espía no reino de Galicia* (A Spy in the Kingdom of Galicia) (2004), both of which tackle the clichés of Galician identity in an ironic key. What this suggests, as Cristina Sánchez-Conejero writes, is that if Galician literature is to be perceived 'as global and not just local or peripheral, first there needs to be a change to the way Galicia is typically perceived' (Para [conseguir] el acercamiento a la literatura gallega como literatura global y no exclusivamente local o periférica, se hace necesario primero un cambio en el concepto tópico de identidad gallega).[35]

A good example of this concern with making space for the local while simultaneously opening it up to the world can be found in Rivas's treatment of *saudade*, a sweetly paralyzing nostalgia and yearning for home that Emily Apter consecrates as culturally 'untranslateable'[36] and which Miguélez-Carballeira places at the heart of the sentimental aesthetic. While *saudade* is undoubtedly present as a localizing element in Rivas's collection, in 'Manifesto' it is evoked more bathetically than sentimentally as 'cruel',[37] while in 'Mayday' it is a fleshless bone and poor sustenance.[38] In the opening poem of the collection there is 'another kind of longing' (outra saudade) and 'a dispossessed yearning' (una saudade desposeída) that exists in connection with an earthier and more rebellious mode of speaking, remembering and imagining than sentimentality would allow.[39] Sentimentality's old nemesis, humour, is central to this reformulation, and indeed the poems are frequently wry, full of the irony known in Galicia as 'retranca' that is the stereotypical counterpart (or perhaps corrective) to *saudade*. In this particular collection the quality of this humour is most explicitly characterized by the epigraph from Keats's 'A Song of Opposites', 'And hear a merry laugh amid the thunder', a poem that also features among its emotional opposites a 'sweet heart-ache' that seems to encapsulate the sentimentality of Galician *saudade* ('Oh the sweetness of the pain! ... let me slake / All my thirst for sweet heart-ache'). In this way the localized, oppositional dynamic of *retranca* and *saudade* is brought into dialogue with a broader Romantic tradition that, for all the words' supposed untranslatability, moves them beyond local boundaries. A local element both de-sentimentalized and de-naturalized (discovered outside the boundaries of the local), *saudade* therefore remains an affective and cultural touchstone in Rivas's collection, but it is stripped of its passivity and put to work instead in a poetic landscape of laughter and thunder which, notwithstanding the debt to Keats, owes as much to Surrealism as it does to Romanticism. Indeed throughout the collection the essentially emotional opposites of Keats' song – 'I love to mark sad faces in fair weather ... Fair and foul I love together' – unite with the sensory and conceptual opposites of the surrealists, of whom Rivas says in his inaugural speech to the Galician Academy:

Os surrealistas sabían o que dicían cando amosaban a súa preferencia polas asociacións dos antónimos máis extremos ou os termos e imaxes máis contraditorios e afastados. Non soamente se produce un efecto estético de choque, senón que tamén produce máis verdade.[40]

(The surrealists knew what they were doing when they staked everything on bringing together the most extreme opposites or the most contradictory and irreconcilable images. This doesn't just generate an aesthetic clash, it also generates more truth.)

The significance of this concern with opposites may be read not only into the collection's mood – characterized by 'choque' or 'clash' rather than sentimentality – but also as the mobilizer of an ecological poetics of connections and strangeness, bringing diverse and apparently opposing forces into relationship with one another, and opening up the *terra nai* to alternative configurations.

The traditional landscape of Galician poetry is a rural one, and consequently any reimagining of the local environment is also a reimagining of the natural one, with which it is associated via the sentimental aesthetic. Key to these alternative configurations therefore is the relationship between nature and aesthetics, which encompasses not only the relationship between nature and artifice, but also between nature and its representation, rethinking both the parameters of the 'natural' as well as the ways in which nature is represented in art. In 'Historia del arte' (A History of Art), a poem that begins with an image of the flood and ends with one of television, we seem at once to be given a brief account of human history and an equally brief account of art's relationship with nature. At first, nature seems to come looking for art, in an image that might refer us to Romanticism – 'The floodwaters invaded the painter's studio / in search of landscapes' – but art is overwhelmed, overcome by nature (by Realism?), such that the painter, who is 'custodian of all the vanguards', must fight 'against the flood' and rescue 'the paintings from the deep'.[41] His studio becomes a field hospital for shipwrecked paintings. The poem ends with what feels like the false logic of Surrealism, moving us on through art history, though in fact it is less a case of false logic than an evocation of a reparative relationship between nature and art which extends the possibilities of both:

> Quería que os seus cadros fosen felices.
> [...]
> Talvez por iso o primeiro que reparou
> foi as cordas dos violíns
> da serie inconclusa das *Naturezas vivas*,
> onde había tamen bidueiras, cabalos, garzas,
> postes telefónicos, máquinas de coser,
> e o par de botas do pai,
> que andaba os camiños de lobo
> para sandar electrodomésticos
> e orientar as antenas
> dos primeiros televisores.[42]

> (He wanted his paintings to be happy.
> [...]
> Perhaps for that reason the first things he repaired
> were the violin strings
> in an unfinished sequence of Still Lifes
> that also included birch trees, horses, herons,
> telegraph posts, sewing machines,
> the pair of boots belonging to his father,
> who walked the paths of wolves
> to heal domestic appliances
> and tune the aerials
> of the first television sets.)[43]

This reparative relationship between nature and art is also a recovery of the life of all things, of lives rather than still lives ('Naturezas vivas' rather than 'mortas'), in the image of the artist as countryman engaged in the husbandry of electrical appliances. The kind of relationship imagined here between nature and art centres on the inconclusive, the various and the extension of care to all things. It is unconcerned with an idea of nature as distinct from the man-made, and unconcerned with an idea of art as a faithful representation of nature. Bearing in mind not only Morton's suspicion of mimesis but also his observation that many of the words we use to describe nature are in fact drawn from art – 'picturesque' means 'looking like a picture' while 'landscape' is a 'word for a painting, not actual trees and water'[44] – we can observe that this false naturalness is absent from Rivas's conception of either nature or art. The poems of this collection offer us not landscapes but land: ground, earth, rock, metal, mineral. And this material substance is fully, inextricably enmeshed with the memory of human existence, its objects and its lives:

> Unha presa de terra,
> un rescaldo de invernos,
> o mundo antigo a soñar
> na elevación da estruga,
> da herba de cego,
> no molde dunha man.
> ('Herba do cego')[45]

> (A handful of earth,
> embers of many winters,
> an ancient world that dreams
> of the elevation of the nettle,
> blind man's grass
> in the mould of a hand.)
> ('Blind Man's Grass')[46]

> Percorreremos o álbum de familia
> cun detector de metais.
> Un amor incrustado,
> soterrado,
> arqueolóxico.
> Un anaco cego de lóstrego
> entobado.
> ('Meu amor puxo unha bomba do baleiro')[47]

> (Let's scan the family album
> with a metal detector.
> An embedded love,
> subterranean,
> archaeological.
> A fragment of lightning
> blind in its mind-shaft.)
> ('My Love is a Suction-Force Pump') [48]

Undoubtedly it is the land of Galicia, with its lighthouse and ocean, crafts and industries, smugglers, artists, exiles and famines; but these images are diffuse, disjointed, never cohering into a landscape either pictured or picturesque.

In spite of the persisting myth of the maternal earth in Rivas's work, then, the natural world in this collection is not organic, pristine and separate from culture, civilization or industry, but ugly and impoverished,[49] rebellious, playful and full of art and artifice. The blurb to *A boca da terra* (Mouth of the Earth), published a few years after *A desaparición da neve*, reads like a manifesto that could also apply to the earlier collection:

> es una poesía de naturaleza insurgente. Porque aquí la naturaleza habla, murmura, grita o blasfema con ironía en el eco de las campanas… Es una naturaleza que abarca las personas humanas y las no humanas, y también las entrañas de las máquinas… Y abarca el lenguaje, las palabras que escarban boca arriba, que llueven con los pies descalzos y luchan contra la extinción en la línea fósil del horizonte.[50]

In [these] poems …, nature is insurgent. Because nature speaks, murmurs, and shouts, wryly blaspheming into the echo of the bells … Here nature incorporates people, human and non-human, and the bowels of machines … And it incorporates language, words that mine upwards and rain downwards with their feet bare, fighting their own extinction on the horizon's fossil line. In *A desaparición* 'Mother earth' is a Medusa, a 'bizca' (cross-eyed), a smuggler and a bomber, while the landscape is characterized as much by electrical appliances, ironmongers and neon lights as it is by sea, snow and heather. We might argue that Rivas's vision of nature is more akin to Seamus Heaney's in 'Death of a Naturalist' – where mawkish images of daddy and mammy frogs give way to the humorous horror of 'farting' heads and clutching frogspawn – than it is to Wordsworth's in 'Lines Written in Early Spring', where the poet's soul is linked to nature's 'fair works' among primroses. Yet there is no evidence in Rivas's work of the urban and urbane contempt for the countryside sometimes detectable in Morton, whose epigraph to *Being Ecological* (2018) reads: 'Grass is hard and lumpy and damp, and full of dreadful black insects.' The line is from Oscar Wilde's 'The Decay of Lying', a Socratic dialogue in which one character responds to the other's injunction to 'enjoy Nature' as follows: 'Enjoy Nature! I am glad to say that I have entirely lost that faculty.'[51] The ugliness and artifice that Rivas introduces into his collection undermine sentimentality and the picturesque, unite the natural with the man-made and give a positive charge to the impoverished and the forgotten, but they do not reveal a horror of the natural world per se; quite the reverse. By analogy, we could observe that both Galicia and the Galician language are 'de-naturalized' through ugliness and artifice, as well as through translation, but not in order to devalue them. Rather they are reinvigorated in this new configuration of languages and images.

If nature is exposed to new ways of imagining its relationship with art, so too is language and its relationship with the land. If we return, for a moment, to the national and nationalist context that so inevitably presents itself in both the multilingual framing of this collection and in the Galician poetic tradition on which it draws, it is worth noting that not least among the Romantic claims to Nature is the idea that 'individuals and social formations' possess one 'true' language only, their 'mother tongue', and that 'through this possession' they are 'organically linked to an exclusive, clearly demarcated ethnicity, culture, and nation'.[52] Such a notion of organic possession and belonging is, of course, precisely what Morton seeks to move away from in his rejection of Nature and the environment in favour of ecology. Yet as I have already suggested in the context of Rivas's concentric circles, such a view has implications for the existential claims of minority languages and cultures, which rely on a degree of demarcation if they are to avoid absorption and erasure; as such the multilingualism of the collection preserves the space of the local – the Galician language – while acknowledging the wider (linguistic) ecosystem to which it belongs. At the same time, the poems move us past the political claims of particular languages, and even beyond human claims to the possession of language, to evoke Language as an organism in itself. Words in Rivas's poetic world are a living force and a material substance, a physical and shaping presence on the land, embedded in the earth. While it would clearly not be impossible to read this nationalistically (in terms of an organic link between place and language), the poems offer us too many modes of communication, both human and non-human, for this to be satisfactory. Part of the land's nature – but also its artifice – is that it speaks, not in pathetic fallacies, but in words and images that are cheerfully but powerfully insubordinate. The first poem of the collection opens with an image of words 'that come to reclaim what is theirs, / all that was taken from them' (Veñen as palabras reclamar o seu, / o substraído). This poem is a manifesto for the 'mouth of literature' that is also the central image of Rivas's speech to the RAG, a 'mouth' that gives voice not only to 'o substraído' (the subtracted, removed, taken away) but also to 'o máis estraño' (the strangest things).[53] Throughout the collection, land and language are united through memory to become a force of the articulate imagination:

> Meu amor enche o ventre
> de seixos silábicos,
> de runas, de aghoams,
> de voces baixas,
> pictogramas coprófagos
> que crían nos excrementos da lúa.
> ('Meu amor contrabandista')[54]

> (My love fills her womb
> with syllabic shingle,
> with runes, ogham stones,[55]
> hushed voices,
> coprophagus pictographs
> hatched in the moon's faeces.)
> ('My Smuggler-Love')[56]

Language is everywhere in the land, from the 'seething mouth of the well, / viscous, foul-mouthed' to the 'peat of dead tongues' (turba das linguas mortas) ready to be dynamited from under layers of rock.[57] It is present in the orality of breath, voice, onomatopoeia and storytelling, in the written markings of the pictogram, the cave painting and the rune, and also in the intangible radio signal. Sound and speech are everywhere in the collection, conveyed in ubiquitous images of mouths and their constituent parts, including teeth, tongue, gums and saliva. This is a world in which everything speaks, and so listening must become the poet's primary mode of reception – for Rivas 'listening … is the most beautiful job on earth' (escoitar … é o traballo máis fermoso do mundo)[58] – while sight is often hampered, evoked in terms of blindness, squinting, blinking or braille. Not all sound is articulate, though its expressiveness seems to bring it into the frame of language, and it is not just present in nature, but also in man-made structures. In 'O monte do faro' (Lighthouse Hill), the poem gives voice to one of Galicia's most ancient and notable buildings, the Roman lighthouse in A Coruña known as the Tower of Hercules or Breoghan's lighthouse, its names evoking figures of the Roman and Gaelic traditions respectively and so reaching deep into Galicia's history and mythology. Its beam of light is evoked consistently and synaesthetically through sound, which is at once mechanical (the typographer's punch) and animal (warbling, bellowing, buzzing, murmuring). Among the most interesting of these evocations are those of breath and phonics, of asthma and onomatopoeia, because in their approximation to language they evoke the communicative power of the lighthouse beam:

Oes o traballo da luz?
O asmático alampar,
[...]
as onomatopeas somnámbulas no odre dos ventos.
[...]
O seu ulululú de curuxa mariña,
o seu xxxxssssss de narval
[...][59]

(Can you hear the working of the light?
Its asthmatic illumination,
[...]
the somnambulant onomatopoeias in the winds' wineskin?
[...]
its sea own to-wit to-whoo
its narwhal whoosh
[...])[60]

The metaphor of asthmatic breath not only evokes the rhythm of the pulsing light, but also animates, literally breathes life into, the lighthouse itself. The onomatopoeic sounds further animate it, animalize it, while bringing its messages into the realm of human language, embodied in the form of words. Onomatopeia offers a direct connection between sound and sense which is otherwise absent from the abstractions of language; the evocation of the light's beam as onomatopoeic creates a circuit of connection between the sign (the beam of light), the inarticulate but expressive sounds of the world around it, and the communicative power of language, which in Rivas is always connected to memory. As the poet has explained, the lighthouse beam 'is an ecological light, because it is a human insertion into nature, and because it generates language. It is the bearer of signals, the bearer of information, the bearer of meaning. And at the same time it is a light that remembers'.[61]

The poem 'Así se fai un poeta' (How to Make a Poet), which brings together scenes of ecological destruction with the loss of both language and the imagination, depicts a comic-book world where people speak in smoke rings or geometric speech bubbles:

Mesmo a auga era muda.
Un aeroplano sulfatou os pentagramas
e o pesticida matou os pronomes persoais.
Os homes falaban con bocados de fume
e onomatopeas de banda deseñada
con moitas caídas
polo oco da néboa,
chissst, plaf, catacroc, tumba.
Había mulleres que pronunciaban cores,
triángulos marelos,
círculos azuis
e cadrados negros.
Os beizos eran dúas lachas
de pedra das ánimas.
O neno durmía cunha buguina
debaixo da almofada.
E Lela da Pastora
díxolle de ollos en verdes labaradas:
  --Ti, rapaz, sempre a facer torres no ar![62]

(Even the water was speechless.
A plane dusted the stars
and the pesticide killed all the personal pronouns.
Men spoke in mouthfuls of smoke
and comic-book onomatopoeias
with lots of falling
through gaps in the fog,
wheeee, splat, crash, ka-boom.
There were women who spoke in colours,
yellow triangles,
blue circles
and black squares.
Their lips, two chips
off the old block of souls.
The boy slept with a conch
beneath his pillow.
And Lela da Pastora,[63]
with green flames in her eyes, said:
'Don't ever give up building castles in the air'.)[64]

If in the previous poem onomatopoeia was a form of ecological connection between different modes of both existence and communication, here it is the visual representation of empty, meaningless human speech, its sounds limited to those of falling, fighting and destruction. In this context, the image of the seashell or conch under the boy's pillow (the future poet's pillow) might evoke several things: the preservation of a fragile organism; the sound of the sea inside the conch; the listening ear itself; and the possibility of a clarion call. At the same time it is an object that 'remembers', like the lighthouse, because it articulates cultural memory: 'In the fishing towns the sailors who got on well with the sea were called listeners, and the best of them were said to have one ear larger than the other, shaped like a sea snail'.[65] A microcosm of the sea, at once the vessel of sound and the means of listening to it, an ear, a mouth and a memory, the conch becomes a symbol of ecology and ecological thinking, and supplies the boy with what he needs to become a poet.

In conclusion, the multilingualism of the collection is more than just a synonym for biodiversity, functioning instead as a kind of ecosystem in its own right. Reading the collection through the lens of ecology rather than biodiversity allows for a reconnection of the poems themselves with their multilingual framing, itself an ecological act, bringing into focus their concern with nature, art and language. As Hooper notes, for the reader there is something disorientating, even perhaps diminishing, about approaching a collection that is partly inaccessible, an inaccessibility heightened perhaps by the poems' surrealist, elliptical quality. There is also something potentially isolating about the sequentially organized individual language sections, which makes the reader's experience of the collection very distinct from reading a translation, a parallel text or a bilingual edition. And at the same time this isolation and this smallness are only experienced within the multilingual ecosystem that is the book, so that smallness is referred immediately back to largeness, isolation to interconnectedness. Furthermore the organization into separate language sections gives an equal legitimacy to all languages, notwithstanding the primacy of Galician; and though Hooper rightly cites her sense that Galician is the collection's first language, I myself had no qualms – or fewer qualms than if I had simply read the poems in translation – about focusing my attention on the poems in Castilian (the language I know best), in spite of the fact that I kept losing my page as I moved irresistibly forwards and backwards between the language sections. (In this sense the collection is, to quote the poet Erín Moure in the context of a different multilingual book, 'a kinetic sculpture that includes our hands'.[66]) Nonetheless I have rather dishonestly quoted the poems in Galician, with English translations by Lorna Shaughnessy, in deference perhaps to that sense of 'originality' that Hooper acknowledges, though more particularly to the dignity of the language in which Rivas chooses to compose. If the linguistic organization of the collection works against isolation, the poems themselves do the same thanks to an eclectic mix of juxtapositions that bring together ugliness and beauty, creativity and destruction, sight and blindness, incorporating also a wide range of intertextual references and loan words that channel into a variety of art forms, artistic movements and languages. The sequencing of languages allows for the audibility of the local as well as the visibility of the ecosystem of which it is a part, constructing a local universalism out of a series of concentric circles. Inherently local, multilingual and translational, the collection speaks in meaningful ways to tensions in world literature between the local and the global, while staging this encounter in linguistic terms.

Notes

1. Manuel Rivas, *A desaparición da neve/La desaparició de la neu/Elurraren Urtzea/La desaparición de la nieve*, trans. Manuel Rivas (Castilian), Biel Mesquida (Catalan) and Jon Kortazar (Basque) (Madrid: Alfaguara, 2009).
2. Concha Carrón, 'Manuel Rivas publica 'La desaparición de la nieve'', *El Mundo*, 14 April 2009. Available online: www.elmundo.es/elmundo/2009/04/14/cultura/1239722042.html (accessed 28 August 2020).
3. Miguel Ángel Villena, 'Manuel Rivas, la poesía como "célula madre"', *El País*, 14 April 2009. Available online: https://elpais.com/diario/2009/04/14/cultura/1239660007_850215.html (accessed 28 August 2020).
4. 'What is ecology?' Available online: www.britishecologicalsociety.org/about/what-is-ecology/ (accessed 20 June 2019).
5. M. Colyvan, S. Linquist, W. Grey, P. Griffiths, J. Odenbaugh and H. P. Possingham, 'Philosophical Issues in Ecology: Recent Trends and Future Directions', *Ecology and Society* 14.2 (2009). Available online: www.ecologyandsociety.org/vol14/iss2/art22/(accessed 25 July 2018). The source is not paginated, but the citation comes from the section entitled 'Environmental Ethics'.
6. Manuel Rivas, 'A boca da literatura. Memoria, ecoloxía, lingua' (Inaugural address to the Real Academia Galega, 12 December 2009), 27, 31.
7. Alexander Beecroft, *An Ecology of World Literature: From Antiquity to the Present Day* (London: Verso, 2015), 21. Ecology is offered as an alternative to Pascale Casanova's economic metaphor of the market to describe the circulation of world literature, on the basis that 'where economics tends to simplify our understanding of complex systems in order to make them easier to understand, ecology is more comfortable accepting that the complexity may be inherent to the system' (18).
8. Ibid., 21, 28
9. Neil Lazarus, 'Cosmopolitanism and the Specificity of the Local in World Literature', *The Journal of Commonwealth Literature* 46: 1 (2011): 119–37, 134.
10. Timothy Morton, *The Ecological Thought* (Cambridge, MA: Harvard University Press, 2010), Kindle edn., loc. 207.
11. Rivas, 'A boca', 11.
12. Morton, *Ecological Thought*, loc. 176.
13. Isabel Castro-Vázquez, *El lenguaje ecológico de Manuel Rivas: Retranca, resiliencia y reexistencia* (PhD diss., 2004), 7.
14. Morton, *Ecological Thought*, loc. 371.
15. Ibid., loc. 118.
16. 'Manuel Rivas ve el gallego "en riesgo de autodestrucción por bioperversidad"', Europapress, 7 Sept 2014. Available online: www.elcorreogallego.es/hemeroteca/manuel-rivas-ve-gallego-riesgo-autodestruccion-bioperversidad-HECG888438 (acccessed 28 August 2020). All translations are the author's own unless otherwise stated.
17. Carrón, 'Manuel Rivas publica …'; Villena, 'Manuel Rivas …'
18. Rivas, 'A boca', 9.
19. Castilian Spanish is of course spoken widely in the Americas, while Galician is, thanks to the region's history of economic migration, a diasporic language that found a particular home in Buenos Aires. Catalan is spoken not only in Catalonia but across the *Països Catalans* or Catalan Countries (which include Valencia, the Balearic

islands, Rousillon in France, and Andorra), while the Basque country and language extend across the Pyrenees from Spain into France.

20 Dolores Vilavedra, 'La obra literaria de Manuel Rivas: Notas para una lectura macrotextual', *Romance Notes* 51: 1 (2011): 87–96, 89.
21 Kirsty Hooper, '*A desaparición da neve* (2009) de Manuel Rivas: ¿Hacia una po/ética relacional?', in *Voces de Galicia: Manuel Rivas y Suso de Toro*, ed. Sadi Lakhdari (Paris: Indigo et Côté-Femmes, 2012), 120–7, 123–4.
22 Morton, *Ecological Thought*, loc. 160.
23 Hannes Bergthaller, '"Trees Are what Everyone Needs": The Lorax, Anthropocentrism, and the Problem of Mimesis', in *Nature in Literary and Cultural Studies*, ed. Catrin Gersdorf and Sylvia Mayer (Amsterdam: Rodopi, 2006), 155–77, 159, 156.
24 Morton, *Ecological Thought*, loc. 165.
25 Ibid.
26 Helena Miguélez-Carballeira, *Galicia, A Sentimental Nation: Gender, Culture and Politics* (Cardiff: University of Wales Press, 2013), 2–3.
27 Ibid., 32.
28 Ibid., 207, 85.
29 Morton, *The Ecological Thought*, loc. 57; loc. 107.
30 Rivas, 'A boca', 25.
31 Miguélez-Carballeira, *Sentimental Nation*, 33.
32 Elizabeth Nash, 'Manuel Rivas: Spirits of the Sea', *The Independent*, 1 February 2003. Available online: www.independent.co.uk/arts-entertainment/books/features/manuel-rivas-spirits-of-the-sea-134702.html(accessed 28 August 2020).
33 Manuel Rivas, *A cuerpo abierto* (Barcelona: Alfaguara, 2014), Kindle edn., loc. 2521.
34 Vilavedra, 'La obra literaria', 89.
35 Cristina Sánchez-Conejero, 'De la identidad gallega nacional a la identidad gallega global: "Galicia, el bonsái atlántico" (1989) de Manuel Rivas y "Finisterre" (1998) de Xavier Villaverde', *Revista Hispánica Moderna* 57, no. 1/2 (2004): 223–39, 227.
36 Emily Apter, *Against World Literature: On the Politics of Untranslatability* (London: Verso, 2013), 138. Apter does this with reference to Portugal, which neighbours Galicia geographically and with whose language Galician has at least as much in common as it does with Spanish.
37 Manuel Rivas, *The Disappearance of Snow*, trans. Lorna Shaughnessy (Bristol: Shearsman Books, 2012), 43.
38 Ibid., 106.
39 Ibid., 18; 19.
40 Rivas, 'A boca', 28–9.
41 Ibid., 77.
42 Ibid., 78.
43 Ibid., 79.
44 Morton, *Ecological Thought*, loc. 85; loc. 141.
45 Rivas, *Disappearance*, 22.
46 Ibid., 23.
47 Ibid., 24.
48 Ibid., 25.
49 This lacks the political or moral overtones of such modernist landscape poetry as Antonio Machado's *Campos de Castilla* (1917), where impoverishment suggests a nation brought low.

50 Manuel Rivas, *A boca da terra/La boca de la tierra* (Madrid: Visor, 2015).
51 Oscar Wilde, 'The Decay of Lying' (New York, 1889; Brentano, 1905).
52 Yasemin Yildiz, *Beyond the Mother Tongue: The Postmonolingual Condition* (New York: Fordham University Press, 2011), 3.
53 Rivas, 'A boca', 9.
54 Rivas, *Disappearance*, 28.
55 Ogham is an ancient rune-like writing system created during the Roman Empire to represent Gaelic. It can be found carved into stones across Ireland.
56 Rivas, *Disappearance*, 29.
57 Ibid., 18, 19, 24, 25.
58 Rivas, 'A boca', 11.
59 Rivas, *Disappearance*, 36.
60 Ibid., 37.
61 Rivas, 'A boca', 13.
62 Rivas, *Disappearance*, 112.
63 Mother of Antón Avilés de Taramancos (1935–92), poet and Galician cultural icon, to whom the poem is dedicated. Lela da Pastora is quoted in the epigraph to his poetry collection *As torres no ar* (Towers in the Air): 'Ai, meu fillo: / ti sempre a facer torres no ar …' (Oh, my son, always building towers in the air …)
64 Rivas, *Disappearance*, 113.
65 Rivas, 'A boca', 11.
66 Erín Moure, 'River to the Sea: A Commentary by Erín Moure', in Wilson Bueno, *Paraguayan Sea*, trans. Erín Moure (New York: Nightboat Books, 2017): 107–12, 112.

6

Monolingualizing the multilingual Ottoman novel: Ahmet Midhat Efendi's *Felatun Bey ile Rakım Efendi*

Keya Anjaria

In the introduction to his recent book, *What Is a World?*,[1] Pheng Cheah argues: 'It should be evident that we should not take the presentation of the world for granted because, it, at the very least, is given to us by imagination.'[2] His intervention into the debates within the field of world literature draws our attention to a hitherto overlooked aspect of the field: the world. Whether it is by charting circulation, waves within the world-system, or mapping the meridian of the world of letters – to reference the most famous, but certainly not the only models – world literature has relied heavily on 'normative understandings of the world',[3] where the world remains a conceptually stable and seemingly objective unit of analysis. As Cheah asserts 'world literature as a world-making activity',[4] he refocuses our attention on the field of world literature itself, highlighting that it is a critical activity, one which produces and reinforces not only definitions of literature but also of the world.

Cheah, of course, is not the only scholar to draw attention to world literature as world-making. Francesca Orsini, for example, points to the biases and privileges that have not yet been fully accounted for in the revival of world literature at the turn of the twenty-first century: '"World literature," a famously slippery, apparently expansive yet surprisingly narrow category, has been much theorized and re-theorized in recent years as comparative literature for the global age, with one foot in the US university curriculum and the other in theories of globalization.'[5] Orsini's work takes aim particularly at the monolingual conception of the world in the twenty-first century revival of 'world literature', where it cannot seem to, or does not want to, accommodate the fact that 'literary cultures have indeed been multilingual in most parts of the world since the second millennium'.[6]

Building on the above interventions in world literature, this chapter will consider world literature and multilingualism with regard to the late-Ottoman novel.[7] Its starting point is to emphasize that multilingualism is the contextual reality, linguistic scaffold and thematic interest of the Ottoman novel, particularly in *Felatun Bey ile Rakım Efendi* (1875). It will argue that, for the Ottoman novel, the multilingual ecology of the form may be defined as cosmopolitanism, where, according to Cheah it is 'about viewing oneself as part of the world',[8] even as this connection to the world, as Rebecca Walkowitz has argued, might also be 'a model of perversity, in the senses of obstinacy, indirection, immorality and attitude'.[9]

Despite the novel being indebted to Ottoman multilingualism, this fact has been obfuscated, if not occluded, by the two major lines of critical enquiry that have dominated its reading and reception. First is the secularizing, nationalist, monolingualist criticism emerging from the Turkish Republic. This branch of criticism had two primary (albeit, often unconscious) outcomes: to seek legitimacy and authenticity in literary expression and to demonstrate the success of Republican modernization efforts, such that the Turkish novel would always be superior to its Ottoman origins. Its conclusions often rely on identitarian[10] or nationalist evaluations based upon dichotomies between self/other and East/West, while its evaluative thrust tends to consider the novel as either good or bad. The second is the revival of world literature under which a new home has been found for the international study of Ottoman and Turkish novels. Particularly, Moretti's 'Conjunctures on World Literature'[11] opened up a critical framework which offered genuine possibilities to recontextualize Ottoman and Turkish literature in broader terms than those offered by national(ist) frames. However, what we have come to see is that even as world literature attempts to identify connections beyond the national paradigm, it, at least in the case of the Ottoman novel, unintentionally reverts to a similar identitarian dichotomy: foreign/local. These literary critical frameworks, which have been most interested in the Ottoman and Turkish novel, have not yet managed to recognize its multilingual origins, let alone critically activate them.

The focus on criticism rather than the Ottoman novels themselves in the first part of this chapter is not accidental. My approach can be situated in the wake of Felski's *The Limits of Critique* and the huge inroads the book makes into understanding how criticism functions on texts as its 'dominant metalanguage'.[12] Felski's redeployment of Ricoeur's 'hermeneutics of suspicion' and focus on the 'style and sensibility' of critical storytelling help open up the language of nationalist republican criticism that has dominated and determined the Ottoman novel in very particular ways. While Felski is not addressing multilingualism, per se, her reorientation of reading so that we may emphasize a 'language of addition rather than subtraction, translation rather than separation, connection rather than isolation, composition rather than critique'[13] inspires new potential for reading the Ottoman novel through its multilingualism. In this vein, we may find a way to relieve ourselves from the suspicion that multilingualism is the unfortunate, unspeakable, accident of the Turkish novel's birth, a failure of its modernity and a stain on its role in building the national language and culture. Instead, we might speak to multilingualism in this 'language of addition' and transform our critical activity on the basis that multilingualism was (and is) the life-giving conditions of the novel's origins and success.

This chapter will thus consider this occluded aspect of the novel through a reading of Ahmet Midhat Efendi's canonical, *Felatun Bey ile Rakım Efendi*.[14] It will read the novel using multilingualism as its focal point, showing that there is an important, if more ambiguous, conceptualization of the cosmopolitan that is awakened through multlingualism and which seems to refute, or at least complicate, the dominant reading of the novel as proto-nationalist and identitarian. It will furthermore assert, in line with Cheah and Orsini, that world literature is world-*making*, and that by pivoting around the axis of multilingualism we learn more about the unacknowledged interests of its body of criticism.

The Ottoman novel: National and world literary criticism

In order to understand how criticism has managed to overlook multilingualism in the Ottoman novel, it is worth starting first with a brief description of its contribution to the landscape and composition of the Ottoman novel. To this end, the fact of multilingualism in the late-Ottoman empire is well known, and it is of particular interest in the study of Istanbul's print culture at the end of the nineteenth century. Johann Strauss's seminal research on readership in Istanbul in the late nineteenth century shows the labyrinth of languages and scripts, organized around ethnic and religious groups, as well as print publications such as periodicals and books which were being exchanged and circulated.[15] Strauss begins his study by showing a transformation taking place during the nineteenth century. At its beginning, the written languages of Istanbul were predominantly classical: Ottoman Turkish, Persian, Arabic, Greek, Armenian and Hebrew.[16] But as the century progressed, witnessed by significant modernization reforms and a new engagement in nationalism, written language went through significant reform. The ensuing developments of written language at this time were four-fold. Firstly, there was a vernacularization of 'sacred' languages, particularly Armenian. Secondly, there was a further separation made between ethnic and classical languages (i.e. Turkish was utilized distinctly from Arabic and Judeo-Spanish from Hebrew). Thirdly, this period saw the beginnings of the nationalization of languages, particularly Bulgarian and, finally, French was introduced as both a written and spoken language.[17]

Alongside the burgeoning of new written languages, the Ottoman print culture also had a complex exchange of scripts.[18] The primary scripts were Arabo-Persian; Greek; Hebrew; and with the addition of French, Roman. Language itself had a flexible relationship to its script. For example, Turkish was written in multiple scripts such as Arabo-Persian as well as Armenian and Greek.[19] This exchange of script was partly fuelled by a productive and dynamic enterprise of translation and publication between the reading communities, because the knowledge of multiple languages did not necessarily entail knowledge of multiple scripts.[20] Interaction varied from community to community in the nineteenth century and script was an important meeting-point for cross-community, cross-lingual interaction, while also sometimes demonstrating inequality and inaccessibility across communities and readerships.[21]

As it emerged from this multilingual scene, it is not surprising that the novel should be marked by such linguistic and script mixing. *Felatun Bey ile Rakım Efendi* does not disappoint. The novel not only refers to multiple languages, including Armenian, Circassian, Arabic, Persian English and French, alongside Ottoman Turkish, but also is mainly written in two: Ottoman-Turkish, interspersed with dialogue and words in French, and in addition, one scene where Persian is used. To capture this, the novel uses the two corresponding scripts: Arabo-Persian and Roman. When dialogue takes place in French, the translation is put in parenthesis next to it. Multilingualism is also a useful trope and serves the narrative's comedic, dramatic and dialogic ambitions, as will be discussed in greater detail towards the end of the chapter.

Yet, multilingualism in *Felatun Bey ile Rakım Efendi* has been almost entirely overlooked. While Midhat's use of Turkish language has indeed been a focus of study – for its hasty, colloquial style which brought the written and spoken versions of the language into contact with each other[22] – its narrative and linguistic engagement in this multilingual context has never been fully considered. Such an oversight seems to be designed not by the novel itself but rather by the terms of criticism and the primacy of a certain type of suspicion. As Felski writes, for the critic, '[a] toolkit of methods lies ready to hand to draw out what a text does not know and cannot comprehend. The scalpel of political or historical diagnosis slices into a literary work to expose its omissions and occlusions, its denials and disavowals'.[23] In the case of *Felatun Bey ile Rakım Efendi*, however, the question is not what the text does not know; instead, it is what the text knows but the critic cannot fathom.

The discussions surrounding the 'first' Ottoman-Turkish novel are helpful as a way into investigating this point. This is Yusuf Kamil Paşa's 1862 translation of Fénelon's *Les Aventures de Télémaque*. That the novel arrived into Ottoman-Turkish through translation is not, on its own, a particularly striking or controversial fact. Yet, as the fields of Turkish and Ottoman literary studies developed through the twentieth century, this mere fact has proved to be a continual challenge. Recently, Azade Seyhan has summed up the situation aptly: 'Practically every work on Turkish literary history cites the birth of the Turkish novel from translation as an inauspicious beginning, as an almost embarrassing fact that is best left unexamined or glossed over.'[24]

We might add to Seyhan's point that when this fact is not 'glossed over', the novel becomes an unpayable 'debt',[25] to which all innovation and development of the novel must neatly be brought back. And as a result, interwoven within literary criticism of the Ottoman and Turkish novel, is a perpetual anxiety about its foreign form. For example, Ahmet Evin has argued that the introduction of the novel to the Ottoman intelligentsia 'played an important role in the development of modern Turkish literature by becoming a topic of dispute between progressives and traditionalists'.[26] Robert Finn takes a more progressive approach but nonetheless sees the Turkish novel as influenced by translations:

> The first novels published in Turkish were translations from the French. …. With the publication of Şemsettin Sami's *Taaşşuk-i Talât ve Fitnat* (The Romance of Talat and Fitnat) in 1872, Ottoman writers began their endeavors in this field. The early novels in Turkish, although modelled on French examples …, nevertheless include[d] certain elements, both in form and development which have as their antecedents the Near Eastern Story-telling tradition and the rich intellectuality of classical Ottoman poetry, the Divan tradition.[27]

Most influentially, Ahmet Hamdi Tanpınar, often considered the first Turkish literary critic, in 1936 verbalized the anxiety of the borrowed novel: 'Bir Türk romanı niçin yoktur?'[28] (Why isn't there a Turkish novel?). His question continues to reverberate in criticism, which Nurdan Gürbilek recently labelled the criticism of 'lack': 'The criticism of lack is torn between two extremes. The first one assumes the original is elsewhere ("outside" namely in the West) while the second insists that we do have an authentic literature and a genuine native thought but in order to appreciate it we have to leave aside all those lifeless imitations and snobbish efforts related with the West.'[29] The fact of the novel's translated origins has entrenched in criticism a seemingly immutable anxiety about the 'lack' of native identity, culture and expression, while also forcing its gaze towards identitarian politics in East versus West terms.

Suspicion-fuelled criticism has had two major outcomes for the reading of the Ottoman novel. Firstly, critics have derided the novel.[30] Secondly, reading the novel has tended to confirm the *a priori* of the critical act itself: namely, that the primary labour of the novel is to address and possibly resolve the ambivalences around identity and culture, embedded in the novel's original Westward gaze.[31] For example, Mardin writes, 'the central theme of *Felatun Bey ile Rakım Efendi* is the difference between two types of westernization'.[32] Of course, Westernization is thematized and embodied in *Felatun Bey ile Rakım Efendi*'s characters, but seeing it as the central theme provides a tautology where the ambivalence surrounding the origins of the novel must necessarily be its main theme. All of this is not to suggest that critical inquiries into the evaluation of the Ottoman novel are inadequate, but rather they have been determined by a 'certain orientation', that the act of 'digging down' is one conditioned by the problem of foreignness and authenticity as it encounters ideologically driven national monolingualism.[33]

The other side of the story lies in the twenty-first-century revival of world literature. Here, the Ottoman and Turkish novel has been largely ignored as a genre, with the singular exception of Orhan Pamuk who has received a lot of individual attention. Most famously, the genre has been discussed in Moretti's 'Conjectures on World Literature'. In the article, he footnotes two scholars of the Ottoman Turkish novel, Evin and Parla, to support his argument about the 'rule' of the world novel: 'it's *always* as a compromise between foreign form and local materials'.[34] As it is explained above, Moretti's 'conjecture' fits neatly with Ottoman-Turkish criticism's own perspective on the development of the novel, while removing the anxieties of authenticity that have dominated local criticism, because it is the 'rule'. As Ertürk cautiously argues, Moretti's compromise allows for 'dynamism and violence, rather than some Orientalized evolutionary plateau of "backwardness"'.[35] Of course, 'Conjectures' has received a certain amount of criticism as well. Joseph Slaughter has shown that Moretti's 'rule' is determined by the criticism upon which he builds, that 'reflect[s] the condition and history of comparison from the periphery'.[36] In other words, the rule of compromise fits so well in the Ottoman-Turkish context not accidentally, but rather because it is founded in Ottoman-Turkish scholarship which has always argued such a point.

It is not the point of this chapter to rehash arguments for or against Moretti's 'Conjectures'. Instead, it is brought up here to illustrate the minute space – quite literally in the footnotes – which the Ottoman and Turkish novel has been given in discussions of world literature. On the one hand, Moretti does allow for a refocusing of the reading of the conditions of the novel in the late Ottoman Empire – mobilizing those troublesome notions of importation, imitation and debt – to make way for formal uniqueness, originality and therefore, authenticity. On the other hand, the 'act of hospitality'[37] in bringing the Ottoman novel to this world stage, as Rey Chow argues, is another 'level of complication: that of the hierarchical frameworks of comparison – and judgement – that have long been present as universals, that tend to subsume otherness rather than deconstruct their processes of operation from within'.[38] These two lines of critical enquiry – the dedicated Ottoman-Turkish one and the larger world literary one – are both dogged by a search for authenticity and the politics of comparison, leaving little space for the multilingualism of the Ottoman novel to be considered on its own terms.

Finally, it is worth pointing out here, with regards to Moretti, that the compromise of form and content determines what is understood about the imaginative possibilities of individual novels themselves.[39] We might make an assumption about Moretti's compromise: since the form is foreign but the content is local, the world the novel conjures is likewise *always* local and never worldly.[40] Such limitations on the non-Western novel's imaginary are clearly different from the wanderings of the colonial travelogue, for example, and its more contemporary novel iterations that serve as authoritative guides to unexplored lands. It is a strange paradox, then, in Moretti's notion of the world novel, that it is recognized to travel the world and yet, at least for the non-Western novel, it cannot imagine it. In the end, Ottoman-Turkish criticism leaves little space to read the novel outside of a foreign/local dichotomy and Moretti's 'Conjectures' never quite manages to relieve it of the suspicion of its inauthenticity, its borrowed-ness, and its limits.

Back to the beginning: Multilingualism and the Ottoman novel

The cul-de-sac of suspicion and the reiteration of a foreign/local dichotomy are nevertheless not necessarily unresolvable. Ertürk sums up her discussion of Moretti by pointing to another limitation of his theory: namely, 'the real and unavoidable complexities of linguistic mediation'.[41] For her, a necessary pivot for understanding the rise of the Ottoman novel is in a turn towards language in the late nineteenth century: namely, the development from logocentric language to the rise of phonocentric vernacular.[42] Ertürk's turn is particularly useful for considering multilingualism in the Ottoman novel. She writes, 'conventional critical models of literary influence, which turn on the dissemination of European genres such as the novel or European literary currents such as realism, Romanticism, and modernism, are incapable of explaining the emergence of new Ottoman Turkish literary forms, which are *foremost* contingent on the transformation of writing practices accompanying their development'.[43] In a similar vein, this chapter too sees the multilingual as a fulcrum by which criticism might be shifted away from the suspicion of inauthenticity.

To this end, it is worth revisiting the *Télémaque* translation through the prism of multilingualism. If on the one hand, its importation and translation from the French has been dominated by identitarian-oriented criticism, on the other, Strauss's study considers the translation in a rather different way. His focus is on the multiple local print cultures and leads him to conclude that this translation as the first novel is 'less striking a choice if we consider the fact that it has been immensely popular among all communities in the Levant before'.[44] Arzu Meral's study of *Télémaque* in the Ottoman empire likewise highlights that the 'Turks' acquaintance with the novel predates its translation into Ottoman-Turkish, not only through the French original, but also because the Greek and Arabic translations were popular and well known in the Empire.[45] Strauss and Meral's detailed literary histories emphasize that while East–West exchange was indeed part of the story, the exchange between various language and reading communities within Istanbul and the Ottoman Empire was far more significant for the conditions of what and when the first Ottoman novel would be.

The significance of this for the reading of the Ottoman novel is likewise important as it suggests that dominant readings which have privileged the thematization of West–East identities, as well as ones that favour the question of identity, do so outside of the immediate and contemporary context of the readership and the languages of the Ottoman novel. Of course, large parts of the early novel are indeed dedicated to these themes. However, the fact of multilingualism provides a platform to see greater interests and appeal of the novel, which have been almost completely circumvented for the sake of East–West identitarianism and Westernization.[46]

(Re)reading *Felatun Bey ile Rakım Efendi* through multilingualism

Ahmet Midhat's *Felatun Bey ile Rakım Efendi* is primarily discussed in three ways: first, in terms of Ahmet Midhat's contribution to the proliferation of the Ottoman novel; second, in the context of his work as a late-nineteenth-century reformer; thirdly, for his work as a translator of European literature. At the same time, Jale Parla points out that Midhat was only recognized for his contribution to the development of the Turkish novel in the 1970s, and since then, has been seen as a key figure for anchoring the Turkish novel within local language and culture, as opposed to centring its foreign influence.[47] Among other points, this is what makes *Felatun Bey* such an interesting point of discussion. On the one hand, it is seen as an example of the domesticated novel, whose impact is felt throughout the generations which come after it,[48] and, on the other hand, its themes and plot – the content of its story – are widely regarded as measuring the effects of foreign influence and cautioning against its excesses. In this sense, *Felatun Bey ile Rakım Efendi* is seen in almost conflicting ways – as part of the initiative that domesticated the novel form and as one that warned against cultural and social Westernization.

The story of *Felatun Bey ile Rakım Efendi* follows the lives of the two eponymous characters, Felatun and Rakım. Most of the narrative is given to describing random conversations, the coincidences and encounters between friends and family around famous Istanbul locations (i.e. the contingencies of unexceptional daily life), but if there is one overarching narrative, it is the love story between his slave, Canan, and Rakım. Ahmet Evin, however, has argued more broadly: 'The main plot of the novel revolves around Rakım's spectacular success as an intellectual entrepreneur paralleled by his popularity with women.'[49] Either way, narrative focus is primarily given to Rakım who is torn between his duty as educator and guardian of Canan and his burgeoning love interest in her. Although there are no catastrophic obstacles, at least in the sense that Canan and Rakım stay emotionally true to each other, Rakım's attractiveness creates some jealousy and despair, not least with Felatun.

Unsatisfied with the vague plot, which is 'conceived more as a story told in an informal circle than as a novel',[50] and suspicious of the narrative style, scholarship has tended to emphasize a particular reading of *Felatun Bey ile Rakım Efendi*, which centres its characters. Evin continues, 'The two principal characters, Felâtun and Rakım, are creatures of a difference universe thrown together between the two covers of a book for the purpose of a parable; they only meet coincidentally in the Ziglas house. Characterization is achieved by means of hyperbole ....'[51] In this way, Felatun and Rakım provide useful signposting and significance for a novel 'thrown together' in a haphazard composition. They serve as anchors for critical inquiry, which compares their characteristics and the trajectories of their lives, through East–West identitarian anxieties. Mardin sums up the comparison in a similar vein: 'Thus the central theme of *Felâtun Bey ile Râkım Efendi* is the difference between two types of Westernization, one approved by the author, the other selected for ridicule.'[52] Berna Moran argues that the comparison between Felatun and Rakım amounts to a comparison between the over-Westernized dandy and ideal Ottoman man.[53] Evin sees a different emphasis, however: 'The problem with Felâtun is not that he is Westernized, but that he has fundamentally misunderstood what the West means'.[54] As for Rakim, he 'is more of a Westernized type in that he has the intellectual curiosity and the work ethic of the European bourgeois'.[55] While these approaches consider the meaning of the novel in overlapping but slightly different ways, they rely on a similar critical position: namely, that there is a didactic thrust of the novel which provides its readers with stable and singular knowledge about Ottoman society and the West.[56] This arises from the juxtaposition of the two characters, despite the anxiety over Ahmet Midhat's skill as a novelist.[57] In other words, the story is a cautionary tale: one that champions one way of living over the excesses of another, while also reiterating the seemingly irreconcilable difference between East and West.

This idea, that *Felatun Bey ile Rakım Efendi* delivers a stable 'moral'[58] is intensified by another much-discussed feature of Ahmet Midhat's writing style: namely, his pronounced, playful and involved narrators. For Parla, it is not so much the narrator but the authorial voice which interrupts his narratives: 'In an almost frenzied effort to ensure the undivided attention of his readers, Ahmet Mithat interrupts his narrative to inform them on a topic he thinks significant, to moralize, to discuss his novelistic concerns and problems, or to offer autobiographical details.'[59] Seen as descendent from the *meddah* tradition [coffee-house, story-tellers], Midhat's author/narrator is one of the most prominent features of *Felatun Bey ile Rakım Efendi* as well. In Ertürk's discussion of Midhat's '*meddah*-author' she makes the further argument that the involved and interrupting author persona gives his 'ear to the world', distributing the rumours and events that are encountered in the landscape of daily lives.[60] For Ertürk, then, the *meddah* tradition shapes the role of the narrator who primes the reader, engages and holds their interest.

It might then be argued that the story's moral is rather less the focus of the novel than its interest in exploring storytelling, for the sake of storytelling. Take, for example, the opening lines of *Felatun Bey ile Rakım Efendi*: 'Have you heard of Felatun Bey? You know who I'm talking about, old Mustafa Meraki Efendi's son! Doesn't ring a bell? Well now, he's a lad worth meeting.'[61] And again, when the narrator introduces Rakım in the beginning of Chapter 2: 'The previous section informed us pretty well about the specific personality of one of the two individuals we named our story after. Now, here briefly once again we need to take a look at Râkım Efendi's situation.'[62] Such a pronounced narrative voice serves the purpose of not only introducing the characters, but conditioning the reader to the assertive, interactive and, above all, light-hearted and teasing voice of the narrator. Here, it is the salaciousness of storytelling that is being asserted, more than a strictly informed morality.[63]

This is not to say that morality does not play a part in storytelling, but that the dialogue between narrator and reader is often at the forefront of novel's attention. Take this moment when the narrator is describing Felatun and Rakım's last encounter, after Felatun has wasted away all his money and has been compelled to take up a job outside of Istanbul:

[…Rakım] went all the way down to Hendekbaşı.
Who do you suppose he ran across there?
Felâtun Bey!
Oh, no, put the waster aside!
How can we? How can we abandon the fellow who is a partner to half our story?
We should never have included him in this story in the first place.
We shouldn't have…but we already did. Besides, where is this animosity towards Felâtun Bey coming from? Is it that you can't stand his *alafranga* ways? If Felâtun Bey didn't exist, how could the mayonnaise incident have occurred? What about the Hotel J-----? Would it be able to host such a rich *alafranga* Ottoman if not for Felâtun Bey? Would the two bands have played in front of the lady's carriage in Kağıthane?
What good is it if he's going to rack and ruin?
It's all right! We assure you that he is not going to go rack and ruin anymore.
He can't anyway!
We fear that his money…
Instead of worrying, listen to this[64]

This narrative break in the plot is a conversation, imagined by the narrator as between himself and the reader(s). It certainly can be seen as moralizing, insofar as it is asking about whether 'we' should have included Felatun in the story. Yet, and moreover, by its very words, it questions this morality. It poses questions; it tells us, the readers, to reserve judgement. And above all else, it tells us that a good story – Felatun's mayonnaise, the hotel, the two bands – is more important than a morally unimpinged world. Moreover, the novel is also mimicking – here, mimicking as slippage and excess[65] – the technique of dialogism which, to borrow Ertürk's phrase, has the effect of setting words free, as it was 'both enchanted by *and* fearful of open communicability and translatability in Ottoman Turkish'.[66]

The two major points of critical engagement – authorial/narrator's voice and the obvious juxtaposition between the two main characters – have typically been seen to confirm a moralistic and proto-nationalist, identitarian worldview or the novel and novelist. Such a perspective confirms the suspicions that the Ottoman novel is neither a 'good' novel nor is its society quite 'ready' for it. However, considering the *meddah/* author/narrator as 'mimicking the moralizing voice of [an] older mode of authority'[67] is a useful clarification to these identitarian and nationalist criticisms of hindsight, because it opens up the ways in which we might also read Rakım and Felatun. Instead of thinking of their stories as straightforwardly educative, we might think of excess, not only in Felatun's over-Westernized ways, but also in how the excesses of language and dialogue construct society and interpersonal relations that quite literally caution the reader against digging past the story to get to a moral.

This is where multilingualism re-emerges in the discussion of the Ottoman novel and its criticism. As I have already mentioned, from Ertürk's discussion of Midhat, we see that the novel was a 'kind of public overhearing of the gossip, rumor and news of a language disseminated in oral and written media'.[68] As we have already established through Strauss's work, 'oral and written media' were multilingual and multi-scripted. It is thus not surprising that *Felatun Bey ile Rakım Efendi* is both thematically and prosaically multilingual. This multilingual composition is employed in primarily three ways: comic relief; communication and knowledge building; and dialogue. It is worth mentioning that as Ertürk shows, multilingualism should not be read in the late Ottoman empire as utopic heterogeneity. Instead, she sees modern identitarian movements emerging from this heterogeneity with Midhat himself aligned with 'imperial Ottoman identity in promoting the hegemony of Turkish-Islamic values'.[69] This is to add that the question of multilingualism is not, in the Ottoman context, one inherently poised against national and monolingual criticism of twentieth-century Turkey. In fact, its ambivalence is precisely the point for thinking about the novel outside of the hermeneutics of suspicion, for it, like the *meddah*/narrator is part of a 'network of actors that bring new things to light'.[70] Finally, that it has been almost wholly overlooked in the canonical novel and readings of *Felatun Bey ile Rakım Efendi* speaks to the ways in which it fits uncomfortably with criticism which sought to draw a singular line of development to the Turkish novel, nationalism and the era of monolingualism.

Thus, multilingualism is a fact of *Felatun Bey ile Rakım Efendi*, reflective of a stratified society and entwined with Midhat's experimentations with the novel. To give one example of how it appears, in the second chapter which introduces Rakım, his education is described:

> [H]e thoroughly learned the fourth annotated Arabic textbook. He was especially well trained in logic. He acquired a substantial knowledge of Hadith and Quranic exegesis. He even dipped into Islamic jurisprudence. Quite apart from finishing the Persian works of Saadi's *Gulistan* and *Bustan*, Jami's *Baharistan*, Attar's *Pandnameh* and the poetry of Hafez and Saib, he memorized the most famous selections of these works. Now, about French: he achieved a good grasp of the language. Later … he mastered the basics of physics, chemistry, and biology; in his Armenian friend's library in Beyoğlu he accumulated additional knowledge of geography, history, law and international agreements. He never stopped reading French novels, plays, poems, and literature.[71]

What is immediately striking is how knowledge and language are tied together. Arabic, Farsi, French and Ottoman Turkish are not merely languages, but connected to epistemologies. In this passage, Parla points to a divide between positivist sciences in the French-Armenian language-sphere and Islamic sciences in the Arabo-Persian one.[72] Her analysis supports a metonymic relationship between language and knowledge, where French, Arabic and Persian stand in for positivist science, Islamic logic and poetics, respectively. This is not accidental, as *Felatun Bey ile Rakım Efendi* follows a common perspective on what different languages/knowledges might have contributed to the Ottoman Empire. Taken further, modern identitarianist formations reinforce this analysis, particularly in an assertion of different types of knowledge clashing, between Islamic ontology and morality, on the one hand, and Western science and governance on the other.

At the same time, the focus of multilingualism might also give us new ways of reading this description. Instead of metonymic, language can be read as *synecdochical*, representing part of (the whole world of) knowledge. In this passage – but indeed throughout the various language exchanges in the novel – the depiction of languages and knowledges is syncretic, rather than clashing, even when there is no clear distinction between types of knowledges and its designated languages: French represents literature as much as Persian and both Arabic and French represent law and logic. The lack of competition suggests that there is no real *clash* between knowledges in *Felatun Bey ile Rakım Efendi*. In other words, each language brings something (i.e. a specific type of knowledge) and together they represent a whole world. This is a world forged in multiple languages, not in contest with each other, but in play.

Clearly, reading the multilingual in such a way echoes cosmopolitanism in its ability to imagine 'the whole of deterritorialized humanity'.[73] Yet, neither the novel nor cosmopolitanism necessarily have to do this imagining in utopic terms, as is often supposed. As Walkowitz writes in relation to her idea of critical cosmopolitanism: 'I argue that the syncretic but less-than-national tradition of cosmopolitanism, which is often associated with aestheticism, dandyism, and *flânerie* at the fin de siècle, helped to establish a new analysis of perception and alternative tones of political consciousness amount early modernist writers'.⁷⁴ These texts unfold with 'aesthetic decadence, a repertoire of excessively and purposefully deviant cultural strategies which include pleasure, consumption, syncretism and perversity'.⁷⁵ Although she addresses European literature in particular, Walkowitz might well be speaking directly to *Felatun Bey ile Rakım Efendi*. Her insistence that syncretism comes with (not despite) aesthetic decadence, political consciousness and excess speaks largely to a recent rethinking of cosmopolitanism that goes beyond the 'abstract universal normative view of the ideal unity of the world'.⁷⁶

While Rakım is a master of both multiple knowledges/languages and communication, Felatun is ridiculed for not knowing Turkish properly and only speaking in French.⁷⁷ In one scene, for example, he forgets that Ottoman has the letters 'p', 'ç' and 'z' in addition to the letters from the Arabic alphabet,⁷⁸ the narrator describes this oversight in knowledge as such:

> It seems that when Felatun Bey had seen these letters at first he had thought that they did not exist in the old alphabet, so in order to sound 'like Plato' to the English he supposedly lampooned and ridiculed quite a bit the teacher, whom he didn't even know, by putting forth the ideas that the girls would not learn any Turkish if they studied with such a man; and that this man who they found as a teacher didn't know Turkish anyway.⁷⁹

As a counterexample to Rakım's supremacy in knowledges/languages, we can see how Felatun is targeted as small-minded, petty and spiteful, and this is instrumentally unfolded around his lack of languages/knowledges. This scene represents, from Felatun's 'failure', what happens when knowledges are in competition. Here, there are two indictments against Felatun: the mimicking of 'Plato' and his confusion between the Arabic and Turkish alphabets. This, indeed, can be read as both over-Westernization and a kind of self-loathing. However, it is not without importance that his failures arise because he is located in *one* language and his horizon is therefore blocked. If we may conclude something from the narrator's mockery of Felatun in this scene, it is that the monolingual man cannot understand and does not know, and that the excesses of dandyism here are less that he speaks French and more that he is *only* monolingual.

This reading of *Felatun Bey ile Rakım Efendi* shifts the novel away from the hitherto emphasized discussion of East and West and towards one that highlights the novel as an affirming envisioning of the syncretic – but not necessarily utopic – ways in which language, knowledge and communication are performed. Rakım is an idealized character but together with Felatun, the contemporary world imagined is neither ideal or demonic, East or West, Ottoman or French, translated or original.

It is hard in the Ottoman-Turkish context, and perhaps in the Middle East more generally, not to go back and read a 'clash' of civilizations into its turn-of-the-century literature. Yet, the Ottoman novel rarely imagines the world in such simplistic terms; it sees humour, danger, excess and fun in its multiple knowledges and languages. The multiplicity of languages can equally construct harmony as well as confusion, arrogance and small-mindedness. If suspicion has always led us to read the Ottoman novel as caught in the crisis of an Empire's downfall, deluged with unwanted Westernization and suffering from a breakdown of its own cultural and identitarian-based authenticity, then *Felatun Bey ile Rakım Efendi*'s multilingualism casts the terms of these themes differently. Instead of crisis, deluge and breakdown, the novel imagines a world forged of multiple languages, which some of its citizens navigate and some do not manage. On this final point, it might be said that the crisis of identity in the Ottoman novel belongs not to *Felatun Bey ile Rakım Efendi* but to criticism itself; and that the syncretic system that makes up the novel and its characters imprints it, not as half-foreign, borrowed or translated, but as a negotiation between the many languages and knowledges that makes up its world.

Notes

1 Pheng Cheah, *What Is a World? On Postcolonial Literature as World Literature* (London: Duke University Press, 2016).
2 Ibid., 2.
3 Ibid.
4 Ibid.
5 Francesca Orsini, 'The Multilingual Local in World Literature', *Comparative Literature* 67, no. 4 (2015): 345–74, 345.
6 Ibid., 346.
7 The designation here of 'Ottoman' is made to situate these novels, and in particular *Felatun Bey ile Rakım Efendi*, in a particular linguistic and literary moment. As Nergis Erturk states, its historical period is defined from its past by 'the lexical and grammatical simplifications of Ottoman Turkish, during the nineteenth century' and precede 'the extensive language reforms of the twentieth, which saw the new Turkish Republic undertaking to thoroughly rationalize modern Turkish, overcoming the gap separating its spoken from its written registers'. Nergis Ertürk, *Grammatology and Literary Modernity in Turkey* (Oxford: Oxford University Press, 2011), x.
8 Cheah, *What Is a World?*, 3.
9 Rebecca Walkowitz, *Cosmopolitan Style: Modernism beyond the Nation* (New York: Columbia University Press, 2007), 13.
10 I am borrowing this term from Nergis Ertürk, who, in turn, builds on Derrida. Like Ertürk, I mean 'nativist politics'. Ertürk, *Grammatology and Literary Modernity in Turkey*, 44n41.
11 Franco Moretti, 'Conjectures on World Literature', *New Left Review* 1 (2000): 54–68.
12 Rita Felski, *The Limits of Critique* (Chicago: University of Chicago Press, 2015), 5.
13 Ibid., 182.
14 This chapter relies on the recent English translation of the novel for its quotations, because the English translation is particularly invested in highlighting the multilingual and multi-script composition of the novel. In the two Turkish translations/transliterations consulted, there has been more of an effort to consolidate the text into standard Turkish. In one case, the French dialogue was replaced with Turkish and, in another, examples of specific authors and texts in Persian literature

were edited out. This itself speaks to an interesting language politics that is carried out in transliteration and should be further studied, while also confirming the larger point about nationalist monolingual criticism that this chapter is making. Ahmet Midhat, *Felatun Bey and Rakım Efendi*, trans. Melih Levi and Monica M Ringer (Syracuse: Syracuse University Press, 2016), 1 Ahmet Midhat, *Felatun Bey ile Rakım Efendi*, ed. Rukiye Şahin (İstanbul: LM Leyla ile Mecnun Yayıncılık, 2018) and Ahmet Midhat, *Felatun Bey ile Rakım Efendi*, ed. Tacettin Şimşek (Ankara: Akçağ Yayınları, 1998).

15 Johann Strauss, 'Who Reads What in the Ottoman Empire (19th–20th Centuries)?', *Middle Eastern Literatures* 6, no. 1 (2010): 39–76.
16 Ibid., 40.
17 Ibid., 42.
18 Ibid., 53.
19 Benjamin Fortna, *Learning to Read in the Late Ottoman Empire and the Early Turkish Republic* (London: Palgrave Macmillan, 2012), 10–11.
20 Strauss, 'Who Reads What', 54.
21 For example, Strauss explains that Greek and Armenian communities read Turkish works, like *Felatun Bey ile Rakım Efendi* but Armenian and Karamanlı writing did not have equal appeal in the Turkish readership community. Strauss, 'Who Reads What', 53.
22 Ahmet Evin, *Origins and Development of the Turkish Novel* (Minneapolis: Bibliotheca Islamica, 1983), 82.
23 Felski, *The Limits of Critique*, 16.
24 Azade Seyhan, *Tales of Crossed Destinies: The Modern Turkish Novel in a Comparative Context* (New York: Modern Language Association of America, 2008), 31.
25 Jale Parla writes, 'The presence of "foreign interference" has an alienating effect upon working on their native literature. Local specialists, if they are educated within the native philological tradition […] are embarrassed by and, therefore, tend to dismiss as insignificant all kinds of discrepancies, tensions, and contradictions that they diagnose to be the outcome of foreign interference, or "foreign debt" …' Jale Parla, 'The Object of Comparison', *Comparative Literature Studies* 41, no. 1 (2004): 116–25, 124.
26 Evin, *Origins and Development of the Turkish Novel*, 43.
27 Robert Finn, *The Early Turkish Novel 1872–1900* (Istanbul: İsis Yayımcılık LTD, 1984), 1.
28 Ahmet Hamdi Tanpınar, 'Bizde Roman', in *Edebiyat Üzerine Makaleler* (Istanbul: Milli Eğitim Basımevi, 1998): 46–7, 46.
29 Nurdan Gurbilek, 'Dandies and Originals: Authenticity, Belatedness and the Turkish Novel', *South Atlantic Quarterly* 102: 2/3 (2003): 599–624, 600.
30 For sure, this minimization of the Ottoman novel and early efforts in the genre is somewhat out of fashion. For example, Finn writes in his conclusion, 'That such a remarkable development [of the Turkish novel] could have been made in the span of one generation is mainly a function of the imitative nature of the Turkish novel in this period. In addition, the development was neither chronologically nor developmentally adherent to that of the French novel, but, as might be expected, haphazard and arbitrary.' Finn, *The Early Turkish Novel*, 1.
31 Felski calls this the 'tireless tautology, rediscovering the truth of its bleak prognoses over and over again'. Felski, *The Limits of Critique*, 35.

32 Şerif Mardin, 'Superwesternization in Urban Life in the Ottoman Empire in the Last Quarter of the 19th Century', in *Turkey: Geographical and Social Perspectives*, ed. P Benedict and E. Tumertekin (Leiden: Brill, 1974): 403–43, 406.
33 Felski, *The Limits of Critique*, 115.
34 Moretti, 'Conjectures on World Literature', 60, 62.
35 Ertürk, *Grammatology and Literary Modernity in Turkey*, 20.
36 Joseph Slaughter, 'Locations of Comparison', *Cambridge Journal of Postcolonial Literary Inquiry* 5, no. 2 (2018): 209–26, 221.
37 Ibid., 221.
38 Rey Chow, 'The Old/New Question of Comparison in Literary Studies: A Post-European Perspective', *ELH* 71.2 (2004): 289–311, 304.
39 Moretti's interests lie in 'distant reading' and it is clear why he does not emphasize the individual novel. Yet, when we come back to national literatures, on which he is building his argument, we also inevitably return to the individual novel.
40 To borrow Moretti's emphasis on the 'always' of the law of compromise. Moretti, 'Conjectures on World Literature', 60.
41 Ertürk, *Grammatology and Literary Modernity in Turkey*, 20.
42 Ibid., 13.
43 Ibid. Author's italics.
44 Ibid., 49.
45 Arzu Meral, 'The Ottoman Reception of Fénelon's Télémaque', in *Fénelon's Enlightenment: Traditions, Adaptations and Variations*, ed. Cristoph Schmitt-Maaß, Stephanie Stockhorst and Doohwan Ahn (Brill/ Rodopi, 2014): 211–35, 211. Available online: https://brill.com/view/book/edcoll/9789401210645/B9789401210645-s012.xml (accessed 8 August 2019).
46 The seminal criticism of Berna Moran is a good example of this. While he rightly points to how the Ottoman novel had a problem of Westernization that needed to be addressed, in order for the novel to be relevant, he overlooks the larger more diverse linguistic universe from which these novels were emerging. For example, Moran argues that *Felatun Bey ile Rakım Efendi*'s influence as an early novel can be attributed to two points: its characterization of Westernization through the dandy figure and its view of Westernization as excess. Both points, while of course important contributions to the discussion of the Ottoman novel, reiterate Westernization as the most significance aspect of the novel's context. Berna Moran, *Türk Romanına Eleştirel bir Bakış* (Istanbul: İletişim Yayınları, 1983), 48.
47 Parla, 'The Object of Comparison', 123.
48 Moran, *Türk Romanına Eleştirel bir Bakış*, 48.
49 Evin, *Origins and Development of the Turkish Novel*, 84.
50 Ibid., 81.
51 Ibid., 85.
52 Mardin, 'Superwesternization in Urban Life in the Ottoman Empire in the Last Quarter of the 19th Century', 406.
53 Moran, *Türk Romanına Eleştirel bir Bakış*, 48–9.
54 Evin, *Origins and Development of the Turkish Novel*, 87.
55 Ibid.
56 What Evin calls a 'parable', Moran calls a 'fable'. Moran, *Türk Romanına Eleştirel bir Bakış*, 58. Both give the sense that two characters' juxtaposition brings about a singular message and educative experience from reading the novel.

57 Evin, for example, says, '[The] banal and surprisingly colloquial opening is indicative of Ahmet Mithat's approach to the novel [...]. It has often been pointed out that the uneven nature of his prose resulted from his preference for speed over accuracy in composing his articles as well as his fiction.' Evin, *Origins and Development of the Turkish Novel*, 82.
58 Parla, 'The Object of Comparison', 122.
59 Ibid., 121.
60 Ertürk, *Grammatology and Literary Modernity in Turkey*, 13, 46–7.
61 Midhat, *Felatun Bey and Rakım Efendi*, 1.
62 Ibid., 9.
63 We are not introduced to the characters as 'good' and 'bad', for example.
64 Midhat, *Felatun Bey and Rakım Efendi*, 126–7.
65 Homi Bhabha, 'Of Mimicry and Man: The Ambivalence of Colonial Discourse', *October* 28 (1984): 125–33, 126.
66 Ertürk uses this phrase specifically for the 'initial phase of phonocentrist venacularization' of which Midhat was a huge contributor. Ertürk, *Grammatology and Literary Modernity in Turkey*, 13.
67 Ibid., 58.
68 Ibid., 33.
69 Ibid., 44n42.
70 Felski, *The Limits of Critique*, 174.
71 Midhat, *Felatun Bey and Rakım Efendi*, 10–11.
72 Jale Parla, *Babalar ve Oğullar: Tanzimat Romanının Epistemolojik Temelleri* (İstanbul; İletişim Yayınları, 1990), 32.
73 Cheah, *What Is a World?*, 3.
74 Walkowitz, *Cosmopolitan Style*, 13.
75 Ibid.
76 Cheah, *What Is a World?*, 3.
77 Ibid., 6.
78 Midhat, *Felatun Bey and Rakım Efendi*, 31.
79 Ibid., 31–2.

7

Thinking in French and writing in Spanish: Rubén Darío's multilingualism

Carlos F. Grigsby

The story is commonplace in Hispanic literary history: when Spanish-language literature seemed to have stagnated toward the end of the nineteenth century, Rubén Darío shook it out of its slumber and put it back in conversation with the literatures of the West. As Pedro Henríquez Ureña puts it, as a result '[o]f any poem written in Spanish it can be told with certainty whether it was written before or after him'.[1] The conventional narrative goes on to explain that Darío was greatly influenced by French literature, and that through his learning and imitation of its models and forms, he managed to transpose and reinvent them in his own language, forever changing the face of literature in Spanish.

This chapter will show how Darío's relationship to French is more complex. As neither he nor his contemporaries could, we cannot think of Darío's writing in Spanish without considering its imbrication with French syntax and lexicon. This has been discussed by scholars before.[2] Nevertheless, what has often been overlooked is Darío's own ambition to write in French alongside Spanish, as well as his understanding of his Spanish-language writing as – paradoxically – French. Darío also incorporated elements from other languages into his writing, such as Latin, Provençal and Early Modern Spanish, imbuing his poetry with multilingual echoes.[3] What's more, Darío's notion of what he called *el movimiento cosmopolita* (the cosmopolitan movement), which he used to refer to a contemporary world literature of sorts that spanned the literatures of the West and had its literary capital in Paris,[4] shows us how Darío's multilingualism was based on a transnational conception of literature. The Nicaraguan writer sought to include *Modernismo* – the continental literary movement he spearheaded – into that wider *movimiento cosmopolita* by, through his writing, creating a conversation with his French counterparts which both he and his fellow Spanish Americans read and translated fervently thanks to a network of journals, periodicals and magazines that circulated on a continental scale.[5] Since then, Darío's writing has been influential for major Hispanic writers who followed, such as Gabriela Mistral, César Vallejo, Pablo Neruda, Federico García Lorca, among others. In this sense, in the context of world literature, it is telling to regard the history of modern Spanish-language literature as the outcome of a highly charged point of contact with French.

French language in Rubén Darío's writing

Quite literally, Darío wanted to write in French. In an elegiac book called *A. de Gilbert*, written in 1889 for a deceased friend, he writes:

> Oh, cuántas veces en aquel cuarto, en aquellas heladas noches, él y yo, los dos soñadores, unidos por un afecto razonado y hondo, nos entregábamos al mundo de nuestros castillos aéreos! Iríamos á París, seríamos amigos de Armand Silvestre, de Daudet, de Catulle Mendes; le preguntaríamos á éste por qué se deja en la frente un mechón de su rubia cabellera; oiríamos á Renán en la Sorbona y trataríamos de ser asiduos contertulios de madama Adam; y escribiríamos libros franceses! eso sí.[6]

> (Oh, how often in that room, during those cold nights, he and I, two dreamers, brought together by a deep and reasoned affection, would throw ourselves into the world of our aerial castles! We would go to Paris, we would be friends with Armand Silvestre, with Daudet, with Catulle Mendes; we would ask him why he always has a lock of his blonde hair hanging over his forehead; we would listen to Renan at the Sorbonne and we would strive to participate in madame Adam's salon; and we would write French books! that, we would do.)

One year later, after the first edition of *Azul* ... (Azure ...) had sold out, a second edition appeared in Guatemala with added corrections and new writings. It now included Spanish writer Juan Valera's famous letters to Darío from 1888, which had conferred the book and its author some renown at the time. The true novelty, however, lay in that the second edition included three poems written in French, presented under the section 'Echos': 'Chanson Crépusculaire' (Twilight Song), 'A Mademoiselle' (To Mademoiselle) and 'Pensée' (Thought). Unfortunately, Darío made more than one metrical mistake in the poems, as he recognizes in his autobiography:

> Yo ignoraba cuando los escribí muchas nociones de poética francesa. Entre ellas, pongo por caso, el buen uso de la "e" muda, que, aunque no se pronuncia en la conversación, o es pronunciada escasamente según el sistema de algunos declamadores, cuenta como sílaba para la medida del verso.[7]

> (When I wrote them I ignored many notions of French poetics. Among them, for instance, the correct use of the silent 'e', which, though it is not pronounced in conversation, or is scarcely pronounced depending on the system of some reciters, counts as a syllable for the measurement of verse.)

They were therefore suppressed from subsequent editions. Nevertheless, despite the failure those three poems represented in Darío's endeavour to write in the language of Hugo, in 1896 (about six years later) he would argue against Paul Groussac that 'Azul es un libro parnasiano, y por lo tanto, francés' (Azure is a Parnassian book, and therefore, French), after acknowledging that 'mi sueño era escribir en lengua francesa. Y aún [*sic*] versos cometí en ella que merecen perdón porque no se ha vuelto a repetir' (My dream was to write in French. And I even committed verses in that language which deserve forgiveness for it did not happen again).[8] Clearly, Darío suggests that his mistakes in French verse dissuaded him from further attempts to write in the language.

As a result, he would not publish in French again until 1907, after more than seven years in Paris, when a poem called '«Helda»' came out as part of the collection *El canto errante* (The Wandering Song). Afterwards, he would only do so again seven years later in 1914: the poem 'France-Amérique' (France-America) was published in *Mundial* (Worldwide), the magazine he edited, and was later included in the collection *Canto a la Argentina y otros poemas* (Song for Argentina and Other Poems) of the same year. As Mariano Siskind notes, the poem 'has been utterly ignored by critics of *modernismo*'.[9] The poem is noteworthy because it associates France with translation:

> Marseillaises de bronze et d'or qui vont dans l'air
> Sont pour nos cœurs ardents le chant de l'espérance.
> En entendant du coq gaulois le clairon clair
> On clame : Liberté ! Et nous traduisons : France ![10]

> (Marseillaises of bronze and gold who go through the air
> Are for our ardent hearts the song of hope.
> Listening the clear clarion of the Gallic cock
> There is a shout: Freedom! And we translate: France!)

For Siskind, the use of the term *traduisons* in the poem reveals how French translation is, in Darío's poetics, a condition for aesthetic modernity:

> Of course, Darío is not a French poet, and *Azul* and *Prosas profanas* are not, literally, French books. Their Frenchness results from an operation of translation. If France is immediately modern, in and for itself, in Darío's books of the 1890s ... Latin America is modern *through* France—France as mediation, as the instance that enables a Latin American translation of modern forms, images, and desires. Darío's literature is *Latin Americanly French* ... Darío returned to this idea of French translation as the condition that makes aesthetic modernity possible in Latin America toward the end of his life, after he had made Paris his adopted home, in a poem he wrote in French, 'France-Amérique'.[11]

While much of what Siskind argues is true when it comes to Darío's poetic aims of the 1890s, he over-interprets the term *traduisons*. If we read the whole text, it becomes clear that 'France-Amérique' is an anti-war poem like many others which Darío wrote late in life, around the time the First World War began. Below is the stanza that immediately precedes the one above.

> Il semblerait que tous les démons du passé
> viennent de s'éveiller empoisonnant la terre.
> Si contre nous l'étendard sanglant s'est levé,
> c'est l'étendard hideux de ce tyran: la Guerre;[12]

> (It would seem that all the demons of the past
> have just woken poisoning the earth.
> If against us the bloody flag is raised,
> it is the hideous flag of this tyrant: War)

'Marseillaises de bronze et d'or' in line 13 turns out to be an allusion to the French Revolution, just like the mentions of 'Liberté' (l.16) and 'Fraternité' (l.25). Through its rhetorical flourishes painstakingly set in alexandrines, the poem suggests that the Americas and France join strengths to overcome war. The cry 'France!', which is – according to Darío – how Spanish Americans translate 'Liberté!', refers not to aesthetic but to political freedom granted by the social conquests of the French Revolution. In spite of this, Siskind interprets these lines as an aesthetic commentary on the worldview of *Modernismo*:

> 'On clame: Liberté! Et nous traduisons: France!': we translate France, *for* and *in* Latin America, and we translate liberty as France, and France as liberty. Darío's translational intervention makes France and freedom interchangeable, where freedom is understood as the pillar of the discourse of modernity and, in the case of Latin American *modernismo*, points to the idea of freedom from want and from aesthetic and cultural marginality. This, in turn, makes possible the nontransparent, nonmimetic translation that constitutes the *modernista* aesthetic formation.[13]

However, according to Darío's contemporary, Chilean writer Francisco Contreras, the poem was written to be read on a diplomatic event:

> Rubén Darío compuso estos versos para ser leídos en fiesta de una institución de carácter panamericano: el "Comité France Amérique" y acaso también en la secreta esperanza que el pobre poeta abrigaba todavía de volver a ser diplomático.[14]

> (Rubén Darío composed these verses to have them read at the celebration of a Pan-American institution: the 'France-America Committee' and perhaps in the secret hope, still harboured by the poor poet, of becoming a diplomat again.)

Saavedra Molina explains that the poem was read on May 1914 and was then self-translated into Spanish as 'Oda a la Francia' (Ode to France) and published in the Cuban newspaper *El Fígaro* on 4 October 1914.[15]

Still, it is curious that Darío chose the term *traduisons*. At the very least, it belies Darío's position vis-à-vis French culture and language as a Spanish American immigrant in Paris who must translate the world around him. Furthermore, we can use the term heuristically to think about Darío's relation to French. To go back to Darío's article in reply to Groussac, after having confessed that it was his dream to write in French, he writes that:

> Al penetrar en ciertos secretos de armonía, de matiz, de sugestión, que hay en la lengua de Francia, fué mi pensamiento descubrirlos en el español, o aplicarlos [...] Y he aquí como, pensando en francés y escribiendo en castellano que alabaran por lo castizo académicos de la Española, publiqué el pequeño libro que iniciaría el actual movimiento literario americano.[16]

> (By penetrating into certain secrets of harmony, of nuance, of suggestion, which exist in the tongue of France, it was my notion to discover them in Spanish, or to apply them ... And this is how, thinking in French and writing in a Spanish that would be praised for its purity by scholars of the Royal Academy, I published the small book that would initiate the current literary movement of the Americas.)

It is revealing to look at what Valera famously called Darío's *galicismo mental* (intellectual Gallicism) in the shadow of his failure to write in French;[17] not to regard it as a second-rate solution compared to writing in French proper, but to consider it in terms of literary traditions. When Darío claims that *Azul ...* is a French book, despite not being written in French, more than saying that it is 'Latin Americanly French' as Siskind suggests, Darío seems to position himself within French literary tradition in spite of the language barrier: poetics, such as that of *Symbolisme* or *Parnasse*, take precedence over language and national tradition, whose boundaries become porous in Darío's multilingual poetry. If his ambition was to live in Paris and to write in French, it is because he literally wanted to become a French-language writer; however, he failed, for both cultural and personal reasons.[18] Despite that, and instead, he wrote as if he were part of the tradition of French poetry – but did so in Spanish. That is to say, he wrote poems that engaged with French themes and motives and can be read as a direct response to them. In a letter to Spanish writer Miguel de Unamuno, he writes the following:

> Le confesaré, desde luego, que no me creo escritor *americano*. Esto lo he demostrado en cierto artículo que me vi forzado a escribir cuando Groussac me honró con una crítica. Mejor que yo ha desarrollado el asunto el señor Rodó, profesor de la Universidad de Montevideo. Le envío su trabajo. Mucho menos soy castellano. Yo ¿le confesaré con rubor? no pienso en castellano. Más bien pienso en francés. O mejor, pienso *ideográficamente*; de ahí que mi obra no sea castiza. Hablo de mis libros últimos. Pues los primeros, hasta *Azul*, proceden de innegable cepa española, al menos en la forma.[19]

> (I will admit, certainly, that I do not believe to be an *American* writer. This I have proved in an article I was forced to write when Groussac honoured me with a

critique. Mr. Rodó, professor of the University of Montevideo, has elucidated the matter better than I. I send you his work. Even less am I Castilian. I – shall I say so without blushing? – do not think in Castilian. Rather, I think in French. Or better yet, I think *ideographically*; hence my work is not pure. I speak of my latest books. For the early ones, until *Azure*, come from undeniable Spanish roots, at least as regards form.)

The letter is remarkable despite the affectation. Darío is masquerading as someone who literally does not think in Spanish but in French – and, what's more, says he does so ideographically, echoing Valera's claim regarding his style as the result of a *galicismo mental*. The somewhat theatrical claim can be construed as referring to Darío's literary intent to transpose French forms and motifs into Spanish, hence 'ideographically'. On the other hand, it is worth noting that this francophone guise was part of Darío's self-fictionalization as the hero of *Modernismo*, a literary persona he began to cultivate in the 1890s and which he developed throughout the Spanish-language iterations of the debates around *Décadence* and *Symbolisme* that were taking place in world literature at the turn of the century. This persona changed over time. Later in his life, particularly from 1905 onwards, Darío wrote of himself as a 'hijo de América … nieto de España' (son of America … grandson of Spain).[20] In other words, he was not so French anymore, and fervently Hispanic instead. This was possibly a result of his failure to enter the literary milieu of Paris, which contrasted sharply with the admiration he roused, and the stimulating intellectual exchanges he found, in Spain. I have discussed Darío's *modernista* campaign in Paris elsewhere, in relation to its effort in becoming part of *el movimiento cosmopolita*.[21] Nevertheless, it is worth pointing out that the Nicaraguan's understanding of literature as multilingual and transnational was the corollary of his notion of *patria* [homeland]:

> La patria no se define por los límites naturales; no se define por la lengua, por la raza; no tiene que ver casi con la geografía, la lingüística, la etnografía. La patria se constituye por el libre y mutuo consentimiento de hombres que quieren vivir bajo un régimen político y social que han libremente creado ó adoptado.[22]

> (One's homeland is not defined by natural limits; it is not defined by language, by race; it barely has anything to do with geography, linguistics, ethnography. A homeland is constituted by the free and mutual consent of men who wish to live under a political and social regime which they have freely created or adopted.)

The passage explains why Darío considers *Azul …*, despite being a text written predominantly in Spanish, a French book: because its author has chosen French literature as its tradition. Darío probably held this view because of his desire to become a citizen of Paris in spite of his uncertain command of French – hence, language could not be the centre of a writer's home, otherwise he would have no claim to life in the *Ville Lumière*. In doing so, however, Darío suggests that a writer's home is not even fixed in the language they choose, for they can always write within a tradition that is different from it. This radical understanding of a writer's relation to nationality and language in Darío has often been overlooked. At best his writing has been read as that of a cosmopolitan pan-Hispanic writer. However, revising George Steiner's words, unhoused poets like Darío are not only wanderers across languages, but across traditions.[23]

As with so many of Darío's political and literary views, José Martí is a key influence for his insight into the possibilities of multilingualism. When Martí wrote about the Irish-Colombian poet Diego Fallon (1882), he advised his fellow Spanish Americans as follows:

> Para hablar bien nuestra lengua, no hay como conocer otras: el contraste nos enamora de la nuestra; y el conocimiento nos habilita para tomar de las ajenas lo que a la nuestra le haga falta, y curarnos de los defectos que ella tenga y en los demás estén curados.[24]

> (To speak ours well, there is nothing like knowing other languages: the contrast makes us fall in love with our tongue; and the knowledge enables us to take from the other ones what is missing in our own, curing us from whatever defects it may have and which in others are cured.)

There is a familiar ring of Martí's words in Darío's 'Historia de mis libros':

> Y yo, que me sabía de memoria el Diccionario de galicismos de Baralt, comprendí que no sólo el galicismo oportuno sino ciertas particularidades de otros idiomas, son utilísimos y de una incomparable eficacia en un apropiado trasplante.[25]

> (And I, who knew Baralt's Dictionary of Gallicisms by heart, understood that not just a fitting Gallicism, but also certain particularities from other languages, can be extremely useful and of an incomparable efficacy in an adequate transposition.)

However, even if we try to countenance Darío's assertion regarding Baralt's dictionary, it is clear that no one could have committed its pages to memory. Not only is it a colossal task, but a futile one from a literary point of view – it includes vast amounts of useless information. On the other hand, the preface *is* interesting: Baralt warns the reader that an excessive use of Gallicisms in Spanish would lead to a new language, altogether different from both Spanish and French:

> Si continúan como hasta hoy y se van extendiendo estas y otras varias especies de galicismos; si seguimos tomando del francés palabras de buen ó mal sonido, y olvidamos por ellas las de uso corriente; si á las voces castellanas que conservemos se aplica significación que nunca tuvieron; y al formar la oración gramatical y el período distribuimos y enlazamos los términos de otra manera que la usual hasta ahora; el feliz resultado de tantas y tan graves innovaciones habrá de ser la formación de un idioma nuevo.[26]

(If they go on as they have until today, and these and other various sorts of Gallicisms are spread widely; if we go on taking from the French words that sound good or bad, forgetting those of common use; if, to the Castilian terms we preserve, we apply meanings they never possessed; and by forming a grammatical sentence and its period we distribute and link the terms together in a way that is different from the usual; the happy result of such and many grave innovations shall be the formation of a new language.)

From *Azul* ... (1888) onwards, that is precisely what Darío would do: write in Baralt's fearful new Spanish – a Spanish ridden with French. It is impossible to know whether Darío fabricated the claim above; however, if he did not, it does not seem far-fetched to posit that Darío may have read Baralt's preface motivated by his admiration for French writers; heeding Martí's words, he might have inverted the negativity of its warning to make it a positive claim of how to come to a new style. As Darío knew well, the Spanish language needed a change; he would find that change in French.

While Darío gave up on writing in the language of Hugo, he found a way of writing in Spanish that used French calques and borrowings, thereby offering what would comprise a renovation of Spanish-language literature. As a result, he imbued Spanish with echoes of French; his writing became, in a sense, multilingual.

Darío's poetry as a conversation with France

Since Darío's writing is multilingual, it is also multilayered insofar as it offers at least two experiences of reading. On the one hand, we can imagine the experience of a Spanish-language reader at the turn of the century. In Darío's verse Spanish must have appeared rarefied; its rules were bent and its vocabulary made strange. On the other hand, if that reader also had French, certain words, tropes, metres and themes belonging to French language and literature would come through Darío's Spanish as echoes at once familiar and new. Within the wider context of Western literature, this corresponds to two distinct ways of representing literary history. In the former case, when Darío's oeuvre is read only from the locus of Spanish-language literary tradition, it seems to emerge as a ground-breaking body of work that renewed the literature of the language. In the latter, when the reader goes beyond national and linguistic boundaries, reading the Nicaraguan's oeuvre with French literary tradition in mind, a continuity across languages and traditions comes to the fore – as mentioned earlier, what Darío called el *movimiento cosmopolita* (The Cosmopolitan Movement), or in other words international *Symbolisme*, which at the time was spreading across France, England, Italy, Portugal, Spain and Spanish America.[27] Traditionally, Darío's oeuvre has mostly been read and represented only according to the former, even when recognizing its 'debts' to and 'influences' from French literature. As has been made clear throughout this chapter, however, Darío aimed at achieving the latter as much as he did the former. The Peruvian critic Julio Ortega comments on this blind spot present in much Darío scholarship:

Si bien Rubén Darío, como él mismo explica, se documentaba para escribir algunos poemas, el rastreo de sus fuentes ha ofrecido siempre una versión limitada de su proceso de composición. El problema de cómo leer esas fuentes, a la luz del poema, no está resuelto, ni siquiera bien planteado, y cada vez que la crítica académica ha creído demostrar las referencias de un poema suyo, ha reincidido en la simplificación y hasta en cierta pobreza conceptual... De modo que se puede adelantar que esa interacción con las fuentes es otro tejido de la resonancia del poema en tanto objeto de arte, figura artística y precipitado asociativo que lo convierte en texto articulado entre las artes.[28]

(Though Rubén Darío, as he himself explains, documented himself to write certain poems, the tracing of his sources has always offered a limited version of his process of composition. The problem of how to read those sources, in light of the poem, has not been solved, not even framed well; and every time scholars have thought they had proved the references that are present in one of his poems, they have fallen into a simplification and even a conceptual crudity of sorts ... Thus we can now say that such interaction with its sources is another layer of resonance of the poem as artwork, artistic figure and associative precipitate which transforms it into a text articulated in the midst of other arts.)

To be sure, the authorities on the subject of Darío's sources and influences – Arturo Marasso, Erwin K. Mapes, among others – study those sources as a means of explicating Darío's originality. Unlike them, I will explore the latter possibility of reading I have just described, by closely reading two poems which illustrate the rich conversation Darío held with his French counterparts.

Before delving into the poems, it is worth remembering Derek Attridge's definition of 'creative reading' as an articulation in words of a response to a text, 'as if the work being read demanded a new work in response'.[29] The poems in which Darío rewrites Théophile Gautier and Théodore de Banville seem to fall within this kind of response – spurred, no doubt, by the fact that nothing quite like what these writers were doing in French existed in Spanish. The following poems appear to emerge like responses to the French literature of Darío's time. These poems are rewritings, rejoinders, glosses, versions, translations – displaying an engagement with their source that is reminiscent of what was formerly understood as *imitatio*.[30] To a certain degree, one could argue that this is a trait that all poets show in their work. As the poet and critic Craig Morgan Teicher explains:

> Poetry is a conversation, an extended one, occupying, perhaps, the span of an entire life. Poets converse, first and foremost, with their language [...] and with the idea of language itself.[31]

For a poet like Darío, poetry was also a conversation with other languages. Teicher elaborates on how considering the conversational dimension of poetry might bear on how we conceive of literary influence:

> We tend to define poetic influence in terms of how a later poet is shaped by an earlier one. This definition perhaps oversimplifies what poetic influence is: the internalization and adaptation of other poets' work into a new style. Poetry is a reader's art: poets make poems in response to the poems they've read.... Poems take place in many kinds of conversations, whether with other poems and poets, with an imagined reader, with the culture at large, or with the poet's own previous, current, or future selves.... Poetic influence occurs as an aspect of these conversations, a volleying between poets living and dead.[32]

Teicher's musings on poetry as a reader's art are fitting for a reading of Darío's poems.

I will look at two poems from *Prosas profanas*. Although the texts of *Azul...* include some of the elements I mentioned as part of this second possibility of reading Darío's oeuvre, they do so to a lesser degree. Also, in *Prosas profanas* there is a clear change with regard to Darío's Spanish. Though the language of *Azul...* is already scattered with French words (*esmaragdin* appears as *esmaradigna* in 'El rey burgués' (The Bourgeois King); *farandole* as *farandola* in 'El velo de la reina Mab' (The Veil of Queen Mab); *chartreuse* in 'La ninfa' (The Nymph); and so forth) for the most part, the vocabulary employed was already part of Spanish.[33] By contrast, a survey of *Prosas profanas* shows at least thirty-eight borrowings from the French. This does not include all the Greek words that Darío clearly borrowed from Parnassian diction (Leconte de Lisle, one of the most influential poets of *Parnasse*, was a prolific translator of Classical Greek literature). Nor does it include the many words typical of the diction of *Romantisme* (French Romanticism), which the Nicaraguan most likely came to by way of Victor Hugo. Any reader of Darío would naturally recognize *d'or, sonore, vague, brume, harmonie, lyre, soupir, l'azur, l'aube,* and so forth, as recognizable *modernista* terms. While in *Azul...* Darío is writing from within the French tradition, his ambition seems to be to write in both languages. In *Prosas profanas*, however, he has given up for the time being on the dream of writing in French, and in turn has radically transposed elements of French language and literature into the Spanish. One language is brushed against another.

'Canción de carnaval' (Carnival Song) is a poem that is both a translation and a rewriting of another poem by Banville called 'Mascarades', from the collection *Odes funambulesques* (Funambulist Odes) (1857). The title itself is telling: 'Mascarades' (Masquerades) is a poem about the famous carnival of Paris, a fact which sheds light on Darío's own choice of title: 'Canción de carnaval'. What the majority of critics have failed to recognize is that Banville's poem is not merely a source or an influence for the Nicaraguan: it is a 'hegemonic' text that Darío, from the 'periphery', creatively reads, translates and rewrites. The poem's epigraph is a line from 'Mascarades'; by citing Banville, the author is pointing the reader to the French text. Further, in 'Historia de mis libros' Darío acknowledges that 'La Canción de Carnaval es también a lo Banville, una oda funambulesca, de sabor argentino, bonaerense' (The Carnival Song is also Banville-style, a funambulist ode with a Buenos Aires, Argentine flavour).[34] Thus it is a poem that is expected to be read in tandem with Banville. Darío freely translates many passages of Banville's poem, rewriting it with added Argentine elements and, interestingly, with Banvillesque elements that transcend 'Mascarades' and are found elsewhere in Banville's poetry. Below is a parallel comparison of the corresponding fragments:

Musa, la *máscara* apresta,	Le *Carnaval* s'amuse !
ensaya un aire *jovial*	Viens le chanter, ma *Muse*,
y goza y ríe en la fiesta	Sur un rhythme *gaillard*
del *carnava*l.	Du bon Ronsard !
Ríe en la danza que gira,	Chante ton dithyrambe
muestra la *pierna rosada*,	En laissant voir ta *jambe*
y suene, como una lira,	Et ton sein arrosé
tu carcajada.	D'un feu *rosé*.
Mueve tu espléndido *torso*	Mets ta *ceinture*, et *plaque*
por las calles pintorescas	*Sur le velours* d'un claque
y juega y *adorna* el corso	Les rubans querelleurs
con rosas frescas.³⁵	*Jonchés de fleurs*!³⁶
(*Muse*, ready your *mask*,	(The *Carnival* is at play!
play a *jovial* song	Come sing along, my *Muse*,
and enjoy and laugh in the feast	With a *spicy* rhythm
of the *carnival*.	From old Ronsard!
Laugh in the twirling dance,	Sing your dithyramb
show your *rosy leg*	While you show your *leg*
and may it sound, like a lyre,	And your fêted breast
your guffaw.	Of a *rosy fire*
Move your splendid *torso*	Put your *hip* into it, and *press*
through colourful streets	*On the velvet* with a smack
and play and *adorn* the parade	The feisty ribbons
with fresh roses)	*Strewn with flowers*!)

I have emphasized the most visible parallelisms between the poems. In the first stanza, both speakers refer to a muse, inviting her to enjoy the carnival each poem celebrates. Banville's *Muse* corresponds to Darío's *Musa*; *Carnaval* to *carnaval*; *gaillard* to *jovial* – and in the first line, Darío inserts the word of Banville's original title, *máscara*. In the other stanzas Darío displaces the description he translates; instead of *feu rosé* he opts for *pierna rosada*; in the third he writes *torso* in lieu of *ceinture* and *adornar* instead of *joncher*. Darío also 'translates' the metre: the Spanish lines are longer, but he keeps the abridged fourth line of each stanza to preserve the playful rhythm of Banville's *Odes funambulesques*. He also changes the rhyme scheme: while Banville's is AABB, Darío opts for ABAB.

As mentioned earlier, Darío also includes characters found in other poems by Banville: *Pierrot*, *Polchinelle* (which Darío translates as *Pulchinela*), *Colombine* (*Colombina*), *Arlequin* (*Arlequín*) and *Le Clown* (*un clown*). Mapes has imaginatively described this as the result of Darío not finding Banville's poem Banvillesque enough for his own version.[37] However, Mapes plainly considers it 'une imitation des *Mascarades*' (an imitation of *Mascarades*), in which Darío 'reproduit admirablement l'impression donnée par le poème de Banville, mais comme nous l'avons dit, c'est le Banville de tous les poèmes de carnaval qu'il imite, plutôt que les *Mascarades* seules' (admirably reproduces the impression given by Banville's poem, but as we said earlier, here it is the Banville from all the carnival poems whom he imitates, rather than only *Mascarades*).[38] Arturo Marasso also reads it as an imitation:

> Darío imita así los nombres de poetas y contemporáneos, de cosas parisienses, que brotan a cada instante de la pluma del ilustre rimador francés, a quien tanto admira.[39]

> (Darío imitates thus the names of poets and contemporaries, of Parisian matters, which spring at every moment from the pen of the illustrious French writer, whom he so admires.)

What leads both Mapes and Marasso to read the poem as an imitation is their disregard of the Argentine elements that Darío includes in his version of Banville. For instance, in the fourth stanza we find:

> Y que en tu boca risueña
> que se une al alegre coro,
> deje la abeja porteña
>   su miel de oro.

> (And may, upon your smiling lips
> which join the happy chorus,
> the porteño bee leave
>   its golden honey.)

Later on, in the tenth and twelfth stanzas:

> Sé lírica y sé bizarra
> con la cítara sé griega;
> o gaucha, con la guitarra
>   de Santos Vega.

> (Be lyrical and be daring
> with a zither be Greek;
> or gaucha, with the guitar
>   of Santos Vega.)

De perlas riega un tesoro
de Andrade en el regio nido,
y en la hopalanda de Guido,
        polvo de oro.[40]

(Drop pearls upon the treasure
of Andrade in the splendid nest,
and upon Guido's houppelande,
        golden powder.)

Darío includes, on the one hand, *lo porteño*; on the other, he inserts three allusions that change the meaning of the poem. The allusion to 'la guitarra / de Santos Vega' refers to the poem 'Santos Vega' by Rafael Obligado from 1885. The allusion to Andrade refers to the poet Olegario Víctor Andrade, whereas Guido is the poet Carlos Guido y Spano. All three poets are important figures of Argentine Romanticism. In that sense, Darío's Banvillesque muse will not only be *griega* but *gaucha*, as the mythical Santos Vega was, and will embellish the works of Andrade and Guido with *perlas* and *polvo de oro*. Contrary to what Mapes and Marasso claim, Darío is not merely imitating Banville. The bawdy gaiety of the Frenchman's frivolous muse, which merely celebrates France as opposed to other nations, becomes in the hands of Darío the muse of new poetry, which carries the accents of French verse in order to improve upon its Argentine predecessors. In other words, this clearly is not merely imitation; Darío is translating and rewriting Banville in order to produce new meaning. He does so overtly, pointing the reader to the elements from the French text that are used in his own, so as to have his poem read as one which is in conversation with its French counterpart. In the poem we can also hear echoes of Banville's collection *Odes funambulesques*: many of its most colourful characters parade before our eyes. However, this is a Spanish-speaking Banville that does not celebrate the exquisiteness of French culture; it speaks of Argentine literature to come.

We find a second case of rewriting in the poem 'Bouquet'. Unlike 'Canción de carnaval', here Darío only rewrites another poem conceptually. The title itself is a Gallicism. As with the previous poem, in the first stanza Darío points the reader to the author whose writing he will cast anew:

Un poeta egregio del país de Francia
que con versos áureos alabó el amor
formó un ramo harmónico, lleno de elegancia,
en su *Sinfonía en Blanco Mayor*.[41]

(An eminent poet from the country of France
who with golden verses praised love
formed a harmonious bouquet, full of elegance,
in his *Symphony on White Major*.)

He is referring to Théophile Gautier, the title of whose poem 'Symphonie en blanc majeur' he translates for the reader. Commenting on Darío's use of intertextuality in this poem, Alberto Julián Pérez notes that:

> En el poema "Bouquet" Darío ... informa al lector sobre la "escuela" poética de su texto, y crea un "entretejido" intertextual con la tradición francesa reivindicada por los parnasianos ... Vemos que en "Bouquet" Darío está tratando el paratexto modelador como un texto codificable, susceptible de ser continuado.[42]

> (In the poem 'Bouquet' Darío ... informs the reader about the poetic 'school' of his text, and creates an intertextual 'interweaving' with the French tradition reclaimed by the Parnassians ... We see that in 'Bouquet' Darío is using the modelling paratexts as a codifiable text, susceptible of being continued.)

Though the intertextual interweaving is undeniable, there is more to it than meets the eye. The poem continues as follows:

> Yo por ti formara, Blanca deliciosa,
> el regalo lírico de un blanco bouquet,
> con la blanca estrella, con la blanca rosa
> que en los bellos parques del azul se ve.[43]

> (For you I would form, delicious White woman,
> the lyrical gift of a white bouquet,
> with the white star, the white rose
> that in the beautiful parks of blueness one sees.)

As Julián Pérez notes, Darío establishes a continuity: Gautier wrote *un ramo harmónico* and he in turn will write *un blanco bouquet*. The reader is made complicit in his witnessing of this volleying between one poet and the other. However, significant differences separate the two. In his poem, Gautier explores the semantic possibilities of the colour white, seemingly covering its whole connotative spectrum. From:

> De ces femmes il en est une,
> Qui chez nous descend quelquefois,
> Blanche comme le clair de lune
> Sur les glaciers dans les cieux froids

> (Of these women she is one,
> Who descend among us at times,
> White like the moonlight
> Over the glaciers of cold skies)

to:

> Sphinx enterré par l'avalanche,
> Gardien des glaciers étoilés,
> Et qui, sous sa poitrine blanche,
> Cache de blancs secrets gelés?⁴⁴

> (Sphinx buried by the avalanche,
> Guardian of starry glaciers,
> And who, under her white chest,
> Hides white frozen secrets?)

He does so not only through the repetition of the word *blanc*, but by extending it through metaphors that entail glaciers, snow, camellias, boreal regions, swans, satin, among other indicators of whiteness. It is a virtuosic display of poetic skill. Also, he uses those metaphors to describe a mythical *femme-cygne* (woman-swan) from *les contes du Nord* (tales from the North).⁴⁵ By contrast, Darío's poem is simpler, as it seems to use repetition and alliteration of a single word, namely 'blanca', as the generative force of the poem. Also, though the echoes of 'Symphonie en blanc majeur' can be heard in 'Bouquet', Darío's poem is notably less rich in metaphors. However, despite the appearance of flippancy, he takes intertextuality a step further: he does not merely create poetic continuity between one poem and another, as Pérez suggests, but answers to Gautier's last stanza with a rejoinder in his own poem. Gautier's poem ends with the following lines:

> Sous la glace où calme il repose,
> Oh! qui pourra fonder ce cœur!
> *Oh! qui pourra mettre un ton rose*
> *Dans cette implacable blancheur!*⁴⁶

> (Under the ice where calmly it rests,
> Oh! who could melt this heart!
> *Oh! who could strike a rose tone*
> *Upon this ruthless whiteness.*)

To which Darío writes:

> Yo, al enviarte versos, de mi vida arranco
> la flor que te ofrezco, blanco serafín.
> *¡Mira cómo mancha tu corpiño blanco*
> *la más roja rosa que hay en mi jardín!*⁴⁷

> (I, in sending you verses, tear from my life
> this flower which I offer you, white seraphim.

Look how I stain your white bodice
with the reddest rose in my garden!)

I have emphasized the last two lines of each stanza to foreground Darío's ingenious rewriting of Gautier. Clearly, only the multilingual reader who has access to both texts in their original language can be complicit in Darío's mischievous turn: while Gautier presents the whiteness of his *femme-cygne* as immaculate and unattainable for its mythic quality, rhetorically asking who could change its cold whiteness to a mellow *rose*, Darío claims that he will stain the immaculate white with his reddest *rose* – a symbol of sensuality, voluptuousness and desire. As with 'Canción de carnaval', the term 'imitation' falls short in describing what takes place between the two texts. Darío clearly writes a less ambitious poem, taking only what most interests him from Gautier: in this case, the rhythmic qualities of repetition more than its imagistic possibilities. However, after pointing the reader to the French text, so as to show how the poem is meant to be read, Darío inserts a rejoinder to Gautier in the ending of his poem.

As the analysis of these poems shows, there is ample ground for new and productive readings of the *modernista*'s work which go beyond monolingual and national categories, demanding us to re-evaluate our notions of literary influence and imitation in the process. Writers like Darío bridge gaps between literary traditions by making their languages mesh; thereof multilingualism arises as both the process and the result of the conversation of world literature. To be sure, as Darío's work proves, a writer is not bound to the language in which they write, nor to the nation in which they were born.

Notes

1. Pedro Henríquez Ureña, *Literary Currents of Hispanic America* (Cambridge, MA: Harvard University Press, 1945), 169.
2. See for example Erwin Mapes, *L'influence française dans l'œuvre de Rubén Darío* (Paris: H. Champion, 1925); and Juan López-Morillas, 'El "Azul" de Rubén Darío: ¿Galicismo mental o lingüístico?', *Revista Hispánica Moderna* 10 1/2 (1943): 9–14.
3. I discuss his use of these languages in detail in my doctoral thesis. See Carlos F. Grigsby, 'Rediscovering Rubén Darío through Translation', PhD diss. (University of Oxford, 2019).
4. See for example Rubén Darío, 'Las letras hispanoamericanas en París', in *La caravana pasa libro tercero*, ed. Günter Schmigalle (Berlin: Edition Tranvía, 2000): 69–104.
5. Gerard Aching, 'The Temporalities of Modernity in Spanish American Modernismo: Darío's Bourgeois King', in *The Oxford Handbook of Global Modernisms* (Oxford: Oxford University Press, 2012): 109–29, 115.
6. Rubén Darío, *Obras completas*, vol. II (Madrid: A. Aguado, 1950), 34. All literal renderings henceforth are my own.
7. Rubén Darío, *Obras completas*, vol. I (Madrid: A. Aguado, 1950), 98.
8. Rubén Darío, *Escritos inéditos de Rubén Darío*, ed. Erwin Mapes (New York: Instituto de las Españas en los Estados Unidos, 1938), 121.

9   Mariano Siskind, *Cosmopolitan Desires: Global Modernity and World Literature in Latin America* (Evanston, Illinois: Northwestern University Press, 2014), 214.
10 Rubén Darío, *Poesía*, ed. Ernesto Mejía Sánchez (Caracas: Biblioteca Ayacucho, 1977), 419, lines 13–16.
11 Siskind, *Cosmopolitan Desires*, 214.
12 Darío, *Poesía*, 419, lines 9–12.
13 Siskind, *Cosmopolitan Desires*, 216.
14 Francisco Contreras, *Rubén Darío: su vida y su obra* (Barcelona: Agencia mundial de librería, 1930), 238.
15 Julio Saavedra Molina, 'Poesías y prosas raras de Rubén Darío compiladas y anotadas', *Anales de la Universidad de Chile* 29–30 (1938): 96–197 (135).
16 Darío, *Escritos inéditos de Rubén Darío*, 121.
17 Rubén Darío, *Azul … Cantos de vida y esperanza* (Madrid: Cátedra, 2000), 122.
18 See Carlos F. Grigsby, 'El fracaso de París: Rubén Darío's Modernista Campaign in France', *MLR* 114.4 (October 2019): 614–33.
19 Quoted in Jorge Eduardo Arellano, *Azul … de Rubén Darío: Nuevas perspectivas* (Washington, DC: Organización de los Estados Americanos, 1993), 106.
20 Darío, *Poesía*, 263.
21 See Note 17.
22 Rubén Darío, *La caravana pasa libro tercero*, ed. Günther Schmigalle (Berlin: Ediciones tranvía, 2000), 52–3.
23 George Steiner, *Extraterritorial: Papers on Literature and the Language Revolution* (London: Faber and Faber, 1972), 11.
24 José Martí, *Obras Completas: Edición Crítica, vol. 13, 1881–1882* (La Habana: Centro de Estudios Martianos, 2010), 90.
25 Darío, *Obras completas I*, 196.
26 Rafael María Baralt, *Diccionario de galicismos, ó sea de las voces, locuciones y frases de la lengua francesca que se han introducido en el habla castellana moderna* (Madrid: Imprenta Nacional, 1855), x.
27 For an overview written by Darío on the international outlook of *Symbolisme*, see Rubén Darío, 'Al Dr. Max Nordau', *Crónicas desconocidas 1901–1906*, ed. Günter Schmigalle (Managua: Academia Nicaragüense de la lengua, 2006), 241–53.
28 Julio Ortega, *Rubén Darío* (Barcelona: Omega Ediciones, 2003), 167.
29 Derek Attridge, *The Singularity of Literature* (London: Routledge, 2004), 92.
30 I am thinking here of *imitatio* as it was understood by Horace and Seneca, and later theorized by Quintilian and Dionysius of Halicarnassus. For an indepth treatment of the subject see David West and Tony Woodman, eds., *Creative imitation and Latin literature* (Cambridge: Cambridge University Press, 1979).
31 Craig Morgan Teicher, *We Begin in Gladness: How Poets Progress* (Minneapolis: Graywolf Press, 2018), 4.
32 Ibid., 91–2.
33 Whereas the Gallicisms of *Azul …* are mostly syntactic and, as it were, stylistic, in the Spanish of *Prosas* the lexicon is ridden with Gallicisms. For a detailed discussion of the former, see Mapes, *L'influence francaise*, 39–58, and López-Morillas, 'El "Azul"'.
34 Darío, *Obras Completas I*, 208.
35 Rubén Darío, *Prosas profanas* (Madrid: Alianza Editorial, 1992), 58–61, lines 1–4, 5–8, 41–4.

36 Théodore de Banville, *Odes funambulesques* (Paris: A. Lemerre, 1874), 35–7, lines 1–4, 9–12, 41–4.
37 Mapes, *L'influence francaise*, 70.
38 Ibid., 70–1.
39 Arturo Marasso, *Rubén Darío y su creación poética* (Buenos Aires: Kapelusz, 1954), 59.
40 Darío, *Prosas profanas*, 58–61, lines 13–16, 37–40, 45–8.
41 Ibid., 64, lines 1–4.
42 Alberto Julián Pérez, *La poética de Rubén Darío: Crisis post-romántica y modelos literarios modernistas* (Madrid: Orígenes, 1992), 156–7.
43 Darío, *Prosas profanas*, 64, lines 5–8.
44 Théophile Gautier, *Émaux et camées* (Paris: G. Charpentier, 1874), 33–7, lines 9–12, 68–71.
45 Ibid., 32, lines 1–4.
46 Ibid., 37, lines 69–72; emphasis added.
47 Darío, *Prosas profanas*, 65, lines 17–20; emphasis added.

8

Multilingual maelström: Re-reading Primo Levi's 'Canto of Ulysses'

Dominique Jullien

Ulysses ... must not forget the Odyssey.

(Calvino)[1]

The figure of Ulysses and the Dantean Canto at the centre of *If This Is A Man* have been analysed extensively in terms of the memoir's conflicted relation to humanist values. The Babelian curse of the Lager has also been the focus of much critical attention. This essay attempts to connect them: to interface the humanist dilemma embodied by the crucial (but also problematic) Ulysses self-image[2] with the linguistic mix displayed in Levi's chapter, where language switching is pervasive and broken bits of German, French, Polish, Italian, Hungarian float along the classic Odyssean narrative. The essay also points to an overlooked yet important intertext, which provides a bridge from the Auschwitz testimonial to the Odyssean trope of shipwreck and survival: Edgar A. Poe's story 'A Descent into the Maelström' where the sailor's escape from the vortex-shaped abyss is attributable to intellect and ingenuity. The chapter's central shipwreck trope seems relevant as a traditional site for teleological doubt, while linguistic plurality appears connected to two major diverging paradigms: on the one hand, the defeat of human intelligence and agency by the biblical forces of linguistic confusion and the anti-Providential camp narrative; on the other hand, a post-Holocaust, anti-totalitarian reshaping of the traditional humanist bond between classic and audience in the context of broken languages, damaged memory and fallible transmission protocols. This essay revisits the famous 'Canto of Ulysses' (together with *The Drowned and the Saved* which looks back at *If This Is A Man* forty years later, forming with it a 'macrotext')[3] in the framework of a discussion of multilingualism, where the intermingling of languages is not simply a reflection of the Lager reality but signals the possibility of transforming that violent heterogeneity into a creative rethinking of literary agency.

The Babel trope: The multilingual curse

The multilingual Lager experience is an indispensable starting point. Linguistic confusion is the first form of violence the prisoners encounter.

> La confusione delle lingue è una componente fondamentale del modo di vivere di quaggiú; si è circondati da une perpetua Babele, in cui tutti urlano ordini e minacce in lingue mai prima udite, e guai a chi non aferra a volo.[4]

> (The confusion of languages is a fundamental component of the way of life here: one is surrounded by a perpetual Babel, in which everyone shouts orders and threats in languages never heard before, and you're in trouble if you fail to grasp the meaning.)[5]

Throughout Levi's writings, Auschwitz is obsessively described as a Babel; its tower built by slave labour is known to the inmates as the Babelturm:

> L'odio li ha cementati; l'odio e la discordia, come la Torre di Babele, e cosí noi la chiamamo: *Babelturm, Bobelturm*.[6]

> (Its bricks ... were cemented by hate, hate and discord, like the Tower of Babel; and that is what we call it: *Babelturm, Bobelturm*.)[7]

Because the men thrown together have a multiplicity of vernaculars, a hideous lingua franca has developed out of necessity.[8] Against this background, the imperial language, German, is dominant in absolute terms. Not only is it the language spoken by the authorities, but knowledge of it is directly and brutally linked to the men's chances of surviving. In the later book *The Drowned and the Saved*, Levi is harshly explicit about this: 'Il sapere o no il tedesco era uno spartiacque'[9] (Knowledge of German was a dividing line);[10] to the point where

> La maggior parte dei prigionieri che non conoscevano il tedesco, quindi quasi tutti gli italiani, sono morti nei primi dieci-quindici giorni dal loro arrivo.[11]

> (Most of the prisoners who did not know German – almost all the Italians, in other words – died within the first ten to fifteen days of their arrival.)[12]

This dominance is clear in the case of Jean Samuel (the Pikolo of the 'Canto of Ulysses' chapter), who, as an Alsatian native, is bilingual in French and German and as such has secured a position of prominence in the group, and of Primo Levi himself, who demonstrates his competence in two useful skills, chemistry and German, in the preceding chapter, 'Chemistry examination'. (That German is the language of the Nazis as well as the language of science is for the scientist Primo Levi one of the many linguistic ambiguities of the story.) Conversely, in *The Drowned and the Saved*, Levi recalls:

In questo Lager, ancora piú mistilingue di Auschwitz, il nerbo di gomma si chiamava 'der Dolmetscher', l'interprete: quello che si faceva capire di tutti.[13]

(At the Mauthausen camp, which was even more multilingual than Auschwitz, the rubber whip was called *der Dolmetscher*, the interpreter: the thing that could make itself understood by everyone.)[14]

At the other end of the multilingual spectrum, in *The Truce*, Levi introduces the poignant figure of three-year old Hurbinek, 'un figlio della morte, un figlio di Auschwitz'[15] (a child of death, a child of Auschwitz),[16] who cannot talk but whose eyes shine with the 'urgenza esplosiva'[17] (explosive urgency)[18] of his need to communicate, to 'rompere la tomba del mutismo'[19] (shatter the tomb of his muteness).[20] Hurbinek dies repeating a single word in a language none of the men can understand: in him the Lager babble reaches its vanishing point.[21]

Multilingualism, and incomprehension, are prominently showcased and performed in Levi's first book, *If This Is A Man*, from the arrival chapter where the newcomers leaving the cattle cars are greeted by the 'barbarici latrati'[22] (barbaric barking)[23] of German guards, to the cacophony of translated terms for bread,[24] or the Canto of Ulysses chapter which opens on the prisoners' multilingual questions to Jean, and closes on the multilingual soup of cabbage and turnips.[25] The chapter itself revolves around questions of translation, from Levi's quixotic attempt to teach Italian to Jean through Dante's poetry, to the bi- or multilingualism of numerous characters (Levi and Jean especially), or the constant translation (or non-translation) moments.[26] Decades later, the 'meta-book',[27] *The Drowned and the Saved*, the last book published before Levi's death, takes the language question to a higher theoretical level, confronting it directly and systematically. The chapter 'Communication' contains a sustained reflection on language as a vital necessity, equal in importance and in fact analogous to food. Scraps of words retrieved from the meaningless noise of the camp's languages are like potato peels scavenged near the kitchen:

L'equivalente mentale del nostro bisogno corporeo di nutrimento', 'una inconsapevole preparazione per il 'dopo', per una improbabile sopravvivenza.[28]

(The mental equivalent of our bodily need for nourishment', 'an unconscious preparation for 'after', for an unlikely survival.)[29]

Levi's insistence on communication as an ethical imperative is rooted in part in his view of language as a vital necessity.[30] The chapter 'Communication' also contains an analysis of the camp language, mediated by a reflection on linguist Victor Klemperer's *Lingua Tertii Imperii* (the language of the Third Reich), a treatise on Nazi Germany's distortion and perversion of the German language.[31] That the German spoken by the guards, 'scheletrico, urlato, costellato di oscenità e di imprecazioni'[32] (skeletal, shouted, sprinkled with obscenities and curses)[33] represents 'une variante particolarmente imbarbarita'[34] (a particularly barbarized variant),[35] not only of Klemperer's LTI, but even more of what Primo Levi, revealingly, calls the 'tedesco di Goethe'[36] (Goethe's German),[37] is also significant in light of the other, rival imperial language at the heart of the chapter: Italian. More specifically, Dante's Italian.

The multilingual paradigm, I suggest, while it is intensely dramatized in 'The Canto of Ulysses', and explicitly and insistently theorized in the later book, *The Drowned and the Saved*, is vitally linked to the question of humanism (what can literature do?) and its incarnation, Ulysses, the multilingual hero of layered intertexts from Homer to Virgil, Dante and Eliot. Through the overdetermined (and much analysed) figure of Ulysses, this essay aims to connect two issues: the question of humanism (survival through literature) and the question of the survival of the 'classic' itself in a new, hostile, multilingual environment.

Struggling to remember Dante's lines, Levi does not forget Ulysses's famous words to his men:

> Considerate la vostra semenza:
> Fatti non foste a viver come bruti,
> Ma per seguire virtute e conoscenza.[38]

> (Consider well the seed that gave you birth:
> You were not made to live your lives as brutes,
> But to be followers of worth and knowledge.)[39]

A majority of earlier readers have tended to favour a humanist interpretation of the chapter, and of Levi's narratives generally, as heroic affirmations of human capacities. An exemplary case is Philip Roth, who, in his conversation published in the *London Review of Books*, celebrated Levi's 'profoundly civilized and spirited response' to Nazi barbarism.[40] Jonathan Druker even talks of a 'critical consensus' in favour of an optimistic reading of Ulysses as an 'unproblematic standard-bearer for Levi's humanism'.[41] The interpretation of the 'Canto of Ulysses' chapter as a triumph of the human spirit's resilience, which aligns the Dantean Ulysses's proud words with Levi's own fleeting experience of transcendence above the misery of the Lager ('Per un momento, ho dimenticato chi sono e dove sono'[42] (or a moment I forget who I am and where I am)),[43] is to some extent supported by Levi himself, in various letters and interviews, as well as in the essay entitled 'The Intellectual in Auschwitz',[44] a rebuttal to fellow writer and survivor Jean Améry's nihilistic assessment of the inadequacy of mind and literature in the camp, *At the Mind's Limits*.[45] If for Améry, 'in the camp the intellect in its totality declared itself to be incompetent',[46] for Levi instead 'il Lager è stata una Università'[47] (the Lager was a university),[48] and furthermore, he maintains,

> A me, la cultura è stata utile; non sempre, a volte forse per vie sotterranee ed impreviste, ma mi ha servito e forse mi ha salvato.[49]

> (Education was useful to me. Not always, and sometimes in subterranean and unexpected ways, but it served me and may have saved me.)[50]

More recently, however, scholars have tended increasingly to question what Nancy Harrowitz characterizes as hagiographic criticism of Levi's account,[51] and Bryan Cheyette as the 'appropriation' of Levi as a kind of secular saint,[52] interrogating Levi's paratexts and the texts themselves as the site of an ongoing tension (or 'restless negotiation')[53] between a humanist narrative and a counter-narrative of doubt. I propose to read 'The Canto of Ulysses' as an exemplary nexus of Levi's 'skeptical humanism',[54] where these tensions play out in connection with the multilingual paradigm.

The multilingual chaos of the Lager, the Babel trope, is closely connected to the particular horror of irrationality. Primo Levi's first encounter with this aspect of life in Auschwitz is narrated in an early episode, in which a thirsty and naïve Levi asking why he is forbidden to drink is told by the Nazi guard that *'hier ist kein warum'*, here there is no why.[55] Auschwitz is a place without reason, and also, as has often been noted, a hell where innocents are punished, instead of sinners as in Dante's *Inferno*.[56] Levi's attempts to use Dante as a 'conceptual grid'[57] to make sense of the incomprehensible world into which he has been thrown are repeatedly curtailed by an unfathomable unreason. The lesson is carved on the bottom of an older prisoner's soup bowl: 'ne pas chercher à comprendre',[58] don't try to understand. The search for a reason is not only bound to fail but dangerous as well, ultimately jeopardizing survival. Thus the Babelian cacophony is both a cause of the incomprehensible nature of Auschwitz and an image of it, trapping the prisoners in a special kind of catch-22 where rationality is doomed and irrationality spells death, turning men into empty shells, *muselmänner* enslaved to the here and now of the moment.

This is why the master trope of the chapter, and to a lesser extent the entire narrative, overlapping with the drowning trope, is the confrontation of intellect against brute force.[59] This is pictured by the conflict between Ulysses and Polyphemus, in particular Ulysses's successful escape from Polyphemus's cavern thanks to his intelligent trick of the sheep.[60] (Aptly, the gigantic Nazi guard in charge of the washhouse is nicknamed Polyphemus).[61] The audacity of the two young men 'che osiamo ragionare di queste cose con le stanghe della zuppa sulle spalle'[62] (who dare to talk about these things with the soup poles on our shoulders),[63] has justifiably been read as a reference to Kant's aphoristic summation of the Enlightenment, *sapere aude*, dare to know,[64] just as the brief voyage across the camp to the soup distribution place can be read as an escape narrative. Poetry, Dante's Canto of Ulysses remembered along the way, makes the prisoners forget Auschwitz for an hour: the trope of the sea voyage is thus escapist on multiple levels, allowing them to substitute temporarily the grim Polish landscape with the Mediterranean sea, 'ferocemente lontane'[65] (cruelly distant)[66] yet brought into the text through an effort of memory. (Significantly, in their postwar correspondence Jean Samuel and Primo Levi referred to themselves as the two Ulysses, and their first reunion, in 1947, was held in the border city of Menton, allowing Jean to see the Mediterranean for the first time, and turning the metaphor into reality.[67])

The intertextual choice of Dante's Canto 26 introduces the sub-theme of the shipwreck. Ignorant of Homer, Dante condemned his Ulysses to perish in a shipwreck with all his crew, seduced into the mad adventure by Ulysses's smooth rhetorical skills; this is the reason why he finds himself in the eighth circle of Dante's hell among the seducers and false counselors. Thus while the sea voyage as a theme, and the attempt at reciting Dante's poem, serve as an escape route away from the camp, the lines meet up at the end, with Primo Levi and Jean's rude awakening from their poetic interlude as they join the starving prisoners in line for the watery soup of cabbages and turnips. Levi's chapter ends, memorably, with Ulysses's account of drowning: 'Infin che'l mar fu sopra noi richiuso'[68] (Until the sea again closed – over us).[69] The episode also brings to mind another scene evoked in *The Drowned and the Saved* where an Italian prisoner who dared to return a blow is drowned in the soup vat.[70] It also loops back onto the metaphor used pervasively in *The Drowned and the Saved*, where Levi remembers his 'compagni italiani ... annegando ad uno ad uno nel mare tempestuoso del non-capire'[71] (Italian comrades ... drowning one by one in the stormy seas of incomprehension).[72]

Several readers have remarked that the shipwreck of Ulysses coincides with the shipwreck of literature against reality, Améry style. The harsh reality of Auschwitz, then, reasserts itself over Dante at the end of the chapter.[73] And yet, I would argue, things are more complex, for, just as the intertexts collide (Levi, unlike Dante, knows Homer's *Odyssey* and the successful *nostos* narrated in the Greek original) the endings of both voyages are incompatible, placing the chapter in a richly ambiguous light. On the one hand the cacophonic multilingualism of the soup ending becomes the symbolic vehicle for the multiple defeats of Primo Levi – the failures of his memory, where scattered fragments of the shipwrecked poem bob up like cabbages and turnips in a soup, the failure of his bizarre pedagogical attempt to teach the Italian language in one hour using broken bits of misremembered *Inferno* and more generally the limits of the mind in Auschwitz, to paraphrase Améry's bitter title. But on the other hand, it is a victory of memory over oblivion, since Levi finally remembers the line he was searching for. Triumphantly flashing its magnificent Italian against the backdrop of the pitiful Lager jargon, this is a cry of victory – and yet one that speaks of utter defeat. The ambiguity of the ending, I would suggest, is the text's way of accomplishing what for the writer is by definition an impossibility: to be both among the drowned and among the saved.[74]

The high seas of Auschwitz: Unpacking the shipwreck trope

The same ambiguity enriches the sustained shipwreck metaphor. On the one hand, it provides a paradigm of helplessness and lack of human agency, the sea being characterized, in Hans Blumenberg's classic study *Shipwreck with Spectator: Paradigm of a Metaphor for Existence* (1979), as an environment 'stubbornly withdraw[n] from the sphere of determinable forces', hence well suited to the camp narrative.[75] But on the other hand, it provides a metaphoric escape route from that same camp narrative, since, as shown earlier, the seafaring images work to replace, however precariously, the Polish landscape with a Mediterranean seascape. Considerable scholarly attention has been devoted to Coleridge's 'Ancient Mariner', from which Levi borrowed the epigraph to *The Drowned and the Saved* ('And till my ghastly tale is told / This heart within me burns'),[76] relating it to the compulsion or duty of the testimonial narrative.[77] By contrast, it would seem that the Poe intertext, the allusion to 'A Descent into the Maelström' (a survivor's tale like Coleridge's poem), has been overlooked. Levi's famous statement in the Preface to *Stories and Essays* (published in 1985, shortly before *The Drowned and the Saved*), reads:

> Sono un uomo normale di buona memoria che è incappato in un vortice, che ne è uscito piú per fortuna che per virtú, e che da allora conserva una certa curiosità per i vortici, grandi e piccoli, metaforici e materiali.[78]

> (I am a normal man with a good memory who fell into a maelström and got out of it more by luck than by virtue, and who from that time on has preserved a certain curiosity about maelströms large and small, metaphorical and actual.)[79]

Indeed 'maelströms metaphorical and actual' are ubiquitous in this story about drowning, from the funnel-shaped Dantean Inferno to the 'cisterna interrata'[80] (underground gas tank)[81] out of which the young heroes emerge, to the whirlpool that sucks Ulysses's ship into the abyss, and even to the vat of watery soup on which the chapter climaxes. Remarkably, Poe's story 'A Descent into the Maelström' also hinges on the redemptive agency of the intellect. The narrator's survival is linked to his use of intelligence in the face of the greater force of the natural cataclysm: even as he is sucked into it, he is able to observe the mechanics of the maelström and devise a strategy to escape, while his brother yields to panic and is drowned.[82] Poe's character's intellectual drive resonates strongly with Primo Levi, possessed by an equal (and equally 'unnatural') desire to understand:

> I have already described the unnatural curiosity which had taken the place of my original terrors. It appeared to grow upon me as I drew nearer and nearer to my dreadful doom. I now began to watch, with a strange interest, the numerous things that floated in our company.[83]

The human 'seed' *(semenza)* is the same, from Ulysses's contagious curiosity for the unknown, to Poe's successful mariner, in whose intelligent mind curiosity displaced fear. Curiosity here is set against ethics (survival 'more by luck than by virtue', as Levi repeatedly claimed) and it reinforces the lesson of Ulysses (triumph of intelligence over brute force) while also negating the providential narrative (the virtuous saved by God.)

Poe's story is therefore a relevant (albeit implicit) element in the larger shipwreck intertext. It is also worth noting that the story's ending resonates strongly with Levi's situation in postwar Italy as an unwelcome witness: Poe's narrator is neither recognized nor believed by his sailing mates upon his return.[84] As a trope, shipwreck is overdetermined (as is the Odyssean trope with which it overlaps in important ways) because it is linked both to the providential paradigm and to the multilingual paradigm. As is critically well established, the shipwreck trope and the genre of shipwreck narratives since antiquity have been a vehicle for providential interpretations of history, and also for their opposite: either shipwrecks are God's way of testing humanity and offer a chance for spiritual rebirth and renewal, or they are evidence that history is not governed by a providential, benevolent hand. For Voltaire, for Byron, for Auden, shipwrecks are rather emblematic of man's struggle in a chaotic, random cosmos.[85] Josiah Blackmore reminds us as well that shipwreck narratives had a political role to play in a tightly controlled imperial discourse, undermining the master narrative by opposing 'a counter-historiographic impulse to the official textual culture of imperialism'.[86] This counter-narrative resistance also applies to the evil empires that loom so large in Primo Levi's text, Hitler's Third Reich and Mussolini's fascist Italy. The multilingual paradigm is also at the heart of the shipwreck trope, since, as critics have noted, ships were the first global environment.[87] Long before *Moby Dick* and its cosmopolitan mix of sailors, the topos of the motley crew – a haphazard community thrown together in a confined, inescapable space – bridged history and poetry, and in literary shipwrecks the topos of the distraught seamen praying to disparate gods in a cacophony of creeds was a staple of the genre.[88] So, in Levi's memoir, the heterogeneous crowd of doomed men imprisoned in the Reich's sinking jail ship.

Another important overlap between shipwreck and Holocaust narratives is the relationship to memorializing, since the disappearance of victims into the abyss, and the resulting lack of funerary markers, create comparable conditions of loss and a similarly precarious position for the testimonial poet whose words assume a compensatory status in the absence of a physical grave. Boris Dunsch reminds us that an entire poetic subgenre developed in Hellenistic antiquity, the *nauagikon*, an epitaph memorializing the empty tomb of a drowning victim.[89]

In *Shipwreck with Spectator: Paradigm of a Metaphor for Existence*, Hans Blumenberg observes that the shipwreck topos is accompanied by that of the spectator. In fact, surviving a shipwreck, the necessary condition for narrating it, turns the survivor into a spectator of the event, forming what he calls a shipwreck-spectator configuration. 'Shipwreck, as seen by a survivor, is the figure of an initial philosophical experience', leading to the bigger question of the limits of humanity.[90] This speaks directly to the foundational conundrum at the heart of Levi's testimonial writing. The safety of the spectator position is at odds with the deathly danger experienced by the survivor, just as the spectator's relative detachment is at odds with the dreadful duty of bearing witness. As he stated with quiet despair in the preface to *The Drowned and the Saved*, Levi was caught between the duty to bear witness and the inability to do so because he had not experienced the worst:

> Si può oggi bene affermare che la storia dei Lager è stata scritta quasi esclusivamente da chi, come io stesso, non ne ha scandagliato il fondo. Chi lo ha fatto non è tornato, oppure la sua capacità di osservazione era paralizzata dalla sofferenza e dall'incomprensione.[91]

> (Today ... we can safely say that the story of the Lagers has been written almost exclusively by people who, like me, did not plumb the depths. The ones who did never returned, or if they did their capacity for observation was paralyzed by pain and incomprehension.)[92]

The survivor must testify, yet cannot testify, so Levi's persona as a testimonial writer is put into crisis.[93]

Humanism and multilingualism

The guiding intuition of this essay is that the multilingual angle can afford us a fruitful insight into the vexed question of Primo Levi's humanism. The initial translational relation between the chapter's two characters – the Italian lesson for the Frenchman Jean, the attempt to translate the Canto of Ulysses and explain the *Inferno* – endeavours to counter the languages of the camp – the dominant language, German, and the monstrous Lager jargon – with another 'imperial' language, Italian, one that is chosen for its cultural value. Italian is also a mother tongue for Primo Levi, of course: significantly, the discussion of Dante is preceded by the memory of the young men's mothers ('Come si somigliano tutte le madri!'[94] (How all mothers resemble one another!)).[95] The affective investment in the linguistic choice carries over into the cultural memories, since memorizing Dante was something that young cultured Italians of Levi's generation did in school.[96]

Against the barbaric Nazi German and the Lager's lingua franca, then, Dante's luminous Italian stands as a bearer of humanist values. However, as Druker and other critics have observed, it is also fraught with ambiguity, since Dante and in particular the Ulysses figure were also claimed by the Mussolini regime. Attaching mental and moral survival to the Canto of Ulysses therefore also requires rescuing the classic from fascist appropriation.[97] Another complication stems from the fact that the clashing languages are hardly monolingual entities themselves: the Lager jargon is a hideous mix of all the languages spoken by both victims and perpetrators (III: 2481), while Dante's Italian, extolled by the fascist propaganda in favour of nationalistic purity, is itself a multilingual composite (on which more later). Moreover, the camp experience reveals to Levi the paradoxical importance of Yiddish, second only to the perpetrators' language, German.[98] Most painfully, in the camp Italian Jews are scorned for their ignorance of it, even unrecognized as Jews.[99] Levi's engagement with Yiddish would later lead him to write the novel *If Not Now, When,* with 'the ambition to be the first (perhaps the only) Italian writer to describe the Yiddish world'.[100] In addition to being a paradoxical index of Jewishness, Yiddish is a source of fascination for Levi because of its multilingual, hybrid nature and history. It is

> intrinsecamente una multilingua ... la lingua di gente errante, spinta dalla storia di Paese in Paese, e di ogni sua stazione porta i segni[101]

> (intrinsically multilingual ... the language of a wandering people, pushed by history from one country to another, and it bears the marks of every station along the way)[102]

Heteroglossia is another distinctive feature of Yiddish speakers: Levi points out the 'forzato multilinguismo'[103] (enforced multilingualism)[104] of Eastern European Jews who, beyond the *mame loshen,* the mother tongue, Yiddish, learned Hebrew and Aramaic, as well as the dominant language of the country.[105]

Therefore, multilingualism is at the centre of a complex linguistic-political nexus: it is tightly bound up with Primo Levi's effort to rescue Dante from fascist culture, and with his becoming 'the Dante for our time' as Risa Sodi put it.[106] Sandra Bermann pointed out that translations of Dante multiplied in the twentieth century, proposing that contemporary translators were attracted in particular to the multilingual qualities of Dante's poem. Primo Levi's chapter (where Canto 26 is translated, however poorly, into French, against a Babelian backdrop) can be seen as an example of this highly multilingual Dante that fascinated twentieth-century translators. Moreover, Dante himself, as Bermann emphasized, was a determined early advocate of multilingualism: he championed vernaculars over Latin (the imperial dominant language of culture), and by piecing together several dialects, he created today's Italian language, a composite, a 'highly polylingual' hybrid[107] that centuries would eventually meld into the pure, pristine, monolingual classic celebrated, rather improbably, as 'the immediate product of universal Latin' by T. S. Eliot.[108] And of course the *Commedia* itself is a teeming multilingual text where Latin, Provençal, French, various dialects and the demons' gibberish can be heard in all corners of hell. The dialogue between Ulysses and Virgil in Canto 26, we may remember, is supposed to be conducted in Greek.[109] Famously, Dante, dismissing any parochial belief in the superiority of the motherland or the mother tongue in *De Vulgari eloquentia*, saw himself as a citizen and poet of the world: 'To me the whole world is a homeland, like the sea to fish.'[110]

The multilingual hybridity of the Dantean classic is well known: I am suggesting that this feature can be considered as a paradoxical dimension of Primo Levi's survival strategy, and can also be related to the post-humanist debate of which Levi's text, itself now a new classic, is a nexus. J. M. Coetzee's essay 'What is a Classic? A Lecture' (published in *Stranger Shores* in 2002), coming at the end of a venerable chain of essays on the classic, from Charles-Augustin Sainte-Beuve ('Qu'est-ce qu'un classique?', 1850) to T. S. Eliot ('What Is A Classic?', 1944), interrogates the humanist survivability of the classic, represented in both cases by Virgil rather than Dante. Writing after Eliot and also writing back to him, Coetzee picks up the consecrated title 'What is a classic?' and turns the circumstances of Eliot's essay into a counter-argument. Coetzee points out that Eliot delivered his lecture under German bombs, and was prevented by the war from doing preparatory research in the libraries; in particular, he could not read or re-read Sainte-Beuve's prior essays.[111] Eliot's controversial celebration of Virgil as the universal Western classic, Coetzee argues, is both much more radical than Sainte-Beuve's ('who in *his* lectures on Virgil only claimed Virgil as "the poet of all latinity", of France and Spain and Italy but not of all Europe')[112] and likely out of step with the new cultural world order. Instead, Coetzee proposes a less triumphant and more precarious definition of the classic, as a text that survives 'interrogation': 'The classic defines itself by surviving. The interrogation of the classic, no matter how hostile, is part of the history of the classic, inevitable and even to be welcomed.'[113] Following Walter Benjamin's tradition as laid out in his landmark essay 'The Task of the Translator', which emphasizes the afterlife of the classic above its original language, context and meaning, Coetzee posits both translation and criticism as prerequisites of the classic's survival.[114] The classic is thereby defined, like Ulysses himself, by its ability to survive extreme odds. Of course it is entirely appropriate that Primo Levi's chosen classic, Dante's *Inferno*, is already a text about 'esperienze estreme'[115] (extreme experiences), as he pointed out in the later book *The Drowned and the Saved*.[116] The Dantean classic, learned in school, is here subjected to the 'test' of modern hell.[117] The opposition between the classic and barbarism remains but the fault lines keep shifting: as ideological appropriations of the classic press-gang them into the service of modern forms of barbarism (far-Right, antisemitic, fascist ideologues laying claim to Virgil or even Dante, as culture wars intersect world wars)[118] we are reminded that the 'barbarian' (etymologically the one excluded from multilingualism, whose language is not recognized as a language at all but is considered as just noise) may have a new role to play in this post-humanist reconfiguration, as both the classic's traditional counter-reference (Coetzee's discussion climaxes on the example of Polish poet Zbigniew Herbert, writing in a nation with 'an embattled Western culture caught between intermittently barbarous neighbors') and, paradoxically, as a downwardly mobile version of it: a newly barbarized version of the classic – multilingual, babelic and broken, yet despite this or indeed perhaps because of this, surviving because 'generations of people cannot afford to let go of it and therefore hold onto it at all costs'.[119]

In her well-known essay 'Literature for the Planet' (2001), Wai-chee Dimock comes to a similar view from a different starting point. Her theory of the *Inferno* as a 'centrifugal' classic originates in Stalin's Russia: she reflects on poet Osip Mandelstam, who carried a pocket *Inferno* everywhere in case he was arrested away from home (which in fact happened; he died in Siberia three years later) – and who even tried to teach himself Italian in order to read Dante in the original.[120] On the basis of the Mandelstam case, Dimock builds a theory of world literature as deterritorialization, and of the classic as a 'continuum' able to radiate 'across space and time, messing up territorial sovereignty and numerical chronology',[121] a transnational, multilingual space in which both Dante and Mandelstam are 'denationalized'.[122] In her view, 'global transit extends, triangulates, and transforms' the meaning of literature, challenging 'the power of the territorial as a determining force in literature'.[123] Her analysis of Mandelstam's decontextualized reading of Dante applies uncannily well to Primo Levi. In both cases the classic is subjected to what Coetzee terms 'interrogation', which we should understand, I think, as great violence done to it (as in 'enhanced interrogation' perhaps). This includes poor linguistic competency either in the source or the target language, broken memory, lack of books, fallible attention, competing needs – in sum, less than optimal reading conditions overall. And yet, as Levi pointed out forty years later in *The Drowned and the Saved*, this increases the classic's value instead of devaluing it (Levi compares this experience with the book-deprived dystopia of Ray Bradbury's *Fahrenheit 451*).[124] Gone is the familiar reliance on books, reading and a cohesive national, social, linguistic and cultural community. In its place, a 'new' – or rather a return to an older, archaic – and precarious kind of community tentatively takes shape, reliant on person-to-person transmission, orality and even movement. The correlation between the oral recitation of the canto from memory and the walk to the soup in Levi's narrative, noted by Zvi Jagendorf,[125] was also verified in the experience of Osip Mandelstam, who remarked in his 'Conversation about Dante' on the walking rhythm of the *Commedia*, and whose wife, Nadhezda, committed her husband's poems to memory in anticipation of the destruction of his books.[126] Paradoxically, the new community of readers (the ragged, starving, babel-crazed inmates, imprisoned in the sinking ship of the camp, but ready to give up today's soup for another line of the poem) ensures a new and heightened relevance for the text. Saving even scraps of the poem from oblivion contradicts in a small but unmistakable way the Nazi project of erasure and oblivion.[127] 'È assolutamente necessario e urgente che ascolti'[128] (It is vitally necessary and urgent that [Pikolo] listen):[129] before they sink back into the crowd of starving *häftlinge*, the storyteller and the listener, both deficient yet possessed of a sense of 'exaltation'[130] not found in the school room, will share a fleeting experience ('qualcosa di gigantesco'[131] (something gigantic)[132] albeit undisclosed) of the classic speaking still from the flames.

Absent the unspeakable horror, Borges intuited the same definition of the classic as a text which can survive mistreatment: 'The page that becomes immortal can traverse the fire of typographical errors, approximate translations, and inattentive or erroneous readings without losing its soul in the process.'[133] Common to these various reassessments of the classic is a certain awareness that the classic's survival is dependent upon two paradoxical conditions: breaking away from the monolingual and national textual boundaries, and accepting that a writer's peripheral position – the Argentine Borges, the American Eliot, the South African Coetzee or the Jewish Levi in fascist Italy – may offer a privileged vantage point from which to rethink and orchestrate the classic's afterlife.[134]

Echoing the multilingual mistreatment to which the classic is subjected, Levi's memoir itself shows evidence of multilingualism, not only in its mottled appearance (it is a text riddled with untranslated italics), but also in its compositional history, as early drafts were sent out to readers in the United States or France even before the original Italian publication.[135] And the main supporting character, Jean Samuel renamed 'Pikolo' (a playfully Germanized version of the Italian term of endearment), is further proof of the creative multilingualism at play in Levi's reshaping of the Lager experience.[136]

In this unfinished epiphany that throws up no answers for anyone, only more questions (to paraphrase Piero Boitani's analysis),[137] the canto of Ulysses turns away from the confidence of the imperial great book à la Eliot. This is a classic in rags, disguised as a beggar. Multilingualism – Levi's is a book about a multilingual experience, conceived and drafted in a form that pulverizes the national monolingual borders – is the sign of this brokenness and dispersion, yet also the only possible kind of poetry after Auschwitz (in response to Adorno's grim aphorism).[138] It is the afterlife of Dante in a modern and worse kind of hell, a crashing and splintering wreck of a classic, but nevertheless a post-humanist refounding of the classic's legitimacy.

Notes

1 Italo Calvino, *The Uses of Literature: Essays*, trans. Patrick Creagh (San Diego: Harcourt Brace Jovanovich, 1986), 137.
2 The second text featured in Levi's personal anthology *La Ricerca delle radici*, directly after the excerpt from the Bible's *Book of Job*, is from *Odyssey* 9, Ulysses' confrontation with the Cyclops (Primo Levi, *La ricerca delle radici, Antologia personale* (Torino: Einaudi, 1981), 19–21).
3 Gian Paolo Biasin, '"Till my ghastly tale is told": Levi's Moral Discourse from *Se questo è un uomo* to *I sommersi e i salvati*', in *Reason and Light, Essays on Primo Levi*, ed. Susan Tarrow (Ithaca, New York: Center for International Studies, Cornell University, 1990): 127–41, 128.
4 Primo Levi and Pier V. Mengaldo, *Opere*, Torino: Einaudi, 3 vols, 1987, I, 32.
5 Primo Levi, *The Complete Works of Primo Levi*, ed. Ann Goldstein, 3 vols (New York: Liveright, 2015), I, 34.
6 Levi, *Opere*, I, 72.
7 Levi, *Complete Works*, I, 69. On Auschwitz as a modern-day Babel, see in particular Zaia Alexander, 'Primo Levi and Translation', in *The Cambridge Companion to Primo Levi*, ed. Robert S. C. Gordon (Cambridge, New York: Cambridge University Press, 2007): 155–69, 158; Isabella Bertoletti, 'Primo Levi's Odyssey: The Drowned and the Saved', in *The Legacy of Primo Levi*, ed. Stanislao Pugliese (New York: Palgrave Macmillan, 2005): 105–18, 112; Jonathan Druker, *Primo Levi and Humanism After Auschwitz: Posthumanist Reflections* (New York: Palgrave Macmillan, 2009), 43; Fabio Girelli-Carasi, 'The Anti-Linguistic Nature of the Lager in the Language of Primo Levi's *Se questo è un uomo*', in *Reason and Light*, 40–59, 54; Anna Laura Lepschy and Giulio Lepschy, 'Primo Levi's Languages', in *The Cambridge Companion to Primo Levi*, ed. Robert S. C. Gordon (2007), 132; as well as translator Stuart Woolf's Afterword, in *The Complete Works of Primo Levi*, ed. Ann Goldstein, 3 vols (New York: Liveright, 2015), I: 195–6.
8 On the Lager jargon, see especially Sander L. Gilman, 'The Special Language of the Camps and After', in *Reason and Light*, 61; and Alexander, 'Primo Levi and Translation', 158. On the destruction of 'the prisoners' sense of linguistic efficiency', see Patricia Sayre and Linnea Vacca, 'On Language and Personhood: A Linguistic Odyssey', in *Memory and Mastery: Primo Levi as Writer and Witness*, ed. Roberta S. Kremer (Albany: State University of New York Press, 2001): 115–30, 117.
9 Levi, *Opere*, I, 722.
10 Levi, *Complete Works*, III, 2474.
11 Levi, *Opere*, I, 724.
12 Levi, *Complete Works*, III, 2476.
13 Levi, *Opere*, I, 723.
14 Levi, *Complete Works*, III, 2475.
15 Levi, *Opere*, I, 226.
16 Levi, *Complete Works*, I, 225.
17 Levi, *Opere*, I, 227.
18 Levi, *Complete Works*, I, 225.
19 Levi, *Opere*, I, 227.
20 Levi, *Complete Works*, I, 225.

21 On 'non-language' and the impossibility of testimony, see Giorgio Agamben, *Remnants of Auschwitz: The Witness and the Archive* (New York: Zone Books, 2002), 39.
22 Levi, *Opere*, I, 12.
23 Levi, *Complete Works*, I, 15.
24 Ibid., I, 35.
25 Ibid., I, 103, 109.
26 Zaia Alexander describes life in Auschwitz as consisting of untranslatable moments ('Primo Levi and Translation', 162). The key noun itself, *Lager*, is always left untranslated: see Peter Arnds, 'Translating Survival, Translation as Survival in Primo Levi's *Se Questo è Un Uomo*', *Translation and Literature* 21.2 (2012): 162–74, 169.
27 As critic Gian Paolo Biasin calls it ('"Till my ghastly tale is told"', 127).
28 Levi, *Opere*, I, 725–6.
29 Levi, *Complete Works*, III, 2477.
30 On Levi's insistence on communication and his stern rejection of the idea of incommunicability, see Alexander, 'Primo Levi and Translation', 156, as well as Mirna Cicioni, '"Labour of Civilization and Peace": Primo Levi Looks at Interpreters and Interpreting', in *Interpreting Primo Levi: Interdisciplinary Perspectives*, ed. Minna Vuohelainen and Arthur Chapman (Houndsmill Basingstoke: Palgrave Macmillan, 2016): 37–49, 37–8.
31 Victor Klemperer, *Lingua Tertii Imperii: Notizbuch eines Philologen* (1947), quoted in *The Complete Works of Primo Levi*, III: 2479.
32 Levi, *Opere*, I, 728.
33 Levi, *Complete Works*, III, 2479.
34 Levi, *Opere*, I, 728.
35 Levi, *Complete Works*, III, 2479.
36 Levi, *Opere*, I, 728.
37 Levi, *Complete Works*, III, 2480.
38 Dante Alighieri, *Inferno*, trans. Allen Mandelbaum (New York: Bantam Books, 1982), 26, 118–20, 244.
39 Ibid., 245, quoted in Levi, *Complete Works*, I, 108.
40 Philip Roth, 'Interview with Primo Levi', *London Review of Books* 8.18 (1986): 17–19.
41 Jonathan Druker, *Primo Levi and Humanism after Auschwitz: Posthumanist Reflections* (New York: Palgrave Macmillan, 2009). He singles out Joseph Farrell, who views Levi's Ulysses as 'the supreme model of the humanist' (Joseph Farrell, *Primo Levi the Austere Humanist* (Oxford: Peter Lang, 2004), 14).
42 Levi, *Opere*, I, 117.
43 Levi, *Complete Works*, I, 108.
44 Chapter 6 of *The Drowned and the Saved*, *Complete Works*, III, 2503.
45 In many ways Améry's eponymous chapter seems like a mirror image of Levi's 'Canto of Ulysses': the memory of Hölderlin's poem fails to awaken any emotional or mental response; fellow writer Nico Rost's celebration of 'classical literature as a substitute for Red Cross packages' is scornfully dismissed. Even the material details (the watery soup, the absence of an attentive interlocutor like Jean Samuel) pointedly invert Levi's experience. See Jean Améry, *At the Mind's Limits: Contemplations by a Survivor on Auschwitz and Its Realities*, trans. Sidney Rosenfeld and Stella P. Rosenfeld (Bloomington: Indiana University Press, [1966] 1980), 5–7.

46 Améry, *Mind's Limits*, 19.
47 Levi, *Opere*, I, 767.
48 Levi, *Complete Works*, III, 2514.
49 Levi, *Opere*, I, 764.
50 Levi, *Complete Works*, III, 2512. Lynn Gunzberg quotes from Levi's letters to her, concluding that Dante's *Divine Comedy* was 'a cultural vademecum through the tortuous maze of concentration camp life' (Lynn Gunzberg, 'Nuotando altrimenti che nel serchio': Dante as vademecum for Primo Levi', in *Reason and Light*, 82–98, 92).
51 Nancy Harrowitz, *Primo Levi and the Identity of a Survivor* (Toronto: University of Toronto Press, 2016), 64.
52 Cheyette's essay in its entirety is an effort to debunk a certain oversimplified and optimistic image of Levi that has become established in Europe and the United States. See Bryan Cheyette, 'Appropriating Primo Levi', in *The Cambridge Companion to Primo Levi*, ed. Robert S. C. Gordon, 67–85.
53 Ibid., 71.
54 Ibid., 67.
55 Levi, *Complete Works*, I, 25.
56 On the parody of divine (Dantean) justice in the Lager, see especially Uri Cohen, 'Consider If This Is a Man: Primo Levi and the Figure of Ulysses', *Jewish Social Studies* 18.2 (2012): 40–69, 55; and Nicholas Patruno, 'Primo Levi, Dante, and the Canto of Ulysses', in *The Legacy of Primo Levi*, ed. Stanislao Pugliese (2005): 33–40, 36.
57 Lynn Gunzberg, 'Down Among the Dead Men: Levi and Dante in Hell', *Modern Language Studies* 16, no. 1 (1986): 10–28, 27.
58 Levi, *Complete Works*, I, 98.
59 The dichotomy resonates strongly with another wartime reading of a Greek story, Simone Weil's *The Iliad, or the Poem of Force* (1939), which reframes Homer's epic poem in the context of the dehumanizing machine of the Second World War, relentlessly scrutinizing 'the ability to turn a human being into a thing while he is still alive'. See Simone Weil, *The Iliad, or the Poem of Force* (trans. Mary McCarthy 1939) (Wallingford: Pendle Hill, 1945), 5.
60 Homer, *The Odyssey*, 9: 415–70, trans. Richmond Lattimore (New York: Harper Perennial Modern Classics, 2007), 148–9.
61 Levi, *Complete Works*, I, 140.
62 Levi, *Opere*, I, 117.
63 Levi, *Complete Works*, I, 108.
64 Druker, *Primo Levi and Humanism after Auschwitz*, 41.
65 Levi, *Opere*, I, 117.
66 Levi, *Complete Works*, I, 107.
67 Alberto Cavaglion, 'In Memory of Jean Samuel', Centro Internazionale di Studi Primo Levi. Available online: www.primolevi.it/Web/English/Contents/Auschwitz/120_In_memory_of_Jean_Samuel (accessed 28 March 2019); Jean Samuel, *Il m'appelait Pikolo. Un compagnon de Primo Levi raconte* (Paris: Laffont, 2007), 111. Sustaining the sea metaphor, Samuel also described his friendship with Levi as a life-saver in the ocean of memory, 'une bouée de sauvetage dans l'océan de la mémoire' (Samuel, *Il m'appelait Pikolo*, 203).
68 Dante, *Inferno* 26, 142; I, 118.
69 Levi, *Complete Works*, I, 109.
70 Ibid., III, 2434.

71　Levi, *Opere*, I, 726.
72　Levi, *Complete Works*, III, 2478.
73　Druker, *Primo Levi and Humanism after Auschwitz*, 43. The same view is expressed by Fabio Girelli-Carasi: 'Dante's poetry is muted by the Final Solution' ('The Anti-Linguistic Nature of the Lager', 53).
74　Levi's narrative offers an example of a literary solution to a philosophical problem, as formulated by Agamben's witness paradox: 'The authority of the witness consists in his capacity to speak solely in the name of an incapacity to speak' (Agamben, *Remnants of Auschwitz*, 158).
75　Hans Blumenberg, *Shipwreck with Spectator: Paradigm of a Metaphor for Existence* (Cambridge, MA: MIT Press, 1997), 7.
76　Levi, *Complete Works*, III, 2405.
77　See Biasin, '"Till my ghastly tale is told"', 127; Risa Sodi, 'La Terza via: Dante and Primo Levi', *Modern Language Notes*, vol. 127, no. 1: S199–S203, S286, 199; Robert S. C. Gordon, *Primo Levi's Ordinary Virtues: from Testimony to Ethics* (Oxford: Oxford University Press, 2001), 249; and Robert S. C. Gordon (editor), *The Cambridge Companion to Primo Levi* (2007), 39, among others.
78　Levi, *Opere*, III, 833.
79　Primo Levi, *The Mirror Maker: Stories and Essays by Primo Levi*, trans. Raymond Rosenthal (New York: Schocken Books, 1989), 3–4. In the new three-volume edition of Levi's complete works in English, translator Anne Milano Appel stays closer to the original Italian (Levi uses the common word *vortice*: Primo Levi and Pier V. Mengaldo, *Opere*, 3 vols (Torino: Einaudi, 1987), III: 833), but she misses the Poe intertext by translating 'vortex' rather than 'maelström': 'I am an ordinary man with a good memory who fell into a vortex, who came out of it more by good fortune than by virtue, and who since that time has had a certain curiosity about vortexes, large and small, metaphorical and material' (*Complete Works*, III, 2261).
80　Levi, *Opere*, I, 112.
81　Levi, *Complete Works*, I, 103.
82　Poe's narrator observes that the speed at which objects are sucked down is related to their size and shape, and ties himself to a cylindrical barrel, thereby escaping death: Edgar A. Poe, 'A Descent into the Maelström', in *The Fall of the House of Usher and Other Writings* (London: Penguin Books, 1986), 239–41.
83　Poe, 'A Descent into the Maelström', 239.
84　Ibid., 241–2.
85　*Shipwreck in Art and Literature: Images and Interpretations from Antiquity to the Present Day*, ed. Carl Thompson (New York: Routledge, 2014), 11.
86　Josiah Blackmore, *Manifest Perdition: Shipwreck Narrative and the Disruption of Empire* (Minneapolis: University of Minnesota Press, 2002), xxi. Although Blackmore focuses on the specific context of the Portuguese empire, his analysis applies equally well to other narratives of empire.
87　*Shipwreck in Art and Literature*, 18.
88　Boris Dunsch, '"Describe nunc tempestatem": Sea Storm and Shipwreck Type Scenes in Ancient Literature', in *Shipwreck in Art and Literature*, ed. Carl Thompson (New York: Routledge, 2014), 43–53, 53.
89　Ibid., 43.
90　Hans Blumenberg, *Shipwreck with Spectator*, 12.
91　Levi, *Opere*, I, 658–9.

92 Levi, *Complete Works*, III, 2416.
93 Harrowitz, *Primo Levi and the Identity of a Survivor*, 10. This of course is precisely the starting point of Agamben's analysis.
94 Levi, *Opere*, I, 114.
95 Levi, *Complete Works*, I, 105.
96 See Cohen, 'Primo Levi and the Figure of Ulysses', 40; Patruno, 'Primo Levi, Dante, and the Canto of Ulysses', 35; and Ian Thomson, 'The Genesis of *If This Is A Man*', in *The Legacy of Primo Levi*, ed. Stanislao Pugliese (2005): 41–58, 49.
97 See Druker, *Primo Levi and Humanism After Auschwitz*, 39–40; and Wiley Feinstein, *The Civilization of the Holocaust in Italy: Poets, Artists, Saints, Anti-Semites* (Madison: Fairleigh Dickinson University Press, 2003), 336–67.
98 Lepschy and Lepschy, 'Primo Levi's Languages', 126.
99 Girelli-Carasi, 'The Anti-Linguistic Nature of the Lager', 49; Gilman, 'The Special Language of the Camps', 63.
100 Roth, 'Interview with Primo Levi', 18.
101 Levi, *Opere*, III, 785–6.
102 Levi, *Complete Works*, III, 2211.
103 Levi, *Opere*, III, 785.
104 Levi, *Complete Works*, III, 2211.
105 'The Best Merchandise', *Other People's Trades*, in *The Complete Works of Primo Levi*, III: 2211. These essays, many of which share a focus on language (including the important essay 'On Translating and Being Translated') were originally published in *La Stampa*, then collected in 1985, a year before *The Drowned and the Saved*. See also Lepschy and Lepschy, 'Primo Levi's Languages', 127.
106 Risa Sodi, *A Dante of Our Time: Primo Levi and Auschwitz* (New York: Peter Lang, 1990).
107 Sandra Bermann, 'In the Light of Translation: On Dante and World Literature', in *Foundational Texts of World Literature*, ed. Dominique Jullien (New York: Peter Lang, 2011): 85–100, 90. On the contrast between T. S. Eliot's 'hegemonic' and O. Mandelstam's 'denationalized' views of Dante, see also Wai-chee Dimock, 'Literature for the Planet', *PMLA* 116.1 (2001): 173–88, 179.
108 Eliot, 'Dante' [1929], quoted by Bermann, 'In the Light of Translation', 86.
109 Virgil tells Dante to remain silent, as Ulysses and Diomedes would likely despise his vernacular Italian: 'Let me address them (…) Since they were Greek, / Perhaps they'd be disdainful of your speech' (Dante Alighieri, *Inferno*, 26: 73–5, trans. Allen Mandelbaum, 243).
110 Dante Alighieri, *De vulgari eloquentia*, trans. Steven Botterill (Cambridge: Cambridge University Press, 1996), 11, 13, 16, quoted in Dimock, 'Literature for the Planet', 178.
111 Sainte-Beuve's ideas on the classic are developed mainly in 'Qu'est-ce qu'un classique?' (1850) and *Etude sur Virgile* (1857). See Charles-Augustin Sainte-Beuve, 'Qu'est-ce qu'un classique?', in *Causeries du Lundi* (Paris: Garnier Frères, 1923), 3: 38–55; and *Etude sur Virgile suivie d'une étude sur Quintus de Smyrne* (Paris: Calmann Lévy, 1891).
112 'Le poète de la latinité tout entière', Sainte-Beuve, *Etude sur Virgile*, 29; quoted in J. M. Coetzee, 'What Is a Classic? A Lecture', in *Stranger Shores: Literary Essays* (New York: Penguin Books, 2001), 1–16 (2).
113 Coetzee, 'What Is a Classic?', 16. Johan Geertsema borrows Derrida's notion of 'hospitality' (both hostility and hospitality) to describe Coetzee's view of the

translational and critical survival of the classic (Johan Geertsema, 'Between Homage and Critique: Coetzee, Translation, and the Classic', in *Translation and the Classic: Identity as Change in the History of Culture*, ed. Alexandra Lianeri and Vanda Zajko (Oxford: Oxford University Press, 2008), 110–27, 123–4).

114 Walter Benjamin, 'The Storyteller', 'The Task of the Translator', in *Illuminations*, ed. Hannah Arendt, trans. Harry Zohn (New York: Schocken Books, [1968] 1988), 71–4; Geertsema, 'Between Homage and Critique', 121.

115 Levi, *Opere*, I, 664.

116 Levi, *Complete Works*, III, 2421.

117 Zvi Jagendorf, 'Primo Levi Goes for Soup and Remembers Dante', *Raritan* 12.4 (1993): 31–52 (34).

118 See Christopher Prendergast's exemplary Postscript on the far-Right appropriation of Virgil and the Classic debate in French cultural politics post Sainte-Beuve, in *The Classic: Sainte-Beuve and the Nineteenth-Century Culture Wars* (Oxford: Oxford University Press, 2007), 296–308.

119 Coetzee, 'What Is a Classic?', 16.

120 Dimock, 'Literature for the Planet', 173, 176.

121 Ibid., 174.

122 Ibid., 176.

123 Ibid., 177.

124 Levi, *Complete Works*, III, 2513.

125 Jagendorf, 'Primo Levi Goes for Soup and Remembers Dante', 34.

126 Dimock, 'Literature for the Planet', 178, 173. See also Jagendorf, 'Primo Levi Goes for Soup and Remembers Dante', 31–4 on the deathbed transmission of knowledge in Levi's chapter, which he reads through the lens of Benjamin's essay 'The Storyteller'.

127 In the preface to *The Drowned and the Saved*, Levi remembers the SS guards' 'cynical warning' to the prisoners: no one would survive to tell the story, no records would be left, and no one would believe them (Levi, *Complete Works*, III: 2411). On the destruction of memory vs. testimony, see Harrowitz, *Primo Levi and the Identity of a Survivor*, 9–10, and Agamben, *Remnants of Auschwitz*, 157.

128 Levi, *Opere*, I, 118.

129 Levi, *Complete Works*, I, 109.

130 For Jean Samuel's testimony on sharing 'a kind of intellectual exaltation' with Levi, and the comparably redemptive role of mathematics in the Lager, see Samuel, *Il m'appelait Pikolo*, especially 43–7 and 206, and Susan Tarrow, 'Remembering Primo Levi: A Conversation with "Il Pikolo del Komando 98"', *Forum Italicum*, Vol. 28.1 (1994): 101–10 (104–5).

131 Levi, *Opere*, I, 118.

132 Levi, *Complete Works*, I, 109.

133 Jorge Luis Borges, *Selected Non-Fictions*, ed. Eliot Weinberger (New York: Penguin Books, 1999), 54.

134 For an exemplary defence of the creative advantages of marginality, see Borges's seminal essay 'The Argentine Writer and Tradition', in *Selected Non-Fictions*, particularly 425–7.

135 On the multilingual genesis of *If This Is A Man*, see Domenico Scarpa, 'Notes on the Texts', in *The Complete Works of Primo Levi*, III: 2815–83, particularly III: 2818–19. Levi sent drafts sent to his cousin in New York before the publication in Italian; he

also sent an early version of 'The Canto of Ulysses' to Samuel in May 1946 (Samuel, *Il m'appelait Pikolo*, 84).

136 Samuel's narrative emphasizes the multilingual wordplay as a strategy to resist dehumanization: 'A suivi la minutieuse procédure de déshumanisation que j'ai décrite, jusqu'à ce jour où un Italien inconnu qui parlait le français et pas l'allemand m'a donné mon nouveau nom, ma nouvelle identité: Pikolo. Avec un k, comme un pied de nez à l'univers concentrationnaire qui n'a pas eu raison de nous. Comme pour germaniser et alourdir un terme italien et affectueux' (Samuel, *Il m'appelait Pikolo*, 34).

137 Piero Boitani, *The Shadow of Ulysses. Figures of a Myth*, trans. Anita Weston (Oxford: Clarendon Press, 1994), 161.

138 See in particular Jonathan Druker's discussion of Adorno's aphorism ('To write poetry after Auschwitz is barbaric', in his 1949 essay 'Cultural Criticism and Society') in light of Levi's Holocaust writing: *Primo Levi and Humanism After Auschwitz*, chapter 2, 'The Shadowed Violence of Culture', 35–54.

Part III

Multilingual comparative reading: Beyond translation and untranslatability

9

Ghetto, Nakba, Holocaust: New terms (of relationship) in Elias Khoury's *Awlād al-Ghītū*

Nora Parr

Manal didn't know what the word 'ghetto' meant or where it came from. All she knew was that the people of Lydda heard it from the Israeli soldiers.
Elias Khoury, Children of the Ghetto V.1

Words travel across languages, contexts and eras. They are flexible and take on the lived realities of the communities that use them. But when circulating within world literary networks, local usages encounter global frameworks that privilege certain ways of knowing. A host of factors make some narratives impossible to hear on (and in) their own terms: from the gatekeepers of world literature, to the limitations of political action, and the policing of language deemed universal but referring to one particular context. In his 2016 *Awlād al-Ghītū* (translated as *Children of the Ghetto V.I* in 2018),[1] Lebanese author Elias Khoury stages an encounter between the often-flattening frames of global circulation, and an 'impossible'-to-tell story. The story is of Lydda, a small Palestinian city that was 'toppled, fell to pieces and was wiped out'[2] by Zionist forces in 1948.[3] After the city was emptied of most of its inhabitants, it was surrounded by barbed wire and called a ghetto. The word, as Khoury tells it, was previously unknown to Lydda residents, but comes to be (re)defined – given meaning through the lives of the people of the city. Here Ghetto gains a new but inexpressible meaning – inexpressible not because there were no words for the tragedies of Lydda, but because the necessary words were already wrapped up in other structures of narrative that Palestine has been locked out of. Khoury's re-definition and play with the concept of origins bring the idea of 'ghetto' back to its unknown and multilingual etymology. It is a word whose origins scholars continue to debate, findings suggesting it comes from 'Italian metal foundry' after a site one Jewish community was obliged to live in in 1562 Rome, or the Hebrew for divorce, indicating separation.[4] Khoury forces readers to think about where words come from, what they might refer to in different contexts and how they circulate become different and discernible elements of language.

The often-flattening frames of global circulation at which *Awlād al-Ghītū* takes aim represent an intertwined network of physical and discursive regimes. These regimes make it difficult for a novel about the traumatic and generations-long experience of a Palestinian ghetto in today's Israel to be told, heard or acknowledged by a literary or mainstream public. Outlining three major frames – the problematic 'world' of world literature, the exclusionary frames of political legitimacy and language of these systems – we see how they have hitherto excluded the possibility of telling the story found in *Awlād al-Ghītū*. In order to ensure their telling, author Elias Khoury – both personally and textually – strategically positions the story both inside and at odds with the frames that would limit it. The novel then mobilizes the ideological possibilities of world literature, recasting 'world' through the redefinition of language, so that the possibilities of world literature are instead realized – not through its problematic concept of the universal – but through the building blocks of language. Looking at the novel's redefinition of 'ghetto', and the way limiting frameworks are recast through the creation of a multilingual politics, the text offers alternative imaginaries within which to read, understand, but not be limited by exclusionary frames as texts circulate.

Literature

World literature presumes, maintains and polices a set of 'universal' values about the nature and possibility of literary texts that replicate a particular Euro-American creative product. Understanding world literature as that which is held up by what Pascale Casanova calls the 'world republic of letters', texts are accepted when submitted to and judged by what she calls 'a standard that is universally recognized as legitimate'.[5] This standard, Pheng Cheah reminds us, is a European category that postcolonial contexts remain tethered to as 'a form of imprisonment',[6] so that indigenous or non-Euro-American literary artistic practices cannot be read within the 'literary' frame of 'world' unless they submit to its rules and regulations. As Michael Allan reminds us, the ideals of world literature construct 'an entire way of being in language'[7] that at once imposed and imported change the way that 'knowing and apprehending the world'[8] can happen. *Ghītū* sets up a framework whereby the work is understood to have been written outside of this republic, and posthumously submitted, by Khoury, not so much for judgement but to critique the entire system.

This duality – at once inside and out of the world literary networks – is achieved through a brilliantly sustained bit of metatextual theatre. In what appears as an authorial preface, a Lebanese intellectual named 'Elias Khoury' explains that the pages to follow are not written by him. Rather, they are from a series of notebooks written by one Adam Danoun, now deceased. Adam, 'Khoury' tells readers, died in New York City when his apartment caught fire. It was a suspected suicide. The man's notebooks, however, miraculously survive, and are delivered to 'Khoury' via one of his students at NYU, Sarang Lee, a Korean woman who was also Adam's girlfriend. This sets up a condition whereby the notebooks, saved from the fire, are written in a sense outside the networks of the world literary, free from its frames and expectations. In fact, they were not written for global consumption, or for anyone at all. Instead, Adam had set himself the personal task of writing down his life and memories of the ghetto and believed that 'no-one is going to read these words after my death'.[9] The man had a great deal of scepticism that the story even could be written, and has sustained internal dialogues about the problems and pitfalls of writing, and limitations of existing forms to say what he wants to say. Despite this remove from the world literary arena, Adam's notebook experiments enter the world republic of letters as a text to be judged – with 'Khoury' as first arbiter. The seasoned writer-character calls Adam's work and its self-conscious critique of writing 'five star', adding in his foreword that the notebooks did not require any editing from him, and are published 'just as I got them'. In the Arabic, the words 'five star' are rendered in Latin characters, as if to remind the reader that 'Khoury' (and perhaps Khoury) has the literary capital to evaluate the work and bring it to the attention of the world republic. Whatever way of knowing the world Adam has crafted from outside the republic, 'Khoury' deems worthy of the republic's consideration; in many ways it is precisely because of this staged distance that the manuscript becomes important.

This staging reflects reality. The 'real' Khoury certainly holds a cultural position that affords him a unique authority to speak within the global literary scene. He possesses reams of what Pascale Casanova calls 'literary credit', that 'power and authority granted to a writer' by virtue of their perceived and agreed upon 'merit'.[10] To wit, he is Global Distinguished Professor at NYU, was a visiting professor at Columbia University, his fiction (translated into fifteen different languages) is regularly reviewed in top literary magazines. According to his German literary agent Mertin, his most famous novel, *Gate of the Sun*, was named 'Best Book of the Year' by *Le Monde Diplomatique*, *The Christian Science Monitor* and *The San Francisco Chronicle*, and a 'Notable Book' by *The New York Times*.[11] Khoury is a classic example of the sort of postcolonial writer that Huggan describes as providing 'translated products for metropolitan consumers in places like London and New York'.[12] At the same time, Khoury's political commitment draws him to tackle causes, ideas and events generally unrepresented in the mainstream. Where his position as a public intellectual in Lebanon has led him towards involvement in local and regional matters (earlier fiction tackled the Lebanese civil war, the massacre of Palestinians in Sabra and Shatila, Lebanon's religious minorities, Palestinian refugees in Lebanon, Syrian workers in Lebanon, etc.), *Ghītū* shifts target from regional to global knowledge production. It takes aim not at local politics, personal or community memory, but inserts these concerns into the global systems that would allow a Korean student to submit a Palestinian manuscript to a Lebanese professor in New York City. It is this tension between a local logic and global idiom – where the two could not converse with each other – that drives the work.

Politics

At the same time as Khoury is established globally, he is deeply committed to the ideals of liberation and challenging existing political frames that are particular to Lebanon. As he puts it, being born in 1948, and coming of age during the Lebanese Civil War, 'you cannot be an intellectual without taking a stand when there is a national liberation struggle; and I feel all the time that I was part of this struggle'.[13] When it comes to the case of Palestinian liberation, Khoury's participation is not just symbolic. Khoury was a member of the Palestine Liberation Organization (PLO), and in the late 1960s 'joined the Palestinian Fatah movement, fighting alongside leftist forces during the civil war (in which he lost his sight in one eye)'.[14] Khoury later became heavily involved in Palestinian cultural, literary, intellectual circles, even authoring what critics called the first story of the Palestinian catastrophe of 1948, in his most widely known novel *Gate of the Sun*. Khoury has spent a lifetime writing about and fighting for Palestine and Palestinians in a way that has maintained a constant dialogue with Palestinian cultural institutions. This is reproduced in the novel when Adam claims he knows the protagonist of *Gate of the Sun*. Adam criticizes where Khoury left off the story, and adds that *Sun*'s narrator goes on to become a corrupt official in the new Palestinian Authority.[15] The signal is that Khoury is not only producing his narrative in conversation with Palestinians, but is also open to revision and critique by the community he writes about. He is thus deeply embedded in two contexts. What *Ghītū* grapples with is the difference between writing within one context, and having that dialogue heard within another. To read *Ghītū*'s intervention into politics, we must go beyond what it is possible to say and think for a Lebanese intellectual deeply committed to the Palestinian cause of liberation, and focus rather on the level of what it is possible to hear.

As Edward Said so poignantly put it in his 1994 essay 'Permission to Narrate', narratives of Palestinian oppression are subject to a 'disciplinary communications apparatus' that prohibits Palestinian realities from gaining access to a mainstream discourse.[16] This, Said explains, is because existing narratives that Palestinian stories challenge are tightly knit into political discourse – both cannot exist within the same discursive field. For Said it was the McBride commission's 1982 finding of ethnocide during their investigation of the Israeli participation in the Sabra and Shatila massacres,[17] findings that in the American political scene were 'ipso facto justified'[18] because to recognize these acts as wrong would, as Said finds, 'contradict the premises of declared US policy'.[19] Where Said examined the American context, Hawari, Plonski and Weizman explore political terrain of Palestinians in Israel. Here, they found that a regime of 'Knowledge production ... hinges on both productive and repressive practices that work together to render [Israel's] history and present "normal"',[20] so that 'as ways of knowing the world elide with the hegemonic system, it becomes difficult to think outside its existing frames and limits'.[21] These limits actively dis-include Palestinian experiences that might trouble these hegemonies of 'normal' and accepted bases of action. In both cases, constructed ideas of normal preclude the possibility of recognizing harm to Palestinians. This is also the case more broadly when it comes to recognizing what Palestinians call the Nakba.

A word coined in 1948 by Syrian historian Constantine Zurayk, it was used to describe what he called, 'The defeat of the Arabs in Palestine'.[22] While its usage in English has tended to refer to a single 'event' imagined as the 'inverse' of Israel's War of Independence, for Zurayk the Nakba as 'no simple setback or light, passing evil'.[23] Rather, he characterized it as the outcome of forces to which 'the Arabs have been afflicted throughout their long history – a history marked by numerous trials and tribulations'.[24] Contemporary scholars of Palestine have stressed the ongoing nature of the Nakba, given the continued displacement, loss of land and dispossession of the Palestinian people.[25] The Nakba becomes difficult to narrate in the global context for two reasons. The first, as Bashir Bashir and Amos Goldberg draw out in their 2018 volume, *The Holocaust and the Nakba*, is because Nakba is seen as a negating force for the central and founding myths of Israel.[26] The state's internal and external claim to legitimacy 'rests on the metanarrative of the Holocaust, which has, to a large extent, become a central, hegemonic metanarrative of the entire west'.[27] The second is because the Nakba does not fit neatly within existing paradigms of trauma theory so cannot be recognized as the physical, psychological and indeed human catastrophe that it is. As Rosemary Sayigh writes, the role of trauma theory (as exemplified for her by Dominic LaCapra, Nancy Feldman and Veena Das) is to 'delimit what it recognizes as suffering'.[28] So long as 'the holocaust remains a basic reference of exceptional violence',[29] she continues, Palestinian suffering will not be visible. As Khoury himself puts it, if a language and a culture are prohibited from using particular words because they are policed by another group, how then 'are Palestinians to express their tragedy?'[30]

The problem of expression extends, as Adam describes, from the personal directly to the national. As one loaded interaction demonstrates, it is a single and powerful narrative construction that at once erases the discursive possibility of a Palestinian ghetto within Israel, and brushes over the possibility of Adam as a Palestinian when he answers the simple question: where are you from? As a scholar of Hebrew Literature, Adam explains, when he answers with 'ghetto' his Jewish Israeli interlocuters immediately place him within an already-determined category. Being from the 'ghetto', Adam writes, grants him the 'immunity of Warsaw',[31] so that his Palestinian-ness is hidden by the presumption that being born in a ghetto – whether it was Warsaw or Łódź, but not Lydda – indicated a particular and even codified experience. Adam's personal, communal or even national circumstance is erased, Lydda is impossible, and he becomes immune to any further questioning (which he would certainly have undergone had he just said Lydda). There is a validness in what is assumed in the utterance that cannot be questioned – indeed that closes down questions – and the set of assumptions at work in the encounter is paralleled, in reverse, in the narrative of Israel as a nation-state.

As Bashir and Goldberg explain it, the narrative construct of Israel as a 'legitimate' nation-state also rests on the universal recognition of the experience of ghetto. They give the example of 'the expression *meSho'ah le-tekumah* (from Holocaust to rebirth) [which] became a constitutive slogan of Zionist consciousness, and it remains so to this day'.[32] In other words, the trajectory of Israel as a state begins with the suffering of the Holocaust, and the experience of violent 'othering' in Europe. To challenge the singularity of experience of the Holocaust, Bashir and Goldberg go on, becomes akin to challenging the legitimacy of the state. This, they write, creates a 'context of the policing dominance and hegemony of paradigmatic and foreclosed narratives and epistemologies'[33] that close off, deny permission and police the possibility of Palestinian expression. To let in the possibility of a Palestinian experience of ghetto would disrupt the narrative; and certainly disrupt claims to a singular-universal and legitimizing experience.

It is therefore remarkable that *Ghītū* works to tell 'the story of the Nakba in Lydda and the massacre that took place there in language and terms wholly associated with the story of the Jewish Holocaust'.[34] This is a reclaiming of language – not taking it away from existing mythic and discursive formulations, but offering alternatives that instead debunk the myth of these discourses' universalism – the very idea of 'world' in world literature. So, while Palestinian, Arabic-speaking and solidarity writers have mobilized words like 'ghetto', 'extermination', 'ethnic cleansing' and 'genocide' to describe Palestine countless times in the past,[35] *Awlād al-Ghītū* is different. Ghetto is not so much 'domesticated' by Adam or used to describe the realities of Palestine 'as though' they are like the Second World War. Rather, ghetto is totally redefined to hold Adam's experience. Ghetto becomes multilingual and multi-contextual – not least because the word is written in New York City, a place where ghetto has taken on its own life and politics of meaning.

Language

Telling the story of the Nakba becomes a project of claiming appropriate language, then placing the language into the jaw of 'world', so that universalism becomes multilingualism. *Awlād al-Ghītū* mobilizes Khoury's CV not only as a credible teller of a Palestinian tale, but in order to challenge inequalities – not in Lebanon this time – imposed by the very 'world republic of letters' (and the forces that created this republic) that has judged the author credible. Khoury uses his literary 'credit' to secure a sort of permission for his character to narrate. Where Adam struggles with a structure for his story, with words to describe what he feels, and even in gaining access to information to help understand the conditions under which Lydda became a ghetto, Khoury frames these struggles as one – at their heart – about language. It is 'Khoury', in fact, who declares that Adam's story is one about ghetto. In his preface, the fictional author tells readers that it had been left up to him to title Adam's notebooks, and that he originally settles on *The Notebooks of Adam Danoun*. However, 'at the very last minute before I sent the manuscripts to the publisher', this fictional 'Khoury' changes his mind and calls the collected notebooks *Children of the Ghetto Volume I*.[36] The shift, he says, is because:

> the book should expose a truth to which no-one previously had paid any attention, namely that the Palestinian women and men who had managed to remain in their land were the children of the little ghettoes into which they had been forced by the new state that had taken over their country, erasing its name.[37]

Where Adam is focused on a basic writing of memory and experience, 'Khoury' is amplifying these struggles as against a wider set of forces.

Ghītū is not 'writing back' to power with power's tools or metaphors, it is not trying to justify Palestinian inclusion within existing categories. It is giving a platform to Adam, for whom ghetto became a sound signifier filled with the reality of a 'new and strange way of life'[38] that emerged for Palestinians who would become citizens of a new state of Israel. As the word is used, and conditions change, it developed a grammar, meaning and trajectory of its own, separate from what the men guarding the barbed wire understood of the term, and their own particular set of associations. In Arabic, as Khoury's Hebrew translator puts it, ghetto is 'mediated by a colonial regime of continuous Nakba'.[39] The ghetto that *Ghītū* renders not only offers an alternative definition but also crafts a structure of language and telling that prevents the flattening of a specific Palestinian experience as it crosses into the global marketplace. Khoury himself has called the work of translating 'ghetto' akin to 'picking fruit that won't be easy to digest and handing it to the reader who detests the deliberate disregard'.[40] The novel creates in language what Refqa Abu Rimaileh calls 'simultaneous irreconcilables',[41] where words simply come to mean many things, in many languages, at the same time. Looking first at how precisely ghetto is defined in the novel, a final section explores this new meaning in conversation with its European counterpart, ultimately making room for a multiplicity of languages to exist – even if unevenly in a context of ongoing inequality – within the same world of literature.

Defining ghetto

Awlād al-Ghītū writes 'ghetto' so that the word comes to describe the Palestinian experience in Israel; it is at once a place of residence, an act of separation, a process of dispossession and the force (combining all of these parts) that recreated community amid the destruction of the Nakba. Most critically, the word stands independent, it is not a derivative of an other 'original'. In dictionaries of record, 'ghetto' defines 'intentionally and generically ... a place of obligatory Jewish residence'.[42] Though its origins are debated,[43] usage by the late 1500s refer specifically to 'The quarter in a city, chiefly in Italy, to which the Jews were restricted',[44] and the 'Quartier juif de certaines villes d'Europe'.[45] Both the OED and Larousse explain that this specific word defined by European Jewish experience can apply to 'other' minorities separated from a larger population (some cite specifically African American communities in the United States as one such example); such usage is '*transferred and figurative*'.[46] Other contexts can thus make a claim on the term, but the term can never claim them back. In Arabic this general usage holds. When it appears in dictionaries the word (*ghītū*) is transliterated into Arabic script, bringing its specific European meanings with it. This is in part because 'the language of symbols still fresh from World War II and the Holocaust in Europe ... migrated almost naturally to the Middle East',[47] so 'ghetto' came within a much larger set of concepts that were all used to refer to experiences and phenomena elsewhere. In *Awlād al-Ghītū*, a new definition is written; one that is not a subset or derivative of another experience.

In the first instance, ghetto is simply the name of the area where Adam grew up. As the quote that opened this paper lays out, the people of Lydda, allegorized by Adam's mother Manal, 'didn't know what the word "ghetto" meant or where it came from. All she knew was that the people of Lydda heard it from the Israeli soldiers'.[48] Only one person in the wired-off area knew how the word would have been used by the soldiers when they spoke it, Mamoun, the blind schoolteacher. When he hears that this is what Lydda is being called, he rails, muttering to himself, 'these idiots don't know that we don't have ghettos in our towns and call the Jewish districts the "Jewish Quarter" just like any other quarter of our cities, so it makes no sense'.[49] He emphasizes that the Jewish experience of ghetto and the meaning of the word for the residents of Lydda are disconnected. Imposing one meaning 'makes no sense' (bamshish al-ḥāl) for the lived reality of the city. So the residents fill the word with their own.

In calling Lydda a ghetto, residents first assume that the word is used as a replacement for a more familiar concept, and it is mapped on to a practice of neighbourhoods common to Palestine. As Adam explains, 'the general conviction among the fenced-in city's people continued to be that the "ghetto" meant the Arab Quarter [al-ḥayy al-ʿarabī]'.[50] The same word, ḥayy or neighbourhood, or quarter, had been earlier used to describe where the barbed wire was placed, around 'the quarter [ḥayy] embraced by the mosque',[51] and to describe the different neighbourhoods of Lydda. Any ḥayy that Adam references in the work is distinguished by particular characteristics; where a certain family lives, proximity to the mosque or the rail station, for example. Used by the soldiers, residents hear 'ghetto' and use it as a replacement for ḥayy, mapping a sound signifier, (ghītū), onto a Palestinian term. The change in signifier is important, since life for the people of the city would no longer be how it once was. Thus, filling the sound (ghītū) with meaning relevant to the new terms of existence meant ghetto became endowed with meaning directly related and relevant to the Nakba. If the Nakba is an ongoing process, the novel posits ghetto as its lived reality; the cumulative result of the violence that Nakba signifies, but also the process of response and repair – the mapping onto old patterns and existing language, making sense of what Adam calls a 'new fate'.[52]

Filling the sound signifier ghītū with Palestinian meaning in the wake of the Nakba shifts the meaning of ghetto in another important way. Where the dictionary definition describes it as a place of residence and an act of separation, in Ghītū the word describes a force, or a combination of forces that began before the barbed wire was strung, and which continue to the present. Where the experience of Lydda, surrounded by wire in 'a cage with no roof'[53] was exceptional during the Nakba, Adam 'discovered that what had happened in Lydda had been generalised to all the Palestinian cities'.[54] Without the presence of wire, other cities 'were ghettoised [taghawwatat] by the closing off of the Arab districts'.[55] The villages too, he discovered, were 'transformed into closed spaces under military rule'.[56] While the word ghetto was only used by the soldiers to describe the consequences of the wire – which were after all only up for a year – the ramifications of the forces that saw the wire put up (and the military rule in place for eighteen years) 'bore deep into Palestinian consciousness, so that the ghetto became a flag of an entire people'.[57] It was not just the people of Lydda who would 'submit to their new fate'[58] and adapt previous patterns of life to new language. The novel claims ghetto as a word that rather describes the Palestinian experience in Israel. In fact, it is – in this iteration – a word that constituted them as a community amid the destruction of the Nakba.

Gathered around a well, trying to make sense of what was happening, the residents of Lydda named Adam. He was, one resident declared, 'the first child to be born here'.[59] Though he is an orphan, found 'lying under an olive tree in the arms of its mother, who had departed this life',[60] the destroyed city claims him 'like the garden of Eden'.[61] The act of claiming not only gives the orphan an origin, a place of belonging, but it also reconstitutes a community – this new Lydda is made a family by adopting Adam into it. This is also the case for Manal, the nurse who was searching for her lover and found herself in Lydda when the wire was strung up. Adam later describes her as 'a woman fashioned of words, the first word of a sentence with no last word but the ghetto, as though she'd been born there'.[62] As Manal was holding him that morning when the people in the destroyed city saw the barbed wire, everyone assumed she was the infant's mother. And thus she became. 'All of us are children of Adam',[63] one elder declares, and the child himself reflects, 'the people of the ghetto were one family, and I, Adam Danoun, was the first child of the ghetto, so they adopted me, one and all'.[64] In writing the story of the ghetto, Adam once again constitutes place. The story of Adam/ghetto – as intertwined notions – begins with the factors that expelled a pregnant woman from her home, set a blind man on a road alone with an infant, saw a virgin become a mother, and a collective made with the remnants of a city forged to protect each other from the same forces that endangered them in the first place.

But how does this ghetto maintain its particularity in a context where ghetto has one particular meaning? Rising to the challenge set out for the work, within its covers *Ghītū* puts its unique definition into contact with a broader global framework of languages and word meaning that would otherwise see a Palestinian ghetto as a problematic subset of a differently defined original. An analysis of how these terms are variously used, taken up or mobilized as political relationships gives a sense of the flows of power that words circulate within, and how minority/colonized languages and language cultures live, use and mobilize these words across multiple levels of discourse, from the local to the global.

Complex constellations

The relationship of Adam's ghetto to the European term is one of multilingualism, where a multiplicity of languages exists unevenly in a context of ongoing inequality. Setting ghetto into the larger constellation of multilingualism developed within the novel, a method of reading and writing language as situated within its uneven contexts emerges. Where ghetto was redefined entirely, becoming a mere sound signifier for a different experience, 'massacres' (*madhābiḥ*) is appropriated; its meaning in Arabic joined with postwar terminology. In other cases, words with 'other' meanings maintain these definitions, rendered in the novel in Latin script and standing out in stark contrast with the Arabic letters. Still yet, words are given in both their European spelling and their Arabic transliteration. Each difference symbolizes a different relationship between this 'original' and its meaning for Adam – which is often no less 'original'. What is clear in each usage, however, is that transformation is loaded. In claiming, redefining, using and distancing the story of Adam from words variously policed by global forces *Ghītū* centres the imbalances of power in language as part of the story. In this way, even as the words are taken up into the 'world', they are able to retain to some extent the now 'original' context.

Almost reinforcing the distinct and separate definition of ghetto, the use of 'massacre' within the novel pulls consciously from European usage and its associations. The word is most often used when describing the 'Dahmash Mosque massacre',[65] which the narrator asserts, 'one might legitimately compare' with the 'Lydda massacres and the Shatila massacre'.[66] The use of the word massacre indicates in both cases, Adam writes, to 'the organisation of killing'.[67] Rather than the dictionary definition, which focuses on the number or concentration of killing, Adam pulls directly from Holocaust associations and focuses on the intent that drove the violence. Here, usage expands an existing definition, demanding that the word become accountable to other contexts. Adam is not only meticulous in his usage, but also takes time to explain and insist on it:

> I know that the word 'massacres' [*madhābiḥ*] falls unpleasantly on the ear in today's world, which views Israel as the offspring of the Holocaust and as heir to the Jewish pain brought about by savage persecution and mass extermination. Despite this, I can use no other word, for not only is it appropriate to what happened in Palestine in 1948, it is also coextensive with the Nakba that has been ongoing for fifty years in the form of a continuing massacre that has not ceased even now.[68]

The meaning and purpose of the massacre as it was mobilized postwar and its history in Arabic fit neatly, Adam concludes. The children of the Holocaust had taught the children of the ghetto its meaning. But it is not a simple matter of transfer. The meaning of organized massacre (*madhābiḥ*) is also fused with the word's classical Arabic associations of sacrifice; linked to the stories of Abraham and Isaac, the killing of the ram instead of the child and the commemoration of this *madhābiḥ* each year at Eid al-Adha.[69] So that the killing of the men of Lydda is both an organized slaughter perpetrated by an outside force, and for those who remain alive, a sacrifice made by those who died for a larger cause or question.

Adam continually crafts the meaning of words so that they respond – not to their corresponding dictionary definitions – but to the life he has lived and witnessed. These words come to embody power differentials, colonial forces and linguistic histories. Such linguistic crafting is done consciously, as part of the search for a frame within which his story might be expressed. This includes the observation of power as it transforms words and the double meanings that these words take on. As if making a study of the capacity of words to operate as what Abu Rimaileh called 'simultaneous irreconcilables',[70] Adam pauses at the mention of 'sabāba', which 'became a Hebrew word, I've no idea how, even though it's classical Arabic'.[71] He writes an imaginary story about the way the word travelled into Hebrew, loading it with a double significance so that when it is spoken in Hebrew and in Arabic, the meaning differs significantly. The reflection comes as an aside to describe and explain the nicknames of one of the characters, 'Hajj Sababa', who appeared in the scene where Adam gets his name. After mentioning the character, and that sababa became a Hebrew word (indeed, it is likely that most Palestinians remaining within the borders of Mandate Palestine would first know the word through its Hebrew usage) Adam explains it for his reader.

In his aside, Adam reclaims the word as classical Arabic, shows how power can cut off words from their history, but reclaims the compilation as a word of the Nakba. Explaining sababa, he writes:

> In Hebrew it's now a synonym for 'pleasure' combined with the English 'cool'– a word plucked from the Arabic lexicon to which it belongs and which allots it the meanings of 'love' and 'passionate yearning' to be transformed into a Hebrew word that encompasses the senses of 'pleasure' and 'everything's fine.'[72]

Though Adam says he has 'no idea how' the word entered Hebrew, he in fact traces a shift in meaning from a 'passionate yearning' in the classical sense, to the more laissez faire 'everything's fine' in contemporary Hebrew usage. He even uses 'cool' in Latin letters alongside the Arabic *kūl* to denote the foreignness of the concept. Beyond an illustration of the disconnect between meanings, the aside gives critical information necessary to interpret the story of Iliya Batshoun, who comes to be known as Hajj Sababa, who gives 'sababa' to Hebrew, and claims it back for Palestine.

Batshoun had told his wife and children to leave for Lebanon but refused to go because he had preferred to die in Palestine. Ready for death, Batshoun stood up to the guards of the ghetto in its first days to protect a little girl and her devastated mother, who in despair had instructed the soldiers to kill them both, or at least to take the small child so she could die in peace. Her sons and her husband had all been killed in the mosque massacre and she had no one and nothing left with which to take care of herself and her daughter. Batshoun and the woman – a generation younger than he – end up married. It is the first marriage of the ghetto. When Iliyya's son returns to find his father years later and discovers he has converted to Islam and married the once-devastated woman, he asks in anger what he is supposed to tell his mother. The answer, from another elder, is: 'tell your mother sababa', which in its formal context might be rendered: tell your mother its 'passionate love'. Perhaps the overhearing soldiers hear: tell your mother it is what it is, or, everything's fine.

In Hebrew, Adam's story intimates, sababa comes to mean 'relax everything is fine', while the same story in Arabic, in the context of a Palestinian Nakba and the separation of families, takes on a flipped inflection. Sababa, in this case, becomes the possibility of a reconstituted life and continued love in a reality of duress that is also a reality of separation. What Adam doesn't mention is that sababa is also used in metallurgy to mean 'forge', or create an alloy. If 'tell your mother sababa' was interpreted by soldiers as 'tell your mother it is what it is' – which was functionally what was being communicated – it might, taking context and linguistic tradition into account, be rendered differently again. A more long-winded translation, drawing out codes within language and context, might be recorded as: 'Tell your mother that in the context of the Nakba, and your father's decision to stay and fight, that this passionate love has come and brought different elements of a community together. In this case, he must still stay and fight and is now bonded a new configuration of parts and people.' Here it is the power differentials that create the meaning of the word; it is the fact that sababa was appropriated by a colonizing force in a context of Nakba that endows it with its particular meaning, in both Hebrew and in Palestinian Arabic. Read multilingually, sababa tells the story of the Nakba from multiple vantage points, including the power differentials that made it so easy to miss one definition in favour of another.

That ghetto, massacre and sababa are all words created differently in a multilingual and uneven context is never made clearer than with *Ghītū*'s vast and at times disorienting use of Latin characters. These unmistakably place words in a global context, but at the same time pull this global context into the story, showing that these words are necessary to in order to narrate Lydda, which is itself a multilingual story. Similar to 'Khoury''s use of 'five star' to evaluate Adam's manuscripts, Latin characters are used elsewhere as a sort of citation-as-credential. For example, Adam references work he read in the *Middle East Forum*[73] and *Arab Studies Quarterly*[74] (spelled out in Latin characters with English spelling in the Arabic). As common bibliographic practice in many Arabic academic publications, citing journal titles in the language of their publication lends the references in *Ghītū* an air of the official, of referenced and citable fact. Other names and nouns appear in Latin characters, including Fish restaurant '*maṭʿam* Fish *fī shāriʿ balīkar*' (Fish restaurant on Bleecker Street),[75] which notably does not render Bleecker Street in Latin characters. This highlights the restaurant as the central focus, as the thing that is different and notable, not to be confused with any other restaurant, and draws attention to the fact that is a Arabic food purveyor with an English name (the street name, on the other hand, becomes totally domesticated within an Arabic milieu, reminding the reader that New York plays host to Arabic meaning). Rendering the names variously in Latin and Arabic characters emphasizes the point that the story of Palestine unfolds over multiple locations and languages.

These create a foundation of relation between and across languages and language-contexts within which ghetto – a word that is only rendered in Arabic script – can be read within. Other usages only confirm this relationality. The innocuous use of 'kūl cool'[76] uses both Arabic and Latin script, showing that even when the word is 'domesticated' into Arabic it retains for Adam a particular usage and origin. In this case the use of Latin characters and reference to contemporary English convention pin the Arabic word to a particular outside meaning that is at once familiar as 'global English' (indicated by its rendering in Arabic script) but still originating from outside. Other references, like to the British-made Projector, Infantry, Anti-Tank (PIAT), render the word in both Latin acronym and its Arabization: '*biat* PIAT',[77] as if to remind the reader that the thing has a use and a home across contexts. Each example highlights the different ways that language crosses, sometimes taking on entirely new meaning, sometimes retaining a meaning from a separate context, and at other times becoming a complex rendering of many meanings at once. All of these possibilities are necessary to explain Lydda and ghetto, which were likewise produced by so many different complex and uneven crossings.

The novel's final example of Latin-character use poignantly reveals the necessity of reading multilingually and resisting the forces of language, literature and politics that have so obstructed the global narration of Palestine and its Nakba. The phrase in the Arabic text is 'Sonder Kommando', written in Latin characters, and furnishing the name of the novel's second-to-last chapter. It is the German spelling of the name given to Nazi 'special squads composed mainly of Jewish inmates but also of Russian prisoners of war who were forced to work in and around the gas-chambers and crematoria of Auschwitz, in the summer of 1944'.[78] It is used to describe these same Jewish units, and hearkens a parallel with burning squads created by Jewish soldiers in Palestine. In the novel, this first spelling is used three times, once in the chapter title and twice in reference to Holocaust survivors, living men who had been members of the Sonderkommando. The word is used as Adam tries to unpack his encounter with Murad, another resident of Lydda, half a generation older than Adam, who remembers a great deal more of the first days of the ghetto, and was a member of the burning unit.

Where Adam clearly sees 'the transformation of the Palestinian youth of the ghetto into a new form of Sonder Commando'[79] (note the spelling change from the K to a C),[80] it is not a word he claims. Instead he explains that the units created in Lydda are 'a new form' (*naw ʿ jadīd*) of the same thing, but not the same thing. The echoes between one event and another bother Adam, who felt 'perplexed when faced by fate's coincidences',[81] but ultimately declared that he cannot come up with a way to reconcile the two. This discomfort, Khoury's Hebrew translator suggests, is Adam recognizing 'that the term sonderkommandos fits the description of the Jewish victims, but it is not "eligible" for their Palestinian homologues (or not)'.[82] Shanav both suggests and questions whether the words operate as homologues, as referents 'having the same relation, proportion, relative position'[83] to one another. For Shanav, the exact orientation of Sonder Kommando to Sonder Commando remains purposely opaque. Though perhaps a better sense of the relationship would be one that is undetermined.[84] In either case, remaining open allows for both to exist, in some sort of relationship without being reduced to the repetition of a single idea. This is what remains critical in all instances: the refusal of a foreclosure into parallel or comparison.

Conclusion

What makes Palestine 'non-eligible' for Holocaust terminology is that terminology's policing, as well as the inevitable flatting of 'other' experiences or definitions, which fit too neatly into a perceived original so that they are elided or are seen as sub-sets. As Adam himself declares, 'I don't want to draw a comparison between the Holocaust and the Nakba. I hate such comparisons',[85] because the wider reality would mean – beyond the perceived challenge to memory and state legitimacy – the flattening of an actual Nakba experience that relies on the broadening and multiplicity of language in order to be told. For Adam, with his constant questioning of words, language is best not compared; at least when the matrix of comparison is one of fitting in predetermined categories. *Ghītū*, including 'Khoury''s fictional authorial preface challenges world systems to take up Adam's multilingual approach. This echoes, to some extent, Bashir and Goldberg's calls for a 'new grammar of the Holocaust and the Nakba', founded not on comparison but on 'empathic unsettlement' as a tool 'to avoid the posttraumatic collapse of all distinctions [between Nakba and Holocaust] into a single indistinct jumble'.[86] They propose a 'grammar' of relationship whereby Nakba and Holocaust 'do not suppress and deny each other but rather make sense in nexus with one another as part of any meaningful historical utterance'.[87] But Adam goes further than the problem of relationship, and looks to the wider systems that prevent such a relationship from taking form.

Ghītū is a word, a concept and a set of relationships that emerges when world literature and world experiences move outside of the policing norms of discursive systems. It refuses the idea of comparison or similarity (even homologues) and inserts the structures of power that shaped words and word concepts into the stories that they tell, as this context is part of the definition of the words themselves. The novel proposes a literary system with a changed metric of comparison and evaluation, a changed metric that begins with a sense of multilingualism that takes up with language the complex structures that have moved it across contexts and the systems of knowing that have meant that alternatives and alternative relationships had been silenced.

Notes

1 Ilyās Khūrī, *Awlād al-Ghītū, ismī Ādam: riwāyah* (Bayrūt: Dār al-Ādāb lil-Nashr wa-al-Tawzī, 2016). Elias Khoury, *My Name is Adam: Children of the Ghetto Volume 1*, trans. Humphrey Davies (London: Maclehose Press, 2018). All references to the novel refer to these editions.
2 Khoury, *My Name is Adam*, 209; Khūrī, *Awlād al-Ghītū*, 302.
3 Benny Morris, *1948* (New Haven: Yale University Press, 2008), 287–9.
4 Sandra Debenedetti-Stow 'The Etymology of "Ghetto": New Evidence from Rome', *Jewish History* 6, no. 1/2 (1992): 83.
5 Pascale Casanova, *The World Republic of Letters*, trans. M B. DeBevoise (Cambridge, MA: Harvard University Press, 2007), 17.
6 Pheng Cheah, *What Is a World? On Postcolonial Literature as World Literature* (Durham, NC: Duke University Press, 2016), 1.
7 Michael Allan, *In the Shadow of World Literature: Sites of Reading in Colonial Egypt* (Princeton: Princeton University Press, 2016), 17.
8 Ibid., 18.
9 Khoury, *My Name is Adam*, 18; Khūrī, *Awlād al-Ghītū*, 91.
10 Casanova, *The World Republic of Letters*, 17.
11 Elias Khoury's online author page is available at www.mertin-litag.de/authors_htm/Khoury-E.htm (accessed 31 March 2020).
12 Graham Huggan, *The Postcolonial Exotic: Marketing the Margins* (London: Routledge, 2006), 4.
13 Elias Khoury, as quoted in the Israeli daily newspaper *Haaretz*, translated from Hebrew by Yehda Shanav, and republished on US publisher Archipelago Books' website. Available online: https://archipelagobooks.org/2014/05/elias-khoury-interviewed-by-haaretz/ (accessed 31 March 2020).

14 Robyn Creswell, 'Tripoli Nights with a Master of Arabic', in *The New York Review of Books*, 9 March 2017. Available online: www.nybooks.com/articles/2017/03/09/tripoli-nights-master-arabic/ (accessed 31 March 2020).
15 Khoury, *My Name is Adam*, 81; Khūrī, *Awlād al-Ghītū*, 111.
16 Edward Said, 'Permission to Narrate', *Journal of Palestine Studies* 13.3 (1984): 27–48, 30.
17 The Sabra and Shatila massacres of 1982 were perpetrated by the Lebanese Phalangist forces, under the direction of the Israeli army, which had invaded south Lebanon. For more, see Bayan Al-Hout and Nuwayhed, *Sabra and Shatila: September 1982* (London: Pluto Press, 2004).
18 Said, 'Permission to Narrate', 27.
19 Ibid., 29.
20 Yara Hawari, Sharri Plonski and Elian Weizman, 'Seeing Israel through Palestine: Knowledge Production as Anti-Colonial Praxis', *Settler Colonial Studies* 9.1 (2019): 155–75, 155.
21 Ibid., 159.
22 Constantine Zurayk, 'Ma'anā al-Nakba' (The Meaning of Nakba), trans. *The Palestinian Revolution* project (2016). Available online: http://learnpalestine.politics.ox.ac.uk (accessed 27 February 2020). The original Arabic work was written in Beirut in 1948 and published by Dār al-'Ilm li-al-Malāyīn.
23 Ibid.
24 Ibid.
25 See for example Himmat Zubi, 'The Ongoing Nakba: Urban Palestinian Survival in Haifa', in Nahla Abdo-Zubi and Nur Masalha (eds.), *An Oral History of the Palestinian Nakba* (London: Zed Books, 2018): 182–208.
26 Bashir Bashir and Amos Goldberg, *The Holocaust and the Nakba: A New Grammar of Trauma and History* (New York: Columbia University Press, 2019), 4.
27 Ibid.
28 Rosemary Sayigh, 'On the Exclusion of the Palestinian Nakba from the "Trauma Genre"', *Journal of Palestine Studies* 43.1 (2013): 51–60, 52.
29 Ibid.
30 Khoury, 'Foreword', in Bashir and Goldberg, *The Holocaust and the Nakba*, x.
31 Khoury, *My Name is Adam*, 76; Khūrī, *Awlād al-Ghītū*, 89.
32 Bashir and Goldberg, *The Holocaust and the Nakba*, 5.
33 Ibid., 28.
34 Ibid., 13.
35 See for example Michael Rothberg, 'From Gaza to Warsaw: Mapping Multidirectional Memory', *Criticism* 53.4 (2011): 523–48 on mobilization of the Gaza as Ghetto comparison; Nazmi Al Jubeh, 'The Ghettoization of Arab Jerusalem', *Jerusalem Quarterly* 16 (2002): 5–11; or Tom Selwyn, 'Ghettoizing a Matriarch and a City: An Everyday Story from the Palestinian/Israeli Borderlands', *Journal of Borderlands Studies* 24. 3 (2009): 39–55 on the ghettoization of West Bank areas, in particular the case of Jerusalem and Rachel's Tomb in Bethlehem respectively; Ilan Pappé, 'Genocide in Gaza', in *The Plight of the Palestinians* (New York: Palgrave Macmillan 2010), 201–5 on the comparison of Israeli military policy in the Gaza Strip with Nazi genocide.
36 *Children of the Ghetto* is set to have three volumes. Khoury explained to an audience in London in 2018 that the story of Adam was simply too large to fit comfortably

between two bound covers. Each volume has a separate subtitle. Volume One is 'My name is Adam', and Volume Two, which came out in 2019, is 'Najmat al-baḥr, riwāya', translated into English as 'Stella Maris'.

37 Khoury, *My Name is Adam*, 15; Khūrī, *Awlād al-Ghītū*, 17.
38 Ibid., 220; 318.
39 Yehuda Shanav, 'A Translator's Point of View on Children of the Ghetto', in Bashir and Goldberg, 329–52, 342.
40 Da'adli, Tawfiq, 'In this Ghetto for which we have Gathered', *Journal of Levantine Studies* 9.2 (2019): 205–6, 206.
41 Refqa Abu-Remaileh, 'Novel as Contrapuntal Reading: Elias Khoury's Children of the Ghetto: My Name is Adam', in Bashir and Goldberg, *The Holocaust and the Nakba*: 295–306, 297.
42 Ibid.
43 Etymologists have debated extensively the 'origins' of the word (with consensus resting on Italian, but new research suggesting a Hebrew-Italian hybrid), see Debenedetti-Stow, 'The Etymology of "Ghetto": New Evidence from Rome', 79–85, 83.
44 'ghetto, n.', *OED Online* (Oxford University Press, July 2018).
45 'ghetto', *Larousse: Langue Francais* (Larousse, February 2020).
46 'ghetto, n.', *OED Online* (Oxford University Press, July 2018).
47 Bashir and Goldberg, *The Holocaust and the Nakba*, 9.
48 Khoury, *My Name is Adam*, 322; Khūrī, *Awlād al-Ghītū*, 196.
49 Ibid., 220; 319.
50 Ibid., 323.
51 Ibid., 139; 196.
52 Ibid., 221; 320.
53 Ibid.
54 Ibid.
55 Ibid.
56 Ibid.
57 Ibid., 319
58 Ibid., 318.
59 Ibid.
60 Ibid., 83; 112.
61 Ibid.
62 Ibid., 87; 196.
63 Ibid., 156; 223.
64 Ibid., 96; 133.
65 Ibid., 92; 129.
66 Ibid., 150; 214.
67 Ibid., 151; 215.
68 Ibid., 215; 310.
69 See for example Ibn al Manzur's thirteenth-century *Lisan al-Arab*'s (Bayrūt: Dār Ṣādir) extensive definitions around these themes.
70 Abu-Remaileh, 'Novel as Contrapuntal Reading', 297.
71 Khoury, *My Name is Adam*, 244; Khūrī, *Awlād al-Ghītū*, 353.
72 Ibid.
73 Ibid., 188; 272.

74 Ibid., 212; 306.
75 Ibid., 255; 368.
76 Ibid., 244; 353.
77 Ibid., 216; 312.
78 Dan Stone, 'The Sonderkommando Photographs', *Jewish Social Studies* 7.3 (2001): 133.
79 Khoury, *My Name is Adam*, 285; Khūrī, *Awlād al-Ghītū*, 411.
80 This could equally be a way to distinguish the Palestinian experience from the Jewish units in Nazi-controlled Poland. It slightly anglicizes the word, which is occasionally used to refer to the same unit. Alternatively, it is a typo.
81 Khoury, *My Name is Adam*, 284; Khūrī, *Awlād al-Ghītū*, 410.
82 Yehuda Shanav, 'A Translator's Point of View on Children of the Ghetto', in Bashir and Goldberg, 329–52, 338.
83 'homologous, adj.', *OED Online* (Oxford University Press, December 2019).
84 In the novel, the Jewish Sonderkommando are interpreted through Claude Lanzman's film *Shoah* (1985) and his later and lesser known *Tsahal* (1994), which read the establishment of the Israeli military as a redemptive act for those who suffered the humiliation of the Sonderkommando. In *Ghītū*, on the other hand, Murad continues to suffer the humiliation of the memory, 'Screw us and what we'd become!'(276/Arabic 399) he tells Adam, before breaking down in tears and ending the friendship between the men.
85 Khoury, *My Name is Adam*, 284; Khūrī, *Awlād al-Ghītū*, 412.
86 Bashir and Goldberg, *The Holocaust and the Nakba*, 25.
87 Ibid., 6.

10

Multilingual others: Transliteration as resistant translation

Dima Ayoub

The multilingual Arab writer who uses more than one language in their text is often hounded by the question of *which* language to use *when*.[1] Such writers can belong fully to all or neither language, yet they must justify their choices at the same time as they negotiate the fraught boundaries between Arabic and other languages. In *Thou Shalt Not Speak My Language*, Moroccan literary critic Abdelfattah Kilito asks questions that multilingual Arab writers find themselves constantly having to address: 'Can one possess two languages? Can one master them equally? ... How does [one] manage [one's] affairs in perpetual translation?'[2]

Kilito's provocative title, *Thou Shalt Not Speak My Language*, derives from an interaction with an American woman. He is left dumbfounded after realizing that the American not only spoke excellent Arabic without so much as a blemish, but that 'she was able to pronounce letters that bother most non-Arabs, who fail to produce them, such as the qāf, the 'ayn, and the ḥā'. I was surprised, and for the first time I felt that my language is slipping away from me, or rather that the American woman had robbed me of it.'[3] In an effort to unseat parochial literary and cultural notions about Arabic's untranslatability, Kilito advances a hermeneutics of suspicion directed primarily at foreign speakers of Arabic. This hermeneutics is based on an engagement that begins with the West's fixation with Arabic, evoked through a discussion of Petrarch, Dante and Renan, and ends facing the American woman in Morocco – an impressive historical sweep.

For Kilito, the multilingual idiom is thorny because it is inextricably tied to the question of suspicion that pits the self (read: known) against the other (read: foreign). The engagement with notions of linguistic resistance in the works of multilingual postcolonial writers has been famously articulated by Kenyan writer Ngũgĩ wa Thiong'o and Nigerian novelist Chinua Achebe in what has come to be known as the Ngũgĩ-Achebe debate.[4] While their famous debate does not explicitly centre on claims of suspicion, Kilito's meditation on suspicion surfaces a subtle psycho-linguistic dynamic that is typically hinted at rather than discussed outright. The subtlety of this dynamic is often permitted precisely because the subject is foreign – and therefore already suspect by definition. Kilito himself puts it bluntly: 'I dislike having foreigners speak my language.'⁵ Kilito advances the possibility of an exclusive owning of his language, wherein the foreign speaker of Arabic is also an aggressor. But if as Waïl Hassan argues, 'multilingualism, cultural plurality, immigration, and exile are all part of Arab modernity, products of the same historical process, nowhere better documented than in the novel' how can the Arabic language exist as a separate unit from other languages? Multilingual writers like Kilito challenge normative understandings of language and literature because they understand the Arabic language as an inherently multilingual language that is intrinsically tied to other literary cultures and traditions.⁶ Indeed, if linguistic borders are no longer viable categories of analysis, is there still room for suspicion to arise, at least in the way that Kilito imagines it? What are the implications for multilingual writers when suspicion is leveled at them locally in their source language and milieu? What happens to multilingual texts when they are indicted as inauthentic on their soil? In considering the corpus of Maghrebian and African texts written in French, Réda Bensmaïa laments that the question of *which* language forces us to take a 'detour' towards the 'ideological and political'.⁷

The case of Egyptian author, translator and critic Somaya Ramadan shows us that when multilingual authors are rejected from their national and local literary systems, they fall into a state of permanent limbo where they do not belong to either national literature or world literature. After publishing her first novel *Awrāq al-narjis* in 2001 (*Leaves of Narcissus*, 2001), Ramadan faced criticism on the grounds that she betrayed the Arabic language along with its novelistic tradition. *Awrāq al-narjis* rejects outright an adherence to the ideological confines of monolingualism, but also to the very structure of realism that defines a substantial segment of modern Arabic fiction. Written primarily in Arabic, the novel interweaves English and French words and expressions such as 'you think I'm just a pretty face!' and 'يورستوبد' (you're stupid) into the narrative. At times, the Arabic language is superimposed onto the English language through the process of transliteration – a strategy that the author uses to fuse the three languages together, as well as to decentre the dominance of English and French. Centred on the life of its protagonist Kimi, the novel reads like an intertextual interior monologue. A stranger in the midst of her upper-middle class Cairene family, Kimi is sent to Dublin to pursue a graduate degree. While in Dublin, Kimi's engagement with questions of identity and belonging are heightened and her feelings of estrangement, loneliness and madness become more acute. The novel's structure mirrors the life of its protagonist; indeed, *Awrāq al-narjis* defies classification on several fronts. Geographically, it belongs everywhere and nowhere. Linguistically, the text pushes against the limits of monolingualism. It also challenges the very genre of the novel itself and classifying it as such has been the source of contention among critics.⁸

Upon its publication in 2001, *Awrāq al-narjis* received the Naguib Mahfouz Medal for Literature – a highly coveted literary prize that acknowledges and celebrates contemporary literature published in Arabic and not yet translated into English. The prize guarantees translation into English that will be published by The American University in Cairo Press AUC Press. The attention Ramadan garnered by winning the Mahfouz Medal certainly put her on the literary map as a novelist; however, it also exposed her to attacks by critics in the Egyptian literary establishment who acted as gatekeepers.

One major accusation was that the multilingualism in Ramadan's text corrupted her Arabic language and thus made the novel unworthy of the prestigious prize. Among the many charges it received, *Awrāq al-narjis* was decried as a 'national disaster' signaling the downfall of Arabic literature and altogether summoning the 'death certificate' of the famed prize.[9] The attacks on Ramadan expose the extent that critics will go to call her ethnic, cultural, religious, national and linguistic loyalties into question.

A Cairene born in 1951, Somaya Ramadan obtained her Bachelor's degree in English literature at Cairo University and then went on to obtain a PhD also in English literature from Trinity College in Dublin, Ireland in 1983. Prior to publishing *Awrāq al-narjis*, Ramadan published two collections of short stories: *Khashab wa nuḥās* (Wood and Brass) in 1995 and *Manāzil al-qamar* (Phases of the Moon) in 1999. A renowned feminist in Cairo's literary circles, Ramadan is one of the founding members of the Women and Memory Forum, a non-profit organization based in Cairo that focuses on Arab women's history. Among her other notable contributions is her translation of Virginia Woolf's *A Room of One's Own* into Arabic as *Ghurfa takhuṣṣ al-mar' waḥdahu* (1999). Ramadan is also an outspoken believer in Baha'ism in a state that does not recognize the Baha'i faith.[10] Her 2009 publication *Ṭarīq al-mustaqbal: ru'yah Bahā'īyah* (The Way of the Future: A Baha'i's Perspective)[11] is a bold undertaking to translate what it means to be Baha'i from an insider's point of view, especially as Baha'ism is not recognized as an official religion in Egypt.

In this chapter, I read Ramadan's *Awrāq al-narjis* as an example of a 'multilingual local' text as defined by Francesca Orsini in 'The Multilingual Local in World Literature'. Inscribed with Arabic, English, French and intertextual references as varied as James Joyce, W. B. Yeats, Samuel Beckett, Shakespeare, Salah Jahin and Arab folktales, *Awrāq al-narjis* inhabits a multiplicity of linguistic and cultural traditions. Orsini argues that since the second millennium, all literary cultures have been deeply multilingual with 'repertoires of genres in each language that did or did not overlap and circulated along partly shared but often divergent geographies'.[12] Ramadan's is not the first Egyptian novel to re-evaluate Arabic's discreteness or include other languages in the text however, her novel insists on approaching literature's multilingualism as a 'structuring and generative principle' that 'holds *both* local *and* cosmopolitan perspectives'.[13] Egyptian literary critic Sabry Hafez calls attention to Ramadan's literary style by claiming that she is one of the very few writers of her generation to treat the 'once classic' theme of interaction with the West in her text. Hafez locates *Awrāq al-narjis* within a new genre of modern Arabic literature that 'rejects the linear narrative of the realist novel' popularized by Mahfouz.[14] Not only is *Awrāq al-narjis* a non-linear text, but Kimi herself is the embodiment of estrangement, persecution and exile. The plot revolves around her struggle with mental illness, her subsequent rejection by her family and her refusal to belong to a singular language and geography.

At the same time as Kimi occupies a state of non-belonging, the novel insists on reclaiming Kimi as in some way also integral to Egypt. Thus, it is not a coincidence that the name Kimi means Egypt in Coptic – by choosing a Coptic name, Ramadan creates a character that encompasses the duality of belonging and marginalization.[15] While the Coptic community is the largest Christian group in the Middle East, Copts remain a religious minority in Egypt. Notwithstanding her Coptic name, the novel does not explicitly affix a singular religious heritage to Kimi, allowing her to inhabit a multiplicity of voices, influences and attachments that rebuts religious partiality to Islam or Coptism. Ramadan's commitment to the inclusion of Egypt's religious minorities is another element of the text that attempts to move beyond majority culture and language. The exclusion of Baha'is in Egypt is not a topic Ramadan takes up directly in *Awrāq al-narjis*; however, the cruelty of exclusionary nationalism and conformity is a major theme in the text. The novel contains elements of what Mary Youssef calls the 'new consciousness' in contemporary Egyptian literature in *Minorities in the Contemporary Egyptian Novel*. Such works 'broaden the purview of difference to underscore the cultural experiences of marginalized identities at the intersections of race, ethnicity, religion, gender, language, and class'.[16] Youssef explains that this new trend of Egyptian literature includes a diverse scope of representation that 'responds to persistently uniform political and cultural imaginaries and exclusionary practices within Egypt that continue to overlook and/or exacerbate the marginalization of certain groups, most discernible of which are racial, ethno-religious, and women minorities'.[17] Indeed, Ramadan herself suffers from the exclusionary ideology of religious nationalism in Egypt. In a deeply bureaucratic state such as Egypt, Ramadan is unable to obtain a simple document such as a national identity card (*ḥawiya*) because these include religious affiliation as a legal category. Because Islam, Judaism and Christianity are deemed the only formal religions, Ramadan is repeatedly forced to confront her effacement and rejection as an Egyptian.[18]

The Mahfouz Medal: Between ruthlessness and reverence

Established by the American University in Cairo on the occasion of the Nobel Laureate's eighty-fifth birthday, the Naguib Mahfouz Medal for Literature guarantees translation into English of the winning novel. Shortly after the award, *Awrāq al-narjis* was translated into English under the title *Leaves of Narcissus* by Marilyn Booth. The Mahfouz medal, named after the writer whose work is an unequivocal symbol of the Arabic novel, is itself entwined in the ideological struggle against the West's prevailing power system. In more than a century of the Nobel's history, only one Arab writer was awarded the prize for literature – and even this awarding occurred with considerable lobbying and controversy.[19] The Mahfouz Medal thus is a direct response to the dominant English literary canon because of its exclusionary practices towards Arabic literature.[20] While Mahfouz is often celebrated for writing his novels in a standard Arabic accessible to all Arabic readers, he was not only well-versed in European literature, but some critics go as far as to criticize the 'excessive reliance of Mahfouz and his generation on Western fictional models'.[21] The best example of this is articulated by Mahfouz himself. As Shaden Tageldin recounts in *Disarming Words*, in a 1990 interview with the *Sunday Times of London*, and shortly after winning the Nobel Prize, Mahfouz divulged his 'secret passion' for European literature.[22] When asked about the influence of Charles

Dickens, Balzac and other European novelists on his writing, Mahfouz responds, 'Yes, we know Western literature here'. In fact, he adds, 'we love it too much'.[23] Even as many imagine Mahfouz to be a purist for his insistence on writing in standard literary Arabic, his being 'in love with European languages and literatures' shows an awareness of his own multilingual approach towards Arabic, which is in fact 'contaminated', in his own words, by that 'love's excess'.[24] Tageldin understands Mahfouz's conflicted relationship with Western literature as a form of 'translational seduction' or fascination.

In *Awrāq al-narjis,* Ramadan displays an outright rejection of static paradigms of language, nation and identity which in turn made the author vulnerable to a host of allegations. Mahmud Khayrallah, Ramadan's staunchest critic, is a prominent literary commentator and poet in Egypt who describes *Awrāq al-narjis* as 'beginner's literature' riddled with Arabic 'grammar mistakes' that butcher 'our beautiful Arabic language'.[25] These supposed grammatical mistakes are what lead Khayrallah to accuse Ramadan of writing an anti-nationalist work, because for the critic, an allegiance to Egypt corresponds to monolingualism. Indeed, the novel's linguistic interplay between Arabic and English is cited as evidence of Ramadan's substandard command of the Arabic language rather than an expression of the linguistic experimentation that stems from her fluency in multiple languages and familiarity with various literary traditions. Ramadan's reliance on multilingualism and intertextuality gives Khayrallah further reasoning to accuse Ramadan of being 'an elitist and Westward-gazing' author.[26] Such accusations suggest that Ramadan's orientation and bearings as an author are not what they should be, indeed invoking upper-class affiliation as a means of discrediting her work. While the novel is not overtly political, Khayrallah goes further by alleging that *Awrāq al-narjis* espouses 'anti-Nasser politics'.[27]

More telling is the fact that Ramadan's national loyalties were called into question at the same time as her mastery of the Arabic language was criticized. In *Egypt's Culture Wars,* Samia Mehrez examines the contentious reactions to the granting of the Mahfouz Medal to *Awrāq al-narjis.* In a chapter titled 'Children of the Alley', Mehrez exposes the doctrine of gatekeeping that was waged against Ramadan's novel. Mehrez chronicles and compares the reception of Algerian writer Ahlam Mosteghanemi, the first woman to win the medal in 1998 for her novel *Memory in the Flesh,* with that of Ramadan. Mehrez contends that while the awarding of the medal generates critique within the Egyptian literary establishment annually, Ramadan and Mostaghanemi were subjected to an unusually high level of 'post-award antagonism'.[28] The antagonism leveled at these two women writers allows literary gatekeepers to set the standard for who can or cannot be part of Mahfouz's 'alley'.[29] The claim that Ramadan's novel is 'anti-nationalist' further underscores the weight of the ethno-nationalist rhetoric that situates women as the signifiers of cultural identity and positions them as the most susceptible to 'contamination' – Khayrallah's formulation demonstrates the extent to which the slippage between patriarchy and nationalism are often acute.[30] As the bearers of national culture, women are closely tied to nationalist self-imagination,[31] and in the case of formerly colonized nations, where women come to symbolize cultural continuity, the integrity of the national identity and also resistance to Western influence.[32]

Decentring language and nation

From its decentring of the Arabic language and the singular nation, *Awrāq al-narjis* was considered a cultural and national intruder by virtue of its 'hybrid profile' – a charge that disproportionately places the burden of linguistic and cultural authenticity on women writers.[33] A source of great inspiration for *Awrāq al-narjis*, James Joyce's *Ulysses* was also charged with many of the same allegations of linguistic miscegenation – it is perhaps not a coincidence that both novels suffered significant criticism.[34] Echoes of Joyce's own position as a critic of British linguistic and cultural domination in Ireland can be detected throughout *Awrāq al-narjis*, where Ramadan conjures a cacophony of Arabic, English and French as well as identities that struggle to coexist in the cultural limbo experienced by the novel's protagonist.[35] Joyce's influence notwithstanding, Ramadan is also preceded by a generation of Egyptian writers like Idwar al-Kharrat, Sonallah Ibrahim and Gamal al-Ghitani, who were disenchanted with idealized nationalist fantasies of Egypt. Dubbed as *jīl al-sittīnāt* (Sixties Generation),[36] this group of writers produced works that 'underscore the popular spirit of uncertainty, if not despair, among city dwellers, made distraught by persistent regional wars, increasing class differences, atrocious socio-economic conditions, and lack of political and social reforms'.[37] El-Kharrat's 1980 novel *Rama wā-l-tinyn* (*Rama and the Dragon*, 2002) prefigures elements of Egypt's cultural and historic multiplicity that are present in *Awrāq al-narjis*. El-Kharrat diffuses the religious and historical identity of his novel's protagonists, the Muslim Rama and her Coptic lover Mikha'il by invoking 'the Pharaonic, the Nubian, the Coptic, the Islamic, the folkloric, and the modern' in an effort to disrupt essentialist claims to cultural and religious purity.[38]

Egyptian feminist and literary critic Hoda Elsadda reads *Awrāq al-narjis* as an example of the 'postcolonial nomadic novel' in *Gender, Nation, and the Arabic Novel*. A categorization that Elsadda uses to describe certain texts that emerged in post-1990s Egypt, she points to the series of texts published during this time that call into question 'confined' and 'fixed' notions of identity and place as indicative of this postcolonial nomadic existence (168).[39] In every aspect, Kimi resists the confinement of language and national identity. As she narrates her struggle with sanity and madness, the disjointed structure of the novel shapes the reader's experience of both text and protagonist. The novel's chapters and sections invoke scattered '*awrāq*' (leaves or papers) that are dispersed against the landscape of Kimi's lapsed time between Cairo and Dublin. The recounting of Kimi's life occurs within the framework of a series of non-linear sequences written in a densely rhythmic language that often reads like a prose poem. Divided into eighteen chapters, some of which consist of only one paragraph, the impression of finality or closure at the end of the chapters is often absent, even resisted, replaced instead with an open-ended threshold that reflects Kimi's emotional, linguistic and geographic un-rootedness. Elsadda argues that Kimi's madness is 'a metaphor for [an] alternative space that does not operate according to established rules of representation and perception'.[40] Just as Kimi tries to escape the confines of the fatherland she also tries to resist those of the mother tongue and those of imperial monolingualism, refusing to fall into the traps created by nostalgia for language and home.[41]

Despite Mahfouz's cosmopolitan outlook on literature, he nonetheless identifies fully with Arabic, Egypt and Islam.[42] Other canonical writers like Edwar El-Kharrat are not dissimilar in their centring of Egypt, albeit with a Coptic Egyptianness rather than Islam. As a 'new-consciousness' novel, *Awrāq al-narjis* challenges circumscribed notions of representation by 'unsettling the boundaries of a singularly imagined nation-state'.[43] Unlike Mahfouz whose linguistically and culturally dual tongue is masked by a monolingual Arabic, Ramadan challenges 'fixed formulas of identity and belonging that have been prescribed by previous generations, by the state, by social mores or by idealized representations of gendered roles'.[44] In one poignant scene in the novel, Kimi says: 'The walls have no maps here nor there. And I am no longer here, nor there. I am in purgatory with no hope of leaving, not even in the imagination.'[45] By negotiating the paradoxes of language and culture, Kimi maintains a 'dual consciousness' at every interval as defined by her postcolonial global context.[46] Ramadan explores multiple boundaries in the text – what does it mean to occupy multiplicity and reject it at the same time? It means travelling, it means everywhere and nowhere are possible as a home at the same time, but it also means a kind of resilience, because it suggests that it is possible to create a home anywhere and everywhere. Ramadan herself has described Kimi's rejection of sedentary existence by saying that Kimi is not searching for 'an identity, nor does she need to choose one out of the possibilities available to her', but rather, that Kimi encompasses a multiplicity of identities and histories that are 'all integrated inside her'.[47]

Fragmentation, displacement and disintegration are ideas that dominate the thematic as well as the structural elements of *Awrāq al-narjis*. The narrative centres on the life of a young Kimi, raised in Cairo in a conservative upper-middle class family. Kimi travels to Dublin to pursue a graduate degree and this experience forms the basis for a deeper engagement with questions of identity and belonging that recur throughout the novel. Kimi contends with a multiplicity of boundaries that constrain her: linguistic and geographic delineations are blurred alongside the distinction between madness and sanity. There are three main spheres through which Kimi challenges notions of fixity. Linguistically, she hovers between English and Arabic. Geographically, she finds herself unable to claim a home in either Cairo or Dublin. Psychologically, through the interior monologue that forms the main thread of the novel, we follow Kimi as she moves between the realms of madness and sanity.

Kimi resists the concept of belonging, feeling disconnected from both Cairo and Dublin, and both Arabic and English. In this way, she insists on belonging to neither national identity nor language. The non-linear events of the novel parallel Kimi's fragmented relationship with her surroundings, both physical and linguistic. The narrative abruptly switches between Dublin and Cairo; between Kimi's childhood home, her room in the college dormitory and the mental institution in Dublin. These shifts mirror the psychological and linguistic breaks that Kimi endures. As she struggles with the multiplicity of narratives that compete to define her, the theme of language emerges as an element with the potential both to constrain and to free. Kimi oscillates between feeling utterly betrayed by language and at the same time completely dependent on it as a saving force. The last sentence of the novel itself repeats this idea: 'Being demands that we erase and return to writing and life once again, a writing and a life that might be.'[48]

Transliteration, displacement and limbo

Confronted with the alienation from her family, language and country, it is as if Kimi, the young protagonist, anticipates the vexed fate of the prize that befalls the author, where celebration turned into condemnation. Kimi contemplates her predicament saying: 'My passport is Egyptian. I defend it. What is it that I am trying to defend? Whatever loyalties I have are judged suspicious in advance. What am I defending? My passport? My language? My faith?'[49] One of the main accusations levelled against Ramadan is that she glorifies Kimi's life in the West over her life in Egypt.[50] However, anyone who has read the novel closely will quickly understand that Kimi moves back and forth between alienation from her family in Cairo to the cultural and social alienation and otherness she experiences in Dublin. She says, 'I carry on my back my ethnicity and my religion and all the Egyptian, Arab, and Muslim passports, marked by what I imagine others have learned to imagine about my country in jokes and caricatures.'[51] Kimi's estrangement is felt deeply in both geographies – all geographies are exilic to her. Hamid Naficy's concept of 'chronotopes' which collapses time and space together captures the dialectics of displacement and emplacement that epitomizes Kimi's experience. Chronotopes, a concept Naficy borrows from Mikhail Bakhtin, are 'driven by structures of identification and alienation but also eruptions of memory, nostalgia, and the longing to return and by the politics and poetics of acculturation and resistance'.[52] Indeed, one of the novel's central themes is the dismantling of an attachment to the notion of the homeland as a site of refuge. In fact, Kimi clearly states that Dublin and Cairo were equally alienating, and that Ireland is not exempt from the confines of nationalism. She describes a map that hangs on her dormitory room in the following:

خريطة المنفى على الحائط لم تكن حنيناً إلى الوطن: و لم يكن هنالك منفى، كان هناك وطن آخر: تسكنه صوره هو، نفاقه هو و مراءاته هو، وصمت تظاهره هو، بأنه وحده قائم وما كان أبعد من لندن شرقاً أو بوسطن غرباً لا يدخل في عداد الجغرافيا، كم مجهول، من الأفضل أن يظل مجهولاً. وكان الشرط الوحيد هو الصمت و التظاهر بأن هنا هو كل شيء.[53]

kharīṭat al-manfā ʿalā l-ḥāʾiṭ lam takun ḥanīnān ilā l-waṭan: wa lam yakun hunālika manfā, kān hunāka waṭan ākhar: taskunuhu ṣuwarahu huwa, nifāquhu huwa w marāʾātuhu huwa, wa ṣamtu taẓāhurihu huwa, bi-annahu waḥdahu qāʾim wa mā kān ābʿad min landan sharqān aw busṭun gharban lā yadkhul fī ʿidād al-jughrāfiyā, kam majhūl, min al-afḍal an yaẓall majhūlan. wa kāna l-sharṭ al-waḥīd huwa l-ṣamt wa l-taẓāhur bi-anna hunā huwa kull shayʾ.

The map of exile fixed to the wall was not a yearning for the homeland. There was no exile. All there was, in that place, was another homeland, another nation. A nation inhabited by its own images, its own brand of hypocrisy, its own deliberate silences and its own pretense, that it alone existed and that anything east of London or west of Boston had no real place in the calculations of geography.[54]

The intensity of the estrangement Kimi feels in Cairo is perhaps more acute and stands in contrast to the fantasy of filial belonging that her family casts around her. Upon returning to Cairo she asks:

لماذا أشعر بكل هذه الغربة وسط أهلي، و أهلي الناس جميعاً[55]

limādha āsh'ur bi-kull hādhihi –l-ghurba waṣta ahlī, wa ahlī l-nās jamī'an.

Why did I feel this powerful estrangement among my own folk – when my own folk consisted of everyone I know?[56]

The intense alienation that Kimi feels from her family is starkly represented by the fact that we never learn what her last name is. Her parents are largely absent in the novel, and their presence looms only in their persistent absence in Kimi's life. Of her estrangement from them Kimi asks: 'What did they find so painful in me that they needed to isolate me in that way?'[57]

In one of the novel's most significant chapters, titled بيت أبي (*Bayt abī*, My Father's House), we see how Kimi's connection to both Cairo and Dublin is defined by a pervasive sense of non-belonging. Here I want to reflect on the first example of what I am calling resistant transliteration – moments in the text where transliteration supplants or even upends translation. Kimi's use of the word 'limbo' is a case in point. Just after her return to Cairo from Dublin, where she had just spent ten years studying, Kimi sits in her Cairo bedroom while describing her inability to distinguish between what ought to be a familiar location and her college dorm room in Dublin. Commenting on the parallel experience of isolation and non-belonging, Kimi says:

ليمبو، كلمة أوفى لوصف تلك المساحة التي تتخلق عندما يتداخل عالمان.[58]

līmbū, kalima awfā li-waṣf tilka l-masāḥa allatī tatakhallaq 'indamā yatadākhal 'ālamān

'Limbo' is a more accurate word for that space which is made when two worlds intersect and partly merge.[59]

Here, the transliteration of 'limbo' into Arabic upholds, rather than resolves, linguistic difference between Arabic and English. By transliterating 'limbo', Ramadan collapses the clear distinction between source and target language, a strategy that adds alterity to both languages: 'a foreign tongue', notes Moroccan literary theorist, writer and philosopher Abdelkebir Khatibi, 'is not added to the native tongue as a simple palimpsest but transforms it'. Bilingualism, for Khatibi, is 'the space between two exteriorities'.[60] Transliteration allows Kimi to occupy linguistic difference – it further allows her to articulate the duality of what is lost and what is gained in transliterating 'limbo' instead of finding a more faithful Arabic equivalent.

Kimi's meditation on the linguistic faithfulness of the English word – which is transliterated into Arabic – shows her insistence on the conceptual merging of Arabic and English of a multivalent term like limbo that describes temporal and spatial ambiguity as well as religious or moral uncertainty. One important way that Marilyn Booth's English translation *Leaves of Narcissus* preserves the rhetoricity of Ramadan's transliteration of the English word 'limbo' is by placing single quotes around the word in the translation. To the extent that it is possible to foreignize in the translation, Booth allows 'limbo' to stand out instead flattening alongside other English words in the text. Booth's translation is sensitive to Kimi's role as translator in this passage. While it is not possible for the English reader to know that 'limbo' is transliterated in the Arabic text unless one compares source and English target texts, drawing attention to the word in the English translation demonstrates Booth's commitment to surfacing Kimi's predicament. By alerting the English reader that limbo is not a translation, Booth's translation makes the foreign accessible in its attempt to keep the gap between the two languages open. By adding quotes around limbo, Booth approximates the transliteration of the Arabic original by introducing changes to the English language.

The postnational multilingual writer is, as James McGuire points out, 'essentially a translator or, more precisely, a self-translator'.[61] What Kimi attempts to translate into Arabic is not only the limbo or purgatory of not belonging to any place, but also the limbo of not belonging to any language. In the English translation, Booth translates this section by adding that limbo is 'that space which is made when two worlds intersect *and partly merge*'.[62] The word 'limbo' both in its English definition and its Arabic transliteration stands in not only for Kimi's geographical and psychological state of limbo, but more importantly, for the ways in which she interacts with English and Arabic as two languages that flow into one another but that also 'partly merge'. The transliteration of the word limbo mirrors the linguistic image of Bhabha's 'third space' that Kimi inhabits.[63] Arabic and English are imagined as neighbouring units – sometimes the gap between them is closed, while other times, this gap is kept open to show the continuity between the two languages.

In Arabic, there are several words that offer an approximation to 'limbo' but none given an equivalent that describes the term's reliance on the notion of uncertainty.[64] Thus, opting to transliterate rather than translate 'limbo' reflects Kimi's state of linguistic, geographic and psychological indeterminacy. The concept in its specifically Arabic or Islamic understanding was developed by the eighth- to tenth-century Islamic school of thought known as the Mu'tazalites, who believed that the fate of Muslims who were not considered believers (*muʾminīn*) nor considered non-believers (*kāfirīn*) was the 'intermediate position' between the two. The Mu'tazalites called this state of intermediacy or 'limbo' '*al-manzila bayn āl-manzilatayn*', a concept not lost on Ramadan since the concept of '*manzil*' (or dwelling in English) is not only one of the main themes of the text, but several chapters dwell on the words '*manzil*' or '*bayt*'. One chapter in particular, '*manazil al rūḥ*' (Dwellings of the Soul) attests to the duality of the homely and unhomely in *Awrāq al-narjis*, where belonging can very quickly turn into a refusal to belong to any identity paradigm.

Transliteration also figures in the novel when Kimi's maths teacher berates her when she's unable to understand mathematics, she says to Kimi 'يورستوبد' (you're stupid) in transliterated English.[65] Transliteration of admonishing words highlights how Kimi internalizes such words to the extent that Arabic and English here become indistinguishable to her. Other demeaning words levelled at Kimi by her teachers are retained in Latin script and not transliterated such as 'paresseuse', 'méchante', 'imbécile'. These words are interwoven in the text as a way to highlight the impact of their violence. One way to read their insertion in Latin script is as markers of Kimi's alienation, where the language of imperialism retains a certain currency as a linguistic location of primacy from which injury and humiliation can be dispensed.

The novel attempts to expand the conventions of literary Arabic not only in its unique use of English transliteration throughout the text, but also in the extent of its intertextuality. Intertextuality is also where the theme of madness in the novel is most pronounced. As Elsadda argues, Kimi's madness is 'a metaphor for [an] alternative space that does not operate according to established rules of representation and perception'.[66] In addition to referencing Shakespeare, Salah Jahin, Arab and Western folktales, Kimi's hallucinations engage with the giants of Irish literature – James Joyce, Samuel Beckett, Oscar Wilde and W. B. Yeats – all of whom appear as characters (not just historical or literary figures) in the text. Joyce in particular plays a significant role, appearing frequently in the novel.

Joyce provides Kimi a point of entry into her own meditations/hallucinations on the intersecting questions of place, homeland, language and exile. The final chapter of *Awrāq al-narjis* is an homage to Joyce and is titled 'Sirens' – it contains a Joycean mix of allusions, images and concepts that echo a chapter in *Ulysses*, also titled 'Sirens'. Kimi's sirens transport her to a dark, unfamiliar world that is both a threat and a promise. Commenting on Kimi's madness, Egyptian scholar Hala Kamal writes that Kimi's mental state is one of 'consciousness, rebellion' at the same time that it constitutes an 'act of resistance' against a Manichean world view. In Naficy's terms, madness is chronotopic allowing Kimi to transcend boundaries in a world that insists on and dictates her territorialized belonging.

At the end of the novel, James Joyce steps out of the photo hanging on Kimi's wall, and proclaims Kimi mad: 'You're raving' Joyce says[67] and he goes on to respond to an assertion Kimi made in an earlier chapter, when she thinks to herself: 'Egypt is the cradle of civilization'.[68] Joyce contradicts her, saying 'Greece is the cradle of civilization'.[69] This moment marks a rupture between Kimi and Joyce – he disavows her and she in turn rejects him. In signaling her break with Joyce, Kimi gives a nod to Sylvia Plath's novel *The Bell Jar* saying, 'All of us craft for ourselves those bells that protect us and we huddle beneath them for a spell until we begin to suffocate – and then we shatter the bell.'[70]

Conclusion

Let us return now to the earlier question of why Ramadan's *Awrāq al-narjis* became the subject of attacks for its reliance on linguistic and cultural hybridity. In contrast to Ramadan's reception, Ahdaf Soueif, who is a contemporary of Ramadan and writes fiction exclusively in English, was widely celebrated by the same literary establishment in Egypt that rejected Ramadan. Samia Mehrez reminds us that when Soueif was denied the Booker prize for her 1999 novel *The Map of Love*, Egypt's leading literary newspaper *Akhbār al-Adab* (the same paper that smeared Ramadan) published an article claiming that Soueif was the 'real winner' of the prize.[71] Mehrez argues that while critics like Khayrallah staunchly disparaged Ramadan's multilingual and intertextual novel, the Egyptian reception of Soueif's texts, despite being written in English, and despite Soueif's reliance on the genre of the Victorian travelogue, has been overwhelmingly positive. The renowned Egyptian novelist Sonallah Ibrahim even went so far as to refer to Soueif's first novel *In the Eye of the Sun* as 'The Great Arab Novel'.[72]

So why the discrepancy? Why are Soueif's texts so readily embraced and recuperated into 'Egyptian literature' while Ramadan's were castigated? While Soueif positions her protagonists in *The Map of Love* and *In the Eye of the Sun* primarily as anti-imperialists, Ramadan positions her protagonist as a nonconformist both in relation to empire and to the nation. Kimi's linguistic, geographic, familial and mental marginalization encourages subversion of the dominant nationalist narrative creating what Kwame Appiah calls a 'perspectival shift' that is antithetical to the boundaries articulated by Khayrallah.[73] In retrospect, the backlash against Ramadan winning the Mahfouz Medal in 2001 seems to have foreshadowed a heightened anxiety around the protection of Arabic's linguistic boundaries and an insistent conflation of language with nation. Of course, the conflation itself is not new – nor is it unique to the Arab world (one thinks of the conflict over French in Quebec and the rest of Canada, and of those who would insist that English, and never Spanish, is the language of the USA). But when the ideological confines of monolingualism become imbricated in literary criticism, these debates shape approaches to what we think of as the contemporary Egyptian canon. What is the canon going to comprise of and why? Here, Edward Said's axiomatic characterization of Arabic as an 'embargoed' language contains a clue. If an embargo is a blockade, perhaps it is also an impasse that restricts movement both to *and* from that which shores up the borders of Arabic, even against those who call the language their own (writing in the language).

Notes

1 While this chapter analyses Somaya Ramadan's Arabic novel *Awrāq al-narjis* through the lens of multilingualism in her text, I position her alongside the following writers whose multilingualism is often called into question. See here for a host of reviews and interviews that address how multilingual Arab writers, whether they are poets, novelists or academicians, writing between Arabic and English, French and Italian,

are confronted with the question of language choice. For an interview with Iraqi poet and novelist Sinan Antoon, see Asli Igsiz, 'Interview with Sinan Antoon', 14 January 2016, The University of Arizona Poetry Center. Available online: https://poetry.arizona.edu/blog/interview-sinan-antoon#:~:text=Sinan%20Antoon%3A%20Well%2C%20first%20of,been%20translated%20to%20five%20languages (accessed 13 July 2020). See additionally Arabic Literature commentator and blogger Marcia L. Qualey's interview with Inem Yacoubi on writing in English in Tunisia: Marcia Lynx Qualey, 'Imen Yacoubi on Writing in English in Tunisia', 1 November 2011, Arablit.org. Available online: https://arablit.org/2011/11/02/imen-yakoubi-on-writing-in-english-in-tunisia/ (accessed 13 July 2020). See also Al Filreis, 'Review of Ahmad Almallah's "Bitter English"', 15 October 2019, Jacket 2. Available online: https://jacket2.org/commentary/review-ahmad-almallahs-bitter-english (accessed 13 July 2020); Jolanda Guardi, '"I Am My Language". Arabic Language in English Writing in Ahdaf Soueif's Work', Komunikacija i Kultura online no. 9 (2018): 43–58; Marcy Jane Knopf-Newman, 'Interview with Suheir Hammad', MELUS 31, no. 4 (2006): 71–91; Marcia Lynx Qualey, 'Edwar Al-Kharrat: On Books and Writing', 2 December 2019, Arablit.org. Available online: https://arablit.org/2019/12/02/edwar-al-kharrat3/ (accessed 13 July 2020); Zoey Weisman, 'Poet Ahmad Almallah Speaks about Living between Languages at Penn Book Center Event', 27 September2019, The Daily Pennsylvanian. Available online: https://www.thedp.com/article/2019/09/penn-book-center-bitter-english-ahmad-almallah-immigrant-book (accessed 13 July 2020).
2 Abdelfattah Kilito, *Thou Shalt Not Speak My Language* (Syracuse: Syracuse University Press, 2008), 21.
3 Ibid., 91.
4 For further reading on the debate, see Ngũgĩ's challenges to English literature: Ngũgĩ wa Thiong'o, 'On the Abolition of the English Department', in Bill Ashcroft, Gareth Griffiths and Helen Tiffin, *The Post-Colonial Studies Reader* (London: Routledge, 1995): 438–42. 'Translated by the Author: My Life in Between Languages', *Translation Studies* 2.1 (2009): 17–20; 'The Language of African Literature', in *Colonial Discourse and Post-Colonial Theory*, ed. Patrick Williams and Laura Chrisma (Harlow: Prentice Hall, 1993): 435–55. Additionally, see Chinua Achebe, 'The African Writer and the English Language', in *Colonial Discourse and Post-Colonial Theory*, ed. Patrick Williams and Laura Chrisman (Harlow: Prentice Hall, 1993): 428–34, *Morning Yet on Creation Day* (London: Heinemann, 1975); *Things Fall Apart* (New York: Fawcett Crest, 1984). See also Onwuchekwa Jemie Chinweizu and Ihechukwu Madubuike, *Toward the Decolonization of African literature: African Fiction and Poetry and their Critics* (London: KPI, 1985).
5 Kilito, *Thou Shalt Not Speak My Language*, 87.
6 Waïl Hassan, *The Oxford Handbook of Arab Novelistic Traditions* (Oxford: Oxford University Press, 2019), 13.
7 Reda Bensmaïa, 'Multilingualism and National "Character": on Abdelkebir Khatibi's "Bilanguage"', in *Algeria in Others' Languages* (Ithaca: Cornell University Press, 2002), 154.
8 Samia Mehrez, *Egypt's Culture Wars: Politics and Practice*, (Cairo: American University in Cairo Press, 2008), 50.
9 Ibid., 50.

10 See Mona Oraby, 'Authorizing Religious Conversion in Administrative Courts: Law, Rights, and Secular Indeterminacy', *New Diversities* 17, no. 1 (2015): 63–75, 69, where she outlines the long history of the Egyptian state's refusal to recognize Bahaism as a religion: 'Given that only Islam, Christianity, and Judaism are formally recognized by the state, conflicts arose between Baha'is and the Ministry of Interior over the right to indicate their self-proclaimed religious identity on vital records.'
11 My translation.
12 Francesca Orsini, 'The Multilingual Local in World Literature', *Comparative Literature* 67.4 (2015): 345–75, 346.
13 Ibid., 346.
14 Sabry Hafez, 'The New Egyptian Novel: Urban Transformation and Narrative Form', *New Left Review* 64 (2010): 46–62.
15 'Egypt: Kemet', The Fitzwilliam Museum. Available online: www.fitzmuseum.cam.ac.uk/dept/ant/egypt/kemet/virtualkemet/faq/index.html#:~:text=(accessed 1 October 2020). Prior to Europe's involvement which means 'the black land'.
16 Mary Youssef, *Minorities in the Contemporary Egyptian Novel* (Edinburgh: Edinburgh University Press, 2018), 2.
17 Ibid., 2.
18 See Ziler Matthias and Abdul Rahman Ammar. ''اتساع جبهات اضطهاد الأقليات في ظل بمصر الإسلاميين حكم 28, October 2012, Deutsche Welle. Available online: https://www.dw.com/ar/اتساع-جبهات-اضطهاد-الأقليات-في-ظل-حكم-الإسلاميين-بمصر/a-16330032. This is an interview where Ramadan outlines the hardships she faces as a Baha'i and the uncertainty this provokes in her daily affairs. For more on Baha'i's inability to obtain vital records, see Mona Oraby, 'Authorizing Religious Conversion in Administrative Courts: Law, Rights, and Secular Indeterminacy', *New Diversities* 17, no. 1 (2015): 63–75.
19 See Salma Khadra Jayyusi, 'The Arab Laureate and the Road to Nobel', in *Naguib Mahfouz: From Regional Fame to Global Recognition*, ed. Michael Beard and Adnan Haydar (Syracuse: Syracuse University Press, 1993), 10–20.
20 Mahfouz is all over the story of what gets in and what stays out of literary canons. On the one hand, he is everywhere included in Arabic literary canons, but in English, it took many years after winning the Nobel Prize for Mahfouz to become well known in other languages. See Edward Said, 'Embargoed Literature', *The Nation* 17 (1990): 278–81. For a full account of Arabic literary prizes, see Elizabeth Anne Kelley, *Translating the Arab World: Contingent Commensuration, Publishing, and the Shaping of a Global Commodity* (University of California Berkeley, 2014).
21 Muhammad Siddiq, 'Taking the Measure of Egypt's Nobel Laureate', *Los Angeles Times Book Review*, 12 November 1989, 11.
22 Shaden M. Tageldin, *Disarming Words: Empire and the Seductions of Translation in Egypt* (Berkeley: University of California Press, 2011), 4.
23 Ibid.
24 Ibid.
25 Mahmud Khayrallah, 'Ma'raka sakhina hawla l-riwaya l-fa'iza bi ja'zat al-jami'a l-amrikiyya' (Heated Battle over the AUC Award-winning Novel), *Al Arabi* 6 (2002): 15. Additionally, in the chapter on 'Children of Our Alley', Mehrez investigates the

discursive construction of the Mahfouz Medal and her analysis includes a survey of responses to Ramadan's receipt of the medal in 2001. In particular Mehrez cites criticisms made by Egyptian literary critic Mahmud Khayrallah (Mehrez, *Egypt's Culture Wars*, 50).

26 Marilyn Booth, 'On Translation and Madness', *Translation Review* 65.1 (2003): 47–53, 48.
27 Mahmud Khayrallah, 'Riwāyat taḥtaqīr al-miṣrīyyīn wa tuhājim 'Abd al-Nāṣir' (A Novel that Treats Egyptians with Contempt and Attacks Abdel Nasser), *Al Arabi* (2001): 15.
28 Mehrez, *Egypt's Culture Wars*, 51.
29 Direct reference to Mahfouz's novel *Awlād ḥāritnā*.
30 See Hoda Elsadda, *Gender, Nation and the Arabic Novel: Egypt, 1892–2008* (Syracuse: Syracuse University Press, 2012). Elsadda argues that there is a slippage between patriarchy and nationalism. For a similar argument, see Frances S. Hasso, 'Problems and Promise in Middle East and North Africa Gender Research', *Feminist Studies* (2005): 653–78.
31 For more on the connections between nationalism and gendered images and discourses of nation, see Beth Baron, *Egypt as a Woman: Nationalism, Gender and Politics* (Berkeley: University of California Press, 2004); Mehrez, *Egypt's Culture Wars*, in particular 23–89: Part I titled 'Inside the Literary Establishment: Power Struggles and the Dreams of Autonomy'; and Lisa Suhair Majaj, Paula W. Sunderman and Therese Saliba, eds., *Intersections: Gender, Nation and Community in Arab Women's Novels* (Syracuse: Syracuse University, 2002). For non-literary critiques of the ways that women and nation are collapsed, see Baron, *Egypt as a Woman*, and Lisa Pollard, *Nurturing the Nation: The Family Politics of Modernizing Colonizing and Liberating Egypt 1805–1923* (Berkeley: University of California Press, 2005), who both examine the constitutive aspects of gender in the formation of modern Egypt and underscore the dynamics through which men and women were reimagined and remade as national subjects.
32 Fedwa Malti-Douglas, *Men, Women and God(s): Nawal El Saadawi and Arab Feminist Poetics* (Berkeley: University of California Press, 1995).
33 Mehrez, *Egypt's Culture Wars*, 51. See also Amal Amireh, 'Framing Nawal El Saadawi: Arab Feminism in a Transnational World', *Signs* 26.1 (2000): 215–49, and Michelle Hartman, 'Gender, Genre, and the (Missing) Gazelle: Arab Women Writers and the Politics of Translation', *Feminist Studies* 38.1 (2012): 17–49, in addition to Michelle Hartman, *Native Tongue, Stranger Talk: The Arabic and French Literary Landscapes of Lebanon* (Syracuse: Syracuse University Press, 2014).
34 For more on the reception of Joyce's *Ulysses* in Europe and America, see Jeffrey Seagal, *Joyce in America: Cultural Politics and the Trials of Ulysses* (Berkeley: University of California Press, 1993).
35 In her interview with Yasir 'Abd al-Hafiz, Ramadan reflects on Joyce's influence on her work (Somaya Ramadan, 'Interview with Yasir 'Abd al-Hafiz', *Akhbār al-'Adab* 189 (27 May 2001): 10–11, 10).
36 See Yasmine Ramadan, 'The Emergence of the Sixties Generation in Egypt and the Anxiety over Categorization', *Journal of Arabic Literature* 43.2-3 (2012): 409–30.
37 Youssef, *Minorities in the Contemporary Egyptian Novel*, 19.

38 Ibid., 21.
39 Elsadda, *Gender, Nation and the Arabic Novel*, 168.
40 Ibid., 187.
41 Somaya Ramadan and Marilyn Booth, *Leaves of Narcissus* (Cairo: American University in Cairo Press, 2002), 63; Somaya Ramadan, *Awrāq al-narjis: riwāya* (al-Qāhira: Maktabat Madbūlī, 2002), 65.
42 Youssef, *Minorities in the Contemporary Egyptian Novel*, 27.
43 Ibid.
44 Elsadda, *Gender, Nation and the Arabic Novel*, 165–6.
45 Ramadan and Booth, *Leaves of Narcissus*, 59; Ramadan, *Awrāq al-narjis: riwāya*, 61.
46 Elsadda, *Gender, Nation and the Arabic Novel*, 168.
47 Ramadan, 'Interview with Yasir 'Abd al-Hafiz', 10.
48 Ramadan and Booth, *Leaves of Narcissus*, 111; Ramadan, *Awrāq al-narjis: riwāya*, 117.
49 Ibid., 76; 78.
50 Khayrallah, 'Ma'raka sākhina ḥawla l-riwāya l-fā'iza bi-jā'izat al-jāmi'a l-amrīkiyya' (Heated Battle over the AUC Award-winning Novel).
51 Ramadan and Booth, *Leaves of Narcissus*, 44; Ramadan, *Awrāq al-narjis: riwāya*, 46.
52 Hamid Naficy, *An Accented Cinema: Exilic and Diasporic Filmmaking* (Princeton: Princeton University Press, 2001), 155.
53 Ramadan, *Awrāq al-narjis: riwāya*, 62.
54 Ramadan and Booth, *Leaves of Narcissus*, 59.
55 Ramadan, *Awrāq al-narjis: riwāya*, 30.
56 Ramadan and Booth, *Leaves of Narcissus*, 27.
57 Ibid.
58 Ramadan, *Awrāq al-narjis: riwāya*, 61.
59 Ramadan and Booth, *Leaves of Narcissus*, 59.
60 Abdelkebir Khatibi, 'Diglossia' in *Algeria in Other Languages*, ed. Anne Emmanuelle Berger (Ithaca: Cornell University Press, 2002), 158.
61 James McGuire, 'Forked Tongues, Marginal Bodies: Writing as Translation in Khatibi', *Research in African Literatures* 23.1 (1992): 107–16, 112.
62 Ramadan and Booth, *Leaves of Narcissus*, 59; emphasis mine.
63 Homi K. Bhabha, *The Location of Culture* (London and New York: Routledge, 1994).
64 The definition of limbo in Arabic, according to Baalbaki's dictionary, is الْيَمْبُوس. الأعراف؛ سجن؛ إهمال؛ نسيان؛ (*nisyān, ihmāl, sijn, al-a'rāf, al-yambūs*) (Munir Baalbaki, *Al-Mawrid: A Modern English-Arabic Dictionary* (Beirut: Dār al-'Ilm li l-Malayīn, 2001), 530). As explained above, such definitions of limbo give an approximation to the term's meaning in the English language but none fully encompass the way the word limbo describes a state of uncertainty. Significantly, the eighth- to tenth-century Islamic school of thought known as the Mu'tazalites believed that the fate of Muslims who were not considered believers (*mu'minīn*) nor considered non-believers (*kāfirīn*) was the 'intermediate position' between the two or what they term as 'al-manzila bayna l-manzilatayn'. The concept of al-manzila bayna l-manzilatayn is the closest Arabic term to the English concept of limbo. For more on Mu'tazilite definition of al-manzilah bayn al-manzilatayn, see Richard C. Martin, Mark Woodward and Dwi S. Atmaja, *Defenders of Reason in Islam: Mu'tazilism from Medieval School to Modern Symbol* (Oxford: Oneworld Publications, 1997), 26–7, 65–6.

65 Ramadan and Booth, *Leaves of Narcissus*, 8; Ramadan, *Awrāq al-narjis: riwāya*, 13.
66 Elsadda, *Gender, Nation and the Arabic Novel*, 187.
67 Ramadan and Booth, *Leaves of Narcissus*, 108; Ramadan, *Awrāq al-narjis: riwāya*, 114.
68 Ibid., 34; 37.
69 Ibid., 109; 115.
70 Ibid., 108; 114.
71 Mehrez, *Egypt's Culture Wars*, 52.
72 Ibid., 53. Additionally, for a full discussion of how Soueif's English novel *The Map of Love* was recuperated for an Arabic/Egyptian readership by being translated into Arabic, see Dima Ayoub, 'The (un)translatability of Translational Literature: Ahdaf Soueif's *The Map of Love* between English and Arabic', *Translation Studies* 12.3 (2019): 308–20.
73 Kwame Anthony Appiah, *Cosmopolitanism: Ethics in a World of Strangers* (New York: Columbia University Press, 2006), 77.

11

Hauntological versions in Isabel del Río's bilingual *Zero Negative/Cero Negativo*

Ellen Jones

The doubled title of Isabel del Río's 2013 collection, *Zero Negative/Cero Negativo*, is not exactly a translation, though context as well as knowledge of both English and Spanish is necessary to appreciate this fact. The relationship between its two parts is enantiomorphic; just as mirror images appear to be identical until superimposed, at which point their asymmetry becomes apparent, the titles seem to be accurate reflections of one another, but are soon found to be distortions. They exploit a resemblance between the numeral and alphabetic systems to suggest equivalence, though they are in fact quite different in meaning: the blood type known in Spanish as 'cero negativo' is not, in English, called 'zero negative', but 'O negative', with the letter, not the number. 'Zero negative' instead refers to 'zero negative degrees of empathy', a trait associated with the cruel behaviours of narcissistic and psychopathic individuals unable to empathize with others, as del Río explains in her introductions.[1] The title plays on the sonic and visual similarities between two unrelated expressions to create a complex conceit, suggesting metonymically the volume's interlinked themes: bloodshed and human cruelty.

In their doubleness the titles also anticipate the structure of the work itself, which seems to comprise sixteen short stories, each appearing in two versions: the first in Spanish, the second in English. But *Zero Negative/Cero Negativo* differs from typical bilingual editions in that the pairs of stories are, like the titles, not quite translations of each other, but rather 'versions' or 'versiones', which diverge increasingly as the collection progresses. The earliest stories have only slightly modified structures or endings, but the later stories diverge more radically, with one version recounting events from a different perspective, or linking to its pair loosely by theme, meaning that only readers of both languages will appreciate the ways in which the layered narratives are held together in a 'lattice', as the author describes it, of links and cross-references between them.[2] It is better, therefore, to think of the volume as containing thirty-two stories, all written by the same author, each in one of two languages.

Significantly, the two stories that give the volume its title, 'Cero Negativo' and 'Zero Negative', do not appear consecutively. Rather, each of them is paired with a version that has a very different name: 'Cero Negativo' with 'Theatre of Blood' and 'Zero

Negative' with 'Lo dice el periódico' (The Newspaper Says So). The entantiomorphism, or distorted mirror image relationship, between the two parts of the volume's title is borne out in these two stories, which, despite very similar sounding names, turn out not to be a thematic pair. This asymmetry draws attention to the non-isomorphism of the languages they are written in, unsettling readers' assumptions about translation: that it can be easy or transparent, or that formulations such as 'cero negativo' and 'zero negative' will necessarily represent equivalent concepts. The forward slash ('/') in the title implies alternation rather than equivalence.

From the title, then, *Zero Negative/Cero Negativo* insists on being read as a bilingual whole rather than in monolingual parts; each of its stories demands the simultaneous presence of its pair in order to be better understood. In the first section of this chapter I offer a reading of *Zero Negative/Cero Negativo* via its uncertain and multiple identities, using Jacques Derrida's concept of the hauntological to help trace the spectres discernible in not just its thematic content but also its language and its form. The characters in these stories are often unable or unwilling to distinguish between dreams and waking life, imagined and lived experience, absence and presence, living and dead. This thematic concern with states of ontological inbetweenness echoes the volume's linguistic and formal characteristics: its positioning of the stories as neither fully 'original' nor fully 'translation', but rather hauntingly similar 'versions' of one another suggests that they are best read together. This section discusses the stories' narrative structure in the light of their thematic concern with the universality of human cruelty, and argues that *Zero Negative/Cero Negativo* champions reading in multiple languages, over reading in translation, for its ability to promote critical rigour as well as empathetic, open-minded engagement with cultural others.

The second section examines the volume's emphasis on English and Spanish as global languages of late modernity and its questioning of the usefulness of translation as a mode of reading and circulation. This section considers *Zero Negative/Cero Negativo* in the light of debates about world literature, and argues that its 'worldliness' can be located in the intercultural connections it makes, in its refusal to be circumscribed by a single language, and especially in the way it problematizes modes of reading that rely on translation. Del Río dramatizes translation at the level of narrative structure and experiments with ways of making her prose more translatable, while ultimately revealing the limitations of translation as a means of facilitating circulation.

Part I: Hauntological versions

Zero Negative/Cero Negativo can be understood as hauntological – a term coined by Derrida to supplant its near-homonym 'ontological' – from the dedication onwards. The hauntological reconfigures a concern with being and presence as a concern with spectres, which are paradoxically neither dead nor alive, present nor absent – they are unfixed and undecidable.[3] Not only are del Río's stories often populated by the ghosts of characters who have died: to give only a handful of examples, in one pair of versions the speakers have recurring dreams of trying to find their own tombs ('Cuenta atrás' and 'Countdown'); in another, a woman encounters a 'cadáver ambulante' (walking cadaver) ('Hablando de parques'); elsewhere we find an army of 'deathly warriors' ('Landscape and Battle') that 'died and died again'; and the very last version, called 'We'll Never Meet Again', is narrated by a ghost who does not know she has died, though realizes she is living in a haunted house.[4] But more importantly each of the stories, whether it is thematically concerned with ghosts or not, is haunted by the spectre of the other language and the other version in which it exists. Like spectres, these stories have a problematic, intangible and paradoxical textual ontology, whereby each one lingers as a spectral absence-presence in its pair. This is because del Río resists organizing the stories according to oppositions between 'source' and 'target', 'native' and 'foreign', 'original' and 'translation', such that each version must be *both* at the same time, just as a spectre is both alive and dead, present and absent, past and present. The undecidability of spectres is therefore apparent in *Zero Negative/Cero Negativo* far beyond its thematic preoccupation with death and with ghosts. The countless semi-equivalencies, almost-matches, uncanny resemblances and defamiliarized connections between del Río's stories make *Zero Negative/Cero Negativo* a sometimes uneasy reading experience; we cannot identify a sovereign, unitary or self-determining ontology for the work, but rather a restless 'hauntology' that is in large part bound up with its bilingualism and with the way it thematizes and problematizes translation. With their multiple iterations, circular narratives and many perspectives, each story insists that its meaning and identity is at least partly located in another version and another language.

Del Río refuses the hierarchical binary often imposed on 'originals' and their 'translations' insofar as the latter is assumed to be secondary and derivative. One way in which she does this is to refuse to say which in each pair of stories was written first, maintaining that 'en realidad no importa la secuencia de las dos versiones' (the sequence of the two versions doesn't really matter).[5] The linked stories are instead imagined to have emerged simultaneously, rather than one preceding or following the other in the compositional process, as would typically be the temporal relationship between an 'original' and a subsequent 'translation'. By rejecting binaries and accommodating multiplicities, del Río commits to a form of literary production that problematizes chronology as hierarchy and claims equal value for each of the volume's versions and languages. The symbiotic relationship between them is made especially evident in the pair of stories called 'Como te lo cuento' (Believe it or Not) and 'Woman Behind Man'. In the first version, 'Como te lo cuento', a woman crashes her car and kills a passenger. In 'Woman Behind Man', the events of 'Como te lo cuento' are reconfigured as a film script written by two new characters, Al and Alma (a fictionalized Alfred Hitchcock and his wife). This sudden rearrangement, in which the 'first' story emerges from the 'second', decouples the association between original and origin. The second story follows Derrida's logic of supplementarity (when 'a possibility produces that to which it is said to be added on') in the sense that it has conceptual priority over the 'origin' it is supposed to follow.[6] Meanwhile 'Como te lo cuento' interrogates the role we assign chronology in the establishment of authority: before the fictional car accident, the driver discusses fake artwork with her passenger. She remarks that 'en otras ocasiones la obra es más auténtica – valga la impugnación – que el original' (on other occasions, the work is more authentic – if you'll forgive my boldness – than the original),[7] thereby turning the conventional hierarchical relationship between original and derivative on its head. This story and others in the collection suggest that narratives of authorial improvement and translational corruption are obsolete in a bilingual work such as this, authored as it is by a single person. By denying readers a hierarchy of versions, the value of reading *both* rather than *either/or* is reiterated.

Zero Negative/Cero Negativo does not restrict itself merely to two versions of each text, however; each story itself contains multiple, often proliferating layers. Many of the stories are about telling stories and retelling them, about the value of doubling and parallel versions. They thematize all manner of different narratives: written narratives such as short stories, newspaper articles, biographies, detective novels, film scripts and transcripts, and performed narratives such as magic shows, performance art, staged executions and role play. Characters are constantly writing and rewriting their own stories, which are then doubled again by their inclusion in two languages, and they often express a sense of having done things before, or of repeating themselves. One result of this repeated versioning is a characteristically postmodern collapse and distortion of time. The constant layering, repetition and use of revenant images creates a hauntological effect that Derrida calls a 'disjointure of the very presence of the present'.[8] In particular it creates a sense of 'toujours déjà vu', as though we are perpetually bound to return to past moments.[9] Contemporary writing is often characterized by a version of this 'contaminated present', as Mark Currie puts it, whereby temporal distance collapses into simultaneity, particularly through the recycling of the increasingly recent past.[10] *Zero Negative/Cero Negativo* explicitly thematizes the cyclical, forward and backward movement of time, depicting the present as comprised of a series of prolepses and analepses. In doing so it figures bilingual reading as something that allows us to maintain a spectral presence-absence; to occupy multiple positions at once and therefore allow meaning to proliferate. This is illustrated especially clearly by one of the first versions in the collection, 'La autora del fin del mundo' (The Author of the End of the World), which has a version-within-version-within-version structure. It opens with an anonymous frame narrator who argues for the importance of multiple perspectives, and who introduces the first embedded narrative. There follows a short story about the end of the world written by the 'autora' (author) of the title. The frame narrator then introduces the second embedded narrative, which recounts how that same 'autora', now a 'character', comes to write a story about the end of the world. Of course, these are then doubled yet again when they appear in English, in a version called 'The Author of the End of the World'. This proliferation of versions set on the repeated eve of an apocalypse suggests that time is always-but-never-quite running out. Death is an aporia: a non-passage, 'an interminable experience', the impossibility of which generates a spectral cycle of repetitions that is seemingly endless.[11]

Del Río gestures towards this proleptic haunting in her authorial dedication, in which she invokes 'what could have been and never was'.[12] It signals one of the volume's main themes – the persistence of human cruelty across societies and different moments in history – while recalling Derrida's claim in *Spectres of Marx* that post-1989 liberal democracy would continue to be haunted by the spectres of imagined progress – by 'all the lost futures the twentieth century taught us to anticipate'.¹³ We can see this play out in one of the more puzzling pairs of versions in *Zero Negative/Cero Negativo*. These are 'Inocencia' (Innocence) and 'Grammatically Enhanced Transcript for the Purposes of Obtaining a Taxi Cab Licence', by far the most dissimilar of the sixteen pairs, as may be apparent from their titles. They are set in radically different eras: 'Inocencia' in an unspecified premodern civilization, and 'Grammatically Enhanced Transcript' in a present-day global city. The connection between them lies only in their subject matter: violent crimes perpetrated against innocent young people. In the former, an army invades a village and slits the throats of young boys, while in the latter, a homeless teenager with stigmata on his palms is raped and exploited in a number of other deplorable ways. 'Grammatically Enhanced Transcript', in its thematic similarity to its pair, is haunted by the spectre of imagined progress; by a lost future in which the kinds of violence and cruelty detailed in 'Inocencia' would no longer exist. The spirit of social responsibility apparent in these stories and elsewhere in *Zero Negative/Cero Negativo* reiterates Derrida's point regarding the irony of liberal democracy calling itself the 'ideal of human history' when violence, inequality and oppression are so far from being eradicated in contemporary society.¹⁴

The fallacy of progress toward an ideal end point is apparent not just in the content of these stories, but also in del Río's representation of narrative production. The stories' prevailing sense of 'toujours déjà vu' is reiterated at a formal level, whereby the second story in each pair takes us back to the 'beginning' (although, as I have explained, there is no chronological relation of prior/anterior except insofar as it is necessary for them to be printed in a given order). Each version is haunted by its previous and future alternatives, existing in a mutually enriching relationship where no single story is more authoritative than its pair. For this reason del Río claims repeatedly that the ideal reader of *Zero Negative/Cero Negativo* will be bilingual. She insists that readers of all thirty-two stories, who have what she calls a 'tercera lectura' (third reading), will find the collection more compelling than readers of only half, which is to say, of only the English versions, or of only the Spanish versions. She has explained in interview that '[e]sa tercera lectura es mucho más completa (¡y compleja, claro!) porque los relatos versionados se complementan hasta el punto de que a veces la clave del español está en el inglés y al revés' (that third reading is much more complete (and complex, to be sure!) because the paired stories complement one another to the point that sometimes the key to the Spanish is in the English and vice versa), and that 'la trama [es] más intensa y sugestiva' (the plot is more intense and suggestive) when both sets of stories are read.¹⁵ In her English introduction to the collection she also claims that 'the two versions complement each other' to create something 'greater than the sum of their parts'.¹⁶

This argument is illustrated particularly well by the pair of stories called 'Versión oficial' (Official Version) and 'Don't Hang Up!'. The two recount the same events from different perspectives and using different narrative techniques; the first is a journalistic account, the second a one-sided phone conversation. A reader does not know to distrust the 'official' media version, given in Spanish, unless or until she reads the 'unofficial' English version ('Don't Hang Up!'), which reveals the way the event recounted was exploited for political ends: a young girl who dies in an accident is hailed as a martyr for supposedly sacrificing herself in service of a wider cause. Stories like these two support the author's claim that the 'tercera lectura' is fuller and more complete; by highlighting the flaws and misrepresentations in the Spanish, the English reveals the folly of unquestioningly accepting a single narrative. As an alternative to translation, bilingual reading is depicted as ethical precisely because it allows for views to be reversed, altered or simply become more nuanced.

The link between *Zero Negative/Cero Negativo*'s formal organization and its themes of cruelty and bloodshed lies in the suggestion that bilingual reading can promote empathy and openness to others. By maintaining plurality and therefore forcing readers to perceive difference, the collection reminds us that there are always other ways of seeing things. In '¡Tú también, Bruto!' and 'You Too Brutus!', for instance, a woman is persecuted for her political beliefs. Having been betrayed by an ally, she is denied legal representation and tortured, subjected to false executions in order to solicit information. In the Spanish version, the prisoner is an undisputed victim, facing, quite literally, an executioner who wraps a noose around her neck. This version ends not with a blessed escape into death, but back where it began, with the sound of the trapdoor under the gallows creaking open but her not falling to her death, implying that the events of the story are to be repeated in an endless cycle of physical and psychological violence. The prisoner's only solace are the words she regularly recites to herself to fortify her resolve under torture: 'cuerpo lacerado, espíritu intacto'.[17] The English version follows the Spanish up to a certain point. In English, the prisoner repeats to herself the words 'broken body, unscathed spirit'.[18] Soon, however, these words undergo a slight variation, becoming 'untouched soul, ravaged body' – an alternative version of 'cuerpo lacerado, espíritu intacto'.[19] The words, somewhere on the journey from Spanish into English, have lost their fixity, and therefore their power to comfort and reassure, their power of conviction. As though remembering events from a life already lived slightly differently, or a story already told slightly differently, on reciting these words the prisoner thinks: 'Yes, perhaps there were other words for everyday subjects that she had never thought about, other names for people, other ways of seeing things'.[20] The Spanish and English versions begin subtly to part ways: in English, we witness the prisoner beginning to doubt the legitimacy of her beliefs. She notes that, although she has been condemned without trial, she too has been 'beyond the law' for a very long time, that other people's blood has 'been the necessary price' for her to achieve her own ends.[21] Her status as victim is therefore undermined, as we infer that her single-mindedness – or narrow-mindedness – has led her to commit infractions and violent crimes that may be comparable to those inflicted on her.

The effect of this divergence between the two versions is to suggest that there is not always simply a single victim and a single executioner, nor is there ever just one, or even two sides to a story. It is crucial to note that the appearance of an alternative version of 'cuerpo lacerado, espíritu intacto' in 'You too, Brutus!' begins to trouble both the character's and readers' perception of what is just. This is something that happens again and again in *Zero Negative/Cero Negativo*: the English version will represent the same situation as the Spanish but from a different point of view, compelling readers to readjust their impressions, reinterpret and redistribute blame. The volume is constantly working to help readers see from other perspectives in order to reveal the folly of unquestioningly accepting a single narrative. It is not enough just to read a translation; it is necessary to read bilingually.

By invoking Simon Baron Cohen's theory about 'zero negative' personalities,[22] del Río suggests that the injustices detailed in her stories result from a lack of empathy; from an inability to identify with another person's emotions, or to see from another's perspective. Reading bilingually therefore emerges as a process that has the potential to open up a space for understanding. It allows us to see from the perspective of others, including those others who may be, as Derrida has it, 'no longer' or 'not yet there'.[23] Del Río's readers are reminded that reading in more than one language can deliver a healthy blow to narcissism and provide, as the prisoner puts it in 'You Too, Brutus!', 'other ways of seeing things'.[24]

Part II: A bilingual world literature

This section considers *Zero Negative/Cero Negativo* in the light of debates about world literature, and argues that its 'worldliness' can be located in the intercultural connections it makes, in its refusal to be circumscribed by a single language, and especially in the way it problematizes translation as a mode of reading. As we have seen, del Río dramatizes translation at the level of narrative structure; she also experiments with delocalizing her prose to make it more translatable, while ultimately revealing the limitations of translation as a means of facilitating circulation.

Zero Negative/Cero Negativo does not conform to the increasingly hegemonic, US-inflected, often monolingual English version of 'world literature': a version based on the assumption that a book has a single original culture and language beyond which it moves, and which is typified by David Damrosch's definition as 'literary works that circulate beyond their culture of origin, either in translation or in their original language'.[25] Del Río's book challenges this definition in a number of ways. First, as we have already seen, *Zero Negative/Cero Negativo* does not have a single 'original language', but rather is linguistically plural from its inception. Second, it does not have a single 'culture of origin'. It was published in Spain but its Spanish-British author has resided in the UK for a number of decades; and what is more, its stories are mainly set in a placeless no-man's land, avoiding references to cultural practices or social customs. Third, in its regular oscillation between languages, it refuses to acknowledge the global dominance of English or to succumb to its central role in the world literature canon. This section will argue that although it reaches repeatedly for the universal rather than the particular, and for substitutability over individuality, *Zero Negative/Cero Negativo* ultimately constitutes an unsuccessful attempt to delocalize literature in order that it may travel, thus demonstrating the limitations of translation as a means of facilitating circulation.

First, del Río does not identify either English or Spanish as her 'mother tongue' or native language, nor, as we have seen, is it possible to establish primacy or 'originality' for either the English or the Spanish stories in her volume; rather, readers are encouraged to imagine their simultaneous inception. I persist in using the term 'bilingual' rather than 'translingual' to describe *Zero Negative/Cero Negativo* for these precise reasons. Steven G. Kellman defines 'translingual writers' as those who publish in a language that is not their 'mother tongue' or 'native language', a decision, as he understands it, that involves a unidirectional movement from one language to another; the interdependence and supposedly simultaneous emergence of the English and Spanish stories in *Zero Negative/Cero Negativo* renders the term unhelpful here.[26] What is more, both the English and Spanish stories in this volume are at pains to suggest that they could be taking place in any language, or in many languages at once: we are told that newspaper headlines are 'multilingual', words uttered by soldiers in battle seem 'to belong to all languages' and numerous characters hear words spoken in 'a language [they] couldn't understand'.[27] The prose in both Spanish and English is bare of vernacular effects and ideas associated with phonological or etymological patterns. It contains few specialized registers, jargon, colloquialisms or archaisms. It not only abides by formal written standards of Spanish and English, but also tries to avoid lexis and grammatical features that are restricted to specific parts of the Anglophone and Hispanophone worlds, despite much of the narrative being made up of direct speech, where we might expect to find colloquialisms, localized forms and references to cultural practices and social customs. What Rebecca Walkowitz calls the 'surface effects of language' are absent, making del Río's style more easily described by the features it *lacks* rather than those it exhibits.[28] A description by Gilmour and Steinitz captures it well: this is 'language that aspires to be any language: the language equivalent of the empty, placeless space-time of late-modernity, the airport departure lounge or the shopping mall'.[29] Even characters' names – Constance and Constanza, Fortune and Fortuna – denote universal qualities, and seem to have been chosen because they have counterparts in both English and Spanish, rather than because they are typical of naming practices in a particular place or culture. The focus is on substitutability and translatability throughout.

Second, *Zero Negative/Cero Negativo* appears to lack an 'original culture' beyond which it might move, whether in translation or otherwise. On the contrary, the book foregrounds anonymity even in its jacket design: the front cover of the print edition shows an image of blood pumping around a circulatory system. The body has no distinctive features; it is only identifiable as generically human. The back cover shows a naked mannequin: the epitome of substitutability and undistinctiveness. These images anticipate the anonymous, substitutible characters and non-specific locations and temporalities of many of the stories contained in the volume. For instance, of the protagonist in 'You too, Brutus!' we are told that 'Even her real name – both her first and her last – had been erased from her mind, and the same could be said about her background, her family ties, her links with fellow human beings.'[30] The same is true of the speaker in 'Grammatically Enhanced Transcript', who remarks, 'It's been such a long time since I last heard my real name on someone's lips that I can't really say for sure what it is.'³¹ The martyred girl in 'Don't Hang Up!' has no name ('muchos dijeron que habrían preferido personalizar el grito con un nombre' (many people said they would have preferred to personalize the scream with a name)), and in 'Inocencia' we hear shouts from 'una mujer cualquiera' (any woman) and learn that 'todos los niños se parecían' (all the children looked the same).³²

With a few exceptions, the stories in *Zero Negative/Cero Negativo* are set in a literary no-man's land.³³ 'Versión oficial' and 'Don't Hang Up!', for example, recount a protest that takes place outside an embassy in an unspecified country. The Spanish version makes vague references to 'el país anfitrión' (the host country), 'la nación subyugada' (the dominated nation) and 'el país enemigo' (the enemy country), while the English version talks about 'the cause' and 'the demonstrators' without specifying what the protest is about.³⁴ 'Hablando de parques' is similarly set in 'una capital cualquiera' (any capital), while the protagonist in 'You Too Brutus' does not even know in which country or under which authority she is being prosecuted.³⁵ In addition to being set in this strange no-place, many stories seem to take place outside of time. In 'La autora del fin del mundo', for instance, the speaker tells us, 'Ya nada nos permite identificarnos con nuestra era; ahora somos sólo individuos de cualquier época, edad, procedencia; si estamos unidos, es en el desafecto' (Nothing allows us to identify with our own era any more; now we could be individuals from any epoch, age, origin; if we are united, it is in our indifference).³⁶ The recurrence of seemingly universal or universalized experiences at different moments in the volume constitutes another form of haunting, in that it produces, to use María del Pilar Blanco's understanding of the word, 'the disquieting experience of sensing a collision of temporalities and spaces – an experience that is ... riddled with doubt and uncertainty'.³⁷

One effect of the cultural and temporal deracination of del Río's stories is to highlight the continuity of human experience across different communities. Making languages, societies and their institutions interchangeable for one another implies that the same cruelties and injustices persist in all or any of them. For example, in two pairs of stories about war, different causes and armies are kept indistinguishable. During the eponymous battle in 'Paisaje y batalla', 'ni uniforme ni facciones eran ya identificables' (neither uniform nor affiliation was identifiable any more); in that story's pair, 'Landscape and Battle', the conflict culminates in a vision of a single 'universal soldier'.³⁸ Meanwhile, the interviewees in '¿Qué hizo usted en la guerra, Señor Romero?' and 'What Did You Do in the War, Mr. Romero?' refuse to identify which side they fought on during an unspecified civil war, declaring it unimportant.³⁹ The emphasis in all these narratives is on what unites us rather than what divides us; the stories ask readers to perceive common humanity and deep-seated affinity between communities rather than incommensurability.

In recent years critics have begun to celebrate writing that, unlike *Zero Negative/ Cero Negativo*, obstructs easy access, refuses translation and escapes comparison, and therefore resists entering into the market for global literature. Meanwhile, 'the portable work', as Rebecca Walkowitz has it, 'is vilified for having surrendered to that [multinational publishing] pipeline, exchanging aesthetic innovation for commercial success, eschewing the idiosyncrasy of the local for the interchangeability of the global'.⁴⁰

Voices like Emily Apter, Brian Lennon, Tim Parks and Minae Mizumura see the global novel as a simply another commodity vulnerable to capitalist modes of production and consumption.[41] According to this argument, as a result of the 'McDonaldization of the globe', literature has succumbed to standardization and homogenization, abandoning any political agenda, aesthetic innovation, formal difficulty and local particularity.[42] They see writers adopting a style that is excessively fluent in an attempt to be easily readable, translatable or saleable around the world. Tim Parks's much-quoted article skewering what he calls the 'dull new global novel' argues that, increasingly, 'language is kept simple' in order to 'remove obstacles to international comprehension'.[43] This style has been identified in internationally recognized writers whose work is often published (near) simultaneously in a number of languages: Stephen Snyder sees it in Haruki Murakami's writing, which he says has 'few textual and stylistic impediments or difficult cultural contexts', making it 'immediately and readily translatable',[44] meanwhile, Rebecca Walkowitz sees it in the work of Kazuo Ishiguro, whose emphasis on 'drama' rather than 'poetry' as well as his 'simpler diction', she argues, make him more translatable than many writers with more idiosyncratic uses of language.[45] The choice of 'neutral' language anticipates and hopes to facilitate its own inevitable translation.

Zero Negative/Cero Negativo seems to aspire to this portability in an attempt to facilitate the 'translation' of del Río's stories between English and Spanish. And yet, the stories are not really translations at all. The increasing divergence of the pairs as the volume progresses suggests a degree of scepticism about this strategy of deterritorialization, and about the wisdom of relying on translation as a mode of reading at all; as we have seen, the book repeatedly insists that understanding both languages rather than just one will result in a richer, more nuanced reading experience. Despite attempts by del Río to delocalize or deterritorialize her prose in order to facilitate translatability, the volume ultimately suggests the futility of these goals. The title of the collection itself suggests the failure of any attempt to achieve a language that lacks temporal or spatial ties, and reminds us of the multiplicity within each named language. The expression 'cero negativo' is specific to parts of the Spanish-speaking world where 'seseo' is not typically used. 'Seseo' describes an accent in which speakers do not pronounce the letter <c>(where it appears before <e>or <i>) or the letter <z>as /s/, such that pairs of words like 'caza' and 'casa' or 'ciento' and 'siento' are pronounced in the same way. In parts of Spain and across the whole of Latin America, where 'seseo' is typically heard, the blood type 'O negative', since the AIDS epidemic in the 1980s, is described as 'O negativo' rather than 'cero negativo' in order to distinguish it from the homophone 'seronegativo', which means 'HIV negative'.[46] Del Río's usage of 'cero negativo' is therefore specific to contemporary peninsular Spain, undermining the stories' attempts elsewhere to achieve ahistoricity and geographical vagueness. Flashes of specificity of course appear in the stories themselves, too: a fleeting reference to Madame Tussauds or the river Thames, or the use of 'vosotros' rather than 'ustedes' as a you-plural form (again, common in Spain but not the Americas). The spectres of locality cannot help but haunt this writing; it reveals the notion of 'neutral' or 'accentless' language to be a fallacy.

Many of the stories reflect on how translation changes our reading experience; the story titled 'Grammatically Enhanced Transcript' reflects specifically on how the standardization of language in pursuit of translatability can strip narratives of their individuality. We understand from the title of this story that the testimony given – presumably in a 'nonstandard' speech variety – by the young homeless man in this story, has been transcribed by an unknown 'intermediary'[47] into language that better complies with the norms of 'standard' written English expected and accepted by state institutions, such as the one the speaker hopes will grant him a taxi licence. 'Grammatical enhancement' amounts to translation into 'standard' language, which is scrubbed down to its most communicative form, terse and direct:

> Last year I suffered from pneumonia, which meant a stay of three weeks in hospital. But then the summer was good and the lungs recovered. I get a bad cough when it rains, worse when it snows. ... I've a sore on my lip and another on my upper thigh. I've been raped twice. It was painful because of my piles.[48]

The testimony is written in short sentences with simple syntax and widely recognizable lexis ('good' and 'bad'). The resulting tone is at odds with the misfortunes the young man describes (paranoia, chronic illness, abuse), meaning that his account struggles to move us. In this factual, emotionless style, del Río suggests that the idiosyncrasies of speech, along with the human emotions they convey, struggle to survive the process of their transcription.

This story evidently critiques the dehumanization of individuals passing through state institutions (the young man, del Río emphasizes, is 'nobody', barely able to remember his own name) but also the emergence in recent decades of supposedly 'neutral' global lingua franca of bureaucracy, development, international relations and big business: English being the most obvious, but Spanish not far behind it. English in particular is increasingly used in contexts where it is neither an official language nor has any native speakers, such as in large international companies, where it is seen as 'the medium through which communication is effected rather than a culturally laden language allied to a particular nation'.[49] And yet the speaker of this story struggles to understand and make himself heard within this instrumentalized, deracinated English. It is clear that, despite increasing interconnectivity in a globalized world, there remain profound inequalities that are marked by language. The relationship between the speaker's own speech variety and the language of the written testimony is in no way neutral; the 'standard' variety in which the testimony is written is the language of power and prestige, which puts the speaker at a disadvantage when he is unable to understand terms such as 'intermediary' and 'no fixed abode', as he explains.[50] The final line of the story is 'S.O.S.', the international distress signal in Morse code, suggesting precisely the difficulty of expressing himself adequately in the 'grammatically enhanced' language of bureaucracy.[51] This story therefore reflects on the volume's avoidance of linguistic particularity and on the homogenizing trend in which literature is written with a view to translation. That 'Grammatically Enhanced Transcript' and its pair 'Inocencia' are the most dissimilar in the collection clearly demonstrates the limitations to 'neutral' language's ability to facilitate communication and circulation via translation.

As its hauntological characteristics attest, *Zero Negative/Cero Negativo* accommodates ambivalence and contradiction in abundance. In this sense, it is no passive product of globalization, but a knowing response to its diverse effects. It can be considered 'worldly' not because it circulates in translation outside of its 'culture of origin', nor because of its inventive linguistic blending or idiomatic diversity, but rather because of its formal and thematic engagement with the theory and practice of translation at the level of narrative structure, and because of its insistence on being read as a bilingual whole rather than in monolingual parts. Del Río's book dramatizes translation's ability to change the way we read, and is profoundly sceptical about its role in facilitating intercultural understanding. It cautions against reading only translations, and against writing for translation, suggesting that, despite its many advantages of increased interconnectivity and exchange, translation is rarely easy or transparent, and moreover retains the ability to misrepresent, to homogenize, and to strip a literary text of its individuality. By contrast, writing multiple versions in different languages offers an opportunity to go back to the beginning, to tell differently, and to occupy multiple simultaneous positions. Ultimately, *Zero Negative/Cero Negativo* rejects monolingual insularity and complacency, and instead proposes multiplicity (textual as well as linguistic) as a means of achieving critical rigour, committed, open-minded engagement with cultural others and the cross-lingual sharing of ideas.

Notes

1. Simon Baron Cohen, *Zero Degrees of Empathy: A New Theory of Human Cruelty and Kindness* (London: Penguin, 2012). Isabel del Río, *Zero Negative/Cero Negativo* (Valencia: La Bella Araña, 2013), 20.
2. Del Río, *Zero Negative/Cero Negativo*, 20.
3. Jacques Derrida, *Specters of Marx: The State of the Debt, the Work of Mourning and the New International*, trans. Peggy Kamuf (London: Routledge, 1994), 6.
4. Del Río, *Zero Negative/Cero Negativo*, 203; 57; 56; 233–41.
5. Ibid., 17.
6. Jacques Derrida, *Speech and Phenomena and Other Essays on Husserl's Theory of Signs* (Evanston: Northwestern University Press, 1973), 89.
7. Del Río, *Zero Negative/Cero Negativo*, 214.
8. Derrida, *Specters of Marx*, 25.
9. Ibid., 14.
10. Mark Currie, *About Time* (Edinburgh: Edinburgh University Press, 2007), 10.
11. Jacques Derrida, *Aporias* (Stanford: Stanford University Press, 1993), 16.
12. Del Río, *Zero Negative/Cero Negativo*, 9.
13. Mark Fisher, 'What Is Hauntology?', *Film Quarterly* 66, 1 (2012): 16–24, 16.
14. Derrida, *Specters of Marx*, 85.
15. María Luisa Luque, 'Isabel del Río publica "Zero Negative/Cero Negativo" en edición bilingüe', *Madrid Press*, October 2013. Available online: http://madridpress.com/

not/161931/_isabel_del_rio_publica__ldquo_zero_negative_cero_negativo_rdquo__en_edicion_bilingue/ (accessed 4 August 2019).
16 Del Río, *Zero Negative/Cero Negativo*, 19.
17 Ibid., 90.
18 Ibid., 94.
19 Ibid., 97, 90
20 Ibid., 97.
21 Ibid., 94, 97.
22 Baron Cohen, *Zero Degrees of Empathy*.
23 Derrida, *Specters of Marx*, xviii.
24 Del Río, *Zero Negative/Cero Negativo*, 97.
25 David Damrosch, *What Is World Literature?* (Princeton: Princeton University Press, 2003), 4.
26 Steven G. Kellman, *The Translingual Imagination* (Lincoln, NE: University of Nebraska Press, 2000). For a useful critique of Kellman's understanding of 'translingualism', see Maria Lauret, *Wanderwords: Language Migration in American Literature* (London: Bloomsbury, 2014), 13–14. Note that Suresh Canagarajah has a very different understanding of 'translingualism' as communication that 'transcends individual languages', in which 'the semiotic resources in one's repertoire or in society interact more closely, become part of an integrated resource, and enhance each other … mesh in transformative ways, generating new meanings and grammars'. Suresh Canagarajah, *Translingual Practice: Global Englishes and Cosmopolitan Relations* (London; New York: Routledge, 2013), 8.
27 Del Río, *Zero Negative/Cero Negativo*, 45; 57; 167.
28 Rebecca L. Walkowitz, *Born Translated: The Contemporary Novel in an Age of World Literature* (New York: Columbia University Press, 2015), 43.
29 *Multilingual Currents in Literature, Translation, and Culture*, ed. Rachael Gilmour and Tamar Steinitz (New York; London: Routledge, 2017), 3.
30 Del Río, *Zero Negative/Cero Negativo*, 97.
31 Ibid., 191.
32 Ibid., 162, 185, 186–7.
33 Isabel del Río and Susana Medina, 'Writing in Two Languages: Interview with Amanda Hopkinson' (Europe House, London, July 2013). Available online: https://archive.org/details/SusanaMedinaIsabelDelRio.WritingIn2Languages.EuropeHouse.IntroducedByAmandaHopki (accessed 15 July 2019).
34 Del Río, *Zero Negative/Cero Negativo*, 164–5; 165; 164; 169; 167.
35 Ibid., 204, 94.
36 Ibid., 43.
37 María del Pilar Blanco, *Ghost-Watching American Modernity: Haunting, Landscape and the Hemispheric Imagination* (New York: Fordham University Press, 2012), 1.
38 Del Río, *Zero Negative/Cero Negativo*, 53; 57.
39 Ibid., 75, 83.
40 Walkowitz, *Born Translated*, 31.
41 Tim Parks, 'The Dull New Global Novel', *The New York Review of Books* (February 2010). Available online: www.nybooks.com/blogs/nyrblog/2010/feb/09/the-dull-new-global-novel/ (accessed 15 July 2017); Emily Apter, *Against World Literature: On The Politics of Untranslatability* (London: Verso, 2013); Minae Mizumura, *The Fall of*

Language in the Age of English, trans. Mari Yoshihara and Juliet Winters Carpenter (New York: Columbia University Press, 2008); Brian Lennon, *In Babel's Shadow: Multilingual Literatures, Monolingual States* (Minneapolis; London: University of Minnesota Press, 2010); see also Nikil Saval and Dayna Tortorici, 'World Lite: What Is Global Literature', *n+1* 17, The Evil Issue (2013). Available online: https://nplusonemag.com/issue-17/the-intellectual-situation/world-lite/ (accessed 19 July 2017).

42 Damrosch, *What Is World Literature?*, 25.
43 Parks, 'The Dull New Global Novel'.
44 Stephen Snyder, 'The Murakami Effect: On the Homogenising Dangers of Easily Translated Literature', *Literary Hub*, 7 January 2017. Available online: http://lithub.com/the-murakami-effect/(accessed 4 August 2019).
45 Rebecca L. Walkowitz, 'Unimaginable Largeness: Kazuo Ishiguro, Translation and the New World Literature', *Novel: A Forum on Fiction* 40.3 (2007), 216–39, 219.
46 'Dicho de una persona o de un animal: Que no tiene anticuerpos específicos en el suero sanguíneo, frente a un antígeno determinado' (Of a person or animal: lacking specific antibodies in their blood serum with regard to a particular antigen). 'Seronegativo, va', *Diccionario de la lengua española Online*. Available online: https://www.rae.es (accessed 15 July 2019). I am grateful to Omar García Obregón for alerting me to this lexical variation in different parts of the Spanish-speaking world.
47 Del Río, *Zero Negative/Cero Negativo*, 193.
48 Ibid., 190.
49 Braj B. Kachru, *World Englishes and Culture Wars* (Cambridge: Cambridge University Press, 2017); Fiona J. Doloughan, *English as a Language in Translation* (London; New York: Bloomsbury, 2016), 13.
50 Del Río, *Zero Negative/Cero Negativo*, 193; 190.
51 Ibid., 197.

12

transition, untranslatability and the 'Revolution of the Word'

Juliette Taylor-Batty

One of the most urgent problems in Europe, according to Barbara Cassin, is posed by the plurality of languages. She proposes two possible solutions:

> choisir une langue dominante, dans laquelle se feront désormais les échanges – un anglo-américain mondialisé; ou bien jouer le maintien de la pluralité, en rendant manifestes à chaque fois le sens et l'intérêt des différences, seule manière de faciliter réellement la communication entre les langues et les cultures.[1]

> (choose a dominant language in which exchanges will take place from now on, a globalized Anglo-American. Or we could gamble on the retention of many languages, making clear on every occasion the meaning and the interest of the differences – the only way of really facilitating communication between languages and cultures.)[2]

Nearly eighty years earlier, the editors of the modernist magazine *transition* (1927–38) were grappling with a very similar question. Cassin clearly allies her *Vocabulaire européen des philosophes: Dictionnaire des intraduisibles* with the second solution, with a new hopeful Europe 'qui travaille les écarts, les tensions, les transferts, les appropriations, les contresens, pour mieux se fabriquer'[3] (which explores divisions, tensions, transfers, appropriations, contradictions, in order to construct better versions of itself).[4] *transition*, aiming to disseminate a broad range of international avant-garde literature to an Anglophone audience, positions itself at both ends of the scale and at various points in between, finally settling on a fully trilingual editorial policy of non-translation in 1933. Reading *transition* as a 'world literature' project in microcosm, this essay examines the changing translation policy of the magazine.[5] Much as Cassin's dictionary becomes a celebration of the productive distinctions between languages, the transformations and subtle shifts that occur when words travel, so untranslatability in *transition* becomes a productive effect of interlingual difference, the spur to an avant-garde agenda and the basis of a nascent editorial principle that seems to anticipate more recent debates around translation in world literature studies. In this essay, I want to explore the multilingual and translational processes that we find in *transition* and to ask: to what extent does this magazine eventually provide a model for the conceptualization of multilingual literature (rather than translated literature) as world literature?

World literature as a discipline has recently been dominated by the question of translation. David Damrosch argues that '*World Literature is writing that gains in translation*'.[6] So-called 'untranslatable' works, on the other hand, 'are not translatable without substantial loss, and so they remain largely within their local or national context, never achieving an effective life as world literature'.[7] Emily Apter, on the other hand, following Cassin, presents a strident critique of the enduring 'translatability assumption' of world literature studies in the Anglophone academy, critiquing the 'entrepreneurial, bulimic drive to anthologize and curricularize the world's cultural resources', and arguing for 'the importance of non-translation, mistranslation, incomparability and untranslatability' in comparative literary studies.[8] *transition* is especially interesting as a case study in the context of these debates because translation is placed centre stage throughout its existence. The magazine combines a faith in the importance of translation with a growing awareness of 'untranslatability', an impressively international translation project with an increasing interest in the characteristics and aesthetic effects of multilingualism. This essay surveys the changing translation policy of *transition*, from the magazine's early faith in translatability as a mode of literary dissemination through to its final adoption of a multilingual editorial policy. Through close analysis of one pivotal issue, *transition* 21 (1932), I demonstrate that translation, untranslatability, translational mutation and interlingual distortion become the source of productive and playfully experimental literary processes within the pages of the magazine. Indeed, in this issue, we can see how translation in *transition* moves away from its traditional function of making foreign texts comprehensible for the reader – even, at times, serving to make texts *less* comprehensible. By the latter phases of the magazine, it becomes a playfully experimental mode, a mode of literary production rather than dissemination that is integral to *transition*'s growing commitment to a multilingual aesthetic.

transition was founded in 1927 by Eugene Jolas, Maria Jolas and Elliot Paul, motivated by what Eugene Jolas was later to describe as a youthful 'vision of a linguistic and creative bridge between the countries of the Western world'.[9] The magazine is probably now best known for its pioneering publication of extracts from James Joyce's *Work in Progress* (which was to become *Finnegans Wake*), and for its 'Revolution of the Word' manifesto (1929). The aim of the magazine was to promote various forms of 'synthesis': interlingual, intercultural, intercontinental, interracial, psychological and literary. Translation, by facilitating interlingual and intercultural exchange, played a crucial role in its earliest phase. In the first twelve monthly issues of *transition* (1927–8), the magazine aimed to make the latest developments in continental avant-garde literature available in English for an American audience. The work printed in *transition*, particularly in this early phase, was impressively international, including translations not only from French, German, Spanish, Italian and Russian, but also

Serbian, Bulgarian, Czech, Hungarian, Polish, Swedish, Yiddish and Native American texts alongside experimental writing in English.[10] Jolas was the most prolific of the magazine's translators, working to a furious schedule and producing the earliest translations into English of many key modernist works.[11]

On one level, we can relate this early editorial and translational practice to the anthologizing impulse of world literature studies. Translation is held up as a bridge, as a vehicle for dissemination and communication, and a way of bringing together diverse languages and cultures. But any echoes of the universalizing humanism of a Goethean *Weltliteratur* are troubled from the start by an additional, more utopian function: that of 'revolutionizing' language. In a review article marking the first year of *transition*, Jolas and Elliot Paul launch a scathing critique of the state of American letters which they contrast with the vitality of currents in French, German and Russian literature.[12] *transition*'s hostile American reviewers are chastized for being 'timid in the presence of strange names' and perhaps even 'suspicious of foreigners'.[13] They then describe the intentions of the magazine, which are much more far-reaching than broadening American minds:

> What did we hope to achieve by putting, side by side with American and English writers, translations from the works of Europe's most uncompromising revolutionaries? We felt in the beginning that the growing banalisation of the English language, was a grave danger to the development of the new literature. We felt, therefore, that not only an ideological nibbling-offensive was necessary, but that language itself would have to be shaken to its foundation in order to find a more plastic and more organic form of expression.[14]

By using English as a translational bridge between American and continental avant-garde currents, Jolas and Paul hope to do no less than to initiate the destruction and 'decomposition' of 'the traditions of language' with a view to reconstructing the language in a more 'plastic' and 'organic' form. The implication is two-fold: first, that translation into English is itself a means of bringing revolutionary 'foreign' elements into the language, and secondly, that the editorial convergence of international texts within the magazine's pages will itself alchemically produce something 'new'.

This utopian function of translation expressed by Jolas and Paul is flawed, however. The paradox inherent in the early translation policy of *transition* is that translation, by 'bridging' difference and rendering texts in English, has a linguistically homogenizing effect. In 1928, the editors declare the failure of their translational project – 'we feel that our intensified inquiry into international writing is, for the moment, at a standstill'.[15] After a short-lived focus on American Literature, the magazine begins to search for alternatives. From this point onwards, we find three elements that, I argue, are inextricably linked. Firstly, practical and theoretical explorations of a 'Revolution of the Word'; secondly, a gradual editorial move towards non-translation; and thirdly, an increase in contributions that are themselves multilingual. Ultimately, in its later phase, *transition* challenges the translational model of world literature, developing instead a subversive editorial and creative model that critically scrutinizes translation and that challenges the idea of world literature as exchange between defined national literatures and language.

One particularly interesting issue of the magazine, on which I will focus in the second part of this essay, is *transition* 21. It comes at the cusp of *transition*'s shift in translation policy and immediately precedes the next issue's declaration of an explicitly multilingual editorial policy. In *transition* 21, translation becomes a creative, playful process of linguistic mutation and experimentation in itself, and non-translation produces multilingual effects: we find multilingual writing by James Joyce and Samuel Beckett, homophonic translational experiments collected by Raymond Queneau, a translation by James Joyce from English into French, and a 'Revolution of the Word Dictionary' that includes a list of 'Translators' Lacunae'.[16] In all these cases, translation has nothing to do with making texts more comprehensible. Instead, interlingual mutations are celebrated and limited comprehension becomes crucial to avant-garde writing that 'revolutionizes' language by undermining our ability to 'know' or 'master' it.

Eric Bulson has demonstrated that critics of modernism can be too quick to celebrate the seductive notions of transnationalism and cross-fertilizations within modernism. The reality within the context of modernist little magazines is rather more complex, and the editorial and distribution problems faced by magazines, particularly those with transatlantic ambitions, were considerable: 'Texts were not magically flowing from one destination to another: they were getting stopped, tangled up, mutilated, and sunk along the way.' Instead, 'immobility', 'slowness' and 'deceleration' are words that Bulson uses to describe the fate of magazines with internationalist ambitions.[17] His focus is on problems of circulation and distribution, but it is analogous to my own interest in language and translation within *transition*. Jolas held high hopes for *transition*'s possible function as a creative bridge (and 'Bridge' was at one point a favourite possible title for the magazine).[18] Those ideals shift considerably over time, however, and *transition* develops a later ideology and approach to translation that implicitly critiques its own early idealism. Early twenty-first century developments in world literature studies have brought the concept of 'untranslatability' to the fore, most notably with Emily Apter's *Against World Literature: On the Politics of Untranslatability* (2013). Notwithstanding some of the problems with the details of Apter's critique,[19] the questions it raises are important and have been picked up more recently by modernist scholars, arguing that we need to scrutinize the 'pitfalls of connectivity', the limits of translation, and the problems caused by modernist translation, which, as Miller and Rogers point out, 'also produced and created compelling disruptions, internal contradictions, and illustrative gaps that we must consider when recovering or revisiting translational work'.[20]

Eugene Jolas was attuned to such 'pitfalls of connectivity' well before these theoretical approaches were formulated. Growing up as the child of a French father and German mother in the Franco-German disputed territory of Lorraine, Jolas's bilingualism was politicized early on, associated with conflict as well as productive interlingual exchange. When he migrated to his country of birth, America, in 1910, he spoke very little English, but he threw himself into the rich and diverse immigrant cultures of New York, determined to become an American reporter. By the time he founded *transition* in Paris in 1927, he was fully trilingual – a self-styled 'man from Babel' with an acute border-consciousness and ready ambivalence about his own multilingual identity.[21] As well as editorial, journalistic, critical and translation work, Jolas wrote increasingly trilingual poetry and prose, much of which was published within the pages of *transition*. That work – as I have argued elsewhere – presents a fundamental challenge to what Yildiz has defined as 'the monolingual paradigm' according to which 'individuals and social formations are imagined to possess one "true" language only, their "mother tongue"', through which they are 'organically linked to an exclusive, clearly demarcated ethnicity, culture, and nation'.[22] In this essay, I want to examine the extent to which the magazine's later translation policy does as well.

transition is probably best known for the 'Revolution of the Word' proclamation in *transition* 16/17 (1929). The manifesto rejects linguistic 'correctness': it argues that the literary creator should 'disintegrate' words imposed on him by 'text-books and dictionaries', and that he should 'disregard existing grammatical and syntactical laws'. Ultimately, it declares: 'The plain reader be damned'.[23] The 'Revolution' manifesto is absolutely appropriate to the unswervingly avant-garde agenda of the journal and to its increasing multilingualism: although *transition* was dedicated to publishing difficult avant-garde texts from its inception, we do find an increase in neologistic experiments, Dadaist sound-poetry and generally defamiliarizing texts from this point onwards. Although the proclamation does not mention multilingualism, it was specifically related to his own experiences of being 'caught in the labyrinth of idiomatic interfusions and transformations' throughout his life, including the experience of 'two major tongues at war' in his childhood, and his participation in 'the linguistic reorientation of Alsace-Lorraine since the end of the First World War'.[24] And although the proclamation also makes no mention of translation, this 'damning' of the 'plain reader', as Monk has observed, is directly related to the magazine's later development of an editorial policy of non-translation.[25] Indeed, the 'Revolution of the Word' section of that issue contains some of the first instances of non-translated text in the magazine: texts by Léon-Paul Fargue, Arthur Rimbaud, Henry Michaux and August Stramm appear in their original French and German.[26] This is followed up in another 'Revolution of the Word' section in *transition* 18, which contains three contributions in the original French because, as the editors explain, 'the language itself is of intrinsic interest and would lose by translation'.[27]

Rather than any pervasive sense of 'loss', however, we find hope that new forms will grow out of the juxtapositions of languages, cultures and literary styles within the pages of *transition*. An important essay by Jolas in *transition* 16/17, 'Logos', helps to illuminate the political and linguistic perspective behind the idea of the 'Revolution of the Word'. 'Logos' makes an explicit connection between interlingual contact and natural language change, celebrating both in relation to poetic forms of defamiliarization:

> Changes in the organism of language are made as a result of instinctively individual activity and the history of philology shows conclusively, through a vast deduction process, that the linguistic evolution from early days was one of

constant metamorphosis, synthetism, deformation, adjustments. ... The history of Indo-European speech gives us an illustration of the fact that there was a constant growth and mutation through phonetic changes, combinations, duplication of meaning, changes in grammatical canons, sound-transmutations, assimilations, abbreviations. ... In this historic development we find sometimes that one language borrows from another language and assimilates the foreign word completely. In modern history we have the example of the deformations which English, French and Spanish words underwent in America, as in the case of Creole French on Mauritius, Guyana, Martinique, Hayti, Louisiana, and Colonial Spanish.[28]

When Jolas talks about 'synthesis', *this* is really where he is coming from: not homogenization, but a 'linguistic evolution' that is the product of 'constant metamorphosis, synthetism, deformation, adjustments'. It is the direct product of interlingual mixing. Jolas's essay anticipates much later postcolonial perspectives on pidgins and creoles; it also valorizes forms of language that grow in contact zones, through forms of limited mastery and what speakers of hegemonic linguistic forms term 'misuse'.

'Logos' reflects Jolas's perspective on immigration. For him, a city like New York is so powerful precisely because it integrates diverse cultures and languages but resists homogenization: Jolas observes American immigrants who remember their heritages and their languages, and therefore resist full 'translation' into American culture.[29] Like the 'Revolution' manifesto, 'Logos' is not about translation, but it is nonetheless relevant to the magazine's changing attitudes to translation. A policy of transparency in translation might well bring about cultural connectivity, but it is by definition linguistically homogenizing. It will therefore limit the sorts of creolizing processes that Jolas is celebrating here. The early translational editorial model of *transition* (still largely sustained in this edition of the magazine), produces the potential for some interlingual synthesis in the impact of source language upon target language, but it also deliberately presents a relatively linguistically homogeneous target text, whose function is to prevent the Anglophone reader from having to engage directly with different languages.[30] By the time we get to the third phase of *transition* with *transition* 21 (1932), we find translation being used in ways that bring languages very explicitly into contact with each other. Translation begins to function not to make texts more comprehensible, but to deform, distort – even creolize – language.

When the magazine finally settles on a policy of non-translation in *transition* 22 (1933), the editorial reasons seem to be fairly straightforward:

With this issue, transition enters upon a new policy of tri-lingual publication. The crisis of language is now going on in every part of the Occident. It seems, therefore, essential to retain the linguistic creative material intact, and to present constructive work, where possible, in the original.[31]

The avant-garde literature that *transition* is committed to publishing is, in short, difficult to translate. On closer inspection, however, it becomes clear that the move towards untranslatability in *transition* is rather more interesting and far reaching. Instead of merely accepting the 'failure' of translation, I argue that *transition* instead presents a challenge to the essentialism inherent in traditional translational models of world literature. It begins to experiment with another – multilingual – model for the *production* as well as dissemination of world literature. Cassin's dictionary of 'untranslatables' is no lament for interlingual difference: it manifests instead a fascination with the transformations and mutations that are incurred when words travel and when translation is impeded. Indeed, she describes her work on untranslatability in one article as a 'eulogy of translation'.[32] Likewise, *transition*, I argue, embraces the possibilities of interlingual difference and mutation. Untranslatability becomes a source of productivity and possibility.

transition 21: Untranslatability as creativity

At the end of *transition* 21 we find a 'Revolution of the Word Dictionary' entry which includes lists of neologisms to be adopted, defunct words to be 'retired from active service', and redefinitions of existing words.[33] This project of linguistic renewal and redefinition is inextricably linked to translation: the section includes a list of 'Translators' Lacunae' such as 'Weltanschauung', 'unheimlich' and 'esprit'. Up to this point in the magazine, translatability had played a crucial role in furthering *transition*'s utopian linguistic ideals; by *transition* 21, the 'Revolution of the Word' is explicitly associated with *un*translatability. This makes sense: the avant-garde texts within *transition* frequently 'damn' the 'plain reader', just as the 'Revolution of the Word' proclamation declared, and many defy translation because they are themselves multilingual or because they are not written in any identifiable language. However, it is in the magazine's latest phase that untranslatability becomes most explicitly invoked for *transition*'s avant-garde utopian agenda.

Because *transition* 21 comes at the cusp of the magazine's move towards non-translation, it still embodies many of *transition*'s earlier translational ideals. The issue as a whole contains a significant number of translations (many of which were done by Jolas himself), and its pride in its translation work is clearly evident: one editorial footnote points out that *transition* published the first English translation of Kafka.[34] Even with the traditional translations, however, we find a practice that is subtly unsettled and unsettling. A story by Miguel Angel Asturias is described as '*Translated from the Guatemalan* by Adam F. Flecker', and another by Ventura Garcia Calderon as '*Translated from the Peruvian* by Theo Rutra'.[35] In the Asturias, the translator makes a point of retaining Mayan words and words specific to Guatemalan culture, accompanied by explanations in footnotes. This indicates the translator's sensitivity to the importance of autochthonous languages in Spanish America and how they relate to Spanish as a colonial language. To label the language of the stories 'Guatemalan' and 'Peruvian' rather than 'Spanish' indicates an editorial sensitivity to the distinctions between different global forms of colonial language. The Calderon translation also reveals an unsettling attitude to translational attribution: 'Theo Rutra', a frequent contributor to *transition* was, Jolas told his friends, 'a Czech immigrant living in Brooklyn', but was in fact a pseudonym for some of Jolas's most neologistic writing experiments.[36] Why does Jolas perform this translation 'undercover'? The answer is unclear, but it certainly suggests a playful relationship to translation and a way of relating it to different types of immigrant identity. It also subtly undermines the hierarchy of linguistic competence that we are used to attributing to translators: Rutra the 'Czech immigrant' has direct national links to neither source nor target languages; moreover, his contributions to *transition* push English to the limits of comprehensibility and 'correct' usage.

Untranslated texts in *transition* 21 include work in French by Joe Bousquet, Georges Pelorson and Jean-Pierre Brisset, and work in German by Hans Arp and Paul Scheerbart. Perhaps least surprisingly, the sound poems of Hugo Ball and Kurt Schwitters are also left (largely) untranslated because the original texts are in no discernable language in the first place. There are curious inconsistencies in the editorial and translation decisions made, however: Hans Arp's poetry is left in German, but his 'Notes from a Diary' is translated into English; 'difficult' poetry is often left in the original, but Jolas nonetheless includes his own translations of Hoelderlin. And while the title of Kurt Schwitters's 'Lanke Tr Gl: skerzoo aus meiner soonate in uurlauten' is left untouched, Hugo Ball's sound poems are both given translated titles – 'Clouds' and 'Cats and Peacocks' – with the original German titles in footnotes. On the one hand, then, the punning deformations of the Schwitters title are left intact but the reader is not helped into the difficult text; on the other, Ball's titles are made comprehensible so that we are eased into the onomatopoeic relevance of the poems themselves (the softly rounded globular assonance of 'Clouds'; the resemblance of the sounds in 'Cats and Peacocks' to the sounds those animals make). In the case of the Ball poems, though, the effect is still peculiar and unsettling: the English titles provide an illusion of translation that is countered not only by the poems that follow, but by footnotes giving the original German titles. Translational footnotes are usually provided where there is some difficulty or ambiguity in the translation provided. Their very existence suggests the inadequacy of the translation, its existence as a supplement to (rather than replacement of) the original. This practice subtly undermines the fact that, in this case, the English titles offer a pretty straightforward and unproblematic translation of the simple German titles – 'Wolken' and 'Katzen und Pfauen'. Finally, we find two texts that are themselves explicitly multilingual: Samuel Beckett's short story 'Sedendo et Quiesciendo' and Bob Brown's 'Sub-Tropical'. This reflects the magazine's association with the Babelian excesses of Joyce's *Work in Progress*, which *transition* published from the start, while foreshadowing the increasingly multilingual content of later volumes.[37] It makes sense that a move towards non-translation would also produce non-translation within individual texts.

The Anglophone reader of *transition*, then, finds themselves frequently beguiled and bewildered in the face of inconsistent translation strategies: at times helped with clear translations, at times faced with texts in French or German, difficult multilingual texts, or texts that fall outside of any recognizable language. Such inconsistency is not a weakness of the volume, however; it is symptomatic of *transition*'s attempts to explore the limits of translation, as well as the transformative possibilities that it can unleash.

In *transition* 21, translation also appears as a playfully experimental mode. There are a number of examples which I will turn to now, where translation is used not to make texts more comprehensible, but *less* comprehensible. It becomes integral to the doctrine of 'difficulty' and defamiliarization that is inscribed into *transition*'s 'Revolution of the Word'. Translational distortion and mutation in these examples appear not as failure, but as potentially productive processes.

The first of these is entitled 'James Joyce, *Translator*'. A poem in English by James Stephens, 'Stephen's Green', is presented alongside a translation, by James Joyce, in French entitled 'Les verts de Jacques'.[38] Joyce here reverses the usual function of translation: given that *transition*'s target audience is Anglophone, this makes the poem *more* 'foreign' to its readers. Stephens's English title is a pun on his own name as well as a reference to Stephen's Green Park in Dublin, the site of Irish Citizen Army resistance in the Easter Uprising. Joyce's title in French – 'Les verts de Jacques' – means 'Jacques's greens' but also punningly suggests 'Jacques's verses' ('les vers de Jacques'). It therefore brings out the original title's pun on the author's name (Stephens), but instead of translating his surname, Joyce translates his *first* name, James – which also, of course, happens to be Joyce's own name. ('Jacques' is the French equivalent of 'James'.) Joyce thus inscribes his own authorship into the French title, a fact that is consolidated by his authorial signature at the end of the poem: 'James Joyce, after James Stephens'.

Two months later, Joyce sent a set of translations of 'Stephen's Green' to James Stephens in German, Latin, Norwegian, Italian and French, and suggested that Stephens add an Irish version 'so as, with the English, to make a rainbow and we might present it to ourselves in a brochure for our jubilee year'.[39] This playfully grows out of the fact that Joyce and Stephens, as well as sharing a name, were – as a footnote in *transition* points out – purportedly 'born at the same hour, the same day, the same year'.[40] Joyce's letter details some of the creative transformations he has made to the different versions. As in the *transition* translation, Joyce presents himself as 'author' of each version, signing each in the letter as 'J.J.'. 'Les Verts de Jacques', then, is part of a collaborative, creative literary enterprise that reverses the usual function of translation, including its traditional hierarchies of authorship.

The next instance of playful translation is C. K. Ogden's translation of Joyce's *Anna Livia Plurabelle* (part of what was to become *Finnegans Wake*) into Basic English.[41] Damrosch has proclaimed *Finnegans Wake* a 'global work' which cannot be a work of world literature because its 'prose is so intricate and irreproducible that it becomes a sort of curiosity in translation'.[42] As Patrick O'Neill has demonstrated, however, the inevitable transformations produced when translating *Finnegans Wake* form a crucial part of the text's own afterlife. The *Wake*, he argues, is 'a literary machine designed to generate as many meanings as possible for as many readers as possible', and the repeated act of translation extends that process, so that what Joyce initially entitled a *Work in Progress* 'is very evidently still in progress, still moving, still continually changing'.[43] *transition* places *Work in Progress* centre stage of its internationalist agenda from the start,[44] and this experimental translation forms just one part of an important and still influential Joycean project. Ogden's 'Basic English' is an explicitly de-Babelizing project, an 'International Language of 850 words in which everything may be said'.[45] *Finnegans Wake*, on the other hand, famously perpetuates the state of Babel.[46] Ogden, in his Preface, describes it as a translation from 'the most complex' to 'the simplest' 'languages of man'.[47]

When we read the Preface and the translation itself, however, we start to see curious contradictions. Ogden's Preface asserts that his translation gives 'the simple sense' of Joyce's text, but in the very next sentence we learn that '[i]n places the sense of the story has been changed a little'. Moreover, the main principle of Basic English is to use only a highly restricted vocabulary; Ogden's rendition of *Anna Livia Plurabelle*, however, specifically uses a number of words that do not belong to Basic English. Where the names of rivers are perceived to have crucial sonic and rhythmic properties, for example, 'they are put into the Basic story without any change, and underlined'.[48] This is also the strategy for many of Joyce's non-English words: when their sound is important to the text, they are kept, italicized. Translation usually moves from other languages into English; in Ogden's translation, however, most of the translating is done between Joycean English and Basic English rather than between other languages and Basic English.

This is not to say that other languages are not translated: the Basic English version is less multilingual than Joyce's. However, within the extract, a number of words really stand out as foreign. In fact, if we compare them to Joyce's text of *Anna Livia Plurabelle*, we might say that the non-English words used by Joyce end up appearing *more* foreign in the Basic English translation. On the very first page, we find the following words in italics: '*Viel Uhr? Filou!* What time is it? It's getting late'.[49] This is Ogden's translation of 'Fieluhr? Filou! What age is at? It saon is late'.[50] The *Annotations to Finnegans Wake* explain the original text as follows: '"Filou" ("scoundrel"), shouted across Rhine by Frenchman, was heard by German as "wie viel Uhr?" "What's the time?")'.[51] The multilingualism in Joyce's text is used to represent a multilingual misunderstanding incurred by homophonic similarity between two languages. In that sense it is particularly relevant as an 'untranslatable': it combines French and German within sounds that are appropriated within English rhythmic effects. Ogden, however, reinstates German spelling, which, alongside italicization (a conventional editorial marker of foreignness), turns Joyce's hybrid word into one that is unequivocally German.

Another example, also from the first page of the text in *transition*, demonstrates that this increased emphasis on the foreign is not just a one-off. Joyce's 'I'd want to go to Aches-les-Pains' is rendered by Ogden as 'I would go then to Aix-les-Pains'.[52] Joyce puns on the French spa town 'Aix-les-Bains', where you'd get your 'aches and pains' cured, and might eat some French bread. In Joyce's reading of this section of *Anna Livia Plurabelle*, recorded by Ogden in 1929, the pronunciation of 'Aches-les-Pains' is clearly Anglicized; in Ogden's translation, however, there is a reversion to French spelling ('Aches' becomes the explicitly French 'Aix'), and as a result, the bilingual 'pains' is likely to be read first in *French* in Ogden's text (i.e. meaning bread), and in English in Joyce's. In effect, Ogden's translation is more explicitly 'foreign' than the original text. This is not an isolated example. To give a couple more: Ogden turns Joyce's 'Sexaloitez!' into 'Sacheläute'. By reverting to the correct spelling of the

Zürich spring festival, Ogden completely removes the English part of the pun. When Joyce's 'Concepta de Send-us-pray!' is turned by Ogden into 'Concepta de Spiritu', the Latin is highlighted at the expense of the English.[53] Joyce's text works to undermine the boundaries between different languages; its multilingualism works specifically to challenge our idea of 'national' language. It is worth noting that the italicization of 'foreign' words in *Finnegans Wake* is restrained. The editorial practice of italicization functions to mark words as 'foreign', but Joyce's work more broadly undermines and parodies this tendency, making us ask: what is a 'foreign' word anyway? How do we distinguish between the borders of languages? And what is the difference between a loan-word that has been assimilated into the language (therefore not, technically, requiring italicization), and a 'newer' one that is conventionally marked by italics as an interloper? Ogden's translation, on the other hand, is marked by six words and phrases in italics, where we only find one in this section of the *Wake*. In making apparent the present of languages marked *as* 'foreign', Ogden's text is both more explicitly multilingual and less *ideologically* multilingual.

In its move towards a monolingual ideology, Ogden's Basic English might seem to be out of line with the organic multilingualism exemplified in Joyce's text and explicitly celebrated by Jolas in his critical and creative work. I give it here not as an example of a unified ideology of multilingualism within *transition*, but more as evidence of the magazine's openness to interlingual transformations in translation. Joyce himself collaborated in the translation and it is likely that he quite deliberately and playfully worked to undermine the monolingual designs of Ogden's de-Babelizing project. Indeed, it forms part of a series of translations that fed into the compositional genesis of Joyce's text. Between the first printed version of *Anna Livia Plurabelle* in 1925 and its final form in *Finnegans Wake* in 1939, we find translations in French (1931 – based on the 1928 text), Basic English (1932) and Italian (completed 1938, published 1940 – also, oddly, based on the 1928 text; Joyce co-translated this himself).[54] Joyce was directly involved in all of these translations, and was one of the listed translators of the Italian version. As Rosa Maria Bollettieri Bosinelli writes, this creates a peculiar dynamic, whereby the process of translation 'could profitably go hand in hand with the genetic process of a primary text that came to be engaged in a sort of experimental "exchange" with secondary texts'.[55]

In the context of *transition* 21, then, *Anna Livia Plurabelle* in Basic English is an experiment in the transformations and mutations that can be created by translation. For all its monolingual principles, Ogden's translation does not function in any traditional sense of making more comprehensible (and I would even argue that Joyce's text makes more sense than Ogden's in a number of places).[56] The Basic English version, then, is a linguistic experiment, a playful exercise. It also becomes part of the genesis of Joyce's own text, an exercise in translational collaboration that merges into composition.

Perhaps the most explicitly and gratuitously experimental translation play that we find in *transition* 21 comes in the section entitled 'Words from the Unconscious'. For this entry, Raymond Queneau presents a series of extracts from Jean-Pierre Brisset's *Le mystère de Dieu est accompli* (1890) alongside the religious ravings of a madman taken from the *Annales Médico-psychologiques*. Brisset, himself a 'fou littéraire', here presents a delightful cacophony of homophonic word-play, including the following 'translations' between Latin and French:

> *Mets-à-cul le pa*, mea culpa. *Paterne austère*, pater noster. *V t'ai mis ça es-çeu*, ite missa est. *Queue raide os ine-dè homme*, credo in Deum. *D'homme ist nu, ce veau bisque on-meu*, dominus vobiscum.[57]

Brisset's extraordinary work is based on an etymological theory that 'Toutes les idées énoncées avec des sons semblables ont une même origine et se rapportent toutes, dans leur principe, à un même objet' (All ideas spoken with similar sounds have a shared origin and all relate, originally, to a shared object).[58] His writings attempt to demonstrate that puns and similarities between words (and, as in the case above, at times across languages), demonstrate a shared origin, which reveals truths about the origins of the human race. (His most famously crazy conviction was that the human race was descended from frogs, based on the similarity between the words *reine* and *raîne*.[59]) Brisset does not make either language clearer in any way. On the contrary, the French and Latin are equally defamiliarized by his peculiar method of breaking words up into constituent sounds, and associating those sounds, recombined, with other punning meanings. There might be a proliferation of possible referents, but language is rendered other – much as Brisset's stated intentions in his longer text face us with the otherness of an idiosyncratic and eccentric perception of language.

All these examples of playful translation from *transition* 21 push the reader to positions of not knowing, of partial understanding, and the effect is distinctly unsettling. Whatever our levels of trilingual competence (or lack of), they force us to be aware of linguistic plurality and make us engage with that plurality. Even though *transition* moves away from its earlier utopian ideals for translation as a mode of dissemination and transmission, the later phase of the magazine presents an interest in untranslatability that is in fact an exploration of the possibilities of translation when we move away from its traditional function, when we acknowledge its pitfalls, the inevitable transformations that ensue. The effect, in the case of *transition*, is a resolute move towards multilingualism as its editorial model. By making us confront difference directly – by encouraging us to engage with different languages and cultural forms – *transition* begins to function both as a 'bridge' between cultures *and* as what Jolas described as a 'crucible' for the construction of new linguistic and literary forms. Within the magazine, translation holds a parallel function, then: what begins as a mode of communication and dissemination of world literature ends as a mode of experimentation and *production* of multilingual world literature.

Notes

1 Barbara Cassin, ed., *Vocabulaire Européen Des Philosophies: Dictionnaire Des Intraduisibles* (Paris: Le Robert; Seuil, 2004), xvii.

2   Barbara Cassin et al., eds., *Dictionary of Untranslatables: A Philosophical Lexicon*, trans. Steven Rendall et al. (Princeton: Princeton University Press, 2014), xvii.
3   Cassin, *Vocabulaire Européen Des Philosophies*, xvii.
4   Cassin et al., *Dictionary of Untranslatables*, xvii.
5   The role of periodicals in and as world literature goes right back to Goethe's concept of *Weltliteratur*, which was in part a response to international periodicals. See Theo D'haen, *The Routledge Concise History of World Literature* (London; New York: Routledge, 2011), 6. The modernist magazine is receiving increasing attention as a form of 'world literature', for example in the important *Oxford Critical and Cultural History of Modernist Magazines* which has expanded from initial volumes focusing on Britain in Volume 1 and North America in Volume 2 to more expansive studies: Volume 3, which examines a wide range of European magazines (see Peter Brooker et al., *The Oxford Critical and Cultural History of Modernist Magazines. Volume III: Europe 1880–1940* (Oxford: Oxford University Press, 2013)), and a second forthcoming series entitled *The Oxford Critical and Cultural History of Global Modernist Magazines*, the first volume of which, edited by Eric Bulson, Andrew Thacker and María del Pilar Blanco, will focus on magazines in South America and the Caribbean. Thacker argues for a more expansive response to Franco Moretti's question of what 'world genres' of literature might be: 'are there other "material texts" that are worldly, in Moretti's sense, that is, textual forms that cross boundaries and borders and dwell primarily in the *world* of literature, rather than within individual national cultures?' His answer is that the little magazine is one such form. Andrew Thacker, 'Crossing Borders with Modernist Magazines', *Variants: The Journal of the European Society for Textual Scholarship* 9 (2011): 199–210, 200. Further important work in this area has been carried out by Eric Bulson in his book *Little Magazine, World Form* (New York: Columbia University Press, 2017).
6   David Damrosch, *What Is World Literature?* (Princeton: Princeton University Press, 2003), 288.
7   Ibid., 289.
8   Emily Apter, *Against World Literature: On the Politics of Untranslatability* (London: Verso, 2013), 3, 4. For a recent assessment of the role of translation in world literature, including a critique of Apter, see Susan Bassnett, ed., *Translation and World Literature*, New Perspectives in Translation and Interpreting Studies (London; New York: Routledge, 2018).
9   Eugene Jolas, *Critical Writings, 1924–1951*, ed. Klaus H Kiefer and Rainer Rumold (Northwestern University Press, 2009), 121.
10 Craig Monk, 'Eugene Jolas and the Translation Policies of Transition', *Mosaic: A Journal for the Interdisciplinary Study of Literature* 32, no. 4 (December 1999): 17–34.
11 See Céline Mansanti, *La revue transition, 1927–1938: Le modernisme historique en devenir* (Rennes: Presses universitaires de Rennes, 2009), Ebook, 729. Available online: http://books.openedition.org/pur/32713?format=toc (accessed 3 July 2019) ; and Mansanti, 'Between Modernisms: *transition* (1927–38)', in *The Oxford Critical and Cultural History of Modernist Magazines: Volume II: North America 1894–1960*, ed. Peter Brooker and Andrew Thacker (Oxford: Oxford University Press, 2012; published online 2015). Available online from Oxford Scholarship Online, http://dx.doi.org/10.1093/acprof:osobl/9780199545810.001.0001 (accessed 4 September 2020), 1–21. Particularly important translations noted by Mansanti include 'extracts

from Saint-John Perse's *Éloges*, Alfred Döblin's *Berlin Alexanderplatz*, and Carl Einstein's *Bébuquin* (not yet translated into English), Breton's first chapter of *Nadja* (published the same month in English in *transition* and in French in *La Révolution surréaliste*), Desnos's first chapters of *La Liberté ou l'amour!* (only fully translated into English in 1993), and Kafka's *Metamorphosis*, and "Letter to the Father"' (Mansanti, *La revue transition, 1927–1938*, 9–10).

12 Eugene Jolas and Elliot Paul, 'A Review', *Transition* 12 (March 1928): 139–47.
13 Ibid., 146.
14 Ibid., 144.
15 *transition* 12 (March 1928): 182. Monk writes that 'After that single issue, dominated by American submissions that he considered mediocre at best, Jolas quickly and quietly scaled back his commitment to Josephson's suggestion' ('Eugene Jolas and the Translation Policies of Transition').
16 In focusing on one particular issue of *transition* I am in agreement with the argument, recently put forward by Andrew Thacker, for the importance of close reading in studying modernist magazines, which often fail to provide the 'substantial and stable corpus' that would be required for a form of 'distant reading'. Andrew Thacker, 'Spatial Histories of Magazines and Modernisms', in *Historical Modernisms*, ed. Angeliki Spiropoulou and Jean-Michel Rabaté (London: Bloomsbury, forthcoming). In the case of *transition*, it is specifically through close reading that we begin to see the complexity of how translation operates, as the latter part of this essay demonstrates.
17 Bulson, *Little Magazine, World Form*, 80.
18 Eugene Jolas, *Man from Babel*, ed. Andreas Kramer and Rainer Rumold (New Haven: Yale University Press, 1998), 88.
19 For a recent critique of inaccuracies in Apter's analysis of 'untranslatables', see Lawrence Venuti, 'Hijacking Translation: How Comp Lit Continues to Suppress Translated Texts', *Boundary 2* 43, no. 2 (1 May 2016): 179–204. Available online: https://doi.org/10.1215/01903659-3469952 (accessed 9 March 2019).
20 Joshua Miller and Gayle Rogers, 'Translation and/as Disconnection', *Modernism/Modernity Print Plus* 3, no. 3 (11 September 2018): 6. Available online:. https://doi.org/10.26597/mod.0062 (accessed 9 December 2019). Apter is also one of the few critics to have examined Jolas's multilingual poetry in any detail, in *The Translation Zone: A New Comparative Literature* (Princeton: Princeton University Press, 2006), 112–19.
21 Jolas wrote directly about the complexity of his own linguistic heritage in his posthumously published autobiography, *Man from Babel*.
22 Yasemin Yildiz, *Beyond the Mother Tongue: The Postmonolingual Condition* (New York: Fordham University Press, 2012), 2. Juliette Taylor-Batty, 'On the Frontier: Eugene Jolas and Multilingual Modernism', *Dibur Literary Journal* 7 (Fall 2019): 7–20. Rainer Rumold has recently argued for the importance of 'the multilingual and multiethnic borderland regions at the margins' of Europe in the development of the historical avant-garde, with Jolas playing a significant part (*Archaeologies of Modernity: Avant-Garde Bildung* (Evanston, Illinois: Northwestern University Press, 2015), 93). For an insightful analysis of the politics of Jolas's multilingualism, see also Delphine Grass, 'The Democratic Languages of Exile: Reading Eugene Jolas and Yvan Goll's American Poetry with Jacques Derrida and Hannah Arendt', *Nottingham French*

Studies 56, no. 2 (July 2017): 227–44. Available online:. https://doi.org/10.3366/nfs.2017.0183 (accessed 18 September 2018).
23 Eugene Jolas et al., 'Proclamation', *Transition* 16/17 (June 1929), 13.
24 Jolas, *Man from Babel*, 108.
25 Monk, 'Eugene Jolas and the Translation Policies of Transition', 24.
26 As Monk has argued, this reflects a concern with the 'fidelity' of translations in *transition*, but also suggests that 'almost from the outset [Jolas] had been moving away from the idea that a text needed to be translated in the interests of the reader, and was beginning to feel that a reader must negotiate the text as found', a tendency that is felt in the Revolution manifesto's declaration that 'The plain reader be damned' (ibid.).
27 Eugene Jolas, 'Glossary', *Transition* 18 (November 1929): 287.
28 Eugene Jolas, 'Logos', *Transition* 16/17 (June 1929): 25–30, 28.
29 See for example Jolas, *Man from Babel*, 147.
30 Jolas and Paul emphasize the importance of comprehensibility in their introduction to the first volume of *transition*, where they invite non-American writers 'to appear, side by side [with American writers], in a language Americans can read and understand. The result should be mutually helpful and inspiring' (Eugene Jolas and Elliot Paul, 'Introduction', *Transition* 1 (June 1929) 135–8, 137).
31 Eugene Jolas, 'Glossary', *Transition* 22 (February 1933), 177.
32 Barbara Cassin, 'The Energy of the Untranslatables: Translation as a Paradigm for the Human Sciences', *Paragraph* 38, no. 2 (July 2015): 145–58, 155. Available online: https://doi.org/10.3366/para.2015.0154 (accessed 30 August 2019).
33 Eugene Jolas, 'Transition's Revolution of the Word Dictionary', *Transition* 21 (March 1932): 323–5.
34 Franz Kafka, 'Three Tales', trans. Eugene Jolas, *Transition* 21 (March 1932): 58–64, 58.
35 Miguel Angel Asturias, 'Legend of the Tatooed Girl', *Transition* 21 (March 1932): 8–12, 12; Ventura Garcia Calderon, 'The White Llama', *Transition* 21 (March 1932): 42–7, 45.
36 Jolas, *Man from Babel*, 109.
37 For my analysis of the multilingual content of *transition* in later volumes, including Jolas's own multilingual work, see 'On the Frontier: Eugene Jolas and Multilingual Modernism'.
38 James Stephens and James Joyce, 'James Joyce, Translator', *Transition* 21 (March 1932): 257, 257.
39 James Joyce, *Letters of James Joyce Volume I*, ed. Stuart Gilbert (New York: Viking Press, 1966), 317.
40 Stephens and Joyce, 'James Joyce, Translator'.
41 The Basic English translation of *Anna Livia Plurabelle* in *transition* is a reprint: it was first published in Ogden's journal *Psyche* in 1931. For an overview of the Basic English translation and Joyce's involvement in it, see Patrick O'Neill, *Trilingual Joyce: The Anna Livia Variations* (Toronto: University of Toronto Press, 2018), 26–9.
42 Damrosch, *What Is World Literature?*, 289.
43 Patrick O'Neill, *Impossible Joyce* (Toronto: University of Toronto Press, 2013), 3, 5.
44 As Dougald McMillan points out, 'More pages of *transition* were devoted to "Work in Progress", defence and explanation of it than to any other author' ('*transition*': *The History of a Literary Era, 1927–1938* (New York: George Brazillier, 1975), 179).

45 C. K. Ogden, trans., 'James Joyce's "Anna Livia Plurabelle" in Basic English', *Transition* 21 (March 1932): 259–62, 259.
46 Despite this apparent opposition, there are very close links between Ogden, Joyce and Jolas's projects. See Jean-Michel Rabaté, 'Joyce and Jolas: Late Modernism and Early Babelism', *Journal of Modern Literature* 22, no. 2 (Winter 1998/99): 245–52. For analysis of Jolas's own attempts to create a universal language, see Eugenia Kelbert, 'From Babelbank to Atlantica: Eugene Jolas and His Language Laboratory', in *Philologie und Mehrsprachigkeit*, ed. Till Dembeck and G. Mein (Heidelberg: Heidelberger Winter-Verlag, 2014), 275–309.
47 Ogden, 'James Joyce's "Anna Livia Plurabelle" in Basic English', 259.
48 Ibid.
49 Ibid.
50 James Joyce, *Finnegans Wake* (Harmondsworth: Penguin, 1992), 213. Ogden based his version on the 1929 recording that he made of Joyce reading *Anna Livia*, which is very close to the *Wake* in its final published form and which is therefore the version I am using here as an 'original' text – although we cannot identify a stable 'original' here because of the complex and extended period of genesis of the *Wake*. For discussion of the Joyce –Ogden connection, and the significance of the recording to Ogden's version, see Susan Shaw Sailer, 'Universalizing Languages: "Finnegans Wake" Meets Basic English', *James Joyce Quarterly* 36, iv (Summer 1999): 853–68.
51 Roland MacHugh, *Annotations to Finnegans Wake*, 4th edn. (Baltimore: Johns Hopkins University Press, 2016), 213.
52 Ogden, 'James Joyce's "Anna Livia Plurabelle" in Basic English', 259.
53 Ibid.
54 Rosa Maria Bollettieri Bosinelli, 'Introduction: Anna Livia Plurabelle's Sisters', in *Transcultural Joyce*, ed. Karen Lawrence (Cambridge: Cambridge University Press, 1998): 173–8, 175. For a detailed comparative study of the different translations of *Anna Livia Plurabelle*, see O'Neill, *Trilingual Joyce*.
55 Ibid., 173. Bosinelli does not specifically mention the Ogden translation here, but as Jean-Michel Rabaté argues, 'Joyce was not only pleased with efforts such as Jolas's or Ogden's, but he incorporated them into the very substance of *Finnegans Wake*' ('Joyce and Jolas').
56 For example, the Basic English version includes the following passage, which is initially quite hard to understand: 'I'll put some stones on the hotel linen. But that it came from a married bed it would be watered and folded only.' Joyce's text, on the other hand, is much clearer: 'I'll lay a few stones on the hostel sheets. A man and his bride embraced between them. Else I'd have sprinkled and folded them only' (James Joyce, *Finnegans Wake*, 213).
57 Raymond Queneau and Jean-Pierre Brisset, 'Words from the Unconscious', *Transition* 21 (March 1932): 302–3, 302.
58 Cited and translated in Dennis Duncan, *The Oulipo and Modern Thought* (Oxford: Oxford University Press, 2019), 56.
59 See Ibid., 58.

Part IV

Multilingual poetics of world literature

13

How each sound becomes world

yasser elhariry

What was there before the world? What was there before literature? Were there sounds? What's a sound that goes unheard? What's a forgotten sound? What was there before language? Was there silence? What comes after literature? What comes after the end of the world? What comes after bidding language farewell? Can language and literature return to a world before language and literature? Or come close to one? Was there one? What is this literature? What does it look like? What language is it in? What does it sound like? What is sound without an ear?

Call to order

For twentieth-century writers immersed in the ambient internationalism of the avant-garde – 'destructeurs prophétiques' (prophetic destructors)[1] of language like Louis Aragon, René Maran, Georges Henein, Isidore Isou, Christophe Tarkos and PNL – radical reversals, ruptures and undoings constitute committed aesthetic callings. The literary history recounted by this lineage seeks the destruction of destruction – the recuperation, then the collapse, of something akin to the mythical and mystical origins of verbal creation: the first sounds we hear, the first sounds we make. For the waves of destruction that followed in the wake of the undifferentiated sonic 'magma',[2] like the primordial 'waters of a volcano',[3] had long given way to the layered, near-invisible norms and veneers of lingual order, beginning with the invention of words, then the invention of language out of words. Armed with words and rules, cloaked in respectability, logic, decency and coherency, literary transmissions conceal the antecedent sonic dissonance. Which is why our prophetic destructors bring literature face to face, Janus-like, with its pasts and futures. They plunge it headfirst into the sonic magma.

In the sonic retuning of literary history, some literature will never be world literature, because not all languages are of this world. Such a literature respects neither the competing cartographies of lingual-national order; nor the protocols of market-driven literary publishing, translation and prizes; nor the spatialized understanding of a world in which literary artefacts circulate away from a point of origin. For the world is ordered, likes order. It follows order, respects order. 'Languages distinguish between nations', in Denis Hollier's damning assessment.[4] 'In today's world', he clarifies, 'the production and consumption of literature continue to respect the geography of language'.[5] Translation may tilt the picture, but only by so few degrees. David Damrosch's interest in how 'literary works ... circulate beyond their culture of origin'[6] similarly recasts Hollier's view of literary cartography. Or, against 'cartographies of the world', as Pheng Cheah would have it, that 'describe and analyse how literary works circulate around the world or are produced with a global market in mind', producing an epistemology that 'reduces the world to a spatial object', the world may at best be redefined as a 'temporal construct', wherein 'temporalization constitutes the openness of a world, the opening that is world'.[7] Aragon, Maran, Henein, Isou, Tarkos and PNL draw on this openness by exploiting the slow time of linguistic development. They draw on an ancient aural memory, encrypted into the progressive sedimentation of language and the consonantal hardening of the tongue. They counter world literature's spatial constraints with lingual modes of sonic deregulation. And since they compose in riddles and tongues, their attempts at linguistic and literary transmissions take longer, only to be reborn out of the most unexpected of ashes, like the lyric of contemporary hip hop. Their destructive experiments with language sidestep the spatialized world of lingual-national order, organized around principles of translatability and transparency.[8] Irascible irritants, they grate against the epidermis of the world. Counterworldly, they are at a remove from the circulatory logics of the spatial world.

Despite these attempts to counter hegemonies of social order and sovereign national geographies of language, the paradigmatic cachets of world literature – book sales, cultural-linguistic representativity, translatability – constitute a recurrent *Rappel à l'ordre* (Call to Order), in Jean Cocteau's titular formulation from 1926.[9] The avant-garde's thwarted desire for a total linguistic returning of the world would seem all but moot. In Abdellah Taïa's expression, no matter how close you and I may get,

> c'est horrible. C'est triste. C'est dégoûtant. Tout, absolument tout, nous sépare. Le rêve est fini. Les images du paradis entre [nous] sont en train de tomber. De se remplir petit à petit d'amertume, de distance, d'un rappel à l'ordre.[10]
>
> (it's awful. It's sad. It's gross. Everything, absolutely everything, separates us. The dream is over. The images of heaven between [us] are falling. Filling up, little by little, with bitterness, distance, a call to order.)

The muddying of distinct tongues that was dreamt up by some of the most imaginative of vanguardist texts swiftly meets its end in the sobering realities of worldly division and separation. Space, time and lingual difference (what keeps people and their tongues discrete and isolated, even within multilingual contexts) are kept rigorously separate. Even in closest intimacy: 'j'ai introduit ma langue dans sa bouche et j'ai cherché le bon angle pour commencer à jouer avec sa langue à lui' (I slipped my tongue into his mouth and found just the right angle to begin playing with his own tongue).[11] Even in deepest intimacy, in the dissolution of you in me, me in you, everything separates us. Extreme solitude.[12] For separation contains and maintains diversity. And who dreams of the eradication of diversity? Of the total dissolution of ipseity?

Total separation. Total fusion. An irresolvable tension stalks the world's proliferation of tongues and literatures. Multilingualism may very well reflect the realities of today's global cultures, and easily lend itself to a critique and conceptual dismantling of the literary world order. But internally, multilingualism seems untenable without, inseparable from monolingualism. Multilingualism, in practice, maintains and sustains monolingualism: we only ever speak one language at a time.[13] Or, in David Gramling's more incendiary provocation, monolingualism was invented in order to manage and subtend the multilingualism of the world: the threat we pose by never only speaking one language in any given moment, by hubris threatening eternal relapse into babelism, or – what's worse! – alingualism.[14]

In what follows, then, I make a case for the multilingualism of monolingualism in literature that does not readily conform to the definitional standards of world literature. The dual approach, to a difficult literary corpus and the fraught debates of literary worldliness, allows me to demonstrate a longer historical conception of the relationship between sound and sense, sound and language. I do this by closely following the sounds of the human tongue in its emancipation from the single, countable language. This happens intertextually in Georges Henein by way of Louis Aragon, in Isidore Isou by way of René Maran, in the lyrics of hip hop duo PNL by way of Isou and Christophe Tarkos. When taken as an intertextual collective, they showcase a peculiar kind of historical precedent that generates lingual diversity within (imagined) monoculture. Indeed, against the grain of world literature today, wherein translation and success in the literary marketplace represent the yardstick by which to measure the becoming-world of literature, literary circulation across cultures was once (as with the vanguardists) transacted in single – but infinitely malleable – languages that cut through and across multilingual sociocultural strata. Still, lingual and literary order were undone from within, as in the examples that follow. Monolanguage, in other words, always already contains the terrible beauty and poetically destructive germ of lingual fraying. The poetics of sonic transmission, which emerges through my analyses of Aragon, Maran, Henein, Isou, Tarkos and PNL, presents a series of movements that gradually progresses across discrete lingual units – letter, phoneme, vowel – only to uncouple them from the contiguous trappings of the sentence, the word and the consonant, respectively. These movements evoke an aural kind of fuzz, a historical linguistic and sonic mode of expression which has always bristled against the mono/nonmono dichotomy. Its distorted underbelly.

mu

Taking Cocteau's merry title *Le Rappel à l'ordre* and his hard-nosed call to order as a point of departure, let us consider how nonmonolingual monolingualism unveils itself in literature through the example of polyglot Egyptian surrealist and provocateur Georges Henein (Cairo, 1914–Paris, 1973).[15] My sustained reading of his intertextual and sonic gestures illustrates the dual reaffirmation and undoing of monolingualism from within. Henein all but eradicates the difference between mono and nonmono. His oppositional approach to the world and its languages begins with the insertion of a banal, seemingly innocuous vowel – *u* – into Cocteau's title. Henein deforms Cocteau's title into a middle finger – *rappel à l'ordure* (call to trash) – flipped right back at him. 'Cocteau!' he calls at him. 'You piece of trash!' He then adopts the reconfigured *Le Rappel à l'ordure* as the title for a 1935 chapbook of poems.

The barb at Cocteau should be heard as a twenty-one-year-old's juvenile exuberance, amplified in the light of the French author's condemnation of a younger generation of vanguardist poets concentrated around André Breton and his circle. In 'Le secret professionnel', for instance, collected in *Le Rappel à l'ordre*, Cocteau polemicizes in favour of a return to the rules of poetry over *la poésie maudite*, and attacks *l'esprit moderne* for its purportedly uneducated exploitation of Arthur Rimbaud and Stéphane Mallarmé.[16] The unresolved hostility between Cocteau and the vanguardists emanates, in turn, throughout *Les Pas perdus* (The Lost Steps),[17] the Bretonian counterpoint to the texts collected in *Le Rappel à l'ordre*.

By siding with the early-twentieth-century international avant-garde, and the many disputes and polemics that engulfed it, Henein's case points to the movement's unique limits (it was monolingual, untranslated, untranslatable) by today's world literary standards (competitive, multilingual, born translated). In *Le Rappel à l'ordure*, he exhibits an intertextual attunement to the nature and stakes of poetic debates and contexts on both shores of the Mediterranean. From Paris to Cairo and back, the international circulation of vanguardist ideas here remains exclusively monolingual – to a fault, to be sure: it was as if the multilingual milieu of early-twentieth-century Cairo were no more than mere exotic backdrop. If that.[18] At its heart, though, a poetic miracle: a small sonic 'exit'[19] punctures Henein's intertext, boring its way through to far-off languages. Henein pokes a tiny intertextual but sonic hole in monolanguage. And language goes boom.

Let's take a specific example. In 1935, the same year as *Le Rappel à l'ordure*, Henein is busy publishing societal disrespect in all available venues. His contribution to the January 1935 issue of the little magazine *Un effort* was a single poem ('Pompes funèbres'), quickly followed in the February issue by a manifesto ('De l'irréalisme'), a philosophical parody in prose ('Étude physiologique du Noumène') and a harsh critique of Aragon's 1934 novel ('*Les Cloches de Bâle* par Aragon'), published in the aftermath of the surrealist movement's backlash against Aragon for his move into the world of realist historical fiction. Henein's publications in the 1930s take place against the backdrop of *l'affaire Aragon*, triggered by the surrealist author's publication in 1931 of the poem 'Front rouge' in *Littérature de la révolution mondiale*, edited by the Moscow-based Union internationale des écrivains révolutionnaires. The polemic operated on two levels: a public one that involved the legal prosecution of Aragon (there was public outrage at the poem's vicious opening and its depiction of bourgeois vanity, with its protective layers and its superfluous, comfy wrappers, and Aragon faced legal prosecution due to the poem's violent call for the murder of 'tous les médecins social-fascistes' [all social-fascist doctors]); a second one internal to the admixture of æsthetics and politics within the surrealist group. While the surrealists rallied in support of Aragon's poem, Breton found himself ill at ease defending Aragon for a poem that he found bereft of poetic or philosophical merit: the referentiality of

Aragon's poem and its 'retour au sujet extérieur' (return to the external subject) was, in Breton's estimation, at odds with the cutting-edge of poetic evolution.[20]

The polemic places Aragon at the front and centre of Henein's preoccupations in the 1930s, as he attempts to reconcile the sonic signature of Aragon's most derisive texts with Breton's appeal to the internal poetic subject's capacity to transcend reality. Henein embeds an Aragonian sound into the short poem 'Pompes funèbres'. It reads like an illustration of the oppositional streak of anti-social rebellion outlined in his manifesto 'De l'irréalisme',[21] except that it goes much further: armed with the Aragonian intertext, Henein manages to undo the order of the lingual real through sonic permutation. In the fourth stanza, the poet dissects the absurdity surrounding what appears to be an ordinary funeral procession. Anomie may prevail in Henein's poem, but prosody comes out on top.

> Qui donc met-on en terre?
> un homme
> chauve comme une planète
> orné d'un ventre en forme de bidon
> en somme ridicule
> de toute façon ce n'est qu'un numéro
> la société a perdu un numéro
> avec componction elle enterre feu le numéro[22]

> (So who are we tossing into the earth?
> a man
> bald like a planet
> festooned with a can-shaped belly
> in sum ridiculous
> anyway he's just a number
> society's lost a number
> with compunction it buries the late number)

The three closing lines introduce gradual refinements to 'numéro': from the detachment qua the body as autonomous object ('ce n'est qu'un numéro' (he's just a number)), to the closing parody of a compunctious society interring an unidentified 'feu le numéro' (late number), by way of *numéro*'s ultimate social severance ('la société a perdu un numéro' [society's lost a number]). The post-interrogative repetition of *numéro* at the end of the closing lines dwells upon each part of the trisyllabic word, it dwells upon each one of the three syllables, it pulls each of the three syllables apart. Their glitchcore repetition foregrounds the poet's sonic imaginary. With a single word, Henein creates an internal rhyme, evokes the corpse washer's job,[23] even an English nursery rhyme. The three closing lines exaggerate the word's first and final syllables. *Nu nu nu*, they seem to go: the dead body is a nude male body, *un homme nu* (does the corpse washer not strip the dead body in preparation for burial?). *Ro ro ro*, they all end: row row row the coffin, gently down the funerary stream. And in-between *nu* and *ro*, the medial *mé mé mé* rings like *mes mes mes*, the first-person plural possessive *my my my*, but also like a homophone for the *met* in *met-on* in the stanza's first line. *Mets mets mets en terre*: put put put into the earth. Against the comic sonic murmurs of a funeral crowd barely keeping its vocal tics hush and in check, the peanut gallery comprising poem and ill-mannered poet just keep cheering on, they just keep going *nu nu nu mé mé mé ro ro ro*: Nude nude nude Put put put Row row row

The lines then give way to an auditory modulation and a bird's-eye view of the gathering, sinking deeper in its sonic farce. The poem shifts from the oral, labial and rhotic *n*'s, *m*'s and *r*'s (what could be more rhotic, more *rho*, more ǫ than *ro*?), to the sibilant *c*'s and *s*'s of *brise, tristesse, lancer, sonnent, sacrilège, frénésie, renonce, guérisons* and *vaste*. They slip by lips of mouths flung wide open like *numéro*'s tomb. Beginning with *sur*.

> sur une Arête se brise la tristesse des hommes
> angle aigu du deuil qui choit dans le comique
> Des bras se lèvent pour acclamer le diable
> en redingote
> Des bouches s'ouvrent pour lancer des hourras
> qui sonnent comme des glas
> Sacrilège la frénésie disloque tous les corps
> l'homme renonce aux équilibres et aux guérisons
> et dans un vaste rire ouvert comme une tombe
> se livre au mouvement qui jamais ne finit ...[24]

> (on a Crest the sadness of men breaks
> mourning's acute angle sinks comical
> Arms rise to cheer the devil
> in a frock coat
> Mouths open dart hoorays
> that sound death knells
> Sacrilegious the frenzy dislocates all bodies
> man spurns balances and cures
> and in a vast laugh open like a grave
> delivers himself to never-ending movement ...)

The rupture of the singsong-like postlingual cheers and laughs[25] opens up a different kind of interreferential literary movement that never ends: intertextuality. Henein's text insolently echoes Aragon's formative Dadist period from 1917–22, in particular derisive, sonically comical poems such as 'Un monsieur' (A Gentleman). Aragon's text parodies scientific exposition. It presents the character traits of an anonymous creature, almost like a police report, a caricature of reasoning man-in-society, which reduces the titular character, Le Monsieur, to a mere, single, foreign (funny-sounding) character.

> On devine que l'homme, appelons le [*sic*] μ pour simplifier, n'a ni devoirs ni droits.
> Si nous conservons donc la classification droits et devoirs envers autrui, soi-même,

ses parents, ses enfants, sa patrie, son époux ou épouse, etc., entendons que nous n'envisageons là que les rapports du cher μ avec ces diverses entités sans bénéfice de jugement. Nous disons donc *Rapports* ...²⁶

(We may surmise that the man, let's call him μ to simplify, has neither duties nor rights. If we were to thereby retain the classification rights and duties toward another, oneself, one's parents, one's children, one's homeland, one's spouse, etc., let us be clear that we only envisage the relationships of dear μ with these diverse entities without the benefit of judgement. Speaking of *Relationships* ...)

But what kind of sound is *μ*? In Henein, the cascading crescendo of *numéro*, the sonic arsenal of numeric decomposition – part-French, part-English, as *numéro* mushrooms into *nu nu nu mé mé mé ro ro ro* – also turns out to be a decomposed enumeration that's all Greek to me: *nu* [ν], *rho* [ϱ], and ... *mé*? But since *mé* is no letter at all, or, at best, a half-letter – half of a letter like the Arabic م [*mīm*] or the Hebrew ם [*mem*] – or an inverted letter (*m = em → mé*), Henein self-corrects his 'mistake' by way of a furtive sonic allusion to Aragon. This modulates *mé* into *mu* [μ]. It transposes *numéro* into *numurho*, or the thirteenth, twelfth and seventeenth letters of the Greek alphabet, ν-μ-ϱ.

And so each letter becomes sound. Each sound becomes letter in different tongue. Through intertextuality and little else. Each monolingual sound becomes multilingual. Situated within a multilingual sonic field, each sound encompasses a multitude of languages in the world. Each sound becomes world.

oubanguy

Monolingualism, however brittle and surface-scatter, may be unavoidable, for it is foundational to a majority of writing. Yet an underlying sonic magma, akin to the babbling phase of child language, precedes monolingualism, supersedes multilingualism. This basis propagates the kinds of sonic permutations as the one generative in Henein, birthing Greek out of French. Can any language really so easily be, so easily cede to, any other language? Henein's system in this respect prefigures Louis Wolfson's in *Le Schizo et les langues* (1970). As Gilles Deleuze explains it, 'un mot de la langue maternelle étant donné, trouver un mot étranger de sens similaire, mais aussi ayant des sons ou des phonèmes communs (de préférence en français, allemand, russe ou hébreu, les quatre langues principalement étudiées par l'auteur)' (given a word in the mother tongue, to find a foreign word with a similar meaning, but also sharing sounds or phonemes in common (preferably in French, German, Russian or Hebrew, the four main languages studied by the author)).²⁷ Wolfson, Deleuze furthermore suggests, should be read in the lineage of Raymond Roussel (Paris, 1877–Palermo, 1933), who undertakes a similar operation within French, unfurling even further the mono-mother tongue's internal phonemic capacity for lingual multiplicity.²⁸

As part of the transferences that they entail, whether in the form of a return to babbling, doubling, ghosting, shadowing, stalking or physical tongue against tongue,²⁹ languages all but stop distinguishing between nations.[30] Or, for that matter, between anything at all. Beginning with themselves. Beginning with you and me. For indeed the separation of one nation from another, of my tongue from yours, is only discernible within a system of hard, rigid geo-linguistics. Which riles Abdelkébir Khatibi.

> la frontière d'un pays à l'autre est invisible
> c'est ainsi que je césure ta langue sans m'égarer …
> apprends en te dressant la rapidité de mon langage[31]
>
> (the border between two countries is invisible
> that's how I can merge [excise] with your language [tongue] without losing myself …
> confront the rapidity of my language and learn)[32]

In a soft, fluid system, sounds mix and blend and retune the world. The associative rapidity enabling such a system of translingual kinship[33] lies neither in single languages, nor entire languages, nor a general system of linguistics. 'Je césure' (I cut), writes Khatibi. 'Ta langue' (your tongue). In a landscape of chopped tongues, 'la rapidité de mon langage' (the rapidity of my language) befalls the smallest of possible units, as they *césurent* or excise their way out of language. Sonic units such as syllables, phonemes, single letters, vowels, consonants, tics, breaths, whispers, glitches. The sounds of insects and animals. Because even words are de trop. And continue to impose too much of a call to order.

If 'Pompes funèbres' sneaks in a sonic or phonemic destruction of lingual barriers, ushering the way to free lingual kinships that later writers from Wolfson to Khatibi would develop into idiosyncratic modes of verbal expression, their systems remain imbricated with an irreducible overall functionality of monolingualism. Though they effectively smudge lingual separation, they construct fluid, sonic bridges from monolanguage to monolanguage. Because of this, other poets take a different route, leading them less across the bridge than downright plunging them into all that the bridge would have saved them from.

A little over a decade after Henein's 1935 take-down of Cocteau and the sonic rupture of 'Pompes funèbres', Lettrism co-founder Isidore Isou (Botoșani, 1925–Paris, 2007) stages his own institutional disruption, assailing the words of language.

> On January 21, 1946, at the Théâtre du Vieux-Colombier in Paris, Isidore Isou interrupted a lecture by Michel Leiris on the occasion of a production of *La Fuite: poème dramatique en quatre actes et un épilogue* by Tristan Tzara, proclaiming, 'We know all about Tzara, Mr. Leiris, tell us about Lettrism!' After the show, Isou declaimed his theories and read one of his poems on-stage. The incident was calculated with the intent purpose of attracting media attention so that Isou, at this point an unknown author, could promote the publication of his *Introduction à une nouvelle poésie et à une nouvelle musique*. The work appeared in 1947 with Gallimard, forevermore linking Isou to the Pleiades of French poetry and literature.[34]

Introduction à une nouvelle poésie et à une nouvelle musique matches Isou's media stunt in bombast. It announces that *'l'élaboration* [de l'alphabet lettrique] *assumera l'acquisition de lettres inouïes'* (*the elaboration* [of the lettric alphabet] *will take the form of an acquisition of unheard-of letters*), that 'pour le lettriste, *chaque son* qu'il cueillera dans la réalité d'alentour *deviendra lettre*' (*each sound* gathered by the Lettrist in the surrounding reality *becomes letter*), that the art of Lettrie 'peut être considérée comme vague, *mystique et mystérieuse*' (may be conceived of as a wave, *mystical and mysterious*).³⁵ Isou calls the mystical and mysterious language of Lettrism the 'langue étrangère' par excellence' (the 'foreign language' par excellence).³⁶ Entrenched in Dada as a purified form of the avant-garde, and as a forerunner to Situationism, Lettrism sought no less than the erosion of the very fabric of monolingualism, indeed of lingualism tout court – words – and the resurrection, out of their ashes, of a new language composed of an unheard sonic palette, unhindered by the grammar and syntax of the single, countable, human tongue. *Nu nu nu mé mé mé ro ro ro* all the way.

Isou's book is actually three books in one, a tripartite ars poetica (*Introduction à une nouvelle poésie*, *Introduction à une nouvelle musique* and *Sur les possibilitsé d'un art nouveau*) followed by two sets of demonstrations: *Vingt récitations graves et joyeuses* and *La Guerre: première symphonie lettriste*.³⁷ The poems of *Vingt récitations graves et joyeuses* are impossible to emulate here in their graphic entirety: Isou uses a typewriter for the layout of the poems, followed by heavy annotation of the typewritten sheet by hand using a specially conceived alphabet, *le nouvel alphabet lettriste*.³⁸ Contrasted to Dada – deemed the 'simple définition d'une existence destructive' (simple definition of destructive existence)³⁹ by Isou for its reduction of 'poetry to its phonemes (the smallest sound unit that forms meaningful contrasts between utterances)'⁴⁰ – Lettrism as an 'endeavor hinged on the question of bodily intonation, explored as a means by which to divide a phoneme's articulation internally'.⁴¹ The new Lettrist alphabet, which draws on Greek letters and the international phonetic alphabet, solicits certain sounds to be produced by the reader. Isou even provides precise indications for when to fart, sneeze, cough, kiss, pant and hiccup. His handwritten annotations feature extensive underlining, the insertion of macrons, occasional corrections, even the odd temporal marker (or musical rest) '• = pause'. The resulting page of poetry resembles a cross between the lyrics of a song (a poem by Isou will feature creative indentation and several refrains) and musical partition (*La Guerre* in particular is written for seven voices, with three lines of partition of four to five bars each to the page).

Of the '10 poèmes joyeux', at first sight I am baffled by 'Jungle', the sixth poem, for (like Henein) its unexpected (but not really) intertextuality. The intertext curtly forestalls accusations of a racist exercise in exoticism. Just as much as it reads like a move straight out of Henein's playbook.

BALA<u>OUOU</u> u
    mowgli
    howghi !
toukouroukouoù
oubanguy ! guy

oubanguy ! guy
oubanguy ! guy
GOUMBEREGA
TCHIOUMBEREGA
TCHIOUMBER<u>EGA</u> ... a
ipépenguyana
nganiagana
niguérigana
INCANAB<u>AA</u> a
BOZAMBAB<u>AA</u>[42]

The glut of vowels contributes to the poem's purportedly joyous soundscape, which follows ten preceding 'poèmes graves' carrying such titles as 'Cris pour 5.000.000 de Juifs égorgés' (Screams for 5,000,000 Butchered Jews), 'Promenade parmi les mots de mon pays' (Walk Amidst My Country's Words) and '1917'. Isou's 'poèmes joyeux' deride rather than represent. They mimic joy, heard in its most sombre note, viewed from its darkest, most oblique angle, against a backdrop of superlative horror: to a postcolonial mind in the immediate aftermath of the Second World War (Isou was born Isidore Goldstein and clandestinely fled Romania for Paris in 1947),[43] what joy can there possibly be in further debasing the colonized mind barely concealed beneath the guise of Kipling's Mowgli? (Besides, Isou, like Henein with Cocteau, flips things back at Kipling: if the nearby slant rhyme is any suggestion, *howghi !* sounds like *How, guy?!*).[44] What joy can there possibly be in evoking every stereotype of the African jungle? (The poem's opening handwritten didascaly asks for a ' – rythme de tam tam –'.)

Or Caribbean slavery? Despite what seems like the sonic deprivation of sense, Isou's poem explicitly names African and Antillean sites of oppression. (In a sonic retuning of the world, what can be more arbitrary than proper names?) 'Jungle' is one of only a handful of poems in *Vingt récitations graves et joyeuses* to make no use of the new Lettrist alphabet, emphasizing instead the standard monolingual alphabet's destructive capacity to revel in the nonmonolingual and embrace the alingual. While the reference to the West Indies and their peripheries appears, within the poem's sonic system, to be straightforward and easily recognizable (Guyana in 'ipépenguyana'), the evocation of West Africa seems slant in contrast. Like Henein's *numéro*, though, it is told three times.

oubanguy! guy
oubanguy! guy
oubanguy! guy

Isou's covert reference to folkloric 'romans de la jungle' (novels of the jungle) and their repurposing of Kipling[45] is today largely forgotten, relegated to the arcana of endnotes and ancillary lamentations over the collective amnesia of committed literary criticism and its pretence to historicity.[46] Once, though, it was at the forefront of major literary polemic, immortalized by René Maran's landmark novel, *Batouala*

(1921), set in the French colony Oubangui-Chari. Coyly subtitled *véritable roman nègre* (true black novel), lauded in the American press,[47] vindicated by André Gide (as expressed by Maran himself in the 1937 preface to the second edition)[48] against spiteful criticism,[49] and heralded as a precursor to Négritude,[50] *Batouala* received the Goncourt Prize, a first in France for both a black author and a book without a single non-black protagonist. The novel, of course, is far from problem-free. The plot unfolds in the midst of a mythical, mythicized Africa, viewed by and recounted from a most paradoxical perspective: that of a Martinican writer whose official capacity as French colonial administrator from 1912 onward consisted of the irreal role of representing, as a black man, imperial white power to colonized West African subjects.[51] Though the French colony of Gabon dates back to 1842, Oubangui-Chari, where Maran was posted, was established in 1903, lasting until independence in 1960 when it became the Central African Republic. Named for the rivers Oubangui, a tributary of the Congo, and Chari, the principal tributary of Lake Chad, Oubangui-Chari becomes, in *Batouala*, the site of unprecedented sonic and lingual excrescences around monolanguage:[52] the sounds of the natural world and animal kingdom[53] enlarge and elasticize the sonic foundation of lingual expression,[54] paving the way for subsequent radical changes in the way that 'language would be used by citizens of the African states colonized by the French and granted independence'.[55]

And if Maran can make the language of *Batouala* sound like Oubangui-Chari, Isou's transcolonial sonic gesture of identificatory affinity in 'Jungle' further pries opens each sound of *Batouala*'s world. The first page of *Batouala* sets the stage.

> Dehors, les coqs chantent. À leur 'kékérékés' se mêlent le chevrotement des cabris sollicitant leurs femelles, le ricanement des toucans, puis, là-bas, au fort de la haute brousse bordant les rives de la Pombo et de la Bamba, l'appel rauque des 'bacouays', singes au museau allongé comme celui du chien.[56]

> (Outside the cocks crowed. Their 'crowing' mingled with the bleating of the goats for the ewes, with the cackling of the hornbills, and – from father away, from the depths of the high thickets bordering the Pombo and the Bembe Rivers – with the hoarse call of the bacouays, monkeys with elongated muzzles like dogs.)[57]

Midway through *Batouala*, at the outset of the ga'nza, the ceremonial initiation into circumcision, the languages of the animals blend with a secret human tongue, 'paroles gutturales ou nasillardes, que l'on ne comprenait pas' (words, nasal or guttural, that no one understood), 'car ils employaient le "samali", langage sacré'[58] (for they used the Samali, the sacred language).[59] In his deliberate avoidance of words altogether, Isou's sounds-cum-letters in 'Jungle' gush guttural consonants ('gli', 'ghi', 'guy', 'kou', 'rega', 'ngan', 'incan') and nasalized vowels ('a', 'ou', 'ouou', 'ouoù', 'an', 'uy', 'iou', 'uya', 'ia', 'aa'). He invents a secret tongue that draws on the Dadaist insistence of the sonic transformation of words into a phonemic paste. Like 'Ânehâtepâtebûche' (Asshastepastenumpty) and 'Bûchepâtehâteâne/Bêtepêcheflûtecôte' (Numptypastehasteass/Stupidfishfluteshore).[60] He situates the corporeal *césures* (cæsuræ) of articulating a phoneme within an expansive historical field of colonial politics and literary polemics, ongoing ever since *Batouala*, while at the same time going further than Dada's lingual stoppage at the phonemic level. The metapoetic and metalingual exercise of 'Jungle' steers sonic possibility away from exclusion, incomprehension and the destruction of sense, and toward initiation, complicity and a retuning of the ear to the world. How each sound sounds like the world.

coco kéké kakà

In fluid lingual systems, it's not just that monolingualism yields to multilingualism and multlingualism yields to monolingualism: language yields to the alingual and extralingual and vice versa. They bleed into and merge with each other. They fuse with the world. Each of their sounds becomes world. And the human tongue will once again speak in tongues. It will yield to the tongues of the animals and speak in the tongues of the animals. Words, their syllables, and their phonemes, the letters that compose them and the corporeal organs that produce them will create an ever-expansive non-totality of world-sounds. The fluidity of the system washes over the languages of the dictionaries and lexicons. There's nothing hard or set in stone about any of this. How else can Henein write in French but actually speak English and Greek? How else can Isou write *oubanguy* and evoke Maran and the language of cocks, hornbills and bacouays? Languages and species cease being hard and separate.

Tongues, too. 'Ma langue douce, avec ta langue' (My soft tongue, with your tongue).[61] They squish into each other. 'J'enveloppe ta langue dans ma langue' (I wrap your tongue in my tongue).[62] The sonic heritage of Louis Aragon in 1917-22, René Maran in 1921, Georges Henein in 1935 and Isidore Isou in 1947 casts a long shadow over performance and sound poetry, and continues to re-erupt in the extreme contemporary moment. The story told by this lineage recounts the progressive accretions accumulated by language through alternating cycles of destruction, reconstruction and refinement: the sudden violence of the Dadaists and their earliest inheritors; the international avant-garde's more measured circulation among the monolanguages; the progressive vanguardist divergences like the linguistically disembodied, internally divided phonemic articulation.

One notable inheritor to this tradition, Christophe Tarkos (Marseille, 1963-Paris, 2004), goes further still: he defies the assertion, exploited by Isou's strain of Lettrist poetry, that the phoneme is the 'unit of sound in a language that cannot be analysed into smaller linear units'.[63] Between 1993 and 1994, he records a sound poem, 'Le voyage autour du monde' (Voyage Around the World), with Valérie Tarkos. The poem dates from the middle of the first of Tarkos's three primary periods, specifically the 'période "marseillaise" du début jusque 1995/1996 où poésie sonore domine' ('Marseillais' period, from the beginning until 1995/1996, during which sound poetry dominated).[64] While the title 'Le voyage autour du monde' of course references Jules Verne and prefigures Daft Punk, Tarkos hews much closer to the parodic flipside of the travel writing tradition, encapsulated in Xavier de Maistre's irreverent *Voyage autour de ma chambre* (Voyage Around My Room) (1794).[65] Tarkos's voyage curtails the spatiality of travel. It hones and amplifies the sonic. It juxtaposes sounds both geographically specific (the cicadas of southern France, the peacocks and tigers of the Indian subcontinent and southeast Asia) and globally generic (unidentifiable twitter, cooing pigeons or doves). In a sense, the poem wilfully short-circuits the Isouian auditory onslaught of exotic local colour. It cuts it with a heavy dose of the mundane.

The mundane in all its muddy dross. And Tarkos's brand of poetry is particularly well suited for the task at hand. As a sonic tour de force, his poem renders language into a slurry, a sticky, messy, unformed but malleable bulk of sound, which takes on different material and plastic forms.[66] In 'Le voyage autour du monde', lingual form is a fluid, jammy purée of nasty mud: 'c'est de la poisse' (it's sludge), 'la pure pure purée', 'c'est maladif' (it's sickly), 'le malaise boueux' (muddy discomfort), 'tu [la poésie] es poubelle … tu es l'endroit de la merde' (you [poetry] are a trashcan … the place of shit), 'une seule boue' [one and the same mud], 'c'est la bouillie' [it's porridge], 'la merde chiante … la même merde monotone et chiante' (shitty shit … the same monotonous and shitty shit), 'long cadeau merdique' (long shitty gift), 'couleur caca d'oie' (the colour of goose poop), 'une boule close' (a sealed ball).[67]

And since waterfowl and their poop are fair poetic game, the poem layers field recordings of animals, birds and insects against a dual channel recording of Christophe and Valérie's voices. The superimposition of their voices speaking with, over, against and into one another makes for one messy, muddy auditory experience. What exactly are we listening to? How are we supposed to listen to two reading-speaking voices at the same time? Thrown into the face of sense, it's an aural mud that hardens: all it takes are two overlaid monolingual tongues for monolingualism to turn into Babelish brouhaha. For Tarkos, in Christophe Hanna's words, is 'un écrivain qui confère un aspect préhensible aux formes ambiantiques, diffuses, des échanges ordinaires auxquelles on s'est accoutumé au point qu'on n'arrive plus bien à les sentir et à les observer. Il vaudrait mieux se demander quels moyens, quels ressorts, pour parvenir à cela, il a exploités dans l'institution-poésie' (a writer who confers a prehensible aspect to diffuse, ambiantic forms, ordinary exchanges to which we are so accustomed that we no longer feel or observe them. It make you wonder what means, what motivations he exploited in the institution-of-poetry to arrive at this end).[68]

Like the smudge of u and μ in Henein and Aragon, Tarkos's text exploits language from within. It makes extended use of the fluidity of these vowels. And what do we pay less attention to than vowels and the sounds of insects? Vowels and the sounds of animals? Humans may be talking animals, and in that they sure just might be all alone: humans are the only animals whose entire lingual system is premised on the introduction of difference through consonantal articulation in order to form 'meaningful contrasts between utterances'.[69] Language, in other words, exists because of consonants. Humans, in this regard, are the only animals who produce consonants-against-vowels for the purpose of producing language and communication. Even Isou cannot do away with this difference: 'Jungle' would be inconceivable without the sounds, nasal or guttural, that no one understands.[70] Consonants in language come at a premium: they are the bones of language, they harden sound, give it shape, produce meaning out of contrasts.[71] Consonants safeguard language against the vowel's ever-present threat: total communicational fallout.

For Tarkos, that we no longer feel or observe consonants and vowels rings like a truism. And so he liquefies the hard and clear separation of the two. Like the Lettrists, his experience of language throbs within the body. And when he and Valérie simultaneously vocalize two throbbing lingual forces, the liquefied verbal fluid borne of their union becomes the embodiment of verbal poetic experience for both reader/speaker and listener/receiver. Tarkos forces vocal sound back to its original magma, its first fluid state of disorder, before the advent of language. He reliquefies it by structuring the entire opening sequence in 'Le voyage autour du monde' around the vowel *u*. The poem opens with recordings of the cicada, nature's songstress, then gives way to the opening lines, as read by Christophe.

> Il y a   un fluide   chaud dans la tête.
> Quelquefois, les déplacements du fluide se font sentir.
> Les mouvements du fluide contre la tête suivent des différences.
> Le fluide chaud qui se fait sentir sur la tête se déplace différentiellement.[72]

> (There is   a   fluid hot in the head.
> Sometimes, the fluid's displacements are felt.
> The fluid's movements against the head follow differences.
> The hot fluid felt on the head displaces itself differentially.)

'Fl*ui*de', 'fl*ui*de', 'mo*u*vements d*u* fl*ui*de', 's*ui*vent', 'fl*ui*de'. One of the ways by which Tarkos extends the intertextual sonic rupture of Henein's *u* and *μ*, and the transcolonial sonic filiation of Isou's destruction of words and invention of a new psycho-physiological alphabet, is through the compulsory diaresis of *fluide*. In prosody, the diaresis occupies an ambiguous (if not lowly) role as a last resort to syllabic completion. Words like *fluide*, where syneresis is not an option, reaffirm how unusual it is for two unarticulated vowels to follow, to flow from one to the next.

The singularity of the double vowel reverses the long-standing traditions in linguistics and the philosophy of language over the primacy of the consonant over the vowel. Consonants may continue to be hard and vowels soft, but in Tarkos, under pressure, lingual fluid cracks hard skull, like 'small flowers crack concrete'.[73]

> Il existe un fluide chaud dans la tête qui bourgeonne sur la surface du crâne à des endroits différents.
> Le fluide chauffe une partie de la tête.
>
> Les déplacements se font sentir. Il est chaud. Le crâne se fluidifie.
>
> La sensation chaude se déplace lentement; elle est
> En haut à droite de la tête,
>
> à gauche,

derrière la tête,
à droite⁷⁴

(There exists a hot fluid in the head that bulges on the surface of the skull in different locations.
The fluid heats a part of the head.

The displacements are felt. It is hot. The skull fluidifies.

The hot feeling moves slowly; it is
At the top right of the head,

to the left,
behind the head,
to the right)

Igneous rocks form after molten rock has cooled. Like a thick, slow river of flowing magma, fluid lingual poetics forever struggle against the threat of cool ossification. And the only way for it to keep flowing is, well, to keep it flowing. As Tarik and Nabil Andrieu – better known as Ademo and N.O.S of the trillwave hip hop duo PNL – would have it:

Coco joue pas le kéké, humble comme Kaká
Un peu survolté, un dos louche comme Blanka
Sous Jamaïca, j'sors un flow comme Sanka⁷⁵

The alliterative and semantic flow from *coco* (buddy) to *kéké* ('jouer le kéké' (to show off)) to *Kakà* (the Brazilian footballer) is made possible by modulation in vowel alone. The difference between them is reducible to the vowel's variations as it progresses from near-front to back. From *oh* to *eh* to *aah*, a staggering 'évolution' of 'métamorphoses complexes', as Tarkos puts it, foregrounds 'une limite infranchissable entre le a et le o' (an impassable limit between a and o).⁷⁶

The openness of the vowel, in contrast to the constrictions of the consonant, spins a red thread running throughout the motley literary crew of Henein, Aragon, Isou, Maran, Tarkos and PNL, who all skulk around monolanguage. They skulk around Arabic, Banda, English, French and Greek. In fact, they skulk around everything. They skulk around the docile subservience of the (formerly) colonized subject …

Immédiatement, je l'avoue, je me suis mis à faire le gentil, le docile. Le bon immigré bien intégré.⁷⁷

(Immediately, I admit it, I began to play the role of the gentle, docile, well-integrated good little immigrant.)

… as much as they transform then pacifically invade monolanguage. In this view, world literature no longer appears constricted by translation,⁷⁸ circulation,⁷⁹ or even temporality.⁸⁰ A sonic overture defines it, with the immutable vowel at the origin of lingual dis/order. A world literature formed of pure sonic material, infinitely plastic and malleable, forming the deep content of all language. Beyond the strictures of mono/nomono. Even beyond the postlingual.[81] For multilingual literature to be world literature, it must first and foremost be sound. Only then can vanguardist ghosts unexpectedly be heard in the most unlikely of places. Lines like these.

J'ai le flow te3 Boubou, de Kuta à Ubud, yeah
Salam gue3, coucou ouais puta, j'suis fou-fou, yeah
Et j'roule à gauche, oui (et j'roule à gauche, oh)
Appelle-moi Mowgli (woo, woo, ounga, ounga).[82]

Notes

1 Salah Stétié, *Le Français, l'autre langue* (Paris: Imprimerie nationale, 2001), 22. Unattributed translations are mine.
2 Gilles Deleuze, 'Schizologie', pref., in Louis Wolfson, *Le Schizo et les langues* (Paris: Gallimard, 1970): 5–23, 10.
3 Hoda Barakat, *The Stone of Laughter*, trans. Sophie Bennett (New York: Interlink, 1995), 83.
4 Denis Hollier, 'How Can One Be French?', in *A New History of French Literature*, ed. Denis Hollier (Cambridge: Harvard University Press, 2001): 1061–7, 1067.
5 Ibid.
6 David Damrosch, *What Is World Literature?* (Princeton: Princeton University Press, 2003), 4.
7 Pheng Cheah, *What Is a World? On Postcolonial Literature as World Literature* (Durham, NC: Duke University Press, 2016), 5–9. See also Michel Collot, *Pour une géographie littéraire* (Paris: José Corti, 2014).
8 Édouard Glissant, *Poétique de la relation* (Paris: Gallimard, 1990), 130; *Poetics of Relation*, trans. Betsy Wing (Ann Arbor: University of Michigan Press, 1997), 115–16.
9 Jean Cocteau, *Le Rappel à l'ordre; Le Coq et l'Arlequin; Carte blanche; Visites à Maurice Barrès; Le Secret professionnel; D'un ordre considéré comme une anarchie; Autour de Thomas l'imposteur; Picasso* (Paris: Stock, Delamain & Boutelleau, 1926).
10 Abdellah Taïa, *La Vie lente* (Paris: Seuil, 2019), 61.
11 Ibid., 90.
12 Roland Barthes, *Fragments d'un discours amoureux* (Paris: Seuil, 1977), 5 and *A Lover's Discourse: Fragments*, trans. Richard Howard (New York: Hill and Wang, 2010), 1.
13 Only on the surface: see Jacques Derrida, *Le Monolinguisme de l'autre: ou la prothèse d'origine* (Paris: Galilée, 1996) and *Monolingualism of the Other, or, The Prosthesis of Origin*, trans. Patrick Mensah (Stanford: Stanford University Press, 1998).
14 David Gramling, *The Invention of Monolingualism* (New York: Bloomsbury, 2016), 9.
15 The earliest vanguardist efforts in twentieth-century Cairo can be dated to the early 1920s; on surrealism in Egypt, see Sam Bardaouil, *Surrealism in Egypt: Modernism and the Art and Liberty Group* (London: I.B. Tauris, 2016); and Sam Bardaouil and Till Fellrath, eds., *Art et Liberté: Rupture, War, and Surrealism in Egypt (1938–1948)* (Paris: Skira, 2016). In this context, debates and polemics regularly broke out in

the Cairene francophone press; for more on which, see Jean-Jacques Luthi, *Lire la presse d'expression française en Égypte, 1798-2008* (Paris: L'Harmattan, 2019), and the archive on the Centre d'études alexandrines's website (cealex.org), which contains *La Presse francophone d'Égypte numérisée (PFEnum)*, a collection of twentieth-century francophone Egyptian periodicals.

16 Cocteau, *Le Rappel à l'ordre*, 175-233.
17 André Breton, *Les Pas perdus* (Paris: Gallimard, 1924).
18 Paris and Cairo represent only two points of a large and complex network of circulation: for a wider sweep of global modernism from Latin America to the Caucasus, see Harsha Ram, 'The Scale of Global Modernisms: Imperial, National, Regional, Local', *PMLA* 131, 5 (October 2016): 1372-85.
19 See al-Saʿīd Abī al-Qāsim Hibat Allāh ibn Jaʿfar ibn Sanāʾ al-Mulk, *Dār al-ṭirāz fī aʿmāl al-muwashshaḥāt*, ed. Jawdat al-Rikābī, pref. Évariste Lévi-Provençal (Damascus: Dār al-Fikr, 1977); Ryoko Sekiguchi, *Héliotropes* (Paris: P.O.L, 2005); Jean-Marie Gleize, *Sorties* (Paris: Questions théoriques, 2009).
20 For more on *l'affaire Aragon*, see André Breton, 'Misère de la poésie: "l'affaire Aragon" devant l'opinion public' (1932), in Maurice Nadeau, *Histoire du surréalisme suivi de Documents surréalistes* (Paris: Seuil, 1964).
21 On the againstness of the manifesto as genre, see Mary Ann Caws, ed., *Manifesto: A Century of Isms* (Lincoln, NE: Nebraska University Press, 2001).
22 Georges Henein, *Œuvres: poèmes, récits, essais, articles et pamphlets*, ed. Pierre Vilar, Marc Kober, and Daniel Lançon, pref. Yves Bonnefoy and Berto Ferhi (Paris: Denoël 2006), 39.
23 See Sinan Antoon, *The Corpse Washer* (New Haven: Yale University Press, 2013).
24 Henein, *Œuvres*, 39-40.
25 Herman Parret, *La Voix et son temps* (Brussels: DeBoeck Université, 2002), 28; Mladen Dolar, *A Voice and Nothing More* (Cambridge: MIT Press, 2006), 23.
26 Louis Aragon, 'Un monsieur', in *Œuvres poétiques complètes, I*, ed. Olivier Barbarant, Daniel Bougnoux, François Eychart, Marie-Thérèse Eychart, Nathalie Limat-Letellier and Jean-Baptiste Para, pref. Jean Ristat (Paris: Gallimard, 2007), 69.
27 Deleuze, 'Schizologie', 5-6.
28 Ibid., 7-8. See Raymond Roussel, *Locus solus* (Paris: Lemerre, 1914) and *Comment j'ai écrit certains de mes livres* (Paris: Lemerre, 1935); Michel Foucault, *Raymond Roussel* (Paris: Gallimard, 1963).
29 Taïa, *La Vie lente*, 90; Christophe Tarkos, *Oui*, in *Écrits poétiques*, ed. Katalin Molnár and Valérie Tarkos, pref. Christian Prigent (Paris: P.O.L, 2008), 224.
30 Hollier, 'How Can One Be French?', 1067.
31 Abdelkébir Khatibi, *Le Lutteur de classe à la manière taoïste* (1976), in *Œuvres de Abdelkébir Khatibi, II: poésie de l'aimance* (Paris: La Différence, 2008), 22.
32 Abdelkébir Khatibi, *Class Warrior – Taoist Style*, trans. Matt Reeck (Middletown: Wesleyan University Press, 2017), 21.
33 Walter Benjamin, 'The Task of the Translator', trans. Harry Zohn, *Selected Writings, Volume 1: 1913-1926*, ed. Marcus Bullock and Michael W. Jennings (Cambridge, MA: Belknap, 1996): 253-63, 255-7; Dina Al-Kassim, 'The Faded Bond: Calligraphesis and Kinship in Abdelwahab Meddeb's *Talismano*', *Public Culture* 13, 1 (2001): 113-38, 117.
34 Kaira M. Cabañas, 'Pour l'oreille, la pensée, l'œil', trans. Catherine Vasseur, in *Isidore Isou*, ed. Nicolas Liucci-Goutnikov (Paris: Centre Pompidou, 2019): 24-31, 25.

35 Isidore Isou, *Introduction à une nouvelle poésie et à une nouvelle musique* (Paris: Gallimard, 1947), 153, 267.
36 Isidore Isou, *Précisions sur ma poésie et moi, suivies de Dix poèmes magnifiques* (Paris: Aux Escaliers de Lausanne, 1958), 10.
37 *La Guerre* was staged by Lettrism co-founder Gabriel Pomerand in 1947, then recreated by Isou and conducted and recorded by Frédéric Acquaviva in 1999, and finally released on CD in 2004 as *Musiques lettristes* by Al Dante.
38 Isou, *Introduction*, 314–16.
39 Ibid., 151.
40 Kaira M. Cabañas, *Off-Screen Cinema: Isidore Isou and the Lettrist Avant-Garde* (Chicago: University of Chicago Press, 2014), 10.
41 Ibid.
42 Isou, *Introduction*, 350.
43 Nicolas Liucci-Goutnikov, 'Isidore Isou: le nom des noms', in *Isidore Isou*, ed. Nicolas Liucci-Goutnikov (Paris: Centre Pompidou, 2019): 16–21, 17; Cabañas, 'Pour l'oreille', 25.
44 *Cum grano salis*. If Orson Welles's short segment on Lettrism from *Around the World with Orson Welles* (Associated-Rediffusion, 1955) is any indication, Isou had limited (or no) English. Isou performs Lettrist poetry with Jacques Spacagna and Maurice Lemaître (Cabañas, *Off-Screen Cinema*, 6), who responds in English on behalf of the group to Welles's questions.
45 Iheanachor Egonu, 'Les "romans de la jungle" de René Maran', *Neophilologus* 71.4 (1987): 523–30, 526.
46 Keith Walker, *Countermodernism and Francophone Culture: The Game of Slipknot* (Durham, NC: Duke University Press, 1999), 279; Irele Abiola, 'From the French Colonial Novel to the Francophone Postcolonial Novel: René Maran as Precursor', in *French Global: A New Approach to Literary History*, ed. Christie McDonald and Susan Suleiman (New York: Columbia University Press, 2010): 282–97; Felisa V. Reynolds, 'René Maran, Forgotten Father of the Francophone Novel', *Journal of the African Literature Association* 7.1 (2012): 55–65.
47 'The Negro Who Has Won the Goncourt Prize', *Current Opinion* 72.3 (1922): 356–8.
48 André Gide, *Voyage au Congo: carnets de route* (1927) and *Le Retour au Tchad, suite du 'Voyage au Congo': carnets de route* (1928), in *Souvenirs et voyages*, ed. Pierre Masson, Daniel Durosay and Martine Sagaert (Paris: Gallimard, 2001); Christopher Miller and Christopher Rivers, 'Prize Fights: René Maran, Battling Siki, and the Triumph of the Black Man in France, 1922', *Contemporary French Civilization* 36.3 (2011): 219–47, 230.
49 Edmond Jaloux, 'La vie littéraire: Le Prix Goncourt et le Prix "Vie heureuse"', *La Revue hebdomadaire* 31.1 (1922): 106–11; Iheanachor Egonu, 'Le Prix Goncourt de 1921 et la "Querelle de *Batouala*"', *Research in African Literatures* 11.4 (1980): 529–45.
50 Léopold Sédar Senghor, 'René Maran, un précurseur de la négritude', *Liberté, I: négritude et humanisme* (Paris: Seuil, 1964): 407–11; Jane Hiddleston, *Decolonising the Intellectual: Politics, Cultures, and Humanism at the End of the French Empire* (Liverpool: Liverpool University Press, 2014), 52.
51 Chidi Ikonné, 'René Maran, 1887–1960: A Black Francophone Writer Between Two Worlds', *Research in African Literatures* 5.1 (1974): 5–22; 'What Is *Batouala*?', *Journal of African Studies* 3.3 (1976): 373–91.

52　Ibrahima Diouf, 'Un véritable roman barbare? La langue française à l'écoute de la barbarie dans *Batouala* (1921) de René Maran', *Francofonia* 70 (2016): 83–99, 90.
53　Ibid., 93.
54　Ibid., 97.
55　Christopher Miller, 'Francophonie and Independence', in *A New History of French Literature*, ed. Denis Hollier (Cambridge, MA: Harvard University Press, 2001): 1028-33, 1028.
56　René Maran, *Batouala: véritable roman nègre* (Paris: Albin Michel, 1921), 19–20.
57　René Maran, *Batouala*, trans. Adele Szold Seltzer (New York: Thomas Seltzer, 1922), 21–2.
58　Maran, *Batouala: véritable roman nègre*, 80–1.
59　Maran, *Batouala*, trans., 93–4.
60　Louis Aragon, 'La pensée', in *Œuvres poétiques complètes*, I, 62–3, 62–3.
61　Tarkos, *Oui*, 224.
62　Ibid.
63　'phoneme, n.', *OED Online* (Oxford University Press, December 2020).
64　Katalin Molnár, '*Anachronisme*', in *Dossier Christophe Tarkos*, special issue *Cahier critique de poésie* 30 (2015): 29–31, 29.
65　Xavier de Maistre, *Voyage autour de ma chambre* (Turin: n.p., 1794).
66　Tarkos, in the lineage of Aragon's 'Ânehâtepâtebûche' ('La pensée', 62–3), usually calls this concept of poetic language *patmo* (*Oui*, 163–4, 231–2; 'Soleil—Patmot', in *L'Enregistré: performances/improvisations/lectures*, ed. Philippe Castellin (Paris: P.O.L, 2014), 231–5). See David Christoffel, 'Opéra et pas-opéras de Tarkos', *RiLUnE* 2 (2005): 65–77; Félix-Antoine Lorrain, 'L'acheminement vers la parole de la patmo de Christophe Tarkos', *Littérature* 29 (2013): 73–94; Christian Prigent, 'Sokrat à Patmo', pref., in Christophe Tarkos, *Écrits poétiques*, ed. Katalin Molnár and Valérie Tarkos (Paris: P.O.L, 2008): 9–23; Jeff Barda, 'Boules de sensations–pensées–formes in Christophe Tarkos's Poetry', *Nottingham French Studies* 57.1 (2018): 18–32.
67　Christophe Tarkos, 'Le voyage autour du monde' (1993–1994), in *L'Enregistré: performances/improvisations/lectures*, 437–49, 441, 443–7.
68　Christophe Hanna, '200–400', *Dossier Christophe Tarkos*, special issue *Cahier critique de poésie* 30 (2015): 66–72, 71.
69　Cabañas, *Off-Screen Cinema*, 10.
70　Maran, *Batouala*, trans. 80–1 [93–4].
71　Roman Jakobson, 'Les lois phoniques du langage enfantin', in *Selected Writings, I: Phonological Studies* (The Hague: Mouton, 1962): 317–27, 325; Jacques Derrida, *De la grammatologie* (Paris: Minuit, 1967), 444 (*Of Grammatology*, trans. Gayatri Chakravorty Spivak, intr. Judith Butler (Baltimore: Johns Hopkins University Press, 2016), 422–3); Deleuze, 'Schizologie', 10; Michel Chion, *Le Son: ouïr, écouter, observer* (Paris: Armand Colin, 2018), 22 (*Sound: An Acoulogical Treatise*, trans. James A. Steintrager (Durham, NC: Duke University Press, 2016), 15, 250); Jacques Rancière, *Le Sillon du poème: en lisant Philippe Beck* (Paris: Nous, 2016), 47–8 (*The Groove of the Poem: Reading Philippe Beck*, trans. Drew S. Burk (Minneapolis: Univocal, 2016), 44–5).
72　Tarkos, 'Le voyage', 440.
73　Sonic Youth, 'Small Flowers Crack Concrete', *NYC Ghosts & Flowers* (Geffen Records, 2000), 0:07–0:10.

74 Tarkos, 'Le voyage', 440.
75 PNL, 'Blanka', *Deux frères* (QLF Records, 2019), 1:54–2:12, 3:51–4:09.
76 Christophe Tarkos, *Processe*, in *Écrits poétiques*, ed. Katalin Molnár and Valérie Tarkos, pref. Christian Prigent (Paris: P.O.L, 2008), 117–18.
77 Taïa, *La Vie lente*, 27.
78 Hollier, 'How Can One Be French?'
79 Damrosch, *What Is World Literature?*
80 Cheah, *What Is a World?*
81 Parret, *La Voix*; Dolar, *A Voice*.
82 PNL, 'Kuta ubud', *Deux frères* (QLF Records, 2019), 1:53–2:31, 3:47–4:25.

14

Vahni Capildeo's multilingual poetics: Translation, synaesthesia, relation

Rachael Gilmour

> *Who said which language*
> *the book had to be in, anyway?*
>
> Vahni Capildeo, '*From* the End of the Poem'[1]

Though very often excluded from discussions of 'world literature' in favour of a primary focus on the novel as a form,[2] contemporary poetry may certainly lay claim to being counted as *multilingual* literature, in the hands of experimental contemporary poets such as Caroline Bergvall or Uljana Wolf. These are poets whose work tirelessly unsettles and points to the incipient violence in monolingualist language ideologies and the categories and borders they insist on – national, racial, gendered or otherwise – while using poetry's linguistic self-reflexivity to posit other ways of being in language. And this is certainly so for the poet Vahni Capildeo, in whose playful, fraught and experimental work 'English' is forever being interrupted by other languages, or by different versions of itself; its syntax, lexis or lineation disrupted; in poetry that insists on its right not to be in any one language. As Capildeo writes in '*From* the End of the Poem': 'Who said which language / the book had to be in, anyway?' Having grown up in Trinidad and now living and working in Britain, a scholar of translation and Old Norse who has also worked as an OED lexicographer, Capildeo's poetry is self-reflexively concerned with questions of language at a number of levels: aesthetic, political, philosophical, interior and affective. Their poetry considers the problem of English conceived of in monological terms, and as a language of racial and colonial power; while at the same time, it considers the complexities of a multilingual interiority that is not in one language – or, perhaps, Capildeo's work contends, even strictly in language at all.[3] Instead of a multilingualism conceived as movement between an enumerated set of distinct, separate languages, they posit it as a state of being that exists beyond any kind of monolingual assumptions about what 'a language' is, in which many different ways of meaning-making, non-linguistic as well as linguistic, circulate, intersect and interrupt one another. Central to Capildeo's poetics, this vision of language appears via homophones, slippages, mishearings, word games and 'false friends', and in the ways in which language readily becomes other things – sound, shape, colour – as well as in the mixing of English with French, Spanish, Trinidadian Creole, Old Norse, Old English, Latin, Scots.

This chapter will think about how translation and synaesthesia, in particular, work as central figures in Capildeo's recent poetry for imagining the workings of language, and for making sense of a multilingual inner world that is radically heterogeneous, infinitely variable, and prone to surprising and unsettling connections. Translation, rather than being a procedure for finding equivalence, maintaining transparency or carrying across meaning between discrete linguistic systems, operates for Capildeo as something contingent, idiosyncratic and expansive. It is an inherently transformative process that produces newness, strangeness, and unlikeness, including by moving across the supposed boundary between the linguistic and the non-linguistic. Translation thus, for Capildeo, is synaesthetic – a motif which repeats across their work: language calling up not only more language, but also sounds, shapes, colours, sensations. Indeed, Capildeo's poetry often suggests how meaning is always to an extent extralinguistic, working through association, image or sensory memory.

Both translation, and synaesthesia, are fundamental to what Capildeo represents as the everyday operations of a multilingual interiority in which language is expansive and plural, open to that which is unlike itself. In this, their poetics resembles what Édouard Glissant calls *Relation* – a bringing together in improvisatory ways that does not depend on reducing difference to sameness. For Glissant, the meaning of Relation is captured in Creole language, 'whose genius consists in always being open, that is, perhaps, never becoming fixed except according to systems of variables that we have to imagine as much as define'.[4] A poetics of Relation is 'latent, open, multilingual in intention, directly in contact with everything possible'.[5] And, like Glissant, Capildeo's relational poetics posits both a vision of language and a model of connection, even of solidarity, that longs for what is different from itself. Indeed, instead of demanding that we 'speak the same language', Capildeo's poetry asks us to imagine what it means to connect outside the strictures of linguistic comprehensibility, or language as such.

'The fluidity and zigzagging of Trinidadian speech': World histories and travelling language

In a 2014 essay for *PN Review* titled 'Letter not from Trinidad', Capildeo traces an instinctive resistance to formal divisions in poetry – the conventions of 'line break' or 'white space' – to a multisensory experience of language born from an Indo-Trinidadian childhood.[6] Elsewhere, in the prose poem 'Five Degrees of Expatriation', the lyric speaker muses on the experience of playing a party game of word association, in which others produce '[o]utrages and banalities and brilliance', and being stymied by the emergence within their own consciousness of 'another word in a totally inappropriate register or language; more often, several words at once, in a kind of bee dance; most often, no words at all' but a surge of 'sounds and images'.[7] This is not 'an expat phenomenon' – the outcome of a belated linguistic dislocation – but, the speaker muses, maybe a founding principle of their Trinidad-born multilingual consciousness:

Perhaps it was a hypersensitization to the fluidity and zigzagging of Trinidadian speech, where flowery translations of Sanskrit and the formality of the older Christian (mostly Catholic) liturgies naturally mix into the same track as the tricksy shrug and bread-and-curses everydayness of Spanish-French-Portuguese-Syrian-Chinese-Scottish-Irish-(English)'? Was everyone else pretending to have one-word events in their brain, while secretly choosing from a *retentissante* horde?[8]

Returning often to think about a Trinidadian language world – one in which language is not segmented or clearly demarcated but layered and meshed – Capildeo makes claims that are not just about multilingualism itself, but about its relationship to interior consciousness on the one hand, and poetic form on the other. All seem to reveal a common tendency to 'mix into the same track'. In terms of form, Jeremy Noel-Tod has written of Capildeo's fascination with breaching the boundary between prose and poetry, and 'the nameless third thing that it makes'; standing for the troubling of 'taxonomic separation' of all sorts.[9] Something similar could be said for the blurred lines and interstitial spaces in Capildeo's work between poetry and performance text, text and image, original and translation, as well as between what are conventionally determined as discrete languages.

Capildeo emphasizes an approach to poetics that emerges from a particular experience of language; like Edward Kamau Brathwaite in *History of the Voice*, their starting point is the linguistic 'plurality' of the Caribbean.[10] But at the same time, they refuse a straightforward narrative of origins or linguistic collectivity of the kind Brathwaite articulates in 'nation language' in favour of something more contingent and idiosyncratic, connected to place and yet bound up in Relation, in Glissant's terms.[11] Capildeo's is, after all, 'a letter *not* from Trinidad'. Instead they capture a linguistic multiplicity represented but not delimited by Trinidad: that is fluid and 'zigzagging', that contains both understanding and not understanding, and in which language co-exists with the non-linguistic, making its meanings always in conjunction with those of 'sounds and images' and the 'grammar of the body'.[12] In 'Letter Not from Trinidad', Capildeo recalls the childhood experience of chanting Sanskrit words in which semantic meaning, 'painstakingly explicated, never fully understood by me', was made subordinate to an embodied sensation of continuous sound. This experience of language, existing in a multisensory continuum with sounds, gestures, images, objects, sensations, becomes the point of origin for what Capildeo casts as a synaesthetic 'poetics of reverberation and minor noise':

> I find a line does not break so much as hum, the background to the letters (screen or paper) is not flat, but streaming, I want extra words and syllables here and there (as it were, the Caribbean English in which Sanskrit is embedded) which I can fuss over and also ignore, like the necessary and distracting objects which demarcate 'here' from 'theirs'.[13]

This Trinidad, of Caribbean English embedded with Sanskrit, of 'Spanish-French-Portugues-Syrian-Chinese-Scottish-Irish-(English)', stands for a world history of travelling language, and the histories (of travel, trade and above all empire) out of which it comes. The French and Spanish which Capildeo uses in their poetry are languages of Trinidad, of the wider Caribbean world, and of other postcolonial societies, as well as of France and Spain. Fascinated by the history and *techne* of language, Capildeo came to Britain initially to study Old Norse and translation studies at Oxford, and has also worked as an *OED* researcher and lexicographer. Correspondingly, their etymological poetics also recall Europe's multilingual pasts: Old Norse, Old English, Scots, Latin, which conjure up a premodern European linguistic continuum that antedates the ethnolinguistic borders and political boundaries of its nation states, and suggest monolingualism as a recent (and impermanent) phenomenon.[14] Pitting language's constant flux against efforts to pin it down, a poem sequence in *Dark and Unaccustomed Words* (2011) begins with a scene of etymology: a lexicographer trapped and frustrated by the work of 'dis- and rearranging, / suspecting, assessing, keying in and tagging' the historical spellings of 'QUIT'.[15] Others observe that such a task should surely be straightforward: 'QUIT is such a little verb?'. But the lexicographer-poet counters that 'people have been quitting for centuries, and / especially in Scotland, all in different ways'.[16] Language changes with each new scene of use: each instance of a word's utterance, each new set of circumstances governing the need to employ it, produces new layers of signification. You will, in other words, never be able to quit defining 'QUIT'. That this might be true 'especially in Scotland' can be read at least two ways. Scotland is a place of linguistic colonization and struggle, where English secured its place at the expense of Scots and Gaelic. It is also, as any lexicographer knows, a source of English's normative power: it was Scottish writers, grammarians, elocution masters and lexicographers – among them James Murray, first editor of the *OED* – who drove the processes by which a 'standard English' was valorized and codified for Britain and its empire.[17] The violence done in and through linguistic normativity surfaces often in Capildeo's work. In 'Two Foreign', a dazzling sequence of homophonic mis-hearings and double meanings struggle against the monologic power of English as the only language in which the 'war-thrown' may claim sanctuary, a language saturated with inherited prejudice, in which 'words have class issues'.[18] As the poem progresses, it seeks to overcome this monologic 'lesson' both by intralingual associative wordplay and by borrowing promiscuously across English's supposedly firm borders: from the Glasgow Scots of poet Tom Leonard ('it izny / that'), Old English ('thorn'), dialectal English ('pote'), Icelandic ('the stjörnu I stjeer by').[19] Capildeo works in the consciousness of how language – English in particular – disciplines and governs the social world, marking insider from outsider, 'lesson[ing]' and 'lessen[ing]' the speakers who become subject to its logic.[20]

Colonial histories underlie the Trinidadian language-world conjured in Capildeo's poetry; and they are audible too, in a different way, in the raciolinguistic assumptions that greet the Trinidadian 'expatriate' in Britain: '"I don't have an accent! You have an accent!"'.[21] English, meanwhile, particularly where Capildeo is at their most acutely etymologically attuned, appears as a language in and through which colonial and neocolonial violence is done, freighted with history, sometimes burdened with 'class issues' hard to 'e-race'.[22] Nevertheless, Capildeo is wary of essentializing moves that may be entailed in claims to collectivity, even in the name of resistance. In one interview, they recall growing up believing 'that the poet could be a channel for all languages, for any sort of linguistic phenomenon that any literary work encountered', yet in Britain finding the combined forces of 'marketing and identity politics' threatening to obliterate 'the body, the voice, the voice on the page, the biography, the history' in favour of the poet as 'a sort of documentary witness wheeled around and exposing your wounds in the market place'.[23] Resisting fixed labels and definitions is integral to Capildeo's poetic practice. In the performance text 'Shame', a speaker says '**Do not SHE me**', before going on:

> 'You need someone from your own culture,' he said.
> 'What culture is that?' I asked.
> 'Trinidadian,' he said, monotheistically.[24]

Thus, wary of the constraining power of fixed identities and generalized collectivities, Capildeo does not write in the collective voice: their lyric 'I' is always idiosyncratic, never representative. Nevertheless, as Noel-Tod observes, their poetic practice seeks to find ways to write beyond 'a limited lyricism of the personal'.[25] In a poem titled 'On Not Writing as a West Indian Woman', Capildeo's poet-persona enumerates and negates a sequence of stereotypes and conventions: 'not containing oceans', this poet 'hasn't cooked cassava / nor become a mother'.[26] Employing creole grammar while insisting on the right of refusal of stymying categories, Capildeo claims the right to sail, rather than contain, oceans: to 'push the boat out', 'self pull out self, self / issuing the self home'.[27] On one level, the image conjures a mode of poetic subjectivity which is itself multiple: self with self, acting on itself. On another, it also perhaps gestures towards a relational form of solidarity that can recognize both the inalienable selfhood and irreducible difference of another person.

Multilingual modernity, translation and synaesthesia

Though highly experimental in language and form, Capildeo's poetics are nevertheless rooted, as they contend in 'Letter Not from Trinidad', in a claim about the 'everydayness' of language diversity, in a world in which the majority of people speak more than one language and multilingualism, or the everyday encounter with different kinds of language, is a commonplace of human experience.[28] As Capildeo has put it in a radio interview, 'the mother tongue' is 'an evil myth imposed by monoglot societies', and in fact:

> naturally most people in the world grow up with a mishmash of creoles and languages and slangs and high and golden phrases which run together in their heads, and anything which looks like a neat language is a translation.[29]

Yet this is a vision of modernity profoundly at odds with, and threatening to, the ideology of monolingualism, that as Richard Bauman and Charles Briggs contend, vouchsafes the imagining of the modern nation state; which revolves around denying linguistic hybridity, mixing, diversity and change.[30] As Sinfree Makoni and Alastair Pennycook argue, although languages 'do not exist as real entities in the world' but are 'the inventions of social, cultural, and political movements', nevertheless they have 'very real material effects', not least in the shoring up of boundaries and borders and the ways in which 'people have come to identify with particular labels and at times even to die for them'.[31] The conjoined aesthetic and language-political dimensions of Capildeo's poetics are particularly clear at the end of 'Letter Not from Trinidad', when they conclude:

> I write this for an unruly language which is not 'fractured' as with the avant-garde or 'resistant' as with the old-style postcolonial, but may indeed have a politics, as well as a poetics, belonging to a modernity rooted in ways of life still not considered safe, polite or relevant to admit to the canon.[32]

Capildeo's 'unruly language' makes its meanings in unruly ways, by contiguity, substitution, homophony, textual play; as in 'Two Foreign', where English's claim 'on our attention' becomes to 'honour a tension'.[33] Rattling the conventional categories by which English is ordered, by making substitutions based on phonetic resemblance rather than syntactic order or semantic contiguity, the effect, here as elsewhere, is to point at 'tensions' submerged in the language. 'Sycorax W̶hoops' in *Measures of Expatriation* offers its own take on the colonial linguistic predicament as articulated by Shakespeare's Caliban ('You taught me language; and my profit on't / is, I know how to curse' (*The Tempest* Act 2 scene 1)). In Capildeo's poem, a sardonic Caliban surveys a scene of neoimperial power on his invaded island, voiced in language which is half made up of crossings-out, a form of quasi-blackout poetry with the erased words still visible, that when read together offer disjointed and angry glimpses of conflict and white saviourism (like 'Aphrodite, AIDS worker', called on to 'b̶l̶o̶n̶d̶e̶ bond us'):

> Father Zeus airdrops party favours, fractures syntax,
> gettin the glitter out of w̶a̶r̶ where we're s̶t̶r̶u̶c̶k̶ stuck livin,
> [...]
> Turned over a new leaf to indict s̶c̶i̶e̶n̶c̶e̶ silence / siloed w̶h̶i̶t̶e̶n̶e̶s̶s̶ witness[34]

Railing against a monologic linguistic order soaked in histories of racial violence, that has weaponized both 'science' and 'silence', all that Caliban has at his disposal is the seeming 'brokenness' of a stilted and shattered language; while, stuttering over all he cannot say, he scatters a subversive trail of alternate meanings. Finally, he calls on his mother Sycorax to launch a 'pack of languages, fluid as hounds' – reversing the 'divers Spirits, in shape of dogs and hounds' (*The Tempest* Act 1 scene 4) that are conjured to terrorize Caliban in Shakespeare's play – and unleash linguistic multiplicity as an avenging force:

> Mother! plunge your tongue where ever with brokenness we're ~~deaf~~
> ~~en'd defend~~ fed. Take ~~apart~~ our part. Launch in sighted
> darkness our pack of languages, fluid as hounds,
> all ready: bathed: riteful: already intending chase:³⁵

As Capildeo's poem is at pains to make clear, Caliban's linguistic predicament is also a source of expressive possibility insofar as it allows him to connect, albeit under erasure, what is otherwise 'siloed'; even as what is needed in his world, in the end, is a 'pack of languages' set loose on the avatars of monolingualism. Yet as Madeleine Campbell and Ricarda Vidal point out, quoting Walter Benjamin – '"communication in words [is] only a particular case of human language"' – linguistic meaning-making is in fact indivisible from other kinds of communication: image, gesture, touch, scent, sound.³⁶ And as Campbell and Vidal go on to underline, it is 'languages' which are confined by borders, whereas non-word-based forms of communication are able more easily, at least in principle, to transcend those borders.³⁷

In a composition for Campbell and Vidal's project, a 'translation' of Ronsard's poem 'Ode à Cassandre', Capildeo emphasizes not only the unpredictable, nonlinear movement between languages, but also the way the translation process becomes one that is visual, spatial and multisensory. In Capildeo's versioning of Ronsard's poem, printed text alternates with reproduced images of typescript covered in erasures and crossings-out, blotches and scattered handwritten annotations using different coloured inks. As they write in an introduction to the project:

> The techniques used here include: (i) erasure of the source text to produce a new, evocative, playfully minimal text in the source language, which also offers visual space and silence into which the source text can be recalled and from which the next translations may be imagined to be red [sic]; (ii) translation by expansion into a sequence of synaesthetic imagery; (iii) a doubled erasure of the source text into some French words, some English translations, inlaid in compressed stanzas to move in opposition to each other as well as developing a sensuous response; (iv) commentary via a dramatic monologue intended to be read as 'asides' to Ronsard's verses; (v) a playfully minimal English-language text to round off the series by responding to the initial French erasure, including interlineation with empty lines as if for an echo (i.e. further translation of a translation).³⁸

Translation, in Capildeo's playful account, is a process that never ends; the translator cannot afford to be too reverend towards the source which they 'recall' or 'imagine' rather than recreate. As Capildeo puts it in 'After a Hymn to Aphrodite', there must be the latitude in translation to build rather than reproduce, in a process of accommodation or making-room (whether in 'source text' or 'target language' is not clear, which of course is precisely the point): 'Translators tack an extra room on to the roof'.³⁹ This is a process of improvisatory building which has no end point: space must be left for a further 'echo', for 'further translation of a translation'.

The synaesthesia which appears in Capildeo's account of the Ronsard project both as method ('expansion into a sequence of synaesthetic imagery') and as practice ('from which the next translations may be imagined to be red'), is a motif that recurs right across their work. The association between senses – to see a word as colour, or to feel it as a shape – is a refusal of the particular status of language as distinct from other ways of making meaning; and a way of parsing an inner world characterized by contiguity, overlap and surprising connection. In Capildeo's work, just as registers and languages call one another up or dissolve readily into one another, so too do words and colours, shapes, sounds or texture. Synaesthesia in Capildeo's writing serves as a formal analogue to the imagined composition of a multilingual interiority: a psyche moving not between 'languages' as discrete systems but across one continuous field of language, untrammelled by syntactic constraint or fixed signification, and drawn to the affinity of unlike things.[40]

Poetics of multilingual interiority

In *Measures of Expatriation*, Capildeo returns repeatedly to the question of multilingual interiority, seeking to evoke in poetic form and language the operations of a multilingual consciousness. 'COUNTING SHEEP', for example, is an 'INSOMNIA MASHUP' of word-and-image play between French and English, in the dazed listing and tumbling of an insomniac brain:

> coulante – terrific
> one house is a shaded version of another house
> all chemins lead to france
> converge, concentric, intersect
> *le phénix renaît de ses cendres*[41]

The prose-poem sequence 'Five Measures of Expatriation' also takes up the encounter of a multilingual subjectivity with a monolingual order. It charts the dislocated self-invention of a poetic persona leaving Trinidad for Europe, and the experience of being asked to define, for the first time, a country of origin: 'a *patria*, a fatherland'.[42] Faced with the unsettling question so often posed to the migrant, 'Where are you from?', the speaker asks:

> How was it that till questioned, till displaced in the attempt to answer, I had scarcely thought of myself as having a country, or indeed as having left a country? The answer lies peripherally in looming, in hinterland; primarily in the tongueless, palpitating interiority.[43]

To be asked to define a place of origin – to turn the taken-for-granted higgledy-piggledy heterogeneity of 'oil rigs, mobile phone masts, prayer flags, legality of fireworks, likely use of firearms, density and disappearance of forests, scarlet ibis, other stripes of scarlet' into something 'substantial' and 'communicable', corresponding to what one might call 'having a country'[44] – is like having to reduce the multiplicity of a Trinidadian experience of language into English's monolingual mould: to make neatly legible a 'tongueless, palpitating interiority'. The children's game of word association becomes a figure for thinking about how a protean, asyntactic inner language-world – a '*retentissante* horde' of words, 'sounds and images' – clashes with a monolingual social world of shared codes and assumed meanings.[45] 'Language is my home', says Capildeo's speaker, 'not one particular language'.[46] Indeed, language itself becomes subject to synaesthetic association: it is 'ineluctable, variegated and muscular', imagined 'like the world-serpent of Norse legend'.[47] This is a vision of language as agile and denaturalized, shorn of all its conventional givens. As Claire Kramsch contends, whereas 'for monolingual speakers linguistic signs have become so attached to their referents that they seem to be part of the object itself', for multilinguals 'the fact that the same object is called tree in one language, *Baum* or *arbre* in another, makes it evident that the linguistic sign as symbolic form is quite arbitrary'.[48] Thus for Capildeo's speaker, signs are so self-evidently arbitrary that their semantic boundaries may abruptly dissolve – as when they one day lose 'the words *wall* and *floor*'. Why, after all, conceive of them as categorically distinct?

> There seemed no reason to conceive of a division. The skirting-board suddenly reduced itself to a nervous gentrification, a cover-up of some kind; nothing especially marked. The room was an inward-focused container. 'Wall', 'floor', even 'ceiling', 'doorway', 'shutters' started to flow smoothly, like a red ribbed tank top over a heaving ribcage.[49]

With an image as sensuous as it is unsettling, Capildeo suggests how the loss of semantic fixity makes possible other modes of perception. Pointing out how language conditions thought by making what is arbitrary seem natural – as with the distinction between 'wall' and 'floor' – Capildeo also posits the converse: that 'thought is not bounded by language', and that 'languageless perception' is possible.[50] Although, as her speaker observes, given commonplace monolingualist beliefs about the nature of language (that words correspond directly and securely to words or ideas) it's probably best not to mention it: 'I had the sense to shut up about the languageless perception. Procedure for living.'[51]

'Five Degrees of Expatriation' concludes by weighing the associations of a sequence of words:

> Expatriate.
> Exile.
> Migrant.
> Refugee.[52]

Each provokes in the speaker a 'wordless upsurge' of synaesthetic associations. '*Refugee*' conjures the olive-green cover of Bach's *Preludes & Fugues*; 'A path to fall off, a lorry underside to grip to'; 'Sindhi shop-owners' in Trinidad 'working the sharp-edged wordbatch WAR to WARES'.[53] Idiosyncratic, synaesthetic chains of signification connect words, memories, etymologies, images, colours, objects, feelings: 'There is brown and mid-blue, blister-purple, love-scarlet and a great deal of black in this word. There is the insistence on losing and finding, finding and not having, a home'.[54] '*Migrant*' is 'cerulean and khaki and it has a lot to say for itself once encamped temporarily by a river that will do':

> All movement, this word. Out at elbows or tense-thighed: verbal. Absolute: adjectival. In the singular, it implies plurals ....[55]

'Exile' is different in different languages – 'flattened in English. *Exil* in French is yet more clipped: *exil* is a short step from death ... *Exilio, esilio* is one to call from mountain tops' – but it contains 'fire' and 'the word burns me so I cannot use it; it is an hysterical word, I shall weep and do wrong to others in order to avenge somebody if I think hard enough about exile'.[56] Capildeo's speaker lands in the end on 'expatriate', conventionally associated with the freedom of movement and settlement of white people from the global North. Yet this word, for this speaker, proffers the possibility of being liberated from the idea of a 'patria', a homeland; a word without fixed bearings that may for that reason represent a kind of freedom: 'Non *dépaysée, sin saber por qué sé yo*', 'expatriate' claims Othello's '*unhousèd free condition*'.[57] Within this multilingual, 'expatriate' psyche, synaesthesia stands for the inexorable connection between different kinds of language, between the linguistic and non-linguistic, and for 'languageless perception'. It is the idea of 'a language' as such, as much as anything else, which Capildeo's speaker is able to become *unhousèd* from.

'A language that is mine only by scratches'

Capildeo's work is concerned with the internal dimensions of multilingual experience, as in the 'tongueless, palpitating interiority' or the world of dreams. It is here that, as against the impetus to decode, interpret or domesticate, they pose the pleasures and possibilities of being in and with difference. In 'Journal of Ordinary Days', from *Dark and Unaccustomed Words*, a speaker dreams 'in a language that is mine only by scratches':

> but I can get the tune of it, a whole conversation
> between strangers friendly to each other, dawdling behind me
> somewhere outdoors, a sandy cone of syllables
> rising and falling[58]

The 'tunes' of voices blur into one another 'so that the Irish have become Jamaican; the Spanish, Trinidadian; / while the French stay French, but sound maternal, a loving thirty-nine'.[59] In this multisensory dream-world, language not only 'drift[s]' into other kinds of language but becomes other things: sounds, objects, movements, feelings, numbers. The effect is not comprehensible, but it is comforting: 'friendly', 'loving', 'maternal'. In the poem's dream-logic, 'language' is not a distinct system of signification but a shared condition of human meaning-making and connection. The final stanza continues its synaesthetic flow – 'I dreamt that I could no longer see by means of light' – to imagine a human intimacy dependent neither on language nor vision: 'and how, instead of speaking, / you comforted my shoulder, both incandescing white'.[60] Returning to the idea of 'languageless perception', Capildeo suggests this as a possible site of true human connection; as when 'white', no longer signifying colour but heat, loses its position as a visual marker of racial difference to become a shared property of human warmth.

Here in Capildeo's dream-logic, synaesthesia extends as a metaphor for openness to another, for a kind of connection that produces understanding or 'comfort' without the need to reduce difference to sameness.[61] Alison Phipps writes of 'decolonizing multilingualism' by abandoning English's overwhelming dominance, and also the 'elite multilingualism' of 'fluent-in-too-many-colonial-languages', in favour of something more contingent and risky, a 'learning in and through difference'.[62] Phipps argues for the importance, and indeed the ethical value, of uncertain comprehension – of getting by with 'scraps of language', following 'gist and tone',[63] and being forced to depend on the nonlinguistic, somatic communication of gestures, touch and cry:

> These moments lead us out of the politics of identity, or the logics of economics, and into new constellations of social and cultural relations. They are marked ... by the presence of risk, by exigencies of breath and the body, by loss of speech and by a shift in the power relations which dominate everyday life.[64]

It is this kind of moment, I'm arguing, that Capildeo's poetics lean towards. Their work gives articulation to an experience of language – as Claire Kramsch suggests is common to multilingual subjectivity – which is always in the presence of other language; which in turn gives on to a fascination with the affinity of unlike things, and a longing to connect across difference.[65] This comes close to what Glissant calls 'Relation', a concept he grounds in the Caribbean and in the improvisatory, adaptable processes of creolization. Creole language is an expression of Relation in that it is 'always ... open', 'never ... fixed': 'Creole tongues ... vary too much within them to "be conjoined", to be prized as an essence or to be valorized as a symbol of either the mother or the father'.[66] Thus, without being able to be totalized or essentialized, creolization stands for 'the Diverse', for the capacity to connect things together without collapsing difference into sameness: for 'all the threatened and delicious things joining one another (without conjoining, that is, without merging) in the expanse of Relation'.[67]

Capildeo's 'unruly language' offers a way of thinking past languages as such that begins, without ending, in Trinidad.[68] The multilingualism they offer is not an orderly, privileged 'fluent-in-too-many-colonial-languages' (even when colonial languages are their linguistic inheritance) but something far more heterogeneous and contingent – the linguistic analogue of 'oil rigs, mobile phone masts, prayer flags, legality of fireworks, likely use of firearms, density and disappearance of forests, scarlet ibis, other stripes of scarlet'.[69] Freed from notions of linguistic structure and order, its model is synaesthesia, where words can become colours, sound become shapes. This is its model for the interior self – the 'pointilliste self', as Capildeo has termed it – and for external relation.[70] Thus it is a form of poetics, with an implied politics: one which calls for connection across difference, for heterogeneity and overlap, and for a mutuality, or solidarity, that does not seek to collapse otherness into itself.

Notes

1. Vahni Capildeo, 'From The End of the Poem', *Skin Can Hold* (Manchester: Carcanet, 2019), 38.
2. See for example Ben Etherington and Jarad Zimbler, 'Introduction', in Ben Etherington and Jarad Zimbler (eds.) *Cambridge Companion to World Literature* (Cambridge: Cambridge University Press, 2018): 1–20.
3. Capildeo identifies as non-binary and uses the pronouns they/them.
4. Édouard Glissant, *Poetics of Relation*, trans. Betsy Wing (Ann Arbor: University of Michigan Press, 1997), 34.
5. Ibid., 32. For detailed discussion of Glissant, multilingualism and Relation, see Jane Hiddleston's chapter in this volume.
6. Vahni Capildeo, 'Letter Not from Trinidad', *PN Review* 221 (2014): 6.
7. Vahni Capildeo, 'Five Measures of Expatration IV. WORD BY WORD', *Measures of Expatriation* (Manchester: Carcanet, 2016), 101.
8. Ibid.
9. Jeremy Noel-Tod, '"Immeasurable as One": Vahni Capildeo's Prose Poetics', in Jane Monson (ed.), *British Prose Poetry* (Basingstoke: Palgrave, 2018): 211–25.
10. Edward Kamau Brathwaite, 'Nation Language', in *History of the Voice: The Development of Nation Language in Anglophone Caribbean Poetry* (London: New Beacon, 1984): 5–51, 5–6.
11. My warm thanks to Jane Hiddleston for this observation.
12. Vahni Capildeo, 'Language and Reinvention', *Start the Week*, BBC Radio 4, 1 February 2016.
13. Capildeo, 'Letter Not from Trinidad', 6.
14. On the recentness as well as pervasiveness of monolingualism as a concept, see David Gramling, *The Invention of Monolingualism* (London and New York: Bloomsbury, 2016).
15. Vahni Capildeo, 'Journal of Ordinary Days', *Dark and Unaccustomed Words* (Kings Lynn: Egg Box, 2011), 25.
16. Ibid.
17. On the role of Scottish writers, grammarians, lexicographers and elocution masters in the standardization of English and the emergence of 'English Literature' as a field in Britain and the British Empire, see Robert Crawford, *Devolving English Literature* (Oxford: Clarendon, 1991), 23; Tony Crowley, *Standard English and the Politics of Language*, 2nd edn. (Basingstoke: Palgrave, 2003).
18. Vahni Capildeo, 'Two Foreign', in *Venus as a Bear* (Manchester: Carcanet, 2018), 46.

19 Ibid. See for example Tom Leonard, 'Honest', in Tom Leonard, *Intimate Voices: Selected Work 1965–1983* (Wilkes-Barre, PA: Etruscan Books, 2003), 78. Old English voiceless þ (thorn), left over from the ancient runic alphabet and distinct from the voiced ð (eth), was lost in the development of the letterpress that replaced both in English with the digraph ⟨th⟩; a history which the poet Caroline Bergvall suggests offers a 'compressed reminder' of the dense and entwined European linguistic histories that have produced language that now pretends to be a bordered and stable thing; see Caroline Bergvall, *Drift* (New York: Nightboat, 2014), 180. The *OED* gives 'pote' as dialectal English, Scots or Irish (meaning to kick, poke or stamp), originating from Old English and 'probably cognate' with words in Middle Dutch, Middle Low German, Icelandic, Norwegian, Swedish and Danish. Icelandic 'stjörnu' means star and has similarly trans-European etymological connections.
20 Capildeo, 'Two Foreign', 46.
21 Vahni Capildeo, 'Five Measures of Expatriation', in *Measures of Expatriation* (Manchester: Carcanet, 2016), 100. On raciolinguistics, see H. Samy Alim, John R. Rickford and Arnetha F. Ball (eds.), *Raciolinguistics: How Language Shapes Our Ideas about Race* (Oxford: Oxford University Press, 2016).
22 Capildeo, 'Two Foreign', 46.
23 Capildeo, 'Language and Reinvention'.
24 Vahni Capildeo, 'Shame', *Skin Can Hold* (Manchester: Carcanet, 2019), 16; bold in original.
25 Noel-Tod, '"Immeasurable as One"'.
26 Vahni Capildeo, 'On Not Writing as a West Indian Woman', in *Dark and Unaccustomed Words* (Kings Lynn: Egg Box, 2011), 71.
27 Ibid.
28 See for example Adrian Blackledge and A. Creese, *Multilingualism: A Critical Perspective* (London: Continuum, 2010); J. N. Jørgensen et al., 'Polylanguaging in Superdiversity', *Diversities* 13.2 (2011): 23–37, 34. Available online: www.unesco.org/shs/diversities/vol13/issue2/art2 (accessed 1 February 2020); Sinfree Makoni and Alastair Pennycook, 'Disinventing and Reconstituting Languages', in Sinfree Makoni and Alastair Pennycook (eds.), *Disinventing and Reconstituting Languages* (Clevedon: Multilingual Matters, 2007).
29 Capildeo, 'Language and Reinvention'.
30 See Richard Bauman and Charles L. Briggs, *Voices of Modernity: Language Ideologies and the Politics of Inequality* (Cambridge: Cambridge University Press, 2003).
31 Makoni and Pennycook, 'Disinventing and Reconstituting Languages', 2–3.
32 Capildeo, 'Letter Not from Trinidad', 6.
33 Capildeo, 'Two Foreign', 46.
34 Vahni Capildeo, 'Sycorax W̶h̶oops', *Measures of Expatriation* (Manchester: Carcanet, 2018), 121.
35 Ibid.
36 Walter Benjamin, 'On Language as Such', in *Walter Benjamin: Selected Writings 1913–1926*, quoted in Madeleine Campbell and Ricarda Vidal, 'Entangled Journeys – An Introduction', in Madeleine Campbell and Ricarda Vidal (eds.), *Translating across Sensory and Linguistic Borders: Intersemiotic Journeys Between Media* (Basingstoke: Palgrave, 2019): xxiv–xliv.
37 Campbell and Vidal, 'Entangled Journeys'.

38 Vahni Capildeo, 'Pierre de Ronsard's "Ode á Cassandre": Erasure, Recall, Recolouration', in Madeleine Campbell and Ricarda Vidal (eds.), *Translating across Sensory and Linguistic Borders* (Basingstoke: Palgrave, 2019).
39 Vahni Capildeo, 'After a Hymn to Aphrodite', *Undraining Sea* (Kings Lynn: Egg Box, 2009), 19.
40 On multilingual subjectivity, see Claire Kramsch, *The Multilingual Subject* (Oxford: Oxford University Press, 2009); and Aneta Pavlenko, *Emotions and Multilingualism* (New York: Cambridge University Press, 2005).
41 Vahni Capildeo, 'COUNTING SHEEP', *Measures of Expatriation* (Manchester: Carcanet, 2018), 76.
42 Capildeo, 'Five Measures of Expatriation II. THE GOD OF OBSTACLES', *Measures of Expatriation* (Manchester: Carcanet, 2018), 95.
43 Capildeo, 'Five Measures of Expatriation III. GOING NOWHERE, GETTING SOMEWHERE', *Measures of Expatriation* (Manchester: Carcanet, 2018), 100.
44 Ibid.
45 Capildeo, 'Five Measures of Expatriation IV', 101.
46 Capildeo, 'Five Measures of Expatriation III', 100.
47 Ibid.
48 Kramsch, *The Multilingual Subject*, 6.
49 Capildeo, 'Five Measures of Expatriation IV', 101.
50 Capildeo, 'Five Measures of Expatriation III', 100, 101.
51 Ibid., 101.
52 Capildeo, 'Five Measures of Expatriation IV', 101.
53 Ibid., 101–2.
54 Capildeo, 'Five Measures of Expatriation V. A RECORD OF ILLEGITIMATE REACTIONS', *Measures of Expatriation* (Manchester: Carcanet, 2018), 102.
55 Ibid., italics in original.
56 Ibid., 102–3, italics in original.
57 Ibid., 103, italics in original.
58 Capildeo, 'Journal of Ordinary Days', 27.
59 Ibid.
60 Ibid.
61 Glissant, *Poetics of Relation*.
62 Alison Phipps, *Decolonising Multilingualism: Struggles to Decreate* (Bristol: Multilingual Matters, 2019) 6, 11.
63 Ibid., 35.
64 Ibid., 27.
65 Kramsch, *The Multilingual Subject*, 16.
66 Glissant, *Poetics of Relation*, 34, 60.
67 Ibid., 62.
68 Capildeo, 'Letter Not from Trinidad', 6.
69 Capildeo, 'Five Measures of Expatriation III', 100.
70 Capildeo, *Measures of Expatriation*, back cover; Capildeo, 'Language and Reinvention'.

15

'Le mystère de notre présence au monde': Monchoachi, Creole proverbs and world literature as restoration

Christopher Monier

In his intervention into the world literature debates, Pheng Cheah has been critical of a tendency among commentators to understand the world of 'world literature' as the global marketplace. In this approach, a text carries 'worldliness' by its status as an 'object of circulation in a global market of print commodities'.[1] For Cheah, this materialist or 'spatial conception' of literature has been 'part of a broader attempt to reckon with the implications of globalisation for the study of literature'. As he has it, in tandem with globalization and the 'delegitimation of the humanities in universities and public consciousness in the North Atlantic', scholars have felt pressure to 'justify the value of literature as an object of study' – and to clarify 'literary criticism's role in the production process'. It's from this impasse that Cheah finds certain critics (Damrosch, Casanova and Moretti, for instance) adopting a 'global approach', one that uses 'market exchange as a paradigm for understanding the worldliness of literature'. Against this (at the very least, looking to 'supplement' these readings of 'world'), Cheah proposes that the tendency to explore or theorize literature as an 'object of exchange and circulation in the world' has had the effect actually of 'diminishing literature's worldly force', in fact reducing it to a 'displaced and delayed communication of socioeconomic forces at work in the real world'.[2] What is lost here, for Cheah, is what he calls literature's 'normative vocation' or 'dimension', by which he means literature's ability to imagine and remember the 'world' in a way that 'cannot be reduced to the greater facility of global communications and the increased range of spatial circulation'.[3] In turn, and both privileging the postcolonial and calling for a return to universal and 'spiritualist' readings of literature (the hope for universal truth being far from unique to the West, he argues), Cheah proposes that we might see world literature as writing that will somehow 'exemplify the process of worlding'.[4] In other words, he prompts us to ask the question of how a literature itself might open or reveal the expressiveness of the world, as opposed to its management by various political and economic ideologies, and, interestingly, how it might do so 'according to a principle of radical transformation that cannot be erased because it is immanent to the present world'.[5]

Taking inspiration from Cheah's central thesis, I want to explore world literature as a kind of writing that *worlds* (that reveals or opens a world) and that does so through the generative force of a multilingual poetic. This, in some sense, departs from Cheah. For one, I want to focus on poetry and poetics (as Thomas Beebee notes, Cheah's work privileges narrative, not unlike that of the materialist theorists[6]). I also want to look at literature not so much as the source of a world, but as the restoration of or response to another, more central world-revealing force. While Cheah rightly emphasizes literary imagination as bringing 'world' into relief, I shall explore the idea that human language itself (often in its simplest forms) *already* encodes or gives out a world – and it is literary writing then that emerges as a response to this world's force and depth, and as an effort to restore or be 'in accord' with it. My focus here will be on the creative approach of the Creole and French language poet (from Martinique) called Monchoachi.

As we will see, Monchoachi approaches both poetry and thought through the idea that man is not chiefly a speaker (who makes an injunction to the world) but rather a *répondeur*, a 'responder' who listens for forces of communication already active in the world and who speaks best when speaking in response to those communicative forces (*chant-for-chant*, as he sometimes puts it). Above all, this entails a poetic based on listening; and it is through listening that Monchoachi relates to the Antilles, by listening to its *lieux* (its landscapes and places) but also (and most significantly) by listening to its Creole languages.

To explore one way this works in his oeuvre, this chapter will look specifically at how Monchoachi, out of more than an ethnographic curiosity, turns towards Creole proverbs, finding in these the source for both a poetry and poetics. In a series of 'interviews' with these proverbs, the poet explores language itself as intrinsically world revealing. He also models what we might think of as a 'decolonial' relationship with language: here, in a way rooted in the local but with universal implications for poetic practice, Monchoachi imagines a Creole *parole* that speaks in a language distinct from that of the current civilization, able to create meaning in a way that transcends the determinations of language as it is used in the global capitalist arena. This approach underscores how languages themselves (in unique ways, no doubt, if we listen closely to them) might still reveal or give out a world. It also testifies to language as an enduring source for creativity, for remembering 'le mystère de notre présence au monde' (the mystery of our presence in the world). As we will see, Creole for Monchoachi installs certain modes by which the poet will try to abide – and it gives out a sense of the 'real' to which poetry itself can be seen as a response.

Monchoachi and Creole poetics

A central element of Monchoachi's poetic is the idea that, above all else, we must work today to 'restore' language. But here, he calls less for an act of speech, or the imagination of something new, than for an act of listening. This can be better understood by developing some sense of how the poet critiques language in the contemporary world. For Monchoachi, ever since the adoption of a limited alphabetic writing, with its 'unparalleled capacity for *diffusion*', the world has largely known language in a mode of 'representation'.[7] In this mode, language is used like a tool or an instrument. It accompanies progress. It communicates information; it *reports*. This (for the poet) leads to a privileging of the gaze and the visual. Also, it installs and fits nicely with the monotheistic mode. This element of the critique is worth expanding on, for it allows us to see more clearly why Monchoachi makes the move of giving language a world-revealing significance.

Briefly, Monchoachi associates the spread of monotheism (the deferral to a supreme, creator being) with the disenchantment of the world itself (with a loss of 'world'). This has implications for language. For one, since it imagines (as in Genesis) that some supreme, originary language exists, monotheism has the effect of putting the human languages in a utilitarian and secondary position. But for Monchoachi, it is precisely the human languages, 'dans leur multitude et leur diversité' (in their multitude and diversity), that emerge miraculously and that are fundamentally obscure and mysterious.[8] It is languages (perhaps especially in certain forms) that already remember, that indicate to man, 'sur le mode de la gravité, sa relation au monde' (in the mode of gravity, his relation to the world).[9] In a related emphasis, Monchoachi also theorizes that monotheism perpetuates the idea that man (like the maker in Genesis) creates *ex-nihilo*, using words to impose his will or vision onto the world (in a kind of demiurgic or logocentric act). The opposite of this is his idea (inspired by the Creole language) that man does not speak truly from himself but in a kind of interview and empathy and accord with the world.

While the critique of monotheism is just one element of Monchoachi's decolonial analysis of language (he also, for instance, imagines the collision of the conquerors and indigenous peoples as the clashing of different notions of the 'word'), these kinds of readings lead the poet to theorize that, in the modern order, we endure in a state of fundamental 'dislocation'. This means separation from both language and place, or the loss of the position of listening and responding to the world. For Monchoachi, this means the loss of home or shelter; it means we no longer know language in a 'mode of presence' or 'support' (where language speaks back towards and nurtures and 'holds' us). And he sees globalization as only accelerating this erosion, leading us into a space 'deserté de monde' (deserted of world).[10] We also have, of course, the lingering possibility to 'restore language' or to 'return to the word', to encounter or experience the *parole* that might sound itself out in us. For the poet, this remains the essential task. It is here that Monchoachi turns (in various ways) to Creole for inspiration, to begin again to see language as an 'event' or 'vision of the world' and to also listen for how words can remind us of what is most basic yet also most difficult to grasp.

In what he has called a *pensée créole* (Creole thinking), Monchoachi allows Creole to become the foundation for a poetics that he elaborates in French. Here, the fundamental move is *listening*, specifically a listening to Creole itself, the poet (in his own words) 'attentif au monde et au mode qu'elle installe' (attentive to the world and the mode that it installs).[11] As Kavita Singh puts it, Monchoachi wants to offer the non-Creolophone reader a 'pedagogy, in French, of the logics of the Creole language'.[12] This is a way for the poet both to explore Creole and to move towards language itself as a source of creative inspiration.

To give one quick instance of this, Monchoachi theorizes that Creole asks for an especially *relational* way of speaking, and this becomes akin to the poet's understanding of poetry. In a recurring technique, Monchoachi describes Creole in a way that also describes how he sees poetic speech (and he likewise describes poetic speech in a way that reflects on Creole). Both, for instance, ask that the speaker 'let go' while also remaining at the mercy of the other. Both are described as taking place on the other side of everyday discourse. Both ask for a turning, for a going inside out, a going '*au revers*. Là où cela [la langue] est susceptible de s'élargir en nous' (to the other side, there where language is likely to grow within us).[13] In another way of putting it, Monchoachi is interested in how the language (and language more broadly) gives out certain imperatives or installs certain modes, privileging them over others (in Creole, not assertion but *ellipsis*, not celebration but *enduring/remembering*). Again, he is interested in how the Creole language tells about or asks for a certain way of being on the earth, how the language amounts to a certain vision of the world, one with which the poet might try to be 'in accord', a move he sees as foundational to an Antillean writing.

While many examples could be given of how Monchoachi reads Creole as a unique vision, my focus below will be on one especially prominent 'mode' of his approach: notably, Martinican Creole for Monchoachi (and he traces this to its linguistic origins) carries an Amerindian dimension. He frames the language, for example, as 'une approche du monde, un rapport au monde qui puise essentiellement dans le *lien* qui s'est établi entre les Noirs et les Caraïbes, tout au début de la colonization' (an approach to the world, a connection to the world which draws essentially on the *link* established between the Blacks and the Caraïbes, at the very beginning of colonization).[14] As commentators such as Romuald Fonkoua and Lydie Moudileno have noted, this plays out in Monchoachi's work as a particular posture or orientation towards the external world or *lieu*, which he sees as symbolic, sacred, speaking. This orientation is also manifest (and most consistently explored) in his view of language itself. In a number of poetic texts, Monchoachi cultivates what could be called a pre-Columbian sense of *la parole*. Patrick Chamoiseau says, for instance, that Monchoachi's ongoing exploration of the Creole language takes place in an 'Amerindian dimension', telling the poet (in homage) that it is 'en amérindien que vous explorez la langue créole, et c'est en amérindien que vous éprouvez tous les piliers d'une nouvelle fondation' (in Amerindian that you explore the Creole language, and it is in Amerindian that you test the pillars of a new foundation).[15]

Again, this underscores Monchoachi's regard for language not only as a means of communication but as a 'vision of the world', one that we can explore in a relational way (or what Chamoiseau calls a 'horizontal' way). Some of his neologisms for the word include: the 'patrimoine le plus précieux de l'homme' (the most precious home of man); the 'proprement divin de l'humain' (the properly divine of the human); that which 'parle l'homme à travers et au plus près de son corps' (speaks man through and closer to the body).¹⁶ In this light, there is a sense here of the word as open and relational and outside of the speaker. As Malik Noël-Ferdinand puts it, the word that matters to Monchoachi has this external and pre-existing quality, 'non pas créatrice et égocentrée, mais magiquement consubstantielle au cosmos' (not creative and egocentric but magically consubstantial with the cosmos).¹⁷ In one of the best known formulations of his poetic, Monchoachi calls for a return to the *parole sauvage* – the 'wild word' – but this does not mean the poet's spoken word or, as Moudileno puts it, a 'bruit lancé à la face du monde' (a noise thrown onto the face of the world).¹⁸ Rather, it asks for the return to a dynamic of responsiveness, to the position of listening. It privileges the word that is already there, in the sense of the forms of communication and expression already offered by the earth and by human language. For Monchoachi, this is the word that resonates in Creole culture – the Creole word as original poem or source, possessive of a chant unique to a people and place.

Monchoachi's poetics are thus notable for how strongly they emphasize language's role in nurturing the poet's own speech. He sees poetry, for instance, not as the result of the individual speaking but of some contact or encounter with language or word – poetic activity more akin to listening than writing, more a question 'd'*écouter la parole, plutôt que de croire qu'on crée ex nihilo*' (of listening to the word more so than believing that we create *ex-nihilo*).¹⁹ His work abounds with articulations of how, in the hope for poetic speech, this kind of nearly alchemical contact (with language) makes response or answering possible. For instance, in 'Quelle langue parle le poète?', Monchoachi likens poetry to an act of translating the self: the Antillean poet must endure 'l'obligation ... de se traduire, de traduire son corps ... faire passer d'un lieu à un autre lieu' (the obligation ... of translating himself, of translating the body ... passing from one place to the other place). However, to make this move, 'sans perdre la mémoire du lieu que l'on quitte' (without losing the memory of the place that we are leaving) a password is necessary, and this can be acquired only through initiation in the original place, in 'l'abri' (the shelter) – which 'ne peut consister que dans l'écoute de la langue' (which could only consist of listening to language).²⁰ Monchoachi also develops this emphasis via his concept of 'se laisser dire' (letting yourself be told). Singh notes how this Monchoachien process that 'demands the poeticization of one's experience of the world' is possible only via 'baptism elsewhere', coming about by 'simply listening to what is always present but often neglected, the world made possible through the practice of one's *own* language'.²¹ As a final example, one which I will continue with below, various texts make reference to what Monchoachi conceives of as a *preèmyé mo* or *première parole* (a first word): as a Creole proverb has it, the first word is the 'mother of the ear' or the 'mother of listening'. Above all, this refers to a particular, relational kind of encounter or contact that we might have with language, one 'qui met au jour l'écoute et la nourrit, et qui dispense un monde' (which brings listening to light and nourishes it and which gives out a world).²² For Monchoachi, this speaks to how language is fundamentally world revealing, and it anticipates a kind of writing that, in Cheah's phrase, will 'work toward receiving a world or letting it come'.²³

Proverbs and restoration

When we encounter what Monchoachi calls the 'first word' – whose opposite is the second word, 'un langage instrumentalisé' (an instrumentalized language) that leads nowhere[24] – we encounter speech in a way that 'opens onto listening'. He says that this can simply be the word itself, if we hear it in its full depth and resonance: a simple greeting, for instance, even though we would rarely hear it this way, continues to announce, in what he calls the 'mode of gravity', 'the mystery of our presence in the world'.[25] And it might announce that mystery (as in the poet's reading of the Creole greeting *sa ou fè*) in accord with that particular language's vision of the world. But it is also true that we might seek out this 'first word' in places where it has been privileged, preserved, cultivated. This is the premise behind his essay 'Des paroles-qui-disent', which takes shape around a series of Creole proverbs. Here, and in a move that may *at first* seem at odds with the relational ideas of creativity associated with the Caribbean, Monchoachi highlights the importance of 'founding' speech. Popol Vuh, Gilgamesh, the *Mahābhārata* (I return to the question of epic again below) – these are places where the words of a people have been preserved. But the poet also privileges riddles and proverbs: especially among Creole cultures, these have had special communal significance. At least since Lafcadio Hearn's *Ghombo Zhebes* in 1885, they have been a great source of ethnographic interest (and they have their own complex history of reception among Caribbean authors). But Monchoachi takes a novel tack, one that puts into practice his notion that the restoration of language might best be understood not as an active gesture of speaking but one of listening and return, even submission. This is a strategy that gives primacy to words themselves, and to the embodied experience we might have of their various communicative elements (sound, movement, rhythm, shape).

In this way, Monchoachi wants to imbue the proverb with a heightened relationality; it serves as a reserve of language that might open onto listening (and a form through which the poet explores a certain orientation towards language). The proverb here does not so much have the sense of a language within a language, but as a language antecedent to or giving way to language. He finds the Creole variant for proverb, *pawol-ka-di*, expressing this very pertinently. Translatable to 'paroles-qui-disent' or 'words-that-tell', the expression draws out *pro-verb* etymologically, reminding us of something forgotten (or latent) in the proverb's nature. In a literal sense, proverbs are *words-that-tell*: they are words that might come before or nurture speech and action. The proverb, literally, is 'ce qui précède et annonce, ce qui donne accès, ce qui introduit en somme' (that which precedes and announces; that which gives access; that which introduces).[26] A Russian expression that Monchoachi cites – '[s]ans angles, pas de maison; sans proverbes, pas de paroles' (without corners, no house, without proverbs, no speech) – gives this very clearly.[27]

While a philological sensitivity will enrich his approach to them, Monchoachi also situates the proverbs within the sphere of Creole and Amerindian oralities. With support from J. M. G. Le Clézio's anthropological writings, 'Des paroles-qui-disent' catalogues a number of Creole and Amerindian arts of the word, illustrations of how the founding word was once transmitted 'selon un rituel, parfois dans le cadre d'un rite initiatique' (as per ritual, in the context of initiation rites).[28] Citing here the Creole *tim-tim* riddles, the Creole riddles from Mauritius called *sirandane*, and the Mayan language of *Zuyua*, the essay evokes oral practices that were not simply 'parole-pour-rire' (words-for-humour) but rather 'épreuve par la parole' (tests by the word) – 'interviews' with the word that bound the group in common remembering. He quotes Le Clézio, who notes how the *sirandane* – an indigenous 'art de la parole si léger et si grave' (art of the word, both light and serious) – once worked to sustain 'la connivence entre les hommes et leur monde' (the togetherness of men and their world).[29] In this way, and in his own use of proverbs and later sacred materials (in the *Lémistè* epic poems), Monchoachi upholds 'founding' speech not out of an atavistic longing but to insist on the primacy of a relational encounter with language (or one that is nurturing, orienting, world opening). The examples also imply a special challenge to our world order: they put in view a kind of primary, I/Thou relationship with words that we struggle now to take seriously; no doubt, this evokes the 'dislocation' the poet describes elsewhere but also, in a way both engaging and serious, invites a return to listening.

In what then can be seen as a decolonial approach to language, Monchoachi explores the proverb neither with an anthologist's curiosity (quick, pragmatic translations do not suffice here), nor with the celebration of Creole folklore as his main goal (as previous writers have done). Instead, the proverb has its own world-revealing validity, one that still indicates to man, 'in the mode of gravity, his relation to the world'.[30] But as the proverbs also have an actual contemporary usage, the 'interviews' often develop a comparative dimension in order to approach this mode of gravity. For instance, *pawol sé van* (the word, that's wind) is now used to express language's triviality, a usage (and we can no doubt see this in the world around us) which essentially positions language outside the sphere of what really matters in life. But listening unbiasedly to the words themselves, Monchoachi finds this just as well expressing 'le procès de l'homme sur la terre' (the trial of man on the earth).[31] Such shifts in 'intonation' are significant to the poet, emblematic of how, in the 'subject-object' disposition of the modern order, man's 'interview with the word' has become an increasingly impoverished one.[32]

Many examples in this vein could be given, from 'Des paroles-qui-disent', but also Monchoachi's period of cultural activism known as *Lakouzémi*, and from more recent poetic statements, such as 'La vraie vie'. These readings sometimes emphasize semantics (as above) but they just as often de-emphasize meaning, privileging sound, rhythm, alliteration, Creole parataxis, always drawing out the proverbs' obscure qualities (one's concise alternation of consonants and vowels is likened to an opaque and radiant 'black diamond', another's rhythm to a drum sounding out the movement of time). Whatever the stylistic focus, the poet always marvels at how the proverbs bring different worlds into play: as above, one of these worlds is a modern, subject-oriented order that refuses to hear the proverb, or that simply subsumes the words so that they reflect that order's sense of worldliness. The other is always a different possibility, the world opened by the proverb itself. Monchoachi's transformative principle, then – one that, in Cheah's phrase, 'cannot be erased because it is immanent to the present world'[33] – is to listen to the 'words-that-tell' and to record the world that they reveal or give out, and importantly, to understand this as a real way of inhabiting the world now. Again, this reflects his basic idea that language speaks back towards the human: the word, which remembers, must be listened for and allowed to sound itself out – man can move always, he says, 'vers l'obscur d'une parole originelle, celle qu'on souhaiterait entendre sourdre encore en son corps' (towards the obscure of an original/founding word, such a one that might still sound itself out in the body).[34] In this way, for Monchoachi, the proverbs have a gravity that itself determines his poetic, just as they also might help *us* to reorient, to the hear the possibility of new ways of relating to language and world. Other readers have noted this: as French poet Marie-Clare Bancquart puts it, Monchoachi's meditations not only share Creole culture's knowledge (or 'vision' of the world), they are 'souvent empreints d'une gravité initiatique' (often possessive of an initiative gravity).[35] Similarly, Noël-Ferdinand reads the interviews as part of Monchoachi's long-standing interest in the 'magic word', specifically the desire to connect this word 'à la relation qui unit le poète à son art' (with the relation that binds the poet to his art).[36] In this way, Creole's founding words become the decolonial source of a multilingual poetic in Monchoachi's writing, establishing for Monchoachi both a sense the poet's task and the ground of the real itself.

As an example, consider the reading of the proverb *presé kouté, pas presé reponn*, or 'be quick to listen, not quick to respond'. Drawing on B. David's anthology of Creole proverbs, the poet first cites a contemporary usage whereby the proverb gives 'bon conseil' – good advice to make our dealings and exchanges with other people more informed and efficient.[37] Not wrongly, the proverb reinforces that listening well is the pre-condition of good understanding; it gives 'solide sagesse prosaïque utile à notre bonne conduit dans le commerce que nous entretenons, hommes, avec les humains' (solid prosaic wisdom to encourage good conduct in the commerce that we maintain, men, with other humans).[38] In this way, Monchoachi first shows a proverb that not so much brings a world into relief, but that fits into or points towards the already existing one: at this level of resonance, it sees the real as the human sphere of activity and commerce in which we participate and things circulate; and it gives advice for how we might more tactfully navigate those spaces.

But this also refuses to hear it as a 'word-that-tells'; it refuses how the proverb might disclose a world all its own. And as Monchoachi notes, there are problems with the contemporary understanding: for one, if the proverb really commands that we listen more carefully to our interlocutors (if this is really the content of a founding word), this could subject us to endless listening to 'bavardage' (gossip, chatter), which we might think of both in terms of people and the trivial, often institutional uses of language that surround us everyday. Monchoachi then makes an interesting move: he says the contemporary understanding's 'littéralité prudente' (prudent literality) actually acts like a 'garde-fou' (a safeguard) against the proverb's gravity; it protects us from the abyss that we might necessarily come closer to (or the going beyond the subject that we might experience) were these words to fully disclose themselves.[39] In turn, and imploring us to *risk* more in listening, he gives primacy not to the world of etiquette and socialization and commerce that has by now absorbed the proverb, but to the language and form of the expression itself, which takes the form of a command or imperative and therefore might express a richer and more wide-ranging form of communication beyond the languages of the everyday.

In response, Monchoachi hears words that, above all, tell of the urgency to listen. And imagining the expression as a founding word that goes back to the base of the Creole culture, he says that this urgency must be 'constitutive de notre humanité' (constituitive of our humanity).[40] He thus hears the proverb as a primordial injunction, finding the very need for this injunction significant: it implies that there is a real struggle for a certain kind of contact or attention; it makes clear that 'diversion' is likely; it also suggests that we are capable of this kind of contact. Also, and to return to the point above on 'bavardage', it raises the question of what there is to listen to. For Monchoachi, in accord with the proverb's originary status, this would have to also be something 'constitutive of our humanity'. He calls this 'la parole'; the proverb, he says, cannot but tell us to hold fast to language. It tells that to speak well would be the result of listening to the word (both the word itself and the word that nature speaks). In this way, Monchoachi concludes the proverb tells what 'response' really is: the true response is not a response at all but a correspondence. It remembers that speaking (and poetry certainly) is not just talking but rather the 'interview' man has with 'la parole qui l'entretient ... et qui nourrit son humanité' (with the word that sustains him ... and that nourishes his humanity).[41]

In this way, *presé kouté, pas presé reponn* opens a world and announces a deeper form of expression: it elaborates what Monchoachi calls a 'une manière de rester, un mode de séjour, une manière d'habiter la parole et donc une manière d'habiter le monde' (a way of enduring, a mode of living, a way of inhabiting the word and thus a way of inhabiting the world).[42] This proverb itself is at the heart of Monchoachi's poetic inspiration, his sense of the Creole poet's task. Again, in the Creole thinking, the poet is a *répondeur*, a responder who proceeds not by projecting his own voice onto the world but who silences that voice and instead hurries (always) to listen, attuning himself to sources of the real, hoping to receive an answer that is 'accorded'. Importantly, language itself (the proverb) is the source of this orientation, and the injunction to listen and correspond is one that, through its various incarnations, Monchoachi's poetry will practice and explore. This is only one way we might understand the world-opening role that proverbs play in Monchoachi's thought. He also uses them more widely, against the grain of modern ways of knowing, as a means of establishing the ground of the 'real'. This also connects closely with the poet's task and can perhaps be best envisioned by briefly returning to the poet's concept of language.

Recall that when Monchoachi asks for a return to the 'wild word', he does not privilege the word that might be spoken/imagined anew by the poet but, as Simastochi-Bronès puts it, the word that already exists, that reveals a distinct world, that might be 'écoutée avec acuité par tous les sens du poète, recueillie, reçue, prélevée dans le lieu' (listened to with acuity by all the senses of the poet, collected, received, taken in the place).[43] Her emphasis on 'prélevée dans le lieu' (taken in the place) is especially telling. Again, inspired by the Amerindian mode, Monchoachi sees the external world, the *lieu*, as sacred and communicative; nature, for instance, speaks its own language; this is another source of the real for the poet. Indeed, Monchoachi sees the poet as one who listens to the earth or place as if it is a foundation, 'comme l'Indien, l'oreille tendue collée au sol' (like the Indian, his ear lowered closely to the ground).[44] Here, we might also stress, as Simastochi-Bronès notes, how Monchoachi sees language (especially in certain forms) as this earth or *lieu*. As we've seen, words play the role of source in Monchoachi's oeuvre (and his poetry can describe them as rock-like, obscure, deeper in the sediment than we might first imagine). This *sol* then is composed of Creole language itself, especially so in the sense of a 'language of presence', which, like a new ground to stand on, makes a world possible and opens onto listening. As Monchoachi writes, '[d]ans la première parole, le monde est présent dans l'envers de la parole, la nature et les dieux sont dans l'envers de chaque mot' (in the first word, the world is present in the word's other side, nature and the gods are in the other side of each word).

In this way, in addition to determining the poet's task, proverbs for Monchoachi also 'speak out' the ground of the 'real', or bring into relief a fundamental ontology: emphases here include the nature of listening and language (as seen above) as well as the nature of time. But in 'Des paroles-qui-disent', the most prominent focus may well be on finitude, which our age of the subject is keen to forget and which also connects closely with the question (an enduring one for Monchoachi) of the possibility of poetry in our time. As Paul Celan put it, poets today must 'not forget that they speak from an angle of reflection which is their own existence';[45] and Monchoachi sees *la parole* itself (which encodes the real and remembers our situation's fundamental vulnerability) as capable of keeping the poet close or true to this 'angle'. While a number of the proverbs put this theme in view, the poet's response to 'soley lévé, ou pa sav koté i kay kouché' develops this most memorably (and this is roughly translatable to 'sun has risen, we don't know the place it sets').

The reading opens with a comparison of the proverb's basic message with a maxim from Wittgenstein's *Tractatus*: 'it is a hypothesis that the sun will rise tomorrow: and this means that we do not know whether it will rise'. Monchoachi takes this route (through Wittgenstein) for an illustrative reason. As he writes, both folk saying and logical maxim work against a 'faux savoir' (a false knowing); both challenge the modern presupposition that everything can be understood, quantified, explained. They are trickster-like challenges to 'l'arrogance de la science-qui-sait-tout' (the arrogance of a science-that-knows-all); or to a 'totalitarisme technique [qui] veut enclore le monde' (technical totalitarianism that wants to enclose the world).[46] He thus upholds both proverb and maxim as examples of thinking against the order of the day – in fact, he is struck by the similarity here, and it could be said that he sees a Creole kind of wisdom in the Wittgenstein. But ultimately, he chooses to compare the proverb to a logical formulation precisely to make a point about the 'first word', to underscore its world-revealing nature and to explore how the language of presence carries a movement and a trace (caesura-like even) that encodes what is most human and inclines us to deeper listening (and it might be noted here that Monchoachi sees the proverbs as each having a 'key', a felicity of rhythm, grammar, or philology that amazes us and allows their true essence to emerge).

So while they both work towards a similar truth, Monchoachi finds proverb and maxim facing in different directions; they speak to us differently because in their essence they are different. First, while it shares affinity with the Creole thinking, the maxim belongs to a world of logic and hypothesis, and it exists to make a point about causal thinking. As a 'word-that-tells', the proverb speaks more directly to (or 'gives out') a human situation. To this end, Monchoachi explores how the proverb might actually not concern itself at all with the logistics of the sun's rising and setting (we could also say these words at night, when the sun is not out; and the night, after all, is the time of day most associated with the transmission of the Creole word). He offers instead that we think of 'soley lévé' as chanting out how there is a 'grace' with which we are currently in 'accord'. But as if we might too soon abstract from this, the second clause ('we don't know the place the sun sets') counters the first. For Monchoachi, this has nothing to do with the actual setting place or horizon of the star. Rather, it tells us that there is a place outside of the grace (with which we are currently in accord) that exceeds us, that cannot be known. He writes in fact that this might not even be thought of as a location but as 'un lieu qui n'est point un lieu … le lieu même d'éloignement de la grâce, lieu et temps mêlés, ni lieu ni temps, temps et lieu qui s'épuisent et que la parole ni le jour ne peut nommer, ni pointer' (a place which is not a place … the very place of separation from the grace, place and time mixed, neither place nor time, time and place exhausted and which neither the word nor the day can name or point out).[47] In this Creole way, the proverb recalls the basic human situation, and it offers the mystery of finitude as what is real and foundational.

With this example, via the contrast with the logical hypothesis, Monchoachi wants to show how the 'first word' – which poetry attempts to restore but which is present in language itself, even in its simplest forms like greeting and proverb (perhaps most profoundly so there) – does not simply make a point or give information but rather gives out a world. It gives out a possibility, asking that we might listen for how language speaks to us about what is most essential, how it continues (even now) to tell about 'the mystery of our presence in the world … ceaselessly announcing it in the mode of gravity'. His project then upholds language as a source of the real, and we can no doubt see this as existing in an intertextual relationship with poetry itself (which I will consider briefly). Again, the Creole poetic is one that hopes for a restoration of language. This means that poetry (itself based on listening) might give us the chance to encounter language in a way that has gone missing from our world – to see the word again, for instance, as primordial and opaque. But other emphases are possible too. For instance, if language remembers what is most fundamental (and if we no longer hear it in the mode of presence), one task of poetry would be to restore or to *remember* what has been forgotten. In this way, nurtured by listening, poetry can be seen as working towards a restoration of what the word intrinsically knows and remembers (such as a sense of finitude). To put this differently, as poet Joanna Klink says – writing of difficult poets (like Monchoachi) who 'situate their poems close to a symbolic source of meaning … who carry their very existence into language' – poetry should be seen as an effort 'to secure a relationship to the real … [to] that which sponsors our existence in the world'.[48] For Monchoachi, this 'real' can be known through closely listening to language itself. It would not be an oversimplification to say that, in the Creole poetic, it is this encounter with language in the 'mode of presence' that makes poetry possible;

Monchoachi himself stresses that we are often unable to write simply because we have not spent enough time listening to language. In another sense, this ethic of seeking the real in language (as modelled by the proverb interviews) might also be seen as a way keeping the poem 'true'. As Celan said in his famous 'Meridian' speech, the horizon of the 'uncanny' (of what might be called a mimetic escapism) can always tempt the poet, because here the poet can forget what is real, can forget the lived self. The true poem though will find a way to elude the discourses of representation by remembering what is most human, by hewing closely to the real: again, the idea of a pre-poetic listening, as modeled by Monchoachi, can nurture this possibility. As Yves Bonnefoy puts it in one of his readings of Shakespeare (like Celan's, a multilingual poetics concerned with the purpose of true poetry), the false poet gets caught up in appearances and images and eloquence, but the real poet knows 'the important thing is to remember'.[49] For Monchoachi, remembering is a naturally Creole mode; it does not mean the recall of trivial events or detail; it is a learning, or re-learning 'à habiter dans l'ouvert du monde' (how to dwell in the world's openness).[50] Importantly, language itself offers a ground for this remembering; it remembers 'the real' for us and, to paraphrase Walt Whitman, another of Monchoachi's inspirations, it has stopped somewhere, waiting for us.

In Monchoachi's recourse to proverbs, Creole becomes the inspiration for a French-language writing as well as for an exploration of how the *parole d'homme* might nurture poetic listening and speaking. This can be understood as a decolonial approach, part of a broader, global movement towards, as Mignolo and Vàzquez put it, 'the recognition, the dignity of those aesthetic practices that have been written out of the canon of modern aesthetics'.[51] It can also be understood as an approach that privileges some fundamental contact with the word, in an encounter that would nurture and take place before speaking (and to which Monchoachi wants to assign a pre-linguistic character). This brings into relief how very different relations with words are possible, just as it underscores the intrinsic value of language. Herein too lies the great novelty of Monchoachi's defence of language (specifically of Creole), which has been astutely noted by Simastochi-Bronès: unlike his *créoliste* forebears, Monchoachi does not see the Creole word as 'périssable' (perishable).[52] He explores instead how its force endures, giving us insight into how that language, in Cheah's phrase, 'enacts a world' – but also a model for thinking about how much is at stake in our own practices of language and literature. Of course, throughout his oeuvre, there is also an implicit call to value linguistic biodiversity, one that asks us to think boldly (indeed, risking more) about how we might teach, share, and advocate for languages. 'Toute langue est un cas' (each language is an event), Monchoachi says.[53] And each language will no doubt 'remember' differently, in its very structure, in its orality, in its tales and myths and more. When languages disappear, it is not only that numbers of speakers go down, but entire ways of knowing the world and knowing ourselves and beyond ourselves are forgotten and covered up.

On this note, it would be fitting to add that while the poetics explored here are of course reflected throughout Monchoachi's poetry, the influence has become especially palpable in his most recent attempts at epic poetry, called *Lémistè* (Creole for 'mystery'). Here, we can see how the decolonial deferral to proverbs established a creative precedent for Monchoachi. Briefly, *Lémistè* is an acclaimed series of long poems based on forgotten sacred materials (myths, magical practices, orality) from around the world, specifically (in the two volumes so far released) the Americas and Africa/Oceania. Just as with the proverbs, Monchoachi does not approach these materials out of an ethnographic curiosity or a desire to chronicle or anthologize, but as modalities, as ways of knowing and accessing the world, 'en vue d'ébranler la vision calamiteuse du monde charriée par la dite Civilisation' (in order to shake the calamitous vision of the world put forth by the so-called Civilization).[54] This allows for a Creole approach to the epic poem: the 'arcana' become the foundation for a listening and a poetic of response. Importantly, the polyglossic poem that results reads less as a hero's journey than as the transcription of a sacred speech. In the same spirit then as the proverbs or the Mayan language of *Zuyua*, Monchoachi sees epic above all as a 'language of presence' – one that comes from a close listening to what is 'original' and then extends that same opportunity out to the reader.

While these poems no doubt deserve serious critical attention in the years to come, it might for now suffice to stress how *Lémistè*, remarkably, takes shape through the same transformative principle that guides Monchoachi's Creole thinking, the hope to achieve an openness to the expressiveness of the world. And Monchoachi's bold move here is not only to appreciate this approach, but to model for us how such creative materials – how such a reverence for and surrender to language – constitute a genuine way of being in our globalized age of speed and the subject. In a way both local and universal, this approach that exceeds the borders of existing linguistic systems, concerns itself with learning how to listen for and receive a world, and it does so not as an act of regression but as an act of resistance and restoration. As Cheah says world literature must, it reveals a desire to 'criticize the existing world', yes, but it gives more weight and even faith to the 'process that keeps alive the force that opens another world'.[55] In the end, this is a process that wants to let language speak, that gives the weight to language itself and to the unique world that it might disclose. And it prompts us to consider how world literature might be seen as a kind of writing that listens for and responds to (indeed, that draws out) this vision of reality inherent in words, in distinct ways among all of the world's languages, peoples, places.

Notes

1. Pheng Cheah, 'World against Globe: Toward a Normative Conception of World Literature', *New Literary History* 45.3 (2014): 303–29, 305.
2. Ibid., 307–8.
3. Ibid., 318.
4. Pheng Cheah, *What Is a World? On Postcolonial Literature as World Literature* (Durham, NC: Duke University Press, 2016), 212.
5. Ibid.
6. Thomas O. Beebee, '*What Is a World? On Postcolonial Literature as World Literature* by Pheng Cheah (review)', *Comparative Literature Studies* 54.1 (2017): 229–34, 232.

7 Monchoachi, 'La vraie vie', *Nouvelles Études Francophones* 32.1 (2017): 3–18, 13.
8 Ibid., 13.
9 Monchoachi, 'Des paroles-qui-disent', *L'Espère-geste* (Nantes: Obsidian, 2003): 92–115, 93
10 Monchoachi, 'Discours pour la reception du prix Max Jacob 2003', *Agotem* 1 (2003): 102–5, 105.
11 Monchoachi, 'Se laisser dire', *Éloge de la servilité* (Vauclin: Lakouzémi, 2007): 37–44, 39.
12 Kavita Singh, 'Let Yourself Be Told', *Small Axe* 18.3 (2014): 107–14, 107.
13 Monchoachi, 'Se laisser dire', 40.
14 Monchoachi, 'Écouter la parole: Interview with Nicolas Cavaillès', *Recto/Verso* 5 (2009): 1–8, 4.
15 Patrick Chamoiseau, 'Autour des grands mystères; récitation pour M. Monchoachi', in *Dire le réel aujourd'hui en poésie*, ed. Béatrice Bonhomme et al. (Paris: Hermann, 2016): 37–41, 40.
16 Monchoachi, 'Quelle langue parle le poète?', *Nuit gagée* (Paris: Harmattan, 1992): 61–7, 65.
17 Malik Noël-Ferdinand. '*Lémistè* ou la voix magique des codex créoles de Monchoachi', *Cahiers de littérature orale* 75–76 (2014): 2–15, 6.
18 Lydie Moudileno, 'Écopoésie de la Caraïbe', in Bonhomme, et al., *Dire le réel aujourd'hui en poésie*: 43–56, 48.
19 Ibid.
20 Monchoachi, 'Quelle langue parle le poète?', 63.
21 Singh, 'Let Yourself Be Told', 108.
22 Monchoachi, 'Discours pour la reception', 104.
23 Cheah, *What Is a World?*, 212.
24 Monchoachi, 'Discours pour la reception', 104.
25 Monchoachi, 'Des paroles-qui-disent', 95.
26 Ibid., 94.
27 Ibid.
28 Ibid., 95.
29 Ibid., 95–6.
30 Monchoachi, 'Des paroles-qui-disent', 93.
31 Ibid., 101.
32 Monchoachi, 'La vraie vie', 11.
33 Cheah, *What Is a World?*, 212.
34 Monchoachi, 'Des paroles-qui-disent', 94.
35 Marie-Claire Bancquart, 'Review of *L'Espère-geste*, by Monchoachi', *Potomitan*. Available online: www.potomitan.info/bibliographie/monchoachi (accessed 14 August 2019).
36 Noël-Ferdinand, '*Lémistè* ou la voix magique', 6.
37 Monchoachi, 'Des paroles-qui-disent', 102.
38 Ibid.
39 Ibid., 103.
40 Ibid.
41 Ibid.
42 Monchoachi, 'Écouter la parole', 2.
43 Françoise Simasotchi-Bronès, 'Monchoachi, éléments pour une créopoétique: "En chantant creole, savoir"', in Bonhomme et al., *Dire le réel aujourd'hui en poésie*, 73–88, 78.

44 Monchoachi, *La case où se tient la lune* (Bordeaux: William Blake & Co., 2002), 7.
45 Paul Celan, 'The Meridian', in *Paul Celan: Collected Prose*, trans. Rosemarie Waldrop (New York: Routledge, 2003): 37–55, 49.
46 Monchoachi, 'Des paroles-qui-disent', 112.
47 Ibid., 114.
48 Joanna Klink, 'You. An Introduction to Celan', *Iowa Review* 30.1 (2000): 1–18, 1, 3.
49 Yves Bonnefoy, 'Art and Nature: The Background of *The Winter's Tale*', in *Shakespeare and the French Poet*, ed. John Naughton (Chicago: University of Chicago Press, 2004): 28–49, 29.
50 Monchoachi, 'Toute la démesure de l'ordre rationnel transparaît dans cette prétention: protéger la nature', in *Retour à la parole sauvage* (Vauclin: Lakouzémi, 2008): 12–20, 13.
51 Walter Mignolo and Rolando Vàzquez, 'The Decolonial AestheSis Dossier', *Social Text: Periscope*, 2013. Available online: www.socialtextjournal.org/periscope_article/the-decolonial-aesthesis-dossier (accessed 14 August 2019).
52 Simasotchi-Bronès, 'Monchoachi', 85.
53 Monchoachi, 'Se laisser dire', 42.
54 Monchoachi, 'Lettre à François Boddaert', *Potomitan*. Available online: www.potomitan.info/bibliographie/monchoachi/lemiste.php#1 (accessed 14 August 2019).
55 Cheah, *What Is a World?*, 212.

16

Configurations of multilingualism and world literature

Wen-chin Ouyang

The history of English is a fascinating field of study in its own right, but it also provides a valuable perspective for the contemporary study of the language ... This historical account promotes a sense of identity and continuity, and enables us to find coherence in many of the fluctuations and conflicts of present-day English language use. Above all, it satisfies the deep-rooted sense of curiosity we have about our linguistic heritage. People like to be aware of their linguistic roots.

David Crystal[1]

The making of English is the story of three invasions and a cultural revolution. In the simplest terms, the language was brought to Britain by Germanic tribes, the Angles, Saxons and Jutes, influenced by Latin and Greek when St Augustine and his followers converted England to Christianity, subtly enriched by the Danes, and finally transformed by the French-speaking Normans. From the beginning, English was a crafty hybrid, made in war and peace. ... The English have always accepted the mixed blood of their language. There was a vague understanding that they were part of a European language family, but it was not until the eighteenth century that a careful investigation by a gifted amateur linguist began to decipher the true extent of this common heritage.

Robert McCrum, William Cran and Robert MacNeil[2]

The proliferation of the conceptual category of 'nation' and its attendant 'national identity' in the colonial and postcolonial age of nationalism has had a long-lasting impact on how we think and speak both of language and literary expression. Monolingualism, albeit a vision of the human linguistic condition invented to allay the anxiety generated by the imagined 'confusion of languages' in Babel, has imposed itself on our imaginings of language and nation, particularly in the connection between them. An Arab, for example, is someone who speaks the Arabic language, which in turns defines the Arab nation. Monolingualism of the imagined nation and national subject, it may be argued, is the logical ramification, perhaps even radicalization, of the remedy for Babel's 'confusion of languages' offered by 'monotheistic communities' that fantasize about an original language that would serve as the glue of their union and at the same time mark their return to the Godly paradise. Monolingualism may offer comforting coherence and cohesion, as David Crystal observes, but it also suppresses our natural multilingualism and the complexity of our linguistic ecology. It generates the kind of emotional, linguistic and intellectual conundrum Derrida describes and interrogates in *Monolingualism of the Other OR The Prosthesis of Origin*.[3] The discourse of 'identity' and 'coherence', underpinned by the 'nation' in postcolonial identitarian politics, imposes on both the speaking subject and environment the type of monolingualism that pushes aside and suppresses their multilingualism and multiple identities. This monolingualism has persisted in theories and practices of world literature. World literature, vaguely conceptualized as a canon of universal classics, takes shape as national literary works that travel around and arrive in the world by the Casanovan means of translation into English or French in order to reach London, New York and Paris.[4] Recent interventions from the perspective of multilingualism, whether of the world, such as Francesca Orsini's 'multilingual local',[5] or of literature, such as the heterolingualism, plurilingualism and translanguaging we read about in this volume, move away from Damrosch's 'translation' as 'mode of circulation'[6] and Moretti's 'distant' 'mode of reading'[7] to close engagement with the multilingualism of the world outside and created in a literary work, of its author, and even of its nation. The literary work is the site of a confluence of languages and reflects both the multilingual speaking subject and the plurilingual ecology. More importantly, it is the creative effect of languages coming into dialogue.

The locus of multilingualism in these interrogations of world literature remains the speaking subject, the linguistic construction of the literary text, and the language environment in which it is created and gets creative. This chapter rather locates multilingualism in the very fabric of language itself, using the history of each language, such as Robert McCrum, William Cran and Robert MacNeil's notion of English as 'mixed blood', to peel away the monolingual discourse of 'identity and coherence' constructed around the nation, and to theorize world literature variously. Both 'world' and 'literature' are, here, multilingual, so is its worlding. The multilingualism of world literature's inherent worlding allows for extending our field of vision to a longer temporal trajectory inclusive of the contemporary and beyond and to a broader spatial canvas encompassing Europe and elsewhere. The different configurations of multilingualism in each language, when examined comparatively, as I will argue and demonstrate, make it possible to produce meaningful close readings of worldly literary works, to situate their worlding and worldliness in, for example, the words, things, concepts, ideas and ideologies that travel as part and parcel of language, to see a plurality of world literature across time and space, and to delineate the contours of each on the basis of the configuration of multilingualism inherent in its language.

How do we see the Arabic language as inherently multilingual, however? It may be obvious that the Arabic language has lived in a variety of multilingual environments and that the history of its development is a series of interactions with other languages from the ancient Near Eastern civilization and Greek philosophy, biblical Hebrew, medieval Latin, Persian and Turkish, and modern European languages. The Arabic language is, like English, 'a crafty hybrid, made in war and peace' but the Arabic speakers have never acknowledged the 'mixed blood of their language'. This is because Arabic is the language of the Qur'an and as such a *lingua sacra*. Moreover, Arabic has always been able to domesticate any foreignness through its impeccable grammaticality: its systemic grammar can in time smooth out awkward translations from foreign languages and its extensive and complex morphology allows for the creation of Arabic words that parallel their foreign counterparts. Grammaticality, as Kees Versteegh shows, has absorbed other languages into Arabic in a seamless fashion and made it into the *lingua franca* of the educated Arabic speakers worldwide.[8] The grammatical Arabic language is for Karla Mallette an 'Alexandrian' or 'Metropolitan' language that is neither dead nor alive, like Latin in premodern Europe, in that it is used for literary writing not for day-to-day communication, but that it has a farther reach historically and geographically than the living languages surrounding them.[9]

By this logic, Arabic necessarily and inevitably renders multilingualism into monolingualism, making multilingualism traceable only, as I have already noted above, to the speaking subjects, the language environment and the composition of the literary work. The monolingual veneer of grammatical Arabic, even of the highest literary register, is never total. There are moments in the history of Arabic language, more particularly, of Arabic writing, which allow us to catch glimpses of various configurations of multilingualism in Arabic and, more importantly, of the ways in which multilingualism is internalized into monolingualism. For my purposes in this chapter, I look at two different but overlapping moments of Arabic multilingualism. Each moment is what Orsini would call 'multilingual local', however, the 'local' here is not only 'significant geography' but also 'momentous history'. This 'multilingual local' is at the same time connected to a global network of circulation. The triad underpinning this 'multilingual local' – its location in geography, history and global network of circulation – circumscribes the languages in use and gives it a particular configuration of multilingualism.

The first such 'multilingual local' is the eighteenth-century Western Mediterranean represented by Moroccan ambassador and traveller, Muḥammad b. ʿUthmān al-Miknāsī (d. 1799),[10] and the second the nineteenth-century Eastern Mediterranean epitomized by Syrian-Lebanese itinerant translator, Aḥmad Fāris al-Shidyāq (1804–87). Both have left behind a complex body of writing that, if read comparatively – diachronically within the works of the same author and synchronically between the two authors – will give us what we look for. These two authors travelled extensively around the Mediterranean, in Europe and the Middle East. They give accounts of experiences abroad in more than one travelogue and, intriguingly and significantly, recast their travelogues written in the conventional *riḥla* genre into the highly literary but also conventional *maqāma* genre. In what I call the *maqāmatasation* of the *riḥla*, the multilingual fabric of al-Miknāsī and al-Shidyāq's travel writings is transformed into what any unsuspecting reader would see as 'authentic' Arabic, 'grammaticalized', syntactically and morphologically, in such a way that no trace of 'foreignness' is easily detectable. The *maqāma* in the *riḥla* is, however, punctuated by a sense of crisis, here, both moral and intellectual, expressed as an anxiety about sexuality. This sexuality in al-Miknāsī and al-Shidyāq is, upon close scrutiny, the manifestation at once of apprehension of and excitement about cultural encounter, or entanglement with the 'other' not only socially, morally and intellectually, but also linguistically. In the interstices between languages, multilingualism, which is here arguably an entanglement of languages, is associated with sexual promiscuity, even though it is at the same time felt as pleasurable and creative. Sexuality in al-Miknāsī and al-Shidyāq is more akin to Roland Barthes's 'secondary sexuality' that is situated not in sex but in language and thought, or what he calls 'the pleasure of the text', for language is inseparable from thought,[11] and multililingualism from intercultural conceptual entanglement.

Riḥla and *Maqāma*

Al-Miknāsī wrote three travelogues: *al-Iksīr fī fikāk al-asīr* (Elixir for the Ransom of [Muslim] Captives) documents his travels to and from Spain for the purpose of ransoming captives (1778–80),[12] *al-Badr al-sāfir li-hidāyat al-musāfir ilā fikāk al-asārā min yad al-'aduw al-kāfir* (Unveiled Full Moon for Guiding the Traveller to Ransom [Muslim] Captives from the Hands of Their Infidel Enemies) recounts his travels to Spain and the Kingdom of Sicily and Naples for a similar purpose (1781–3),[13] and *Iḥrāz al-mu'allā wa l-raqīb fī ḥajj bayt allāh al-ḥarām wa ziyārat al-quds al-sharīf wa l-khalīl wa l-tabarruk bi-qabr al-ḥabīb* (Lofty Sanctuary and Guardian for Pilgrimage to the Sacred House of God and Visitation of the Noble Jerusalem and Anointed Friends and Seeking Blessings at the Tomb of God's Favourite Messenger) describes his travels to Istanbul as an ambassador and of his pilgrimage to the Islamic holy lands in Palestine and Mecca and Medina (1785).[14] In these works, al-Miknāsī follows in the footstep of the earlier, more than millennium old Arabic travel writing on geographical discovery, adventures at sea and in exotic lands, pilgrimage and the journey in search of knowledge, and of the more recent diplomatic missions to Europe to ransom Muslim captives.[15]

The latter type, the diplomatic missions (to ransom Muslim captives from their Christian captors in Spain, Malta, Kingdom of Sicily and Naples) developed in the aftermath of the Reconquista, most likely after the fall of Granada in 1492. The fall of Granada, and the Jewish and Muslim exodus this precipitated, led to the migration of Andalusis to the Maghreb and their resettlement there. Anadalusi immigrants were linguistically equipped to return to Spain and go to Europe as ambassadors on behalf of the Moroccan Sultans. Al-Miknāsī was heir to a long, complex tradition of travel writing by which the Maghreb is known. Andalusis and Maghrebis (including Moroccans, Algerians and Tunisians) made frequent journeys to the Mashreq, as the prevalent view goes, to learn from the eminent scholars established at the major centres of learning in the Mashreq and, more importantly, to visit the Islamic holy lands. The emergence of 'modern' Europe, and the 'Christian' European empires (Portuguese, Spanish, Dutch, English and French) starting in the fifteenth century and ending only in the twentieth century, redefined Christian–Muslim relations (not to mention

Christian–Jewish, Muslim–Jewish and Muslim–Muslim relations) in a variety of ways. The travellers partook in the process and left records of it for us.

Al-Miknāsī's three travelogues, *al-Iksīr*, *al-Badr al-sāfir* and *Iḥrāz al-muʿallā*, offer a glimpse of the kind of travel writings that were taking shape between the sixteenth and eighteenth centuries: records of ambassadorial missions to Europe, in particular, Spain, Holland, France, Kingdom of Sicily and Naples, including Malta, such as those I have already mentioned; and of those to Istanbul, which necessarily overlap with pilgrimage and journey in search of knowledge.[16] The diplomatic mission underpinning these travel narratives, always explicitly stated but never clearly detailed, distinguishes these Moroccan 'travels to the East' from their Algerian and Tunisian counterparts, even as they all similarly describe the pleasures and hardships of their journey, places, especially 'famous' cities, they visit, and the scholars and luminaries they meet and talk to, and more importantly, they all quote extensively, densely from books they have read about the landmarks on their itineraries and the scholars with whom they come into contact.[17]

Al-Shidyāq wrote two travelogues: *al-Wāsiṭa fī maʿrifat aḥwāl māliṭa* (The Means to Knowledge of the Conditions of Malta, 1836) and *Kashf al-mukhabbaʾ ʿan funūn ūrūbbā* (Revealing the Hidden Arts of Europe, 1866; completed 1857).[18] They are, however, more in line with the Arabic genre of travel writing familiar to readers of journeys of discovery and in search of knowledge.[19] These two texts are the records of al-Shidyāq's experiences in European metropolitan capitals, such as London and Paris and rural towns, such as Cambridge, of his observations of European cultural institutions unfamiliar in the Middle East and North Africa, such as theatre and musical concerts, of the manners and customs in Malta, Britain and France, of his encounters with Orientalists and their knowledge and practices, of his life as a traveller and of his views of culture and civilization and the role of gender relations in them. Like al-Miknāsī, who reiterates *al-badr al-sāfir* in the five *maqāmāt* appended to it, al-Shidyāq re- and parallel-wrote his two travelogues in *al-Sāq ʿalā al-sāq* (1855) in the form of an elaborate game of language play, and again in the four *maqāmāt* embedded in *al-Sāq*.[20]

Al-Sāq is arguably al-Shidyāq's fictionalized autobiography,[21] structured around his travels from ʿAshqūt, the village where he was born in Lebanon under the Shihābīs in 1804 or 1805, to Egypt, more specifically Cairo and Alexandria, then to Malta, England (with focus on London, Cambridge and Oxford) and France (especially Marseille and Paris), followed by Tunis and finally Istanbul, where he died in 1887. The bulk of *al-Sāq* follows the trajectory of his two works on his travels to Malta and Europe, where he gives simultaneously similar and different accounts in *al-Wāsiṭa* and *Kashf al-mukhabbaʾ*. In fact, it does not go beyond the historical and geographical scope of these two travelogues, for it was published in 1855 when he still lived in Paris, while he was still working on *Kashf al-mukhabbaʾ*. It is, however, a complex multigeneric work modelled on the classical Arabic *adab* literary tradition. Made up of chapters (*fuṣūl*) that combine travelogue with poetry, *risāla* (epistle), *maqāla* (as in treatise), *ḥikāya* (story akin to *The 1001 Nights*), interpretation of dreams (*taʿbīr*), debate (*muḥāwara*), *gharīb al-lugha* genre of writing on lexical items and semantic oddities in the Arabic language, lexicography and much more, it is full of digressions that give shape to and are shaped by the variety of linguistic topics and literary motifs and genres he mobilized. It is precisely this feature of *al-Sāq* that has generated much discussion and debate, as we see in the huge body of literature on the nineteenth-century *nahḍa* structured around this text and al-Ṭahṭāwī's (1801–73) *Takhlīṣ al-ibrīz fī talkhīṣ bārīz* (The Extraction of Gold in the Summation of Paris, 1830). Intriguingly, a *maqāma* appears as the thirteenth chapter in each of the four sections of *al-Sāq*.

Maqāma in *Riḥla:* Politics of cultural encounter

Al-Badr al-sāfir and *al-Sāq* are not the earliest or only Arabic works that overlap the travelogue, *riḥla*, with the picaresque, *maqāma*. Rather, they are latecomers to 'play' with genres in Arabic writings. Andalusi Lisān al-Dīn Ibn al-Khaṭīb (1313–74) cast his three travels in al-Andalus and the Maghreb in the form of three *maqāmāt*, including *Khaṭrat al-ṭayf* (Spectral Visions). The *maqāma* is a highly diverse literary genre that has, according to Philip Kennedy, served as 'a nexus of interests' for centuries.[22] Its popularity is attested by its continuous use not only in Middle Eastern languages (Arabic, Hebrew, Persian and Turkish) but also European, especially in Iberia, such as Catalan and Castilian from the tenth century to the twenty-first century, by its expansive geographical spread from Asia across Africa to Europe, and by its openness to any 'topic under the sun'. Its 'fictive', 'rhetorical' and 'polemical' mode or 'irony' has placed it at the forefront of 'subversion'[23] of all and every kind. The *maqāma* is a reiteration of the *riḥla* in both al-Miknāsī and al-Shidyāq. In these *riḥla* texts, the dialogization of *riḥla*, written in a language closer to the vernacular packed with foreign words and concepts, and *maqāma*, rendered in the highly literary ornate rhyme prose with no trace of foreignness, is expressive of cross-cultural politics and an attendant anxiety about cultural encounter. While the *riḥla* delights in cultural encounter and particularly the creative energy generated in intercultural linguistic and conceptual entanglement, the *maqāma* in the *riḥla* dramatizes the encounter with foreignness, with foreign languages, concepts, ideas, worldviews and cultural institutions, but in the form of a staged performance of a sexualized melodrama in which foreignness is at once othered as the alluring European or Europeanized woman and integrated into a grammaticalized monolingualism.

Riḥla: Intercultural linguistic and conceptual entanglement

Al-Miknāsī's European travelogues anticipate the tropes to be found in the genre of '*voyage en occident*' in the nineteenth and twentieth centuries, one of the most famous of which is that of al-Shidyāq. Like all Moroccan travelogues to Europe between the seventeenth and twentieth centuries,[24] *al-Iksīr* and *al-Badr al-sāfir* bring home news of the 'cultural institutions' unique to Europe at the time, from monasteries and nunneries, marriage customs and inheritance laws, border quarantines, to hospitals, weapon factories, elite clubs and even opera houses. Al-Shidyāq does the same in *al-Wāsiṭa* and *Kashf al-mukhabba'*. Their narratives of travel are packed with foreign words and descriptions of European cultural institutions. Names of persons, places and cultural institutions are transliterated, or transcribed in Arabic words according to how the authors heard the European sounds and spoke their own language(s). Al-Miknāsī called the ruler of Malta '*al-ṭāghiya*' (despot), which does not appear in al-Shidyāq, the Spaniards '*Isbāniyūl*' (as opposed to Egyptian and Levantine '*isbān*' or '*isbāniyūl*' with a soft 's'), quarantine '*karanṭīna*' (as opposed to Levantine '*karantīna*'), and opera '*al-wubra*' (as opposed to Egyptian and Levantine '*ūbirā*') and 'al-kumidiya' (as opposed to Egyptian and Levantine '*al-kūmīdiya*'). However, they have to invent a new language to describe the unfamiliar cultural institutions and convey their attendant concepts and practices.

When both al-Miknāsī and al-Shidyāq saw and experienced European opera for the first time, the first European opera house in the Arabic speaking world had yet to be built (the Khedival Opera House in Cairo opened in 1871). This is how al-Miknāsī describes the opera house he was invited to in Naples and the opera he attended:

> The despot (*al-ṭāghiya*) invited us one day to see a spectacle they make called Opera (*al-wubra*), which is known among the Spaniards as Comedia. … We found them [the seats] covered with cushions, looking over a huge roofed room. The seats looking over this room were evenly arranged in seven levels (*ṭabaqāt*). … In one of the corners of the [Opera] House, there was a space lifted by half a human height from the ground. It was paved with wood, and this was the place for play and spectacle (*wa fī iḥdā zawāyā l-dār barāḥ muttasi' murtafi' 'an al-arḍ bi-naḥw niṣf qāma mafrūsha bi-khashab, wa huwa mawḍi' al-la'b wa l-furja*). They had draped a curtain over it, separating it from those in the [Opera] House. … Musicians began to do their work, the curtain was lifted, and a spacious house with chairs, domes, stables and levels appeared, and people, women and men in luxurious dress, emerged from all its corners. A woman came forward and began singing with a man. They took turns and brought us wonder and marvel.[25]

Al-Miknāsī is clearly working hard to find a language to convey his first experience of opera. The Arabic term *Dār al-Ūbira* had yet to become common knowledge, and the same goes for theatre, *masraḥ*, stage, *khashabat al-masraḥ*, and play, *masraḥiyya*. In the absence of the technical terms that would be developed in the nineteenth century and standardized in the twentieth, such as acting, *tamthīl*, he turns to the word *la'b*, to convey the idea of performance.

Al-Shidyāq, who seemed to have had better familiarity with European opera, theatre and musical concerts, had to resort to elaborate descriptions and approximations in order to convey what he experienced. Drury Lane Theatre is *malhā*, a noun of place Arabs of the nineteenth century coined from *lahw*, play or entertainment, to denote theatre. What is represented on stage is *tamthīl*, to make an example of something, before the term became common as acting. A play is *lu'ba*, a literal translation of English, and actors are players, *lā'ibūn*, props, enumerated as the dizzying array of instruments (*ālāt*), tools (*adawāt*) and scenes (*manāẓir*), had to be explained through an elaborate approximation. What if one were to represent the story of al-Samaw'al (first half of the sixth century), legendary for his loyalty to the pre-Islamic warrior poet and prince, Imru' al-Qays (501–44), and al-Ḥārith Ibn Ẓālim, the Ghassanid prince, who was known to have demanded that al-Samaw'al hand over Imru' al-Qays's properties and especially his armour? A castle would have to be built, three actors resembling the historical figures found, trained and dressed appropriately for their roles, the armour brought on stage and two scenes set up. In the first, Imru' al-Qays would entrust al-Samaw'al with his possessions, both reciting from their poetry, and in the second al-Samaw'al would refuse to hand over the armour to al-Ḥārith and watch the latter behead his son, all the while reciting from their poetry.

More importantly, al-Shidyāq carves out words from Arabic roots to explain what 'acting' means.

> The most amazing thing one sees in the actors and actresses (*al-lā'ibīn wa l-lā'ibāt*) is that an old man impersonates a young man (*yatafattā*) through clothing, body language and speech so thoroughly that you think what you see is a young man. And a young man can impersonate an old man (*yatashayyakh*) so well that you imagine that you see an old man before you. If they appear in front of you afterwards you cannot recognize any of them. They even change their voice, accent, face and hair to pretend to be hunchbacked, lame, ill, asleep, blind, drunk, weeping, laughing, stupid, mad.[26]

He gets creative with his explanation in Arabic. Playing with Arabic morphology, he uses form five, *tafaʿʿala*, to give us the sense of impersonation. The pattern itself means 'to inhere a characteristic or quality', and by putting the root of *fatā*, youth, in a verbal pattern of this form and attributing it to an old man, *shaykh*, al-Shidyāq gives us a rather visual and visceral sense of an old man impersonating a young man in the verb, *yatafattā*, to inhere youthfulness. He similarly uses form six, *tafāʿala*, the pattern of which means 'to pretend', to translate 'acting' into Arabic words that conjure up images of physicality but also follow patterns of Arabic rhyming. The examples he gives, to pretend to be 'hunchbacked, lame, ill, asleep, blind, drunk, weeping, laughing, stupid, mad', fall into a pattern that repeats the sounds of 'wa yatafāʿalūn' several times: *wa yataḥādabūn wa yataʿārajūn wa yatamāraḍūn wa yatanāwamūn wa yataʿāmmūn wa yatasākarūn wa yatabākūn wa yataḍāḥakūn wa yataḥāmaqūn wa yatajānnūn*. In each instance, a defect with physical manifestation is evoked.

In this type of creative fun, language and thought are entangled, and multilingualism, here, dialogues among languages, does make for a slippery ground. 'Travelling along linguistic boundaries', Rebecca C. Johnson observes of *al-Sāq*, 'al-Shidyāq pieces together an unruly patchwork of a text whose unity is in danger of disintegration, threatening to dissolve into mere *'ujmah*, or "babble"'.[27] Such a world literature text, 'a dynamic constitutive process', Johnson further notes, 'creates trouble – generic and otherwise – and it is always in danger of collapse'.[28] This trouble, whether linguistic, generic, conceptual or cultural, as I mentioned above, finds expression in the form of a melodrama of man–woman encounter steeped in sexual anxiety. This anxiety is a translation of the contact and interaction with European women in open public space, where European men and women flirt, court and make love expressively and freely, transcribing the sexual mores of the Europeans into the local, the site from which they depart on their journey and to which they return. The local becomes, in al-Miknāsī's and al-Shidyāq's travel narratives, the site of linguistic, conceptual and cultural entanglement, where little stands on firm ground. Al-Miknāsī records in *al-Badr al-sāfir* a moment of moral danger when he finds himself attracted to the lead female singer of the opera he attended and flees.[29] Al-Shidyāq likewise brings up the danger of the European model of gender relationships on his own gendered moral universe. As he extols the educational and cultural value of European theatre, he is apprehensive of its effect on women attendees. 'Women will learn techniques and tricks to attract men's attention and hang on to their attachment', al-Shidyāq cannot help but observe of the charisma of men and women actors, and the type of romantic plays put on stage, 'and they [women] will soon swap their inattentive husbands for the passionate lovers they see before them'.[30] This anxiety-ridden ambivalence pervades the *maqāmāt* al-Miknāsī and al-Shidyāq refashion out of their travelogues and, more importantly, serves as the trope around which each explores the perils and pleasures of cultural encounter.

Maqāma: Crisis of morality in al-Miknāsī

Al-Miknāsī wrote the accounts of his travels in Europe and al-Andalus three centuries after the *Reconquista* and the Andalusi migration to the Maghreb, although more than a century before al-Andalus would become embedded in the Moroccan identity – which would come later in the colonial and postcolonial invention of identity.[31] Coming from a family of learning in Miknas, al-Miknāsī would have easily been heir to the subversive Andalusi tradition of *maqāma* writing. He also lived under the Alaouite dynasty (founded in 1631) and served three sultans: Muḥammad (Ibn ʿAbdallāh) III (1757–90), al-Yazīd (1790–2) and Slimane (1792–1822). Muḥammad III initiated a set of judicial reforms to cleanse the society from corruption.[32] Al-Miknāsī's *al-Badr al-sāfir* is the culmination of three centuries of post-*Reconquista* Muslim travels in Europe – and we have yet to unearth this material fully—and it describes in great detail the European alterity manifest in their cultural, civic, technological, religious and social institutions and practices. The observations, relatively free of judgment, are an integral part of a narrative of, in al-Miknāsī's language, Christian–Muslim encounter that reproduces the names of places, characters, practices and cultural institutions, as I have already explained, in the particular way Maghrebis at the time transcribed French, Italian and Spanish in Arabic letters.

These foreign words and more disappear completely from the five *maqāmāt*. Each *maqāma* focuses on a dramatic moment of al-Miknāsī's encounters not with the foreign but with Muslims residing in Christian lands and whose behaviour invited censure. The expression of indictment of Muslim behaviour, and in fact, moral depravity in turn reflects the practices subject to Muhammad III's juridical reforms. Al-Miknāsī's *maqāmāt* do not subvert his *riḥla*, but tap into an anxiety lurking beneath the surface of the accounts of his travel, precipitated by what he witnessed in Spain, Malta, Sicily and Naples (with France in the background), and heightens this anxiety into a scandal, as I will show, through a process of 'translation', linguistically (there is very little biographical information on al-Miknāsī and it is not clear whether he knew European languages or not) and culturally, which is in turn repackaged through another process of 'translation' visible only in the juxtaposition and parallel reading of his *riḥla* and *maqāma*, of the former's muted descriptions against the latter's vociferous, melodramatic rhetoric – the *maqāma* is the enclave of classical Arabic *badīʿ* rhetorical devices and theatrics.

The *riḥla* records two moments of extreme anxiety for its protagonist. In the first instance, the ambassador meets a certain Muḥammad al-Ḥāfī in Malta, also a Moroccan ambassador sent to gather Muslim captives and await their ransom and transport back to Muslim lands. Al-Ḥāfī seems to have outstayed his welcome but more crucially he treats his fellow Moroccan ambassador with disrespect and manoeuvres to take possession of the ransom money.[33] In the second instance, he meets the star of a concert he is invited to, a female singer, and feels her allure.[34] He bids a hasty farewell to his host and leaves in a hurry in order to escape the trappings of passion, or *qabla al-wuqūʿ fī habāʾil al-hawā wa l-iʿtiqāl* in his own words,[35] which may be translated into 'before falling into the traps of passion and detention' in English. These two episodes are, unlike the rest of the travelogue, rendered in the rhyme prose of the *maqāmāt* punctuated by quotations from the classical Arabic poetic tradition. The two anxieties, the first about the reprehensible behaviour of his fellow Muslim, countryman and diplomat in the land of Christians, and the other about his susceptibility to the sexual temptation of a beautiful Christian woman, are collapsed into one in the *maqāmāt*, a huge anxiety about exposure of private parts in public or to prying eyes. The five *maqāmāt*, written in a highly satirical tone, retell the *riḥla* but transform the encounter with the Christian other to that with the Muslim self and rewrite the two anxious episodes in the *riḥla* into dramas of 'shame'.

The narrator is, one may argue, the alter ego of al-Miknāsī who performs the function of the itinerant narrator-protagonist of the traditional *maqāma* genre, and narrates his travels and encounters with the same eloquent con artist, the other protagonist of the traditional genre, at every city he visits, and together they unravel the absurdity of prevalent dogmas and attendant cultural practices. Muḥammad al-Ḥāfī is fictionalized into Ibn Jallūl al-Ṭayyib, another Moroccan ambassador in Europe. He is portrayed as a dirty old man and a traitor from within, but not in the conventional sense; rather, he is an opportunist who flouts the proper conduct of a Muslim ambassador in the Christians. Instead of carrying himself with pride and dignity, treating others with magnanimity and generosity but in fairness and observance of rank and file, and upholding what is right, he brings ridicule to himself and the Muslims. As would be expected of the *maqāma* genre, the narrator-protagonist meets the narrated-protagonist in every city he visits and sojourns. The first *maqāma*, located in Morocco, sets up the character of Ibn al-Jallūl against the backdrop of a moral canvas according to which a Muslim is judged, but here only relevant to his conduct before the Christian other. The second *maqāma*, also set in Morocco but more specifically in Rabat, introduces Ibn Jallūl's 'malice' (*khubth*), playing with his nickname, al-Ṭayyib, which means both noble and good, and shows the ways in which Ibn Jallūl's penchant for giving false, self-serving evidence invites censure and punishment. He is even ordered to be slapped, '*ṣaf*', which is title of the *maqāma*, al-Ṣafʿiyya, in public. The fourth *maqāma*, called the Crucifix (*al-Ṣalībiyya*), takes place in Malta, and shows us the hypocritical nature of Ibn Jallūl, who would profess to be a Christian under duress, but would be in the end cast out of both communities. What happens to Muslim reputation if such a dirty old man is the Muslims' ambassador to the Christians? The third and fifth *maqāmāt* melo-dramatize this inherent anxiety.

The third *maqāma*, *al-Zaytiyya* or *al-Ṣūriyya*, referring to the wax of stolen candles and the pictorial representation of the thief, takes place in Naples, where the narrator-protagonist arrives as a Muslim ambassador. There he is supposed to meet the con artist, an eloquent man of letters who always inadvertently makes a mockery of ruling political, social and cultural structures, but instead, and yet again, Ibn Jallūl al-Ṭayyib, a dirty old man, who, like Muḥammad al-Ḥāfī, is a traitor from within. This old man, Ibn Jallūl al-Ṭayyib, steals the candles every night as soon as they are lit, and when caught and interrogated, replies that burning candles is 'wasteful' (*īqād al-shamʿ min al-saraf*).[36] Worse, this Muslim old man degrades himself further by eating up a storm at meals he is not invited to, and walking in the streets in tatters that expose his private parts. Portraits are made of him in such a state and hung on the walls of marketplaces for all eyes to see. The narrator has to bribe the portrait maker and have him take down these shameful portraits and promise never to produce more. The reversal of the character of the con artist, one of the two protagonists of the *maqāma* genre, to a shameful, scandalous old man, who does not seem able to stop himself from stealing or baring himself in public and to the Christians in the Lands of the Christians, speaks of al-Miknāsī's anxiety about how the Muslims are viewed by their Christian others. What we read in this particular dialogization of *riḥla* and *maqāma* is a forecast of the Muslim humiliation to come. The Muslims are themselves taken to task for their shameful behaviour. Shame in the *maqāmatisation* of the *riḥla* is expressed in the form of exposure in public of private parts in the very sight of the Christians, strangers to the Muslims, and outsiders to their community, in a multilingual and multicultural context.

The fifth *maqāma*, *al-Dhabiyya*, escalates this fear of exposure to that of entanglement, that of being tempted to have sex with strangers. This last *maqāma*, which is the longest of the five at fifty-eight pages,[37] is yet another melodramatic iteration of the entire *riḥla*, in fact, al-Miknāsī's three travelogues, including their itineraries, but shorn of all references to the other. Dense with references to classical Arabic writings from prose and poetry, it invokes the ethos of Arabic *adab* writings. Two ethical principles are of particular interest: care for fellow Muslims during Pilgrimage or in Christian lands and loyalty to Islam. It understandably indicts hypocrisy, when Muslims kowtow to Christians for self-preservation or gain, or convert to Christianity under pressure. Two vignettes in this long *maqāma* recast *al-Zaytiyya*, which is two and a quarter pages:³⁸ Ibn Jallūl al-Ṭayyib is a thief, but here he steals silk pillows from his Christian hosts;³⁹ and he is a lecherous old man who spies on the private parts of his Christian host's wife when she is relieving herself only to be forced to stand naked in public as his punishment.⁴⁰ These vignettes are woven into one and rewritten from the perspective of *khubth*, or malice as a moral judgement on both Christians and Muslim hypocrites. *Dhabiyya*, the noun in the title of the *maqāma*, is interpreted to mean 'morally reprehensible conduct',⁴¹ and has a wide semantic range in Arabic. Fly, the insect, *dhubāb*, is derived from the same root, so is the verb *dhabba*, which means to move around and not settle in any place, or to push something away from another thing, to defend, particularly women and the harem. All these meanings are collapsed into one and mobilized to produce a satire in the traditional *maqāma* style of two creepy crawlers, one indignant Christian husband and another the Muslim dirty old man, who partake in an act of mutual voyeurism.

The *maqāma* begins thus. The household of Ibn Jallūl, alternately called *al-khabīth*, wakes one morning to a feeling that someone has been crawling around the place at night. The investigation leads to a Christian who suspects that his wife is having a liaison with the man of the house. It then transpires that Ibn Jallūl happened upon the Christian's wife in the toilet and peered at her private parts. He accepts standing naked in public as his punishment but unfortunately a Christian painter makes a portrait of him. The narrator-protagonist, as in *al-Zaytiyya*, bribes the portrait maker and buys off all the copies so as to douse the scandalous fire. The introduction of a woman, and here of someone whose privacy is violated by a stranger creeping about in the sanctity of her own home, is revealing of a moral crisis of a particular type. In the playful overlap of the notions of women folk, *ḥarīm*, their sanctuary at home, *ḥaram*, and sanctity, *ḥarām*, propriety in sexual conduct comes to be synonymous with religious, national and personal honour. The vulgarized sex in al-Miknāsī's *maqāmāt* – the dirty old man's voyeurism and nudity – reads like his overreaction to his own sexual attraction to the European female singer he met in Naples. But as we learn from Barthes, sexuality in literary texts, what he calls 'secondary sexuality', is located not in sex but in language and thought, or 'the pleasure of the text'. The pleasure of this text, al-Miknāsī's *maqāmāt*, is the effect of the cultural encounter between European Christians and Maghrebian Muslims in the eighteenth century that created a stir, in this case, in the language and thought of al-Miknāsī. The apprehension about Muslim honour is tinged with the attraction to the Christian other. The allure of the other can only be spoken of as anxiety-provoking sexual attraction. This anxiety is expressive of the fear of entanglement not only of the body but also of language and thought.

The *maqāma* in the *riḥla* moves cultural and linguistic encounter from exteriority (*riḥla*) to interiority (*maqāma*), from externalization to internalization, from describing and mimicking foreign concepts and sounds to translating these through a language steeped in the Arabic literary tradition, *adab*, grammatically, rhetorically, aesthetically and ethically, into a crisis of morality. In the inward facing *maqāma*, multilingualism is subsumed under monolingualism, and the exuberance of cultural encounter so palpable in the *riḥla* is muted, reduced to unwelcome sexual desire and anxiety of entanglement, as if multilingualism, which unavoidably remaps both language and thought, is promiscuity, but of the 'confusion of languages' type which demands that it be reined in and disciplined into 'coherence'. The dialogism between *riḥla* and *maqāma* in al-Miknāsī dramatizes the tension between multilingualism as exhilaration and confusion on the one hand, and monolingualism as continuity and coherence on the other. The creative craze generated by translanguaging goes hand in hand with multilingualism. The five *maqāmāt* are born in the dialogues taking place between al-Miknāsī's Arabic, its structures of thinking, feeling and socialization, its poetics and ethics, and the Maltese, Italian and Spanish languages he heard, the technologies, cultural institutions and social customs he witnessed and experienced in Europe.

It may not be possible yet to articulate the multilingual poetics in these *maqāmāt* in any concrete sense without us knowing al-Miknāsī's readings in European languages. However, the theme of shameful Muslim behaviour in Christian lands is the product of the eighteenth-century, as it would disappear in nineteenth-century Arabic texts, in which the 'West' and 'East' would also replace 'Christian' and 'Muslim' as descriptors of the two parties of the intercultural encounters. But the paradoxical anxiety about entanglement in language, thought and social world would remain. It is a constant in *al-Sāq ʿalā l-sāq*, al-Shidāq's rewrite or parallel narration of his travels around the Mediterranean. While *al-Sāq* 'barely veils an allusion to sexual positions and raunchy anatomical synonyms that the book lists and relists at length in its opening pages',[42] *al-Wāsiṭa* and *Kashf al-mukhabbaʾ* are free of sexual innuendos even in their observations of European women and gender relations. *Al-Sāq* has been subject to extensive, close scrutiny and is acknowledged as 'inter-linguistic and inter-textual blending of at least two languages and two poetic traditions in one bilingual literary work', which 'translat[ed] European writings and languages within its neologistic, monolingual textual fold', just like *al-Badr al-sāfir*, but more recognizably

> represented a philological, translational, literary and narratological *tour de force* that seamlessly blended the rigid fixed forms and abstruse idioms of high classical Arabic with modern neologisms, the corporeal bawdiness of Rabelais, the blues-tinged poetics of Du Bellay's nostalgia, colourful descriptions of Mediterranean travels, unflattering depictions of the filth of pre-Haussmannian Paris, the sexual mores of nineteenth century Parisians, and unprecedented dialogical forays into gender identity and feminine equality and sexuality in Arabic.[43]

Al-Sāq ʿalā l-sāq: The anxiety of interlingual poetics in al-Shidyāq

Readers and critics of al-Shidyāq have all observed his 'obsession' with women. The body of writing he has left behind is saturated with observations of, comments on and positions regarding women's status in both Europe and the Arab East, their social conditions, familial roles, relationship with men and, more significantly, with their attention to their body, whether in the way they dressed, wore jewellery, held themselves together at home and in public or took care of their physical appearance.

The progressiveness of his views is often situated in his laying bare (*ta'riya*) the Arabic language, stripping it of belles-lettrist embellishments, returning it to its fundamentals and reviving its innate rigour and richness. This is equally seen in his liberal attitude towards women. He advocated women's education, work and social freedom even before, for example, Qāsim Amīn (1865–1908), considered the father of Arab feminism for his pioneering call for the liberation of women in *Taḥrīr al-mar'a* (1899) and *al-Mar'a al-jadīda* (1900). Al-Shidyāq's rather explicit references to sex and sexuality of both men and women, especially in *al-Sāq*, is taken not as a symptom of his debauchery (*mujūn*),[44] but instead as a sign of his profound understanding of the importance of women in subject formation, and the role of subject in social and cultural change, in modernization.[45] Bringing East into modernity, according to the messages between the lines and behind al-Shidyāq words, is necessarily premised on the emergence of a 'modern subject'[46] which requires exposing Eastern masculinity, stripping it bare (*al-ta'arrī*), effected here through impersonating woman, going deep into femininity, in order to begin a 'journey of transformation'.[47] This 'journey of transformation' of the 'modern subject' is understandably seen as the crux of the matter in *al-Sāq*.

His travel accounts in *al-Sāq*, as well as in *al-Wāsiṭa* and *Kashf al-mukhabba'*, are taken in their totality as narrative of an encounter between two cultural spheres informed by a critical distance rather than a bedazzled enthrallment with the European allure. The centrality of women in al-Shidyāq's narratives of European–Arab encounter is responsive not only to a cultural other but also to a profound epistemological and ontological difference. Gender comes to be the site on which this profound epistemological and ontological difference is grappled with and articulated. Here, gender is not merely a signifier of sexual difference but also a way of thinking, gendered thinking and its radical consequences in knowing and living. At stake is what he calls *tamaddun*, a 'civilized' state of living centred in the city, that must be grounded in individual freedom that is too often subject to the hegemony of the authority of political and religious institutions as well as 'Tradition' ('*ādāt wa taqālīd*), and in economic health and social cohesion. What he saw during his travels, in his encounter with difference, is offset against familiar habits and customs, seen, examined, thought of, grappled with and transformed into a vision. This vision is a 'moral universe' articulated in the form of melodrama, or dramatization of woman's struggle to find a balance between virtuous living, including responsibility towards her husband, children and society, and happiness founded on personal freedom. The merits and vices of both European and Arab models of society, seen through the microcosm of man–woman relationships, are served on a platter, chewed, spat out and chewed again, all in an attempt to manage the moral dilemmas thrown up in the liminal space opened up in the meeting between two cultures, in the possibility of choice.

Al-Shidyāq writes at length about courtship and marriage in Malta where he lived for fourteen years in *al-Wāsiṭa*,[48] highlighting the divergent practices between the Maltese and Arabs.[49] He first observes that men and women cohabit for a long time in Malta before they marry, sometimes up to three years or more. He discusses the advantages and drawbacks of such a practice from the perspectives of both the Arab East and Europe. Marriage without (first) seeing the girl and knowing her circumstances is a most disadvantageous custom especially among the Christians because they do not allow divorce. No good can come out of long cohabitation outside marriage either. The girl would conduct herself in such a model way until she is married, when she knows that divorce is possible, she would then behave however she pleases. Maltese women are, in his view, lacking in moral uprightness. They often chase after handsome men without thinking of the consequences. They do not respect their husbands. They often contradict their men, correct them and make them look stupid in the presence of others. When they speak to their men, they often raise their voice to such an extent that an outsider is shocked into silence. These themes recur in his comments on English and French women, many of whom he met in Malta, in *Kasfh al-mukhabba'*. He scrutinizes them further, and in a very class-conscious fashion, during his respective stays in England and France, having been given opportunities to socialize with them. He notes their differing way of managing physical appearance at home and in the street, on an ordinary day or at a dinner party, of relating to their husbands in both private and public, of conducting themselves with men and women outside their immediate family circle, of hosting afternoon tea parties or evening feasts, of conserving or squandering their husband's fortune, and of working, whether farming the lands, selling vegetables and fruits in the street, assisting in shops, serving in restaurants and bars, performing on stage in theatres or even prostituting.

Even though al-Shidyāq is disturbed by the unpredictable outcome of European courtship before marriage and its potential moral depravity, he is an advocate of both mixed society and courtship before marriage. Al-Shidyāq gives a tacit nod in *al-Wāsiṭa* and *Kashf al-mukhabba'* to mixed society in Malta, England and France.[50] He inscribes this in *al-Sāq*. His alter ego al-Fāriyāq's marriage to al-Fāriyāqiyya is preceded by a lengthy courtship on the shared rooftop of their separate abodes.[51] Every time they have a disagreement during their marriage and he gets angry and ready to denounce her, he remembers those days on the rooftop, then calms down and is ready to talk to her again. Falling in love aside, this pre-marital courtship allows the potential couple to get to know each other and find out if they are suitable for a life-long partnership, and to avoid the kind of shock a groom or a bride experience when they come face to face with each other for the first time on their wedding day, as often happens in the East and even in Malta in the past. However, compatibility, both of the individuals concerned and the society of which they are members, is perhaps a more important consideration. He approves of the English practice of pairing young women and men closer in age, as opposed to what occurs in the East, where a man can easily marry a woman at least twenty years younger. Compatibility is here seen as the foundation of good partnership. However, partnership requires, in addition to affection and compatibility, mutual trust, companionship, respect and support.

In these matters, he sees English women as a cut above French women, even though French women are more beautiful and charming – they do pay a great deal more attention to their appearance, wear more glamorous clothes and jewellery and have better conversation in company. He admires an English woman's modesty – she remains plain except at dinner parties, her diligence in the domestic sphere, her economy in expenditure and her willingness to take a job in order to help her husband.

Unlike her French counterpart, she plays no emotionally manipulative games (*ḥiyal wa makāyid*) with her husband or others, and she constantly defers to him. In a telling anecdote, he speaks of exchanging gifts with an English family. 'If you receive a gift from an English family and go the next day to give your thanks, the lady of the house would always defer to the husband, even when he is not at home, and say that the gift is from both of them.'[52] He is similarly impressed with the respect she shows her husband in public. This kind of respect goes both ways among the English. English men are equally respectful of their wives in both private and public.

There is, it is apparent, an idealized men–women relationship informing al-Shidyāq's written observations of English, French and Maltese women. As he watches them and compares them with Eastern women, very rarely spoken of explicitly in his travel writing, he is concocting a recipe for what he would consider a model man–woman relationship that can serve as the foundation of *tamaddun* (civilization, or modernity here). For this relationship is the smallest but most fundamental building block of society. The soundness of this building block, as he later articulates in an article (*maqāla*) he wrote for *al-Jawā'ib*,[53] is reliant on compatibility now defined as based on women's accessibility to education and work. Constructed in the form of a debate between one *zīr al-nisā'* (one who thinks highly of women) and another *bakhīs al-nisā'* (he who belittles women), he makes an argument for women's right to education and work. Education would qualify her to share his views, worries and welfare, which would in turn cement their friendship and love and avert infidelity. It must come from reading and writing first, then mixing in society, including men, from whom she may learn not just information but also how to be wise. She would then be able to steer away from following superstitions in her conduct, gossip mongering among friends and relations, stirring up discord in society and manipulating her husband. Women should work for a living too, for work performs the same function and has the added benefit of improving the economic condition of the household. More importantly, she would now be too busy to think of spending money on unnecessary things, especially those that satisfy only her vanity, such as expensive clothes and accessories, make up and perfume and jewellery. But perhaps what is most important is that she can now be the good mother who will teach what she knows as well as by example.

In this, al-Shidyāq is no different from his nineteenth-century contemporaries, who advocated the liberation of woman through her education for the sake of modernizing the East. He locates the backwardness of the East in women and, more importantly, men's attitude towards them. Their ignorance and idleness are both symptomatic and symbolic of what is wrong. Misogyny informs attitudes of both men and women towards life. For example, treating women as sexual objects – which is seen in encouraging women to care only for their appearance in the East – bespeaks of men's frivolity and ingrains them in a sex-obsessed lifestyle. While European men are working hard towards *tamaddun*, Eastern men think only of sex. For al-Shidyāq, women are the problem in the East, and more importantly, women are men's problem. It is up to men to liberate women, to educate them and to give them work. At the end the debate between *zīr al-nisā'* and *bakhīs al-nisā'*, the latter finally comes around to the former position and decides to educate his wife. He goes around town to look for an educated woman to teach his wife but to no avail. He again turns to *zīr al-nisā'* who comes to his rescue one more time. Lo and behold, he has educated his wife and she is now ready to be the educator. She is promptly dispatched to *bakhīs al-nisā*'s house to teach his wife.

Al-Sāq dramatizes this gendered *tamaddun* discourse, or discourse on modernization, and inscribes the project of *tamaddun* on the relationship between its twin protagonists, al-Fāriyāq and al-Fāriyāqiyya, and places the stake on their success as a couple. As I have already mentioned, their marriage comes at the end of a courtship on their shared rooftop, and he takes on the task of educating her and allowing her to have a voice. His journey to Malta is made to seem entirely up to her. By the time they arrive there, she is his equal, sharing not only his views but also all decisions. They chat, debate, fight and make up. They walk down the street hand in hand. They go to dinner parties together and exchange views about all that they see. She moves freely indoors and outdoors, comes and goes as she wishes, mingles in mixed company openly and often decides to stay behind when he travels on business, as in his first trip to Cambridge, or another trip to Tunis. Everything seems perfect for this very 'modern' couple. Their perfect happiness is, however, constantly threatened by his jealousy and, above all, his insecurity. He is always surprised to come home after a trip to find al-Fāriyāqiyya there, waiting for his return, and not having run off with another man. The fear of infidelity permeates *al-Sāq*. The four *maqāmāt* in *al-Sāq* replay this fear of infidelity.

The narrator-protagonist, al-Ḥārith Ibn Hishām, pronounced al-Hāris Ibn Hithām due to the narrator's speech defect, stays up one night pondering over the meaning of life in the first *maqāma*, and when he finds no satisfying answer in the Arabic 'classics' he takes to the street and chances upon al-Fāriyāq, who recites a long poem of his own composition that the narrator receives as the ultimate wisdom and returns home happy. The second *maqāma*, given the title 'To Make One Sit,' finds the narrator looking for answers about marriage and divorce among the scholars in Christian, Jewish and Muslim communities only to run into al-Fāriyāq again, who confirms in another poem the efficacy of divorce. The third *maqāma*, 'To Make One Stand', offers the trials and tribulations of gender relations from the perspectives of both men and women, which al-Fāriyāq, yet again, confirms as the facts of life. 'A Maqāma to Make One Walk', the fourth, exposes women's wiles and men's fear of infidelity only for al-Fāriyāq to confirm their inevitability and display his insight into women's affairs. The four *maqāmāt*, embedded in and framed by *al-Sāq*, do not add to the substance of *al-Sāq*, or for that matter, his discussions of women and gender in his other works, including his travelogues, *al-Wāsiṭa* and *Kashf al-mukhabba'*. They do, however, simultaneously heighten the fear of infidelity and condense al-Shidyāq's play with word, genre and worldviews, the heart and soul of the entire *al-Sāq*, into four relatively short *maqāmāt*.

These *maqāmāt* confine the mobility inherent in the genre in one city, making the journey a linguistic and conceptual one. The topic here is a more egalitarian relationship between modern men and women, which generates not only debate but also conceptual and linguistic play. It precipitates imaginings of all kinds of new scenarios in which men and women interact, relate to each other and invest in their marriage. This is how the consequences of granting women the right to divorce is drawn out in rhymed prose constructed with parallel sentences and contrasting meanings.

*Inna l-zawjata idhā ʿalimat annahā takūnu ʿinda zawjihā ka l-matāʿi l-muntaqil wa ka thawbi al-mubtadhal mawqūfa ʿalā bādira tafruṭu minhā aw hafwa tanqulu ʿanhā lam takhluṣu lahu sarīratahā wa lan tamḥaḍa lahu mawaddatahā bal taʿīshu maʿahu mā ʿāshat fī inqibāḍ wa ījās wa waḥsha wa btiʿās wa nakd wa yās wa tadlīs wa ilbās [...] wa rubbamā khānathu fī ʿirḍihi wa mālihi wa kādat lahu makīdatan faḍaḥathu bayna aqrānihi wa amthālihi.*⁵⁴

[O]nce a wife finds she's no more to her husband than a disposable chattel or worn-out bit of *kit*, presence hostage to any chance mistake or trivial *slip*, she'll never again honestly share with him her *introspection* or grant to him her sincere *affection*. On the contrary, as long as she's with him she'll be depressed and full of *misapprehension*, lonely, sad, bad-tempered, and prone to *desperation*, practicing deceit and *falsification* ... She may betray him with regard to his honor and his *monies* and lay traps to make him an object of scandal before his peers and *cronies*.⁵⁵

The fear of infidelity, overlapped with interlingual, intertextual and intercultural play with words, genres and worldviews here, is a trope around which al-Shidyāq narrates his *tamaddun* project constructed around gender – woman and woman–man relationship – that allows him to do two things simultaneously: to articulate his vision for *tamaddun*, which is necessarily premised on intercultural entanglement, and at the same time act out the emotional turmoil that accompanies any major change. I draw attention to the exaggerated language of *al-Sāq* and its heightened dramatic moments.

The entire book is a hyperbole. It is, moreover, an exaggeration of what has been iterated and reiterated pushed to extremity. *Al-Sāq* is a melodrama of heart and mind that externalizes the hysteria surrounding the emergence of a modern subject. Al-Fāriyāqiyya, as the *nisba* pattern of her derived name suggests, must be read less as al-Fāriyāq's wife having a separate existence from him but more as his alter ego, the other part of him existing within him that is striving to integrate into its own twin, to find coherence. Fear of infidelity makes a different kind of sense here. It is about insecurity of another sort. It taps into the vulnerability of the subject. What if it never coheres? This is central because *tamaddun*'s success depends on the coherence of the subject. The coherence of the subject, however, is a matter of language, for language is the sum total of epistemology and ontology. 'Idhi 'l-lugha', al-Shidyāq says in *al-Sāq*, 'innama hiya 'ibaratun 'an ḥarakati l-insān wa afʿālihi wa afkārihi' (language is the vehicle of man's movement, action and thought),⁵⁶ and shows us through his play with language in *al-Sāq* and the embedded *maqāmāt*. More significantly, *al-Sāq* is about laying bare the workings of language and how these show up the relationship between language and thought, language and culture, and language and subject.

Gender is central to his interrogation of language and its epistemological and ontological reaches and consequences. The crux of the matter here is less the division of the world into women and men, but more gendered thinking, or the construction of thought premised on polarized categories of thought, such as female v. male, right v. wrong, good v. bad, East v. West, Christian v. Muslim, Tradition v. Modern, to name but a few, and the taboos surrounding transgressing well-established categorical boundaries. The boundary between two polarized categories is not only fuzzy but elastic and, more importantly, it straddles two fabricated faces of the same thing dichotomized for a purpose that becomes clear when political decision, social conduct and ethical judgment are imposed, accepted or resisted as right or wrong, good or bad. The female, for example, is derived from the male, and the male encompasses the female. They are two dimensions of the same human, and it is nearly impossible to insist that the male is superior and the female inferior, and to lay evil at the female's door, on her desire, wile and sexuality.

Sexuality figures so heavily in *al-Sāq*, and also the *maqāmāt* in *al-Badr al-sāfir*, because it is the most convenient taboo issue at the centre of a worldview informing a human's every thought and action. It opens up cultural landscape, social etiquette and moral universe for deterritorialization and reterritorialization. It works on thinking, the configuration of abstract and invisible epistemological paradigms that are at the foundation of ontological choices. It binds two archetypal categories, the female and the male, together in such a way that one flows into another and the two, like Siamese twins, cannot and must not be separated. Thought, language and gender are inextricably twined in *al-Sāq*, where inquiry into language and language use here are framed by two simultaneous narratives: marriage and travel. During courtship, marriage and married life, relevant language is presented as both expressive of cultural norms structuring behaviour and ontological assertions. If a word exists in language, then the practice denoted by the word must be known and experienced and must be open to discussion and not suppressed as taboo. Women–men interaction is natural, for language is full of adjectives describing both men and women that embody their desire for each other. This desire in turn makes women and men naturally knowledgeable of each other. This gender discourse in turn frames, or is framed by another East–West discourse that is part and parcel of the travel account. The practices of the West are necessarily seen from the perspectives of two Easts, one female and another male. The East is in turn examined from the perspectives of new experiences, again female and male, gained in the West.

Configurations of multilingualism and world literature

Sexuality in al-Shidyāq is like that in al-Miknāsī: it is Barthesian 'secondary sexuality' situated not in sex but in text, for 'the pleasure of the text' derives from the interplay between language and thought and, here, creative inter-lingual, inter-conceptual and inter-cultural dialogue and playful interaction that generate both change and pleasure. This intercultural dialogue finds a creative outlet in the *maqāmāt* appended to and embedded in their texts, which re-narrate the *riḥla* in a stringently grammaticalized language that brings within its seemingly monolingual fold the multilingualism of the speaking subjects and their environment. The monolingual veneer of the literary texts born in languages in dialogue is, in al-Miknāsī and al-Shidyāq, punctuated by an anxiety, here, of sexual infidelity that betrays the entanglement of languages, concepts and worldviews in their making. Al-Miknāsī and al-Shidyāq offer two 'multilingual locals,' each with a unique configuration of languages in dialogue. The eighteenth-century Western Mediterranean of al-Miknāsī is mapped by, to name but the main languages, Arabic, Italian and Spanish, and the interactions between Christians and Muslims over the question of captives, whereas the nineteenth-century Eastern Mediterranean of al-Shidyāq is by Arabic, English and French, and the East–West intercultural encounter. Close readings of individual texts show us how each is produced and consumed in multilingualism, all the while reproducing its own configuration(s) of multilingualism. Comparative readings make visible the ways in which each configuration of multilingualism shapes each text and is reshaped in it and, more importantly, creates and is recreated in language.

Notes

1   David Crystal, *The Cambridge Encyclopedia of the English Language* (Cambridge: Cambridge University Press, 1995), 5.
2   Robert McCrum, William Cran and Robert MacNeil, *The Story of English: A Companion to the PBS Television Series* (New York: Viking Penguin, 1986), 51.
3   Jacques Derrida, *Monolingualism of the Other OR The Prosthesis of Origin*, trans. Patrick Mensah (Stanford: Stanford University Press, 1996).
4   Pascale Casanova, *The World Republic of Letters*, trans. Malcolm Debevoise (Cambridge, MA: Harvard University Press, 2007).
5   Francesca Orsini, 'The Multilingual Local in World Literature', *Comparative Literature* 67.4 (2015): 345–74.
6   David Damrosch, *What Is World Literature?* (Princeton: Princeton University Press, 2003); *How to Read World Literature* (Malden: Wiley-Blackwell, 2009).
7   Franco Moretti, 'Conjectures on World Literature', *New Left Review* 1 (2000): 54–68; *Graphs, Maps, Trees: Abstract Models for A Literary Theory* (London and New York: Verso, 2005); and *Distant Reading* (London: Verso, 2013).
8   Kees Versteegh, *The Arabic Language* (Edinburgh: Edinburgh University Press, 2001).
9   Karla Mallette, *Lives of the Great Languages: Arabic and Latin in the Medieval Mediterranean* (Chicago: Chicago University Press, forthcoming).
10 For a quick assessment of his career and travel writing, see Nabil Matar, *An Arab Ambassador in the Mediterranean World: the Travels of Muḥammad ibn ʿUthmān al-Miknāsī* (New York: Routledge, 2015).
11 Roland Barthes, *The Pleasure of the Text*, trans. Richard Miller (New York: Hill and Wang, 1973).
12 References are to Muḥammad Ibn ʿUthmān al-Miknāsī, *al-Iksīr fī fikāk al-asīr*, ed. Muḥammad Fāsī (Rabat: al-Markaz al-Jāmiʿī li l-Baḥth al-ʿIlmī, 1965).
13 References are to Muḥammad Ibn ʿUthmān al-Miknāsī, *al-Badr al-sāfir li-hidāyat al-musāfir ilā fikāk al-asārā min yad al-ʿaduw al-kāfir*, ed. Malīka al-Zāhid (al-Muḥammadiyya: Jāmiʿat al-Ḥasan al-Thānī, 2005).

14 Reference is to Muḥammad Ibn ʿUthmān al-Miknāsī, *Iḥrāz al-muʿallā wa l-raqīb fī ḥajj bayt allāh al-ḥarām wa ziyārat al-quds al-sharīf wa l-khalīl wa l-tabarruk bi-qabr al-ḥabīb*, ed. Muḥammad Bū Kabbūt (Abu Dhabi and Beirut: Dār al-Suwaydī and al-Muʾassasa al-ʿArabiyya li l-Nashr wa l-Tawzīʿ, 2003).

15 These include Aḥmad al-Ḥajarī Afūqāy's *Riḥlat al-Shihāb ilā liqāʾ al-aḥbāb*, also known as *Nāṣir al-dīn ʿalā al-qawm al-kāfirīn* (1611–13), Muḥammad al-Ghassānī's *Riḥlat al-wazīr fī iftikāk al-asīr* (1690–1) and Aḥmad Ibn al-Mahdī al-Ghazzāl, *Natījat al-ijtihād fī al-muhādana wa l-jihād* (1766). Selections from the first two texts are available in English translation in Nabil Matar, *In the Lands of the Christians: Arabic Travel Writing in the 17th Century* (New York: Routledge, 2003).

16 The most famous Moroccan examples of the latter type are ʿAlī Ibn Muḥammad al-Tamagurūtī's *al-Nafḥa al-miskiyya fī al-sifāra al-turkiyya* (The Perfumed Breeze of Turkish Embassy, 1589) and Abū al-Qāsim al-Zayyānī's (1734–1833) *al-Tarjumāna al-kubrā fī akhbār al-maʿmūr barran wa-baḥran* (1817? 'Complete guide to the world of seas and lands).

17 See Nabil Matar, *Turks, Moors and Englishmen in the Age of Discovery* (New York: Columbia University Press, 1999) and *Europe through Arab Eyes 1578–1727* (New York: Columbia University Press, 2009).

18 References are to Aḥmad Fāris al-Shidyāq, *al-Wāsiṭa fī maʿrifat aḥwāl māliṭa* (Beirut: Dār al-Madā, 2007); and the version of *Kashf al-mukhabbaʾ ʿan funūn ūrūbbā* published by Alexandria Library (Cairo: Dār al-Kitāb al-Miṣrī and Beirut: Dār al-Kitāb al-Lubnānī, 2012). These two works were edited by Qāsim Wahba and published together in one volume (Abu Dhabi: Dār al-Suwaydī, 2004).

19 See Ian Richard Netton, *Seek Knowledge: Thought and Travel in the House of Islam* (Richmond, Surry: Curzon Press, 1996); and Houari Touati and Lydia G. Cochrane, *Islam and Travel in the Middle Ages* (Chicago and London: University of Chicago Press, 2010).

20 References are to Aḥmad Fāris al-Shidyāq, *al-Sāq ʿalā al-sāq*, ed. al-Shaykh Nasīb Wuhayba al-Khāzin (Beirut: Dār Matktabt al-Hayāt, n.d.).

21 For studies of this work as autobiography, see Paul Starkey, 'Fact and Fiction in *al-Sāq ʿalā al-sāq*', in *Writing the Self: Autobiographical Writing in Modern Arabic Literature*, ed. Robin Ostle, Ed de Moor and Stefan Wild (London: Saqi Books, 1998): 30–8; and 'Voyages of Self-definition: The Case of [Aḥmad] Fāris al-Shidyāq', in *Sensibilities of The Islamic Mediterranean: Self-expression in a Muslim Culture from Post-classical Times to the Present Day*, ed. Robin Ostle (London: I. B. Tauris, 2008): 118–32.

22 Philip F. Kennedy, 'The Maqāmāt as a Nexus of Interests: Reflections on Abdelfattah Kilito's *Les Séances*', in Julia Bray, ed., *Writing and Representation in Medieval Islam* (London; New York: Routledge, 2006): 153–214.

23 See, for example, Alexander E. Elinson, *Looking Back at al-Andalus: the Poetics of Loss and Nostalgia in Medieval Arabic and Hebrew Literature* (Leiden; Boston: Brill, 2009); James T. Monroe, *The Art of Badīʿ al-Zamān al-Hamadhānī as Picaresque Narrative* (Beirut: American University of Beirut, 1983); Douglas C. Young, *Rogues and Genres: Generic Transformation in the Spanish Picaresque and Arabic Maqāma* (Newark Delaware Juan de la Cuesta, 2004); and David A. Wacks, *Framing Iberia: Maqāmāt and Frametale Narratives in Medieval Spain* (Leiden and and Boston: Brill, 2007).

24 See, for example, Ahmed Idrissi Alami, *Mutual Othering: Islam, Modernity and the Politics of Cross-Cultural Encounters in Pre-Colonial Moroccan and European Travel Writing* (Albany: State University of New York Press, 2013).

25 Al-Miknāsī, *al-Badr al-sāfir*, 185–6.

26 Al-Shidyāq, Kashf al-mukhabba', 428.
27 Rebecca C. Johnson, 'Foreword' in Aḥmad Fāris al-Shidyāq, al-Sāq ʿalā l-sāq, trans. Humphrey Davies, Leg over Leg, 4 vols, Library of Arabic Literature (New York: New York University Press, 2014). References are to the paperback edition, Leg over Leg, 2 vols (New York: New York University Press, 2015), 1: ix–xxxvi, xxxvi.
28 Ibid.
29 Al-Miknāsī, al-Badr al-sāfir, 186–90.
30 Al-Shidyāq, Kashf al-mukhabba', 427–8.
31 See Eric Calderwood, Colonial al-Andalus: Spain and the Making of Modern Moroccan Culture (Cambridge MA: The Belknap Press of Harvard University Press, 2018).
32 This is according to Malīka al-Zāhidī, who edited and introduced al-Badr al-sāfir: 17–102, 37.
33 Al-Miknāsī, al-Badr al-sāfir, 131–40.
34 Ibid., 186–90.
35 Ibid., 188.
36 Ibid., 273.
37 Ibid., 275–332.
38 Ibid., 271–3.
39 Ibid., 312.
40 Ibid., 275–8.
41 See Malīka al-Zāhidī, al-Badr al-sāfir, 275n783.
42 yasser elhariry, Pacifist Invasions: Arabic, Translation and the Postfrancophone Lyric (Liverpool: Liverpool University Press, 2017), 20.
43 Ibid.
44 Sulaymān Jubrān, Kitāb al-fāriyāq: mabnāhu wa uslūbuhu wa sukhriyatuhu (Tel Aviv: Tel Aviv University Press, 1991), 24–8.
45 Fawwāz Ṭarābulsī and Azz al-ʿAẓma, Aḥmad Fāris al-Shidyāq (London: Riad el-Rayyes, 1995).
46 Kamran Rastegar, Literary Modernity between Middle East and Europe: Textual Transactions in 19th Century Arabic, English and Persian Literatures (London: Routledge, 2007): 101–24.
47 Ṭarābulsī and al-ʿAẓma, Aḥmad Fāris al-Shidyāq, 32.
48 He was invited to help translate the Bible into Arabic.
49 Al-Shidyāq, al-Wāsiṭa fī maʿrifat aḥwāl Mālṭa, 71–2
50 Elsewhere, in al-Jawā'ib, he makes an explicit plea for mixed society. A woman may benefit from the knowledge of men with whom she comes into contact. I refer in particular to the essay (maqāla) on 'Fī baʿḍ aḥwāl takhuṣṣu al-nisā'' (observations on women's conditions), in Ṭarābulsī and al-ʿAẓma, Aḥmad Fāris al-Shidyāq, 284–303.
51 Al-Shidyāq, al-Sāq, 391–404.
52 Al-Shidyāq, Kashf al-mukhabba', 171.
53 Collected and published in two volumes as Kanz al-raghā'ib fī muntajāt al-jawā'ib (Istanbul: Maṭbaʿat al-Jawā'ib, 1971–1881). Al-Jawā ib was a newspaper he owned, managed and edited whilst in Istanbul from 1860 to 1884.
54 Al-Shidyāq, al-Sāq, 232, 233.
55 Humphrey Davies, Leg over Leg by Aḥmad Fāris al-Shidyāq (New York and London: New York University Press, 2015), Vols 1 and 2, 284–5.
56 Al-Shidyāq, al-Sāq, 522.

Index

Abu Rimaileh 173, 176
Achebe, Chinua 184
acting and the theatre 289–90
activism regarding world literature 9
adab writings 292
Addison, Joseph 75
Adnan, Etel 54–5
Adorno, Theodor 156
aesthetics 121–2
affiliation of languages 69
Aix-les-Bains 224
'Alexandrian' language 284
alignment of text 76
alingualism 235, 244
Allan, Michael 168
ambivalence when faced with multilingual texts 8
American literature 2
Améry, Jean 148
Amin, Qāsim 295
anamorphism 73, 84–5
Andrade, Olegario Victor 139
Anglophone-Arabic writing 8, 72–6, 82–3
Anjaria, Keya (*author of Chapter 6*) x, 8
anthropocentrism 9
Antoon, Sinan 70–1, 84–5
Apollinaire, Guillaume 45–6
Appiah, Kwame 195
Apter, Emily 8, 70, 99, 210, 216, 218
Arabic language 69–73, 77, 175, 184–7, 193–5, 282–4, 287
  associations with other languages 72
  forms of 72
Arabic script 78, 80
Arabic-French literature 8, 57
Aragon, Louis 233–8, 244–7
Arp, Hans 222
Ascal, Françoise 59
Asturias, Miguel Angel 221
Attar, Farid ad-Din 58
Attridge, Derek 18, 135

Auden, W. H. 152
Augustine, St. 282
Auschwitz 146, 149, 156, 179
avant-garde movements 46, 218–21, 234
Awlād al-Ghītū 167–80
Awrāq al-narjis 185–95
Ayoub, Dima (*author of Chapter 10*) x, 8

Babel and de-Babelization 145, 149, 154, 223–5, 282–3
Baetens, Jan 52
Baha'ism 186–7
Bakhtin, Mikhail 15, 191
Ball, Hugo 222
Balzac, Honoré de 187–8
Bancquart, Marie-Clare 274
Bandia, Paul 14–15
Banville, Theodore de 135–9
Baralt's Dictionary of Gallicisms 133–4
barbarism 153, 155
Baron Cohen, Simon 207
Barthes, Roland 4, 285, 293, 300
Bashir, Bashir 171, 179–80
Basque language 94–5
Bauman, Richard 257–8
Beck, Hashem 70–1, 76–7
Beckett, Samuel 194, 218, 222
Beebee, Thomas O. 2, 268
Beecroft, Alexander 8, 94
Benjamin, Walter 154–5, 259
ben Jelloun, Tahar 57
Bensmanïa, Réda 185
Bergvall, Caroline 253
Bermann, Sandra 154
Berrada, Mohammed 65
Bhabha, Homi 193
bilingualism 5, 57, 70–1, 203–8
  in reading 207
Billeter, Jean François 28–30, 38
Binebine, Mahi 58
biodiversity 8–9, 93–4, 107, 278

Blackmore, Josiah 152
blood types 201, 210
Blumenberg, Hans 150, 152
Boitani, Piero 156
Bonnefoy, Yves 278
book market 75
Booth, Marilyn 187, 193
border-crossing, linguistic 6, 8, 57
Borges, Jorge Luis 156
'born-translated' texts 70, 74–82
Bosinelli, Rosa Maria Bolletteri 225
Bounani, Ahmed 54
boundlessness 54, 62
Bousquet, Joe 222
Bradbury, Ray 155
Brathwaite, Edward Kamau 20–1, 255
Braziel, Jana Evans 21
breaking language 82–4
breaking projections 84–6
breaking script 75–82
Breoghan's lighthouse 105
Breton, André 236–7
Briggs, Charles 257–8
Brisset, Jean-Pierre 222, 225–6
Britton, Celia 15–16
'broken English' 72
Brown, Bob 222
Bulson, Eric 218
Burns, Lorna 52
Byron, Lord 152

Calderon, Ventura Garcia 221–2
calligraphy 28–47
Calvino, Italo 145
Cambridge 286
Campbell, Madeleine 259
capacity of a language 15
Capildeo, Vahni 253–64
    'Journal of Ordinary Days' 262
    'Letter Not from Trinidad' 257–8
    'Measures of Expropriation' 260–1
Caribbean landscape 21
Casanova, Pascale 1, 168–9, 267
Cassin, Barbara 215–16, 221
Castilian language 94–5, 107
causal thinking 277
Celan, Paul 276, 278
Cézanne, Paul 32

Chamoiseau, Patrick 270
Cheah, Pheng 111–13, 168, 234, 267–8, 278–9
Chebaa, Mohamed 56
Cheng, François 27–38, 45–7
Cheyette, Bryan 149
Chinese culture 46
Chinese script 47
'Chineseness' 32, 46
Chow, Rey 71, 116
'chronotopes' concept 191
class-consciousness 296
classics 155–6
Cocteau, Jean 234–6, 240, 242
Coetzee, J. M. 154–6
Coleridge, Samuel Taylor 150–1
combinations of languages 7
compound nouns 83
Confucianism 31
consonants 245–7
'contaminated present' (Currie) 204
Contreras, Francisco 130
'Copernican turn' 93–4
Coptic community 186–7
cosmopolitan consciousness 47
cosmopolitanism 5, 111–12, 121–2, 127, 134
co-translation 225
counter-narratives 85
crafting, linguistic 176
Cran, William 282–3
creative reading 135
creativity 8–9, 55–6, 62, 268
creole languages and culture 5, 7, 13–14, 21, 82, 220, 254, 263, 268–79
Cresswell, Tim 73–4
criticism, literary 115, 267
Crystal, David 282–3
cultural symbolism 46–7
Currie, Mark 204

Dadaism 244
Daft Punk 244
Damrosch, David 1–2, 51, 53, 207, 216, 223, 234, 267, 283
Danoun, Adam 168–79
Dante Alighieri 147–56
Daoism 30–1

Darío, Rubén 127–42
Das, Veena 171
Dash, J. Michael 21
David, B. 274
de Castro, Rosalia 98–9
Defoe, Daniel 75
Deleuze, Gilles 24, 239
de Lisle, Leconte 136
del Pilar Blanco, María 209
del Río, Isabel *see* Zero Negative/Cero Negativo
delocalization of literature 207
Depestre, René 54
Derrida, Jacques 71, 202–7, 283
DeSilva-Johnson, Lynne 74
deterritorialization 210
Diamond Rock 22–3
Dickens, Charles 187–8
diegesis 85
Dimock, Wai-chee 5, 155
discourse 283
divorce 298–9
Druker, Jonathan 153
Dunsch, Boris 152

ecology, linguistic 8–9, 93–8
Un effort (magazine) 236
Egypt 187
El Aroussi, Moulim 62
elhariry, yasser (*author of Chapter 13*) x, 9
Eliot, T. S. 148, 154, 156
elites 75
El-Kharrat, Idwar 189–90
Elsadda, Hoda 189–90, 194
emotionless style 211
English
  basic 224–5
  'standard' 211, 256
English language 3–4, 69, 71, 77, 87, 95, 185, 201–2, 207, 253
  as a global language 202
English women 295–6
Enlightenment, the 149
entantiomorphism 202
environmentalism 94
Ertürk, Nergis 115–20
ethical issues 8–9, 93, 292
étrangeté 45

European linguistic continuum 256, 282
Evin, Ahmet 114–15, 118
exclusionary ideology 187
exophones and exographic representation 46
expression and expressivity 15, 24–5

Fallon, Diego 133
Fargue, Léon-Paul 219
fascism 152–4
Fayadh, Ashraf 70–1
Felatun Bey ike Rakim Efendi 111–23
Feldman, Nancy 171
Felski, Rita 112, 114
feminism 186, 295
Fénelon, F. de S. 114
ferocity, creative 56, 65
films 73
Finn, Robert 114
fixity, semantic 261
Flecker, Adam F. 221
footnotes, translational 222
'foreign' words 225
Foucault, Michel 53, 72
Franco, Francisco 94
Franco-Chinese literature 8, 27–8, 47
French language and culture 3, 8–9, 13, 27, 35, 45–6, 55, 61, 82, 95, 113, 127–36, 139, 142, 185, 219, 222–6, 256, 262, 268, 278, 286
French Revolution 130
friction 74

Galician language and literature 93–5, 98–100, 103, 107
Gallien, Claire (*author of Chapter 4*) x, 8
Gana, Nouri 72, 82
García Lorca, Federico 127
gatekeepers 188
Gautier, Théophile 135, 140, 142
Genesis, Book of 269
German language 4, 146–7, 153, 222
Gharbaoui, Jilali 56
ghetto definition 173–8
al-Ghitani, Gamal 189
ghosts 202–3
Gide, André 243

Gilmour, Rachael (*author of Chapter 14*) x–xi, 9, 208
Glissant, Édouard 8, 13–24, 254, 263
global literature 69, 209–10
globalization 3, 5, 52, 94, 111, 211–12, 267, 269, 279
Goethe, J. W. von 217
Goldberg, Amos 171, 179–80
Gramling, David 3–4, 235
grammar and grammatical features 75, 208
'grammatical enhancement' 211–12
grammatical mistakes 188
grammaticality 284
Greenpeace Spain 93
Grigsby, Carlos F. (*author of Chapter 7*) xi, 8
Groussac, Paul 128–32
Grutman, Rainier 73
Guattari, F. 24
Guido y Spano, Carlos 139
Gürbilek, Nurdan 115

Hafez, Sabry 186
al-Ḥāfi, Muḥammad 291
Haji, Golan 86
Halhed, Nathaniel 75
Hallward, Peter 20
Hamidi, Mohamed 56
Hammad, Suheir 70–2, 82
Hanna, Christophe 245
Harrison, Olivia C. 54
Harrowitz, Nancy 149
Härting, Heike 72, 82
Hartman, Michelle 72
Hassan, Waïl 185
hauntology 202–7, 210
Hawari, Yara 170
Hay, John 36
Hayot, Eric 3
Hearn, Lafcadio 272
hegemony: linguistic and cultural 72
Helgesson, Stefan 5
Henein, Georges 233–47
Herbert, Zbigniew 155
heterolingualism 8, 70, 73–5, 84–5
Hiddleston, Jane (*co-editor, co-author of Introduction and author of Chapter 1*) xi, 8
Hikmet, Nazim 58

history, literary 74, 134, 282
Hitchcock, Alfred 203
Hitler, Adolf 152
Hoelderlin, Friedrich 222
Hollier, Denis 233–4
Holocaust, the 8, 152, 171–3, 176, 179
Homer 150
homogenization 210–12
Hooper, Kirsty 95–7, 107
Huggan, Graham 3, 169
Hugo, Victor 136
humanism 148, 153–6
Hussein, Saddam 77, 84
hybridized language 6–7, 28, 47, 82

Ibrahim, Sonallah 189, 195
identarianism 112–21
idioms 3–4, 7, 13, 17–18, 23, 53
'imagetext' 27, 36
immigration to America 220
imperialism 69, 84
indigenous peoples 269
instrumental language 272
intelligibility 95
intercultural understanding 212
intermeshing between languages 8
internationalism 14, 218, 223
intertextuality 69, 71, 188, 194, 235, 238–9, 294
Iraq 77, 84–6
The Iraqi Nights 77–81
Ishiguro, Kazuo 210
Islamic State 85
Isou, Isidore 233–5, 240–4, 247
Istanbul 113, 285–6
Italian language 153, 225
italicization 224–5

Jagendorf, Zvi 156
Jahin, Salah 194
Jerusalem 285
Johnson, Rebecca C. 289
Jolas, Eugene 216–22, 225
Jolas, Maria 216
Jones, Ellen (*author of Chapter 11*) xi, 8
Joyce, James 189, 194, 216, 218, 223–5
Jullien, Dominique (*author of Chapter 8*) xi, 8

Kacimi, Mohamed 58–9
Kafka, Franz 63, 221
Kamal, Hala 194
Kamil Paşa, Yusuf 114
Kant, Immanuel 149
Keats, John 100
Kellman, Steven G. 208
Kennedy, Philip 287
Khaïr-Eddine, Mohammed 55, 62–6
Khatibi, Abdelkébir 54–5, 240
Khayrallah, Mahmud 188, 195
Khoury, Elias 167–73, 178–9
Kilito, Abdelfattah 184–5
Kipling, Rudyard 242
Klemperer, Victor 147–8
Klink, Joanna 277
Kourouma, Ahmadou 14
Kramsch, Claire 261, 263
Kurdish language 86

Laâbi, Abdellatif 54–62, 65
'labelism' 235
LaCapra, Dominic 171
Lakouzémi 273
language
    Glissant's conception of 13–14
    inequalities marked by 211
    as a medium for communication 211
    'representation' mode 268
language units 94–5
languages covered in the present book 6
'langues' 15–16, 24
Latin 194, 225–6
Lauret, Maria 5
Al-Layalī āl-ʿirāqīyah 77
Lazarus, Neil 94
Lebanon 169
Le Clézio, J. M. G. 272–3
Lémistè 278–9
Lennon, Brian 14–15, 210
Leo, Jeffrey 2
Leonard, Tom 256
Lettrists 241–6
Levi, Primo 145–56
lexicography 256
Li, Shuangyi (*author of Chapter 2*) xi–xii, 8
Li, Xiaofan Amy 45
'limbo', use of word 192–3

lingua franca 146, 153, 211, 284
lingua sacra 284
linguacene era 4
linguistic evolution 220
listening 269
literary work 283
literature
    definition of 41
    value as an object of study 267
localism 98
London 283, 286
Lonsdale, Laura (*author of Chapter 5*) xii, 8
Lumumba, Patrice 56
Lyamlahy, Khalid (*author of Chapter 3*) xii, 8
Lydda, city of 167, 171–9

McBride Commission (1982) 170
McCrum, Robert 282–3
MacDonald, Peter D. 76
'McDonaldization' 210
McGuire, James 193
MacNeil, Robert 282–3
Mahfouz, Naguib 186–90
Mahfouz Medal 185–7, 195
Maistre, Xavier de 244–5
Mallarmé, Stéphane 236
Mallette, Karla 284
Malta 295–8
Mandelstam, Osip 155–6
Mapes, Erwin K. 135, 138
maqāma writing and *maqāmatisation* 290–4
Maraini, Toni 55–6
Maran, René 233–5, 242–4, 247
Marasso, Arturo 135, 138
Mardorossian, Carine 22
market exchange 267
Martí, José 133–4
Martinique 9, 13, 21–2, 268
massacres 176
Massumi, Brian 24
Mauritius 273
Maximin, Daniel 21
maxims 276–7
Mayakovski, V. V. 58
Mayan language 273, 279
meaning-making 253, 255

meddah tradition 118–19
Mehrez, Samia 71, 188, 195
Melehi, Mohammed 56, 65–6
Memmi, Albert 54
Menton, city of 149
Meral, Arzu 117
metaphors 141, 150–2
'Metropolitan' language 284
Meyer, Richard 52
Michaux, Henry 219
Midlat, Ahmet 112, 117–20; *see also Felatun Bey ike Rakim Efendi*
Mignolo, Walter 278
migrant writers and artists 47
Miguélez-Carballeira, Helena 98–9
al-Miknāsī, Muḥammad b. 'Uthmān 284–94, 300–1
Mikhail, Dunyan 70–1, 77
Miller, Joshua 218
'minoritization' of English 70
minority languages 13, 95
mirror symbolism 28
misogyny 297
Mistral, Gabriela 127
Mitchel, W. T. J. 27
Mizumura, Minae 210
Mkoni, Sinfree 258
modernism 218
Modernismo persona 132
Molina, Saavedra 130
Monchoachi 268–79
Monier, Christopher *(author of Chapter 15)* xii, 9
Monk, Craig 219
'monolingual paradigm' 219
monolingualism 3–4, 8–9, 15, 75, 111, 195, 212, 235–6, 239–40, 244–5, 253, 257, 282–4
monotheism 269
moon appreciation paintings 41–2
Moran, Berna 118
Moretti, Franco 1, 3, 52–3, 112, 115–16, 267, 283
Morocco 51–9, 65
Morse code 211
Morton, Timothy 94–8, 101, 103
Mosteghanemi, Ahlam 188
'mother tongue' 4, 208, 219, 239, 257

Moudileno, Lydie 271
Moure, Erín 107
M'seffer, Lahbib 62–4
Mufti, Aamir 3
multilingual interiority 260–2
'multilingual local' 5, 186, 284
multilingualism 2–9, 13–14, 27, 45–7, 52–3, 57, 62, 65–6, 71, 73, 93–7, 107, 111–14, 120–3, 127, 134, 142, 145, 147, 152–6, 168, 175, 178, 180, 184–8, 208, 216–21, 224–6, 235, 239, 244, 248, 253–4, 257, 263, 268, 274, 278, 283–5, 289, 293–4, 301
creative 156
elite 263
enforced 153
hard and *soft* 4, 71
and humanism 153–6
meanings of 71
in the Ottoman novel 116–17
as resistance to national monologism 8
in world literature 13
Murakami, Haruki 210
Murray, James 256
Mussolini, Benito 152–3
Mu'tazalites 193

Naficy, Hamid 191, 194
name, lack of 209
nation states 4
national literatures 1–2
nationality of writers 133
Nature, reification of 98
Nazi regime 147, 149, 152–3, 156
neologisms 221–2
Neruda, Pablo 127
Nesbitt, Nick 20
'neutral' language 210, 212
New York 172, 220, 283
Ngũgĩ wa Thiong'o 184
Nicaragua 134
Noël-Ferdinand, Malik 271, 274
Noel-Tod, Jeremy 255, 257
nonhuman languages 7
nonverbal forms of language 7
Noorani, Yaseen 4
novels written for translation 13

Obligado, Rafael 139
Ogden, C. K. 223–5
O'Neill, Patrick 223
onomatopoeia 105–6
opacity of language 6, 16, 18, 73
opera and opera houses 288, 290
orientalism 75, 84
origin, *culture* and *language* of 207
Orsini, Francesca 5, 111, 113, 186, 283–4
Ortega, Julio 134
other languages, writing in the presence of 17
other ways of seeing things 206–7
Ottoman novels 111–17, 120–3
Oubangui-Chari 243
Ouyang, Wen-chin (*co-editor, co-author of Introduction and author of Chapter 16*) xii, 9
Oxford 286

Palestine 56, 82–4, 167–79, 285
Pamuk, Orhan 115
Paris 1, 127, 130–2, 136, 283, 286, 294
Parks, Tim 210
Parla, Jale 115, 117
parole 268–9
Parr, Nora (*author of Chapter 9*) xii–xiii, 8
Paul, Elliot 216–17
Pelorson, Georges 222
Pennycook, Alastair 258
Pérez, Julián 140–1
philology 272
Phipps, Alison 263
pictographs 30, 47
Pizer, John 53
Plonski, Sharri 170
plurality, linguistic 5, 14–15, 226, 255
plurilingualism 283
    strong 14–15
PNL (hip hop duo) 233–5, 247
Poe, Edgar Allan 145, 150–1
politics in literature 8–9, 65, 77
Pollard, Clare 75
polyglossic poems, 279
Polyphemus character 149
polyphonic fluidity 9
'portable work' (Walkowitz) 209–10
postcolonialism 14

première parole 9
presé kouté, pas presé reponn 274–5
print culture 113, 117
prix Goncourt 243
propaganda 85
proverbs 272–9
public intellectuals 169

Qalandia 82
Queneau, Raymond 218, 225
the Qur'an 284

Rabelais, François 294
Rabi, Abdelkébir 62
Ramadan, Somaya 185–91
ransoming 285, 291
reading strategies for literary texts 7
Reconquista, the 285
'Relation' 21, 254, 263
Renaissance, European 75
'Revolution of the World' proclamation (1929) 219–23
Ricoeur, Paul 112
riḥla, the 287, 291–4
Rimbaud, Arthur 62, 219, 236
Rivas, Manuel 93–107
Rogers, Gayle 218
Ronsard, Pierre 259–60
Rose, Jacqueline 57
Roussel, Raymond 239
Russia 155
Rutra, Theo 221–2

Sadouk, Abdallah 59–62
Said, Edward 2–3, 53, 64, 69, 170, 195
Sainte-Beuve, Charles-Augustin 154
Sami, Şemsettin 114
Sánchez-Conejero, Cristina 99
san-chüeh 36
Sanskrit 75, 255
Saussure, F. de 15
Sayigh, Rosemary 171
Scheerbart, Paul 222
Schwitters, Kurt 222
Scotland 256
scripts 113–14
sectarianism 85
Sefrioui, Kenza 56

Segalen, Victor 45–6
self-translation 70, 193
Sembène, Ousmane 54
semiology 7–8
    visual 8
Serfaty, Abraham 56
'Seseo' accent 210
sexuality 284–95, 300
Seyhan, Azade 114
Shaftesbury, Earl of 75
Shakespeare, William 194, 258, 262, 278
shameful behaviour 294
Shan Sa 27–8, 38–47
Shanav, Yehda 179
Shaughnessy, Lorna 107
al-Shaykh, Hanan 69–70
al-Shidyāq, Aḥmad Fāris 284–90, 294–301
shipwreck metaphor 150–2
Sicily and Naples, Kingdom of 285
Singh, Kavita 271
sinographs 46–7
Siskind, Mariano 129–31
Slaughter, Joseph 115
Snyder, Stephen 210
Sodi, Risa 154
Solomon, J. 74, 86
Sommer, Doris 5
Sonder Kommando 179
Soueif, Ahdaf 195
Souffles-Anfas (journal) 51–4, 57, 65
Souffles generation 51–8, 65–6
Spain and Spanish language 3, 8, 93–5, 134, 202, 211, 256
spectres 202–5
Spivak, Gayatri 3
standardization of language 210–11
Steele, Richard 75
Steiner, George 133
Steinitz, Tamar 208
Stephens, James 223
Stramm, August 219
Strauss, Johann 113, 117, 120
'sub-presence' of a language 71
Suchet, Myriam 73
surface effects of language' (Walkowitz) 208
Su Shi 37
synaesthesia 260–4

syncretism 121–3
systems, linguistic 6, 19, 279

Tabet, Maia 84
Tageldin, Shaden 187
Taïa, Abdellah 234
Tanpınar, Ahmet Hamdi 115
Tarkos, Christophe 233–5, 244–7
Tarkos, Valérie 244–6
Tawada, Yoko 28
Taylor-Batty, Juliette (*author of Chapter 12*) xiii, 8
Teicher, Craig Morgan 135
terrorism 75, 84
Thames, river 219
Thomsen, Meads Rosendahl 27
time, *forward* and *backward* movement of 204
Torga, Miguel 95
Tower of Hercules 105
transculturalism 46
transition magazine 215–26
    intentions of 217 *see also* translation policy
translanguaging 7
translatability 3, 71, 202, 207–12, 221, 223 *see also* self-translation; untranslatability
translation 154–5, 254, 259
    attitudes to 218, 220
    importance of 216–17
    limitations of 8, 202, 207, 212, 222
    limits to 8, 222
    models of 221
    multilingual 8
    problems of 203, 207
    secondary and *derivative* nature of 203
    usefulness of 202
translation policy of *transition* magazine 215–22, 226
translingualism 39, 208
transliteration 185, 194
    'resistant' 192
trauma theory 171
travel writing 116, 195, 285–7, 290, 295
travelling language 255–6
Trinidad 9, 253–6
Turkey 8, 112–14, 117, 120

Tussaud, Madame 219
Tu Wei-ming 46–7

Ulysses figure 145, 148–56
Unamuno, Miguel de 131
unintelligibility 6, 15
universal truth 267
universalism 3, 95, 107, 172, 209
untranslatability 8–9, 184, 209, 212, 215–21, 224, 226
Ureña, Pedro Henríquez 127

Valera, Juan 128, 131–2
Vallejo, César 127
Vàzquez, Ronaldo 278
Verne, Jules 244
Vertsteegh, Kees 284
Vida, Richard 259
Vilavedra, Dolores 95, 99
Villa, Ignacio, Teresa 54
violence, routine 82–3
Virgil 148, 154–5
visual languages 7
Voltaire 152
vowels 247

Walkowitz, Rebecca 14, 55, 74, 111–12, 121, 208–10
war stories 209
Warwick Research Collective 3
Watts, Stephen 86
Weizman, Elian 170
Western literature 188
Westernization 115–18, 122–3

Whitman, Walt 278
Wilde, Oscar 194
Wittgenstein, Ludwig 276
Wolf, Uljana 253
Wolfson, Louis 239–40
women, role and status of 188, 284, 295–6
Women and Memory Forum 186
Woolf, Virginia 186
the world around us, language in 7
world literature 1, 3, 7, 9, 13–14, 17, 45, 47, 52–3, 66, 94–5, 107, 111–12, 115, 155, 167–8, 180, 202, 207, 215–18, 221, 233–5, 247–8, 253, 267, 279, 283
  difference from natioal literature 52–3
world-making 111
'worlding' 283
'worldliness' 2–8, 16, 51, 53, 65, 69, 75, 77, 202, 207, 212, 235, 267, 283
  heterolingual or *plurilingual* 8
Wu Zetian, Empress 43, 45

Yeats, W. B. 194
Yildiz, Yasemin 3–4, 219
Young, Robert 3–4
Youssef, Mary 187
Yūjirō, Nakata 36

Zero Negative/Cero Negativo 201–12
'zero negative degrees of empathy' 201
'zigzagging' 9, 255
Zionism 171
Zurayk, Constantine 170
Zuyua 279

www.ingramcontent.com/pod-product-compliance
Lightning Source LLC
Chambersburg PA
CBHW052148300426
44115CB00011B/1567